HINDUISM AND BUDDHISM

VOLUME II

HINDUISM AND BUDDHISM

AN HISTORICAL SKETCH

BY

SIR CHARLES ELIOT

In three volumes

VOLUME II

LONDON

ROUTLEDGE & KEGAN PAUL LTD

Broadway House, 68-74 Carter Lane

First Published 1921
By Routledge & Kegan Paul Ltd.
Broadway House, 68-74 Carter Lane
London, EC4V 5EL
Reprinted 1954, 1957, 1962, 1968 and 1971
Printed in Great Britain
by Lowe & Brydone (Printers) Ltd., London

ISBN 0 7100 1329 9

CONTENTS

BOOK IV

THE MAHAYANA

BOOK V

HINDUISM

BOOK IV

THE MAHAYANA

CHAPTER XVI

MAIN FEATURES OF THE MAHAYANA

The obscurest period in the history of Buddhism is that which follows the reign of Asoka, but the enquirer cannot grope for long in these dark ages without stumbling upon the word Mahayana. This is the name given to a movement which in its various phases may be regarded as a philosophical school, a sect and a church, and though it is not always easy to define its relationship to other schools and sects it certainly became a prominent aspect of Buddhism in India about the beginning of our era besides achieving enduring triumphs in the Far East. The word[1] signifies Great Vehicle or Carriage, that is a means of conveyance to salvation, and is contrasted with Hinayana, the Little Vehicle, a name bestowed on the more conservative party though not willingly accepted by them. The simplest description of the two Vehicles is that given by the Chinese traveller I-Ching (635–713 A.D.) who saw them both as living realities in India. He says[2] "Those who worship Bodhisattvas and read Mahayana Sutras are called Mahayanists, while those who do not do this are called Hinayanists." In other words, the Mahayanists have scriptures of their own, not included in the Hinayanist Canon and adore superhuman beings in the stage of existence immediately below Buddhahood and practically differing little from Indian deities. Many characteristics could be added to I-Ching's description but they might not prove universally true of the Mahayana nor entirely absent from the Hinayana, for however divergent the two Vehicles may have become when separated geographically, for instance in Ceylon and Japan, it is clear that when they were in contact, as in

[1] Sanskrit, *Mahâyâna*; Chinese, *Ta Ch'êng* (pronounced *Tai Shêng* in many southern provinces); Japanese, *Dai-jō*; Tibetan, *Theg-pa-chen-po*; Mongolian, *Yäkä-külgän*: Sanskrit, *Hînayâna*; Chinese, *Hsiao-Ch'êng*; Japanese, *Shō-jō*; Tibetan, *Theg-dman*; Mongolian *Ütšükän-külgän*. In Sanskrit the synonyms agra-yâna and uttama-yâna are also found.

[2] Record of Buddhist practices. Transl. Takakusu, 1896, p. 14. Hsüan Chuang seems to have thought that acceptance of the Yogâcâryabhûmi (Nanjio, 1170) was essential for a Mahayanist. See his life, transl. by Beal, p. 39, transl. by Julien, p. 50.

India and China, the distinction was not always sharp. But in general the Mahayana was more popular, not in the sense of being simpler, for parts of its teaching were exceedingly abstruse, but in the sense of striving to invent or include doctrines agreeable to the masses. It was less monastic than the older Buddhism, and more emotional; warmer in charity, more personal in devotion, more ornate in art, literature and ritual, more disposed to evolution and development, whereas the Hinayana was conservative and rigid, secluded in its cloisters and open to the plausible if unjust accusation of selfishness. The two sections are sometimes described as northern and southern Buddhism, but except as a rough description of their distribution at the present day, this distinction is not accurate, for the Mahayana penetrated to Java, while the Hinayana reached Central Asia and China. But it is true that the development of the Mahayana was due to influences prevalent in northern India and not equally prevalent in the South. The terms Pali and Sanskrit Buddhism are convenient and as accurate as can be expected of any nomenclature covering so large a field.

Though European writers usually talk of *two* Yânas or Vehicles—the great and the little—and though this is clearly the important distinction for historical purposes, yet Indian and Chinese Buddhists frequently enumerate *three*. These are the *Śrâvakayâna*, the vehicle of the ordinary Bhikshu who hopes to become an Arhat, the *Pratyekabuddhayâna* for the rare beings who are able to become Buddhas but do not preach the law to others, and in contrast to both of these the *Mahâyâna* or vehicle of Buddhas and Bodhisattvas. As a rule these three Vehicles are not regarded as hostile or even incompatible. Thus the *Lotus sutra*[1], maintains that there is really but one vehicle though by a wise concession to human weakness the Buddha lets it appear that there are three to suit divers tastes. And the Mahayana is not a single vehicle but rather a train comprising many carriages of different classes. It has an unfortunate but distinct later phase known in Sanskrit as Mantrayâna and Vajrayâna but generally described by Europeans as Tantrism. This phase took some of the worst features in Hinduism, such

[1] Saddharma-Puṇḍarîka, chap. III. For brevity, I usually cite this work by the title of The Lotus.

as spells, charms, and the worship of goddesses, and with misplaced ingenuity fitted them into Buddhism. I shall treat of it in a subsequent chapter, for it is chronologically late. The silence of Hsüan Chuang and I-Ching implies that in the seventh century it was not a noticeable aspect of Indian Buddhism.

Although the record of the Mahayana in literature and art is clear and even brilliant, it is not easy either to trace its rise or connect its development with other events in India. Its annals are an interminable list of names and doctrines, but bring before us few living personalities and hence are dull. They are like a record of the Christian Church's fight against Arians, Monophysites and Nestorians with all the great figures of Byzantine history omitted or called in question. Hence I fear that my readers (if I have any) may find these chapters repellent, a mist of hypotheses and a catalogue of ancient paradoxes. I can only urge that if the history of the Mahayana is uncertain, its teaching fanciful and its scriptures tedious, yet it has been a force of the first magnitude in the secular history and art of China, Japan and Tibet and even to-day the most metaphysical of its sacred books, the Diamond Cutter, has probably more readers than Kant and Hegel.

Since the early history of the Mahayana is a matter for argument rather than precise statement, it will perhaps be best to begin with some account of its doctrines and literature and proceed afterwards to chronology. I may, however, mention that general tradition connects it with King Kanishka and asserts that the great doctors Aśvaghosha and Nâgârjuna lived in and immediately after his reign. The attitude of Kanishka and of the Council which he summoned towards the Mahayana is far from clear and I shall say something about this difficult subject below. Unfortunately his date is not beyond dispute for while a considerable consensus of opinion fixes his accession at about 78 A.D., some scholars place it earlier and others in the second century A.D.[1] Apart from this, it appears established that the Sukhâvatî-vyûha which is definitely Mahayanist was translated into Chinese between 147 and 186 A.D. We may assume that it was then already well known and had been composed some time before, so that, whatever Kanishka's date may

[1] The date 58 B.C. has probably few supporters among scholars now, especially after Marshall's discoveries.

have been, Mahayanist doctrines must have been in existence about the time of the Christian era, and perhaps considerably earlier. Naturally no one date like a reign or a council can be selected to mark the beginning of a great school. Such a body of doctrine must have existed piecemeal and unauthorized before it was collected and recognized and some tenets are older than others. Enlarging I-Ching's definition we may find in the Mahayana seven lines of thought or practice. All are not found in all sects and some are shared with the Hinayana but probably none are found fully developed outside the Mahayana. Many of them have parallels in the contemporary phases of Hinduism.

1. A belief in Bodhisattvas and in the power of human beings to become Bodhisattvas.

2. A code of altruistic ethics which teaches that everyone must do good in the interest of the whole world and make over to others any merit he may acquire by his virtues. The aim of the religious life is to become a Bodhisattva, not to become an Arhat.

3. A doctrine that Buddhas are supernatural beings, distributed through infinite space and time, and innumerable. In the language of later theology a Buddha has three bodies and still later there is a group of five Buddhas.

4. Various systems of idealist metaphysics, which tend to regard the Buddha essence or Nirvana much as Brahman is regarded in the Vedanta.

5. A canon composed in Sanskrit and apparently later than the Pali Canon.

6. Habitual worship of images and elaboration of ritual. There is a dangerous tendency to rely on formulæ and charms.

7. A special doctrine of salvation by faith in a Buddha, usually Amitâbha, and invocation of his name. Mahayanism can exist without this doctrine but it is tolerated by most sects and considered essential by some.

CHAPTER XVII

BODHISATTVAS

Let us now consider these doctrines and take first the worship of Bodhisattvas. This word means one whose essence is knowledge but is used in the technical sense of a being who is in process of obtaining but has not yet obtained Buddhahood. The Pali Canon shows little interest in the personality of Bodhisattvas and regards them simply as the preliminary or larval form of a Buddha, either Śâkyamuni[1] or some of his predecessors. It was incredible that a being so superior to ordinary humanity as a Buddha should be suddenly produced in a human family nor could he be regarded as an incarnation in the strict sense. But it was both logical and edifying to suppose that he was the product of a long evolution of virtue, of good deeds and noble resolutions extending through countless ages and culminating in a being superior to the Devas. Such a being awaited in the Tushita heaven the time fixed for his appearance on earth as a Buddha and his birth was accompanied by marvels. But though the Pali Canon thus recognizes the Bodhisattva as a type which, if rare, yet makes its appearance at certain intervals, it leaves the matter there. It is not suggested that saints should try to become Bodhisattvas and Buddhas, or that Bodhisattvas can be helpers of mankind[2]. But both these trains of thought are natural developments of the older ideas and soon made themselves prominent. It is a characteristic doctrine of Mahayanism that men can try and should try to become Bodhisattvas.

[1] In dealing with the Mahayanists, I use the expression Śâkyamuni in preference to Gotama. It is their own title for the teacher and it seems incongruous to use the purely human name of Gotama in describing doctrines which represent him as superhuman.

[2] But Kings Hsin-byu-shin of Burma and Śrî Sûryavaṃsa Râma of Siam have left inscriptions recording their desire to become Buddhas. See my chapters on Burma and Siam below. Mahayanist ideas may easily have entered these countries from China, but even in Ceylon the idea of becoming a Buddha or Bodhisattva is not unknown. See *Manual of a Mystic* (P.T.S. 1916), pp. xviii and 140.

In the Pali Canon we hear of Arhats, Pacceka Buddhas, and perfect Buddhas. For all three the ultimate goal is the same, namely Nirvana, but a Pacceka Buddha is greater than an Arhat, because he has greater intellectual powers though he is not omniscient, and a perfect Buddha is greater still, partly because he is omniscient and partly because he saves others. But if we admit that the career of the Buddha is better and nobler, and also that it is, as the Introduction to the Jâtaka recounts, simply the result of an earnest resolution to school himself and help others, kept firmly through the long chain of existences, there is nothing illogical or presumptuous in making our goal not the quest of personal salvation, but the attainment of Bodhisattvaship, that is the state of those who may aspire to become Buddhas. In fact the Arhat, engrossed in his own salvation, is excused only by his humility and is open to the charge of selfish desire, since the passion for Nirvana is an ambition like any other and the quest for salvation can be best followed by devoting oneself entirely to others. But though my object here is to render intelligible the Mahayanist point of view including its objections to Hinayanism, I must defend the latter from the accusation of selfishness. The vigorous and authoritative character of Gotama led him to regard all mankind as patients requiring treatment and to emphasize the truth that they could cure themselves if they would try. But the Buddhism of the Pali Canon does not ignore the duties of loving and instructing others[1]; it merely insists on man's power to save himself if properly instructed and bids him do it at once: "sell all that thou hast and follow me." And the Mahayana, if less self-centred, has also less self-reliance, and self-discipline. It is more human and charitable, but also more easygoing: it teaches the believer to lean on external supports which if well chosen may be a help, but if trusted without discrimination become paralyzing abuses. And if we look at the abuses of both systems the fossilized monk of the Hinayana will compare favourably

[1] *E.g.* in Itivuttakam 75, there is a description of the man who is like a drought and gives nothing, the man who is like rain in a certain district and the man who is Sabbabhûtânukampako, compassionate to all creatures, and like rain falling everywhere. Similarly *ib.* 84, and elsewhere, we have descriptions of persons (ordinary disciples as well as Buddhas) who are born for the welfare of gods and men bahujanahitâya, bahujanasukhâya, lokânukampâya, atthâya, hitâya, sukhâya devamanussânam.

with the tantric adept. It was to the corruptions of the Mahayana rather than of the Hinayana that the decay of Buddhism in India was due.

The career of the Bodhisattva was early divided into stages (bhûmi) each marked by the acquisition of some virtue in his triumphant course. The stages are variously reckoned as five, seven and ten. The Mahâvastu[1], which is the earliest work where the progress is described, enumerates ten without distinguishing them very clearly. Later writers commonly look at the Bodhisattva's task from the humbler point of view of the beginner who wishes to learn the initiatory stages. For them the Bodhisattva is primarily not a supernatural being or even a saint but simply a religious person who wishes to perform the duties and enjoy the privileges of the Church to the full, much like a communicant in the language of contemporary Christianity. We have a manual for those who would follow this path, in the Bodhicaryâvatâra of Śântideva, which in its humility, sweetness and fervent piety has been rightly compared with the De Imitatione Christi. In many respects the virtues of the Bodhisattva are those of the Arhat. His will must be strenuous and concentrated; he must cultivate the strictest morality, patience, energy, meditation and knowledge. But he is also a devotee, a *bhaktá*: he adores all the Buddhas of the past, present and future as well as sundry superhuman Bodhisattvas, and he confesses his sins, not after the fashion of the Pâtimokkha, but by accusing himself before these heavenly Protectors and vowing to sin no more.

Śântideva lived in the seventh century[2] but tells us that he follows the scriptures and has nothing new to say. This seems to be true for, though his book being a manual of devotion presents its subject-matter in a dogmatic form, its main ideas are stated and even elaborated in the Lotus. Not only are eminent figures in the Church, such as Sâriputra and Ânanda, there designated as future Buddhas, but the same dignity is predicted wholesale for five hundred and again for two thousand

[1] Ed. Senart, vol. I. p. 142.

[2] The Bodhicaryâvatâra was edited by Minayeff, 1889 and also in the *Journal of the Buddhist Text Society* and the *Bibliotheca Indica*. De la Vallée Poussin published parts of the text and commentary in his *Bouddhisme* and also a translation in 1907.

monks while in Chapter x is sketched the course to be followed by "young men or young ladies of good family" who wish to become Bodhisattvas[1]. The chief difference is that the Bodhicaryâvatâra portrays a more spiritual life, it speaks more of devotion, less of the million shapes that compose the heavenly host: more of love and wisdom, less of the merits of reading particular sûtras. While rendering to it and the faith that produced it all honour, we must remember that it is typical of the Mahayana only in the sense that the De Imitatione Christi is typical of Roman Catholicism, for both faiths have other sides.

Śântideva's Bodhisattva, when conceiving the thought of Bodhi or eventual supreme enlightenment to be obtained, it may be, only after numberless births, feels first a sympathetic joy in the good actions of all living beings. He addresses to the Buddhas a prayer which is not a mere act of commemoration, but a request to preach the law and to defer their entrance into Nirvana. He then makes over to others whatever merit he may possess or acquire and offers himself and all his possessions, moral and material, as a sacrifice for the salvation of all beings. This on the one hand does not much exceed the limits of *dânam* or the virtue of giving as practised by Śâkyamuni in previous births according to the Pali scriptures, but on the other it contains in embryo the doctrine of vicarious merit and salvation through a saviour. The older tradition admits that the future Buddha (*e.g.* in the Vessantara birth-story) gives all that is asked from him including life, wife and children. To consider the surrender and transfer of merit (pattidâna in Pali) as parallel is a natural though perhaps false analogy. But the transfer of Karma is not altogether foreign to Brahmanic thought, for it is held that a wife may share in her husband's Karma nor is it wholly unknown to Sinhalese Buddhism[2]. After thus deliberately rejecting all personal success and selfish aims, the neophyte makes a vow (praṇidhâna) to acquire enlightenment for the good of all beings and not to swerve from the rules of life and faith requisite for this end. He is then a "son

[1] The career of the Bodhisattva is also discussed in detail in the Avatamsaka sûtra and in works attributed to Nâgârjuna and Sthiramati, the Lakshaṇa-vimukta-hṛidaya-śâstra and the Mahâyâna-dharma-dhâtvaviśeshata-śâstra. I only know of these works as quoted by Teitaro Suzuki.

[2] See Childers, *Pali Dict.* s.v. Patti, Pattianuppadânam and Puñño.

of Buddha," a phrase which is merely a natural metaphor for saying that he is one of the household of faith[1] but still paves the way to later ideas which make the celestial Bodhisattva an emanation or spiritual son of a celestial Buddha.

Asanga gives[2] a more technical and scholastic description of the ten *bhûmis* or stages which mark the Bodhisattva's progress towards complete enlightenment and culminate in a phase bearing the remarkable but ancient name of Dharmamegha known also to the Yoga philosophy. The other stages are called: *muditâ* (joyful): *vimalâ* (immaculate): *prabhâkarî* (light giving): *arcismatî* (radiant): *durjaya* (hard to gain): *abhimukhî* (facing, because it faces both transmigration and Nirvana): *dûramgamâ* (far-going): *acalâ* (immovable): *sâdhumatî* (good minded).

The incarnate Buddhas and Bodhisattvas of Tibet are a travesty of the Mahayana which on Indian soil adhered to the sound doctrine that saints are known by their achievements as men and cannot be selected among infant prodigies[3]. It was the general though not universal opinion that one who had entered on the career of a Bodhisattva could not fall so low as to be reborn in any state of punishment, but the spirit of humility and self-effacement which has always marked the Buddhist ideal tended to represent his triumph as incalculably distant. Meanwhile, although in the whirl of births he was on the upward grade, he yet had his ups and downs and there is no evidence that Indian or Far Eastern Buddhists arrogated to themselves special claims and powers on the ground that they were well advanced in the career of Buddhahood. The vow to suppress self and follow the light not only in this life but in all future births contains an element of faith or fantasy, but has any religion formed a nobler or even equivalent picture of the soul's destiny or built a better staircase from the world of men to the immeasurable spheres of the superhuman?

One aspect of the story of Śâkyamuni and his antecedent births thus led to the idea that all may become Buddhas. An

[1] It occurs in the Pali Canon, *e.g.* Itivuttakam 100. Tassa me tumhe puttâ orasâ, mukhato jâtâ, dhammajâ.

[2] See Sylvain Lévi, *Mahâyâna-sûtrâlankâra:* introduction and passim. For much additional information about the Bhûmis see De la Vallée Poussin's article "Bodhisattva" in *E.R.E.*

[3] Eminent doctors such as Nâgârjuna and Asanga are often described as Bodhi sattvas just as eminent Hindu teachers, *e.g.* Caitanya, are described as Avatâras.

equally natural development in another direction created celestial and superhuman Bodhisattvas. The Hinayana held that Gotama, before his last birth, dwelt in the Tushita heaven enjoying the power and splendour of an Indian god and it looked forward to the advent of Maitreya. But it admitted no other Bodhisattvas, a consequence apparently of the doctrine that there can only be one Buddha at a time. But the luxuriant fancy of India, which loves to multiply divinities, soon broke through this restriction and fashioned for itself beautiful images of benevolent beings who refuse the bliss of Nirvana that they may alleviate the sufferings of others[1]. So far as we can judge, the figures of these Bodhisattvas took shape just about the same time that the personalities of Vishnu and Śiva were acquiring consistency. The impulse in both cases is the same, namely the desire to express in a form accessible to human prayer and sympathetic to human emotion the forces which rule the universe. But in this work of portraiture the Buddhists laid more emphasis on moral and spiritual law than did the Brahmans: they isolated in personification qualities not found isolated in nature. Śiva is the law of change, of death and rebirth, with all the riot of slaughter and priapism which it entails: Vishnu is the protector and preserver, the type of good energy warring against evil, but the unity of the figure is smothered by mythology and broken up into various incarnations. But Avalokita and Manjuśrî, though they had not such strong roots in Indian humanity as Śiva and Vishnu, are genii of purer and brighter presence. They are the personifications of kindness and knowledge. Though manifold in shape, they have little to do with mythology, and are analogous to the archangels of Christian and Jewish tradition and to the Amesha Spentas of Zoroastrianism. With these latter they may have some historical connection, for Persian ideas may well have influenced Buddhism about the time of the Christian era. However difficult it may be to prove the foreign origin of Bodhisattvas, few of them have a clear origin in India and all of them

[1] The idea that Arhats may postpone their entry into Nirvana for the good of the world is not unknown to the Pali Canon. According to the Maha Parin-Sutta the Buddha himself might have done so. Legends which cannot be called definitely Mahayanist relate how Piṇḍola and others are to tarry until Maitreya come and how Kâśyapa in a less active rôle awaits him in a cave or tomb, ready to revive at his advent. See *J.A.* 1916, II. pp. 196, 270.

are much better known in Central Asia and China. But they are represented with the appearance and attributes of Indian Devas, as is natural, since even in the Pali Canon Devas form the Buddha's retinue. The early Buddhists considered that these spirits, whether called Bodhisattvas or Devas, had attained their high position in the same way as Śâkyamuni himself, that is by the practice of moral and intellectual virtues through countless existences, but subsequently they came to be regarded as emanations or sons of superhuman Buddhas. Thus the Kâraṇḍa-vyûha relates how the original Âdi-Buddha produced Avalokita by meditation and how he in his turn produced the universe with its gods.

Millions of unnamed Bodhisattvas are freely mentioned and even in the older books copious lists of names are found[1], but two, Avalokita and Manjuśri, tower above the rest, among whom only few have a definite personality. The tantric school counts eight of the first rank. Maitreya (who does not stand on the same footing as the others), Samantabhadra, Mahâsthâna-prâpta and above all Kshitigarbha, have some importance, especially in China and Japan.

Avalokita[2] in many forms and in many ages has been one of the principal deities of Asia but his origin is obscure. His main attributes are plain. He is the personification of divine mercy and pity but even the meaning of his name is doubtful. In its full form it is Avalokiteśvara, often rendered the Lord who looks down (from heaven). This is an appropriate title for the God of Mercy, but the obvious meaning of the participle *avalokita* in Sanskrit is passive, the Lord who is looked at. Kern[3] thinks it may mean the Lord who is everywhere visible as a very present help in trouble, or else the Lord of View, like the epithet Dṛishtiguru applied to Śiva. Another form of the name is Lokeśvara or Lord of the world and this suggests that *avalokita* may be a synonym of *loka*, meaning the visible universe. It has also been suggested that the name may refer to the small image of Amitâbha which is set in his diadem and thus looks down on him. But such small images set in the head of a larger figure are not distinctive of Avalokita: they are found

[1] *E.g.* Lotus, chap. I.

[2] De la Vallée Poussin's article "Avalokita" in *E.R.E.* may be consulted.

[3] Lotus, *S.B.E.* XXI. p. 407.

in other Buddhist statues and paintings and also outside India, for instance at Palmyra. The Tibetan translation of the name[1] means he who sees with bright eyes. Hsüan Chuang's rendering Kwan-tzŭ-tsai[2] expresses the same idea, but the more usual Chinese translation Kuan-yin or Kuan-shih-yin, the deity who looks upon voices or the region of voices, seems to imply a verbal misunderstanding. For the use of Yin or voice makes us suspect that the translator identified the last part of *Avalokiteśvara* not with *Îśvara* lord but with *svara* sound[3].

Avalokiteśvara is unknown to the Pali Canon and the Milinda Pañha. So far as I can discover he is not mentioned in the Divyâvadâna, Jâtakamâlâ or any work attributed to Aśvaghosha. His name does not occur in the Lalita-vistara but a list of Bodhisattvas in its introductory chapter includes Mahâkaruṇâcandin, suggesting Mahâkaruna, the Great Compassionate, which is one of his epithets. In the Lotus[4] he is placed second in the introductory list of Bodhisattvas after Manjuśrî. But Chapter XXIV, which is probably a later addition, is dedicated to his praises as Samantamukha, he who looks every way or the omnipresent. In this section his character as the all-merciful saviour is fully developed. He saves those who call on him from shipwreck, and execution, from robbers and all violence and distress. He saves too from moral evils, such as passion, hatred and folly. He grants children to women who worship him. This power, which is commonly exercised by female deities, is worth remarking as a hint of his subsequent transformation into a goddess. For the better achievement of his merciful deeds, he assumes all manner of forms, and appears in the guise of a Buddha, a Bodhisattva, a Hindu deity, a goblin, or a Brahman and in fact in any shape. This chapter was translated into Chinese before 417 A.D. and therefore can hardly be later than 350. He is also mentioned in the Sukhâvatî-vyûha.

[1] sPyan-ras-gzigs rendered in Mongol by Nidübär-üdzäkci. The other common Mongol name Ariobalo appears to be a corruption of Âryâvalokita.

[2] Meaning apparently the seeing and self-existent one. Cf. Ta-tzŭ-tsai as a name of Śiva.

[3] A maidservant in the drama Mâlatîmâdhava is called Avalokitâ. It is not clear whether it is a feminine form of the divine name or an adjective meaning looked-at, or admirable.

[4] *S.B.E.* XXI. pp. 4 and 406 ff. It was translated in Chinese between A.D. 265 and 316 and chap. XXIV was separately translated between A.D. 384 and 417. See Nanjio, Catalogue Nos. 136, 137, 138.

The records of the Chinese pilgrims Fa-Hsien and Hsüan Chuang[1] indicate that his worship prevailed in India from the fourth till the seventh century and we are perhaps justified in dating its beginnings at least two centuries earlier. But the absence of any mention of it in the writings of Aśvaghosha is remarkable[2].

Avalokita is connected with a mountain called Potala or Potalaka. The name is borne by the palace of the Grand Lama at Lhassa and by another Lamaistic establishment at Jehol in north China. It reappears in the sacred island of P'u-t'o near Ningpo. In all these cases the name of Avalokita's Indian residence has been transferred to foreign shrines. In India there were at least two places called Potala or Potalaka—one at the mouth of the Indus and one in the south. No certain connection has been traced between the former and the Bodhisattva but in the seventh century the latter was regarded as his abode. Our information about it comes mainly from Hsüan Chuang[3] who describes it when speaking of the Malakuta country and as near the Mo-lo-ya (Malaya) mountain. But apparently he did not visit it and this makes it probable that it was not a religious centre but a mountain in the south of which Buddhists in the north wrote with little precision[4]. There is no evidence that Avalokita was first worshipped on this Potalaka, though he is often associated with mountains such as Kapota in Magadha and Valavatî in Katâha[5]. In fact the connection of Potala with Avalokita remains a mystery.

Avalokita has, like most Bodhisattvas, many names. Among the principal are Mahâkaruna, the Great Compassionate one, Lokanâtha or Lokeśvara, the Lord of the world, and Padmapâni, or lotus-handed. This last refers to his appearance as portrayed in statues and miniatures. In the older works of art his figure

[1] Hsüan Chuang (Watters, II. 215, 224) relates how an Indian sage recited the Sui-hsin dhârani before Kuan-tzŭ-tsai's image for three years.

[2] As will be noticed from time to time in these pages, the sudden appearance of new deities in Indian literature often seems strange. The fact is that until deities are generally recognized, standard works pay no attention to them.

[3] Watters, vol. II. pp. 228 ff. It is said that Potalaka is also mentioned in the Hwa-yen-ching or Avatamsaka sûtra. Tibetan tradition connects it with the Śâkya family. See Csoma de Körös, Tibetan studies reprinted 1912, pp. 32–34.

[4] Just as the Lankâvatâra sûtra purports to have been delivered at *Lankapura-samudra-malaya-śikhara* rendered in the Chinese translation as "in the city of Lanka on the summit of the Malaya mountain on the border of the sea."

[5] See Foucher, *Iconographie bouddhique*, 1900, pp. 100, 102.

is human, without redundant limbs, and represents a youth in the costume of an Indian prince with a high jewelled chignon, or sometimes a crown. The head-dress is usually surmounted by a small figure of Amitâbha. His right hand is extended in the position known as the gesture of charity[1]. In his left he carries a red lotus and he often stands on a larger blossom. His complexion is white or red. Sometimes he has four arms and in later images a great number. He then carries besides the lotus such objects as a book, a rosary and a jug of nectar[2].

The images with many eyes and arms seem an attempt to represent him as looking after the unhappy in all quarters and stretching out his hands in help[3]. It is doubtful if the Bodhisattvas of the Gandhara sculptures, though approaching the type of Avalokita, represent him rather than any other, but nearly all the Buddhist sites of India contain representations of him which date from the early centuries of our era[4] and others are preserved in the miniatures of manuscripts[5].

He is not a mere adaptation of any one Hindu god. Some of his attributes are also those of Brahmâ. Though in some late texts he is said to have evolved the world from himself, his characteristic function is not to create but, like Vishnu, to save and like Vishnu he holds a lotus. But also he has the title of Îśvara, which is specially applied to Śiva. Thus he does not issue from any local cult and has no single mythological pedigree but is the idea of divine compassion represented with such materials as the art and mythology of the day offered.

He is often accompanied by a female figure Târâ[6]. In the tantric period she is recognized as his spouse and her images, common in northern India from the seventh century onwards,

[1] Varamudra.

[2] These as well as the red colour are attributes of the Hindu deity Brahmâ.

[3] A temple on the north side of the lake in the Imperial City at Peking contains a gigantic image of him which has literally a thousand heads and a thousand hands. This monstrous figure is a warning against an attempt to represent metaphors literally.

[4] Waddell on the Cult of Avalokita, *J.R.A.S.* 1894, pp. 51 ff. thinks they are not earlier than the fifth century.

[5] See especially Foucher, *Iconographie Bouddhique*, Paris, 1900.

[6] See especially de Blonay, *Études pour servir à l'histoire de la déesse bouddhique Târâ*, Paris, 1895. Târâ continued to be worshipped as a Hindu goddess after Buddhism had disappeared and several works were written in her honour. See Raj. Mitra, *Search for Sk. MSS.* IV. 168, 171, x. 67.

show that she was adored as a female Bodhisattva. In Tibet Târâ is an important deity who assumes many forms and even before the tantric influence had become prominent she seems to have been associated with Avalokita. In the Dharmasangraha she is named as one of the four Devîs, and she is mentioned twice under the name of To-lo Pu-sa by Hsüan Chuang, who saw a statue of her in Vaisali and another at Tiladhaka in Magadha. This last stood on the right of a gigantic figure of Buddha, Avalokita being on his left[1].

Hsüan Chuang distinguishes To-lo (Târâ) and Kuan-tzŭ-tsai. The latter under the name of Kuan-yin or Kwannon has become the most popular goddess of China and Japan, but is apparently a form of Avalokita. The god in his desire to help mankind assumes many shapes and, among these, divine womanhood has by the suffrage of millions been judged the most appropriate. But Târâ was not originally the same as Kuan-yin, though the fact that she accompanies Avalokita and shares his attributes may have made it easier to think of him in female form[2].

The circumstances in which Avalokita became a goddess are obscure. The Indian images of him are not feminine, although his sex is hardly noticed before the tantric period. He is not a male deity like Krishna, but a strong, bright spirit and like the Christian archangels above sexual distinctions. No female form of him is reported from Tibet and this confirms the idea that none was known in India[3], and that the change was made in China. It was probably facilitated by the worship of Târâ and of Hâritî, an ogress who was converted by the Buddha and is frequently represented in her regenerate state caressing a child.

[1] About the time of Hsüan Chuang's travels Sarvajñâmitra wrote a hymn to Târâ which has been preserved and published by de Blonay, 1894.

[2] Chinese Buddhists say Târâ and Kuan-Yin are the same but the difference between them is this. Târâ is an Indian and Lamaist goddess *associated* with Avalokita and in origin analogous to the Śaktis of Tantrism. Kuan-yin is a female form of Avalokita who can assume all shapes. The original Kuan-yin was a male deity: male Kuan-yins are not unknown in China and are said to be the rule in Korea. But Târâ and Kuan-yin may justly be described as the same in so far as they are attempts to embody the idea of divine pity in a Madonna.

[3] But many scholars think that the formula Om maṇipadme hum, which is supposed to be addressed to Avalokita, is really an invocation to a form of Śakti called Maṇipadmâ. A Nepalese inscription says that "The Śâktas call him Śakti" (*E.R.E.* vol. II. p. 260 and *J.A.* IX. 192), but this may be merely a way of saying that he is identical with the great gods of all sects.

She is mentioned by Hsüan Chuang and by I-Ching who adds that her image was already known in China. The Chinese also worshipped a native goddess called T'ien-hou or T'ou-mu. Kuan-yin was also identified with an ancient Chinese heroine called Miao-shên[1]. This is parallel to the legend of Ti-tsang (Kshitigarbha) who, though a male Bodhisattva, was a virtuous maiden in two of his previous existences. Evidently Chinese religious sentiment required a Madonna and it is not unnatural if the god of mercy, who was reputed to assume many shapes and to give sons to the childless, came to be thought of chiefly in a feminine form. The artists of the T'ang dynasty usually represented Avalokita as a youth with a slight moustache and the evidence as to early female figures does not seem to me strong[2], though *a priori* I see no reason for doubting their existence. In 1102 a Chinese monk named P'u-ming published a romantic legend of Kuan-yin's earthly life which helped to popularize her worship. In this and many other cases the later developments of Buddhism are due to Chinese fancy and have no connection with Indian tradition.

Târâ is a goddess of north India, Nepal and the Lamaist Church and almost unknown in China and Japan. Her name means she who causes to cross, that is who saves, life and its troubles being by a common metaphor described as a sea. Târâ also means a star and in Puranic mythology is the name given to the mother of Buddha, the planet Mercury. Whether the name was first used by Buddhists or Brahmans is unknown, but after the seventh century there was a decided tendency to give Târâ the epithets bestowed on the Śaktis of Śiva and assimilate her to those goddesses. Thus in the list of her 108 names[3] she is described among other more amiable attributes as

[1] Harlez, *Livre des esprits et des immortels*, p. 195, and Doré, *Recherches sur les superstitions en Chine*, pp. 94–138.

[2] See Fenollosa, *Epochs of Chinese and Japanese Art*, I. pp. 105 and 124; Johnston, *Buddhist China*, 275 ff. Several Chinese deities appear to be of uncertain or varying sex. Thus Chun-ti is sometimes described as a deified Chinese General and sometimes identified with the Indian goddess Marîcî. Yü-ti, generally masculine, is sometimes feminine. See Doré, *l.c.* 212. Still more strangely the Patriarch Aśvaghosha (Ma Ming) is represented by a female figure. On the other hand the monk Ta Shêng (c. 705 A.D.) is said to have been an incarnation of the female Kuan Yin. Mañjuśrî is said to be worshipped in Nepal sometimes as a male, sometimes as a female. See Bendall and Haraprasad, *Nepalese MSS.* p. lxvii.

[3] de Blonay, *l.c.* pp. 48–57.

terrible, furious, the slayer of evil beings, the destroyer, and Kâlî: also as carrying skulls and being the mother of the Vedas. Here we have if not the borrowing by Buddhists of a Śaiva deity, at least the grafting of Śaiva conceptions on a Bodhisattva.

The second great Bodhisattva Mañjuśrî[1] has other similar names, such as Mañjunâtha and Mañjughosha, the word Mañju meaning sweet or pleasant. He is also Vagîśvara, the Lord of Speech, and Kumârabhûta, the Prince, which possibly implies that he is the Buddha's eldest son, charged with the government under his direction. He has much the same literary history as Avalokita, not being mentioned in the Pali Canon nor in the earlier Sanskrit works such as the Lalita-vistara and Divyâvadâna. But his name occurs in the Sukhâvatî-vyûha: he is the principal interlocutor in the Lankâvatâra sûtra and is extolled in the Ratnakaraṇḍa-vyûha-sûtra[2]. In the greater part of the Lotus he is the principal Bodhisattva and instructs Maitreya, because, though his youth is eternal, he has known many Buddhas through innumerable ages. The Lotus[3] also recounts how he visited the depths of the sea and converted the inhabitants thereof and how the Lord taught him what are the duties of a Bodhisattva after the Buddha has entered finally into Nirvana. As a rule he has no consort and appears as a male Athene, all intellect and chastity, but sometimes Lakshmî or Sarasvatî or both are described as his consorts[4].

His worship prevailed not only in India but in Nepal, Tibet, China, Japan and Java. Fa-Hsien states that he was honoured in Central India, and Hsüan Chuang that there were stupas dedicated to him at Muttra[5]. He is also said to have been incarnate in Atîśa, the Tibetan reformer, and in Vairocana who introduced Buddhism to Khotan, but, great as is his benevolence, he is not so much the helper of human beings, which is Avalokita's special function, as the personification of thought,

[1] Chinese, Man-chu-shih-li, or Wên-shu; Japanese, Monju; Tibetan, hJam-pahi-dbyans (pronounced Jam-yang).

Mañju is good Sanskrit, but it must be confessed that the name has a Central-Asian ring.

[2] Translated into Chinese 270 A.D.

[3] Chaps. XI and XIII.

[4] A special work Mañjuśrîvikrîḍita (Nanjio, 184, 185) translated into Chinese 313 A.D. is quoted as describing Mañjuśrî's transformations and exploits.

[5] Hsüan Chuang also relates how he assisted a philosopher called Ch'en-na (=Diṅnâga) and bade him study Mahayanist books.

knowledge, and meditation. It is for this that he has in his hands the sword of knowledge and a book. A beautiful figure from Java bearing these emblems is in the Berlin Museum[1]. Miniatures represent him as of a yellow colour with the hands (when they do not carry emblems) set in the position known as teaching the law[2]. Other signs which distinguish his images are the blue lotus and the lion on which he sits.

An interesting fact about Mañjuśrî is his association with China[3], not only in Chinese but in late Indian legends. The mountain Wu-t'ai-shan in the province of Shan-si is sacred to him and is covered with temples erected in his honour[4]. The name (mountain of five terraces) is rendered in Sanskrit as Pancaśîrsha, or Pancaśikha, and occurs both in the Svayambhû Purâṇa and in the text appended to miniatures representing Mañjuśrî. The principal temple is said to have been erected between 471 and 500 A.D. I have not seen any statement that the locality was sacred in pre-Buddhist times, but it was probably regarded as the haunt of deities, one of whom—perhaps some spirit of divination—was identified with the wise Mañjuśrî. It is possible that during the various inroads of Græco-Bactrians, Yüeh-Chih, and other Central Asian tribes into India, Mañjuśrî was somehow imported into the pantheon of the Mahayana from China or Central Asia, and he has, especially in the earlier descriptions, a certain pure and abstract quality which recalls the Amesha-Spentas of Persia. But still his attributes are Indian, and there is little positive evidence of a foreign origin. I-Ching is the first to tell us that the Hindus believed he came from China[5]. Hsüan Chuang does not mention this belief, and probably did not hear of it, for it is an interesting detail which no one writing for a Chinese audience would have omitted. We may therefore suppose that the idea arose in India about 650 A.D. By that date the temples of Wu-t'ai-Shan would

[1] It is reproduced in Grünwedel's *Buddhist Art in India*. Translated by Gibson, 1901, p. 200.

[2] Dharmacakramudra.

[3] For the Nepalese legends see S. Levi, *Le Nepal*, 1905–9.

[4] For an account of this sacred mountain see Edkins, *Religion in China*, chaps. XVII to XIX.

[5] See I-tsing, trans. Takakusu, 1896, p. 136. For some further remarks on the possible foreign origin of Mañjuśrî see below, chapter on Central Asia. The verses attributed to King Harsha (Nanjio, 1071) praise the reliquaries of China but without details.

have had time to become celebrated, and the visits paid to India by distinguished Chinese Buddhists would be likely to create the impression that China was a centre of the faith and frequented by Bodhisattvas[1]. We hear that Vajrabodhi (about 700) and Prajña (782) both went to China to adore Mañjuśrî. In 824 a Tibetan envoy arrived at the Chinese Court to ask for an image of Mañjuśrî, and later the Grand Lamas officially recognized that he was incarnate in the Emperor[2]. Another legend relates that Mañjuśrî came from Wu-t'ai-Shan to adore a miraculous lotus[3] that appeared on the lake which then filled Nepal. With a blow of his sword he cleft the mountain barrier and thus drained the valley and introduced civilization. There may be hidden in this some tradition of the introduction of culture into Nepal but the Nepalese legends are late and in their collected form do not go back beyond the sixteenth century.

After Avalokita and Mañjuśrî the most important Bodhisattva is Maitreya[4], also called Ajita or unconquered, who is the only one recognized by the Pali Canon[5]. This is because he does not stand on the same footing as the others. They are superhuman in their origin as well as in their career, whereas Maitreya is simply a being who like Gotama has lived innumerable lives and ultimately made himself worthy of Buddhahood which he awaits in heaven. There is no reason to doubt that Gotama regarded himself as one in a series of Buddhas: the Pali scriptures relate that he mentioned his predecessors by name, and also spoke of unnumbered Buddhas to come[6]. Nevertheless Maitreya or Metteyya is rarely mentioned in the Pali Canon[7].

[1] Some of the Tantras, *e.g.* the Mahâcînakramâcâra, though they do not connect Mañjuśrî with China, represent some of their most surprising novelties as having been brought thence by ancient sages like Vasishṭha.

[2] *J.R.A.S.* new series, XII. 522 and *J.A.S.B.* 1882, p. 41. The name Manchu perhaps contributed to this belief.

[3] It is described as a Svayambhû or spontaneous manifestation of the Âdi-Buddha.

[4] Sanskrit, Maitreya; Pali, Metteyya; Chinese, Mi-li; Japanese, Miroku; Mongol, Maidari; Tibetan, Byams-pa (pronounced Jampa). For the history of the Maitreya idea see especially Péri, *B.E.F.E.O.* 1911, pp. 439–457.

[5] But a Siamese inscription of about 1361, possibly influenced by Chinese Mahayanism, speaks of the ten Bodhisattvas headed by Metteyya. See *B.E.F.E.O.* 1917, No. 2, pp. 30, 31.

[6] *E.g.* in the Mahâparinibbâna Sûtra.

[7] Dig. Nik. XXVI. 25 and Buddhavamsa, XXVII. 19, and even this last verse is said to be an addition.

He is, however, frequently alluded to in the exegetical Pali literature, in the Anâgata-vaṃsa and in the earlier Sanskrit works such as the Lalita-vistara, the Divyâvadâna and Mahâ-vastu. In the Lotus he plays a prominent part, but still is subordinate to Mañjuśrî. Ultimately he was eclipsed by the two great Bodhisattvas but in the early centuries of our era he received much respect. His images are frequent in all parts of the Buddhist world: he was believed to watch over the propagation of the Faith[1], and to have made special revelations to Asaṅga[2]. In paintings he is usually of a golden colour: his statues, which are often gigantic, show him standing or sitting in the European fashion and not cross-legged. He appears to be represented in the earliest Gandharan sculptures and there was a famous image of him in Udyâna of which Fa-Hsien (399–414 A.D.) speaks as if it were already ancient[3]. Hsüan Chuang describes it as well as a stupa erected[4] to commemorate Śâkyamuni's prediction that Maitreya would be his successor. On attaining Buddhahood he will become lord of a terrestrial paradise and hold three assemblies under a dragon flower tree[5], at which all who have been good Buddhists in previous births will become Arhats. I-Ching speaks of meditating on the advent of Maitreya in language like that which Christian piety uses of the second coming of Christ and concludes a poem which is incorporated in his work with the aspiration "Deep as the depth of a lake be my pure and calm meditation. Let me look for the first meeting under the Tree of the Dragon Flower when I hear the deep rippling voice of the Buddha Maitreya[6]." But messianic

[1] See *e.g.* Watters, *Yüan Chwang*, I. 239.

[2] See Watters and Péri in *B.E.F.E.O.* 1911, 439. A temple of Maitreya has been found at Turfan in Central Asia with a Chinese inscription which speaks of him as an active and benevolent deity manifesting himself in many forms.

[3] He has not fared well in Chinese iconography which represents him as an enormously fat smiling monk. In the Liang dynasty there was a monk called Pu-tai (Jap. Hotei) who was regarded as an incarnation of Maitreya and became a popular subject for caricature. It would appear that the Bodhisattva himself has become superseded by this cheerful but undignified incarnation.

[4] The stupa was apparently at Benares but Hsüan Chuang's narrative is not clear and other versions make Râjagṛiha or Śrâvasti the scene of the prediction.

[5] Campa. This is his bodhi tree under which he will obtain enlightenment as Śâkyamuni under the *Ficus religiosa*. Each Buddha has his own special kind of bodhi tree.

[6] *Record of the Buddhist religion*, Trans. Takakusu, p. 213. See too Watters, *Yüan Chwang*, II. 57, 144, 210, 215.

ideas were not much developed in either Buddhism or Hinduism and perhaps the figures of both Maitreya and Kalkî owe something to Persian legends about Saoshyant the Saviour.

The other Bodhisattvas, though lauded in special treatises, have left little impression on Indian Buddhism and have obtained in the Far East most of whatever importance they possess. The makers of images and miniatures assign to each his proper shape and colour, but when we read about them we feel that we are dealing not with the objects of real worship or even the products of a lively imagination, but with names and figures which have a value for picturesque but conventional art.

Among the best known is Samantabhadra, the all gracious[1], who is still a popular deity in Tibet and the patron saint of the sacred mountain Omei in China, with which he is associated as Mañjuśrî with Wu-t'ai-shan. He is represented as green and riding on an elephant. In Indian Buddhism he has a moderately prominent position. He is mentioned in the Dharmasangraha and in one chapter of the Lotus he is charged with the special duty of protecting those who follow the law. But the Chinese pilgrims do not mention his worship.

Mahâsthâmaprâpta[2] is a somewhat similar figure. A chapter of the Lotus (XIX) is dedicated to him without however giving any clear idea of his personality and he is extolled in several descriptions of Sukhâvatî or Paradise, especially in the Amitâyurdhyâna-sûtra. Together with Amitâbha and Avalokita he forms a triad who rule this Happy Land and are often represented by three images in Chinese temples.

Vajrapâṇî is mentioned in many lists of Bodhisattvas (*e.g.* in the Dharmasangraha) but is of somewhat doubtful position as Hsüan Chuang calls him a deva[3]. Historically his recognition as a Bodhisattva is interesting for he is merely Indra transformed into a Buddhist. The mysterious personages called Vajradhara and Vajrasattva, who in later times are even

[1] Chinese P'u-hsien. See Johnston, *From Peking to Mandalay*, for an interesting account of Mt. Omei.

[2] Or Mahâsthâna. Chinese, Tai-shih-chih. He appears to be the Arhat Maudgalyâyana deified. In China and Japan there is a marked tendency to regard all Bodhisattvas as ancient worthies who by their vows and virtues have risen to their present high position. But these euhemeristic explanations are common in the Far East and the real origin of the Bodhisattvas may be quite different.

[3] *E.g.* Watters, I. p. 229, II. 215.

identified with the original Buddha spirit, are further developments of Vajrapâṇi. He owes his elevation to the fact that *Vajra*, originally meaning simply thunderbolt, came to be used as a mystical expression for the highest truth.

More important than these is Kshitigarbha, Ti-tsang or Jizō[1] who in China and Japan ranks second only to Kuan-yin. Visser has consecrated to him an interesting monograph[2] which shows what strange changes and chances may attend spirits and how ideal figures may alter as century after century they travel from land to land. We know little about the origin of Kshitigarbha. The name seems to mean Earth-womb and he has a shadowy counterpart in Akâśagarbha, a similar deity of the air, who it seems never had a hold on human hearts. The Earth is generally personified as a goddess[3] and Kshitigarbha has some slight feminine traits, though on the whole decidedly masculine. The stories of his previous births relate how he was twice a woman: in Japan he was identified with the mountain goddess of Kamado, and he helps women in labour, a boon generally accorded by goddesses. In the pantheon of India he played an inconspicuous part[4], though reckoned one of the eight great Bodhisattvas, but met with more general esteem in Turkestan, where he began to collect the attributes afterwards defined in the Far East. It is there that his history and transformations become clear.

He is primarily a deity of the nether world, but like Amitâbha and Avalokita he made a vow to help all living creatures and specially to deliver them from hell. The Taoists pictured hell as divided into ten departments ruled over by as many kings, and Chinese fancy made Ti-tsang the superintendent of these functionaries. He thus becomes not so much a Saviour as the kindly superintendent of a prison who preaches to the inmates and willingly procures their release. Then we hear of six Ti-tsangs, corresponding to the six worlds of sentient beings, the gracious spirit being supposed to multiply his personality in

[1] Kshitigarbha is translated into Chinese as Ti-tsang and Jizō is the Japanese pronunciation of the same two characters.

[2] In *Ostasiat. Ztsft.* 1913–15. See too Johnston, *Buddhist China*, chap. VIII.

[3] The Earth goddess is known to the earliest Buddhist legends. The Buddha called her to witness when sitting under the Bo tree.

[4] Three Sûtras, analysed by Visser, treat of Kshitigarbha. They are Nanjio, Nos. 64, 65, 67.

order to minister to the wants of all. He is often represented as a monk, staff in hand and with shaven head. The origin of this guise is not clear and it perhaps refers to his previous births. But in the eighth century a monk of Chiu Hua[1] was regarded as an incarnation of Ti-tsang and after death his body was gilded and enshrined as an object of worship. In later times the Bodhisattva was confused with the incarnation, in the same way as the portly figure of Pu-tai, commonly known as the laughing Buddha, has been substituted for Maitreya in Chinese iconography.

In Japan the cult of the six Jizōs became very popular. They were regarded as the deities of roads[2] and their effigies ultimately superseded the ancient phallic gods of the crossways. In this martial country the Bodhisattva assumed yet another character as Shōgun Jizō, a militant priest riding on horseback[3] and wearing a helmet who became the patron saint of warriors and was even identified with the Japanese war god, Hachiman. Until the seventeenth century Jizō was worshipped principally by soldiers and priests, but subsequently his cult spread among all classes and in all districts. His benevolent activities as a guide and saviour were more and more emphasized: he heals sickness, he lengthens life, he leads to heaven, he saves from hell: he even suffers as a substitute in hell and is the special protector of the souls of children amid the perils of the underworld. Though this modern figure of Jizō is wrought with ancient materials, it is in the main a work of Japanese sentiment.

[1] A celebrated monastery in the portion of An-hui which lies to the south of the Yang-tse. See Johnston, *Buddhist China*, chaps. VIII, IX and X.

[2] There is some reason to think that even in Turkestan Kshitigarbha was a god of roads.

[3] In Annam too Jizō is represented on horseback.

CHAPTER XVIII

THE BUDDHAS OF MAHAYANISM

THIS mythology did not grow up around the Buddha without affecting the central figure. To understand the extraordinary changes of meaning both mythological and metaphysical which the word Buddha undergoes in Mahayanist theology we must keep in mind not the personality of Gotama but the idea that he is one of several successive Buddhas who for convenience may be counted as four, seven or twenty-four but who really form an infinite series extending without limit backwards into the past and forwards into the future[1]. This belief in a series of Buddhas produced a plentiful crop of imaginary personalities and also of speculations as to their connection with one another, with the phenomena of the world and with the human soul.

In the Pali Canon the Buddhas antecedent to Gotama are introduced much like ancient kings as part of the legendary history of this world. But in the Lalita-vistara (Chap. XX) and the Lotus (Chap. VII) we hear of Buddhas, usually described as Tathâgatas, who apparently do not belong to this world at all, but rule various points of the compass, or regions described as Buddha-fields (Buddha-kshetra). Their names are not the same in the different accounts and we remain dazzled by an endless panorama of an infinity of universes with an infinity of shining Buddhas, illuminating infinite space.

Somewhat later five of these unearthly Buddhas were formed into a pentad and described as Jinas[2] or Dhyâni Buddhas (Buddhas of contemplation), namely, Vairocana, Akshobhya, Ratnasambhava, Amitâbha and Amoghasiddhi. In the fully developed form of this doctrine these five personages are

[1] In Mahâparinib. Sut. I. 16 the Buddha is made to speak of all the other Buddhas who have been in the long ages of the past and will be in the long ages of the future.

[2] Though Dhyâni Buddha is the title most frequently used in European works it would appear that Jina is more usual in Sanskrit works, and in fact Dhyâni Buddha is hardly known outside Nepalese literature. Ratnasambhava and Amoghasiddhi are rarely mentioned apart from the others. According to Getty (*Gods of Northern Buddhism*, pp. 26, 27) a group of six, including the Âdi-Buddha himself under the name of Vajrasattva, is sometimes worshipped.

produced by contemplation from the Âdi-Buddha or original Buddha spirit and themselves produce various reflexes, including Bodhisattvas, human Buddhas and goddesses like Târâ. The date when these beliefs first became part of the accepted Mahayana creed cannot be fixed but probably the symmetrical arrangement of five Buddhas is not anterior to the tantric period[1] of Buddhism.

The most important of the five are Vairocana and Amitâbha. Akshobhya is mentioned in both the Lotus and Smaller Sukhâvatî-vyûha as the chief Buddha of the eastern quarter, and a work purporting to be a description of his paradise still extant in Chinese[2] is said to have been translated in the time of the Eastern Han dynasty. But even in the Far East he did not find many worshippers. More enduring has been the glory of Vairocana who is the chief deity of the Shingon sect in Japan and is represented by the gigantic image in the temple at Nara. In Java he seems to have been regarded as the principal and supreme Buddha. The name occurs in the Mahâvastu as the designation of an otherwise unknown Buddha of luminous attributes and in the Lotus we hear of a distant Buddha-world called Vairocana-rasmi-pratimandita, embellished by the rays of the sun[3]. Vairocana is clearly a derivative of Virocana, a recognized title of the sun in Sanskrit, and is rendered in Chinese by Ta-jih meaning great Sun. How this solar deity first came to be regarded as a Buddha is not known but the connection between a Buddha and light has always been recognized. Even the Pali texts represent Gotama as being luminous on some occasions and in the Mahayanist scriptures Buddhas are radiant and light-giving beings, surrounded by halos of prodigious extent and emitting flashes which illuminate the depths of space. The visions of innumerable paradises in all quarters containing jewelled stupas and lighted by refulgent Buddhas which are frequent in these works seem founded on astronomy vaporized under the influence of the idea that there are millions of universes all equally transitory and unsubstantial. There is no reason, so

[1] About the same period Śiva and Vishnu were worshipped in five forms. See below, Book v. chap. III. sec. 3 *ad fin.*

[2] Nanjio, Cat. No. 28.

[3] Virocana also occurs in the Chândogya Up. VIII. 7 and 8 as the name of an Asura who misunderstood the teaching of Prajâpati. Verocana is the name of an Asura in Sam. Nik. I. xi. 1. 8.

far as I see, to regard Gotama as a mythical solar hero, but the celestial Buddhas[1] clearly have many solar attributes. This is natural. Solar deities are so abundant in Vedic mythology that it is hardly possible to be a benevolent god without having something of the character of the sun. The stream of foreign religions which flowed into India from Bactria and Persia about the time of the Christian era brought new aspects of sun worship such as Mithra, Helios and Apollo and strengthened the tendency to connect divinity and light. And this connection was peculiarly appropriate and obvious in the case of a Buddha, for Buddhas are clearly revealers and light-givers, conquerors of darkness and dispellers of ignorance.

Amitâbha (or the Buddha of measureless light), rising suddenly from an obscure origin, has like Avalokita and Vishnu become one of the great gods of Asia. He is also known as Amitâyus or measureless life, and is therefore a god of light and immortality. According to both the Lotus and the Smaller Sukhâvatî-vyûha he is the lord of the western quarter but he is unknown to the Lalita-vistara. It gives the ruler of the west a lengthy title[2], which suggests a land of gardens. Now Paradise, which has biblical authority as a name for the place of departed spirits, appears to mean in Persian a park or enclosed garden and the Avesta speaks of four heavens, the good thought Paradise, the good word Paradise, the good deed Paradise and the Endless Lights[3]. This last expression bears a remarkable resemblance to the name of Amitâbha and we can understand that he should rule the west, because it is the home to which the sun and departed spirits go. Amitâbha's Paradise is called Sukhâvatî or Happy Land. In the Puranas the city of Varuṇa (who is suspected of having a non-Indian origin) is said to be situated in the west and is called Sukha (Linga P. and Vayu P.) or Mukhya (so Vishnu P. and others). The name Amitâbha also occurs in the Vishnu Purana as the name of a class of gods and it is curious that they are in one place[4] associated with other

[1] The names of many of these Buddhas, perhaps the majority, contain some word expressive of light such as Âditya, prabhâ or tejas.

[2] Chap. xx. Pushpavalivanarâjikusumitâbhijña.

[3] *E.g.* Yashts. XXII. and XXIV. *S.B.E.* vol. XXIII. pp. 317 and 344. The title Pure Land (Chinese Ch'ing-t'u, Japanese Jo-do) has also a Persian ring about it. See further in the chapter on Central Asia.

[4] Vishnu P., Book III. chap. II.

deities called the Mukhyas. The worship of Amitâbha, so far as its history can be traced, goes back to Saraha, the teacher of Nâgârjuna. He is said to have been a Sudra and his name seems un-Indian. This supports the theory that this worship was foreign and imported into India[1].

This worship and the doctrine on which it is based are an almost complete contradiction of Gotama's teaching, for they amount to this, that religion consists in faith in Amitâbha and prayer to him, in return for which he will receive his followers after death in his paradise. Yet this is not a late travesty of Buddhism but a relatively early development which must have begun about the Christian era. The principal works in which it is preached are the Greater Sukhâvatî-vyûha or Description of the Happy Land, translated into Chinese between 147 and 186 A.D., the lesser work of the same name translated in 402 A.D. and the Sûtra of meditation on Amitâyus[2] translated in 424. The first of these works purports to be a discourse of Śâkyamuni himself, delivered on the Vulture's Peak in answer to the questions of Ânanda. He relates how innumerable ages ago there was a monk called Dharmâkara who, with the help of the Buddha of that period, made a vow or vows[3] to become a Buddha but on conditions. That is to say he rejected the Buddhahood to which he might become entitled unless his merits obtained certain advantages for others, and having obtained Buddhahood on these conditions he can now cause them to be fulfilled. In other words he can apportion his vast store of accumulated merit to such persons and in such manner as he chooses. The gist of the conditions is that he should when he obtained Buddhahood be lord of a paradise whose inhabitants live in unbroken happiness until they obtain Nirvana. All who have thought of this paradise ten times are to be admitted therein, unless they have committed grievous sin, and Amitâbha will appear to them at the moment of death so that their thoughts may not be troubled. The Buddha shows Ânanda a

[1] See below: Section on Central Asia, and Grünwedel, *Mythologie*, 31, 36 and notes: Taranatha (Shiefner), p. 93 and notes.

[2] Amitâyur-dhyâna-sûtra. All three works are translated in *S.B.E.* vol. XLIX.

[3] Praṇidhâna. Not only Amitâbha but all Bodhisattvas (especially Avalokita and Kshitigarbha) are supposed to have made such vows. This idea is very common in China and Japan but goes back to Indian sources. See *e.g.* Lotus, XXIV. verse 3.

miraculous vision of this paradise and its joys are described in language recalling the account of the New Jerusalem in the book of Revelation and, though coarser pleasures are excluded, all the delights of the eye and ear, such as jewels, gardens, flowers, rivers and the songs of birds await the faithful.

The smaller Sukhâvatî-vyûha, represented as preached by Śâkyamuni at Śrâvasti, is occupied almost entirely with a description of the paradise. It marks a new departure in definitely preaching salvation by faith only, not by works, whereas the previous treatise, though dwelling on the efficacy of faith, also makes merit a requisite for life in heaven. But the shorter discourse says dogmatically "Beings are not born in that Buddha country as a reward and result of good works performed in this present life. No, all men or women who hear and bear in mind for one, two, three, four, five, six or seven nights the name of Amitâyus, when they come to die, Amitâyus will stand before them in the hour of death, they will depart this life with quiet minds and after death they will be born in Paradise."

The Amitâyur-dhyâna-sûtra also purports to be the teaching of Śâkyamuni and has an historical introduction connecting it with Queen Vaidehî and King Bimbisâra. In theology it is more advanced than the other treatises: it is familiar with the doctrine of Dharma-kâya (which will be discussed below) and it represents the rulers of paradise as a triad, Amitâyus being assisted by Avalokita and Mahasthâmaprâpta[1]. Admission to the paradise can be obtained in various ways, but the method recommended is the practice of a series of meditations which are described in detail. The system is comprehensive, for salvation can be obtained by mere virtue with little or no prayer but also by a single invocation of Amitâyus, which suffices to free from deadly sins.

Strange as such doctrines appear when set beside the Pali texts, it is clear that in their origin and even in the form which they assume in the larger Sukhâvatî-vyûha they are simply an exaggeration of ordinary Mahayanist teaching[2]. Amitâbha is

[1] These Bodhisattvas are also mentioned but without much emphasis in the Greater Sukhâvatî-vyûha.

[2] Even in Hinayanist works such as the Nidânakathâ Sumedha's resolution to become a Buddha, formed as he lies on the ground before Dipankara, has a resemblance to Amîda's vow. He resolves to attain the truth, to enable mankind to cross the sea of the world and only then to attain Nirvana.

merely a monk who devotes himself to the religious life, namely seeking *bodhi* for the good of others. He differs from every day devotees only in the degree of sanctity and success obtained by his exertions. The operations which he performs are nothing but examples on a stupendous scale of pariṇâmanâ or the assignment of one's own merits to others. His paradise, though in popular esteem equivalent to the Persian or Christian heaven, is not really so: strictly speaking it is not an ultimate ideal but a blessed region in which Nirvana may be obtained without toil or care.

Though this teaching had brilliant success in China and Japan, where it still flourishes, the worship of Amitâbha was never predominant in India. In Nepal and Tibet he is one among many deities: the Chinese pilgrims hardly mention him: his figure is not particularly frequent in Indian iconography[1] and, except in the works composed specially in his honour, he appears as an incidental rather than as a necessary figure. The whole doctrine is hardly strenuous enough for Indians. To pray to the Buddha at the end of a sinful life, enter his paradise and obtain ultimate Nirvana in comfort is not only open to the same charge of egoism as the Hinayana scheme of salvation but is much easier and may lead to the abandonment of religious effort. And the Hindu, who above all things likes to busy himself with his own salvation, does not take kindly to these expedients. Numerous deities promise a long spell of heaven as a reward for the mere utterance of their names[2], yet the believer continues to labour earnestly in ceremonies or meditation. It would be interesting to know whether this doctrine of salvation by the utterance of a single name or prayer originated among Buddhists or Brahmans. In any case it is closely related to old ideas about the magic power of Vedic verses.

The five Jinas and other supernatural personages are often regarded as manifestations of a single Buddha-force and at last this force is personified as Âdi-Buddha[3]. This admittedly

[1] See Foucher, *Iconographie Bouddhique dans l'Inde.*

[2] The Bhagavad-gîtâ states quite clearly the doctrine of the death-bed prayer (VIII. *ad init.*). "He who leaves this body and departs remembering me in his last moments comes to my essence. Whatever form (of deity) he remembers when he finally leaves this body, to that he goes having been used to ponder on it."

[3] See art. Âdi-Buddha in *E.R.E.* Asanga in the Sûtrâlankâra (IX. 77) condemns the doctrine of Âdi-Buddha, showing that the term was known then, even if it

theistic form of Buddhism is late and is recorded from Nepal, Tibet (in the Kâlacakra system) and Java, a distribution which implies that it was exported from Bengal[1]. But another form in which the Buddha-force is impersonal and analogous to the Parabrahma of the Vedânta is much older. Yet when this philosophic idea is expressed in popular language it comes very near to Theism. As Kern has pointed out, Buddha is not called Deva or Îśvara in the Lotus simply because he is above such beings. He declares that he has existed and will exist for incalculable ages and has preached and will preach in innumerable millions of worlds. His birth here and his nirvana are illusory, kindly devices which may help weak disciples but do not mark the real beginning and end of his activity. This implies a view of Buddha's personality which is more precisely defined in the doctrine known as Ṭrikâya or the three bodies[2] and expounded in the Mahâyâna-sûtrâlankâra, the Awakening of Faith, the Suvarṇa-prabhâsa sûtra[3] and many other works. It may be stated dogmatically as follows, but it assumes somewhat divergent forms according as it is treated theologically or metaphysically.

A Buddha has three bodies or forms of existence. The first is the Dharma-kâya, which is the essence of all Buddhas. It is true knowledge or Bodhi. It may also be described as Nirvana and also as the one permanent reality underlying all phenomena and all individuals. The second is the Sambhoga-kâya, or body

had not the precise dogmatic sense which it acquired later. His argument is that no one can become a Buddha without an equipment (Sambhâra) of merit and knowledge. Such an equipment can only be obtained from a previous Buddha and therefore the series of Buddhas must extend infinitely backwards.

1 For the prevalence of the doctrine in mediæval Bengal see B. K. Sarkar, *Folklore Element in Hindu Culture*, which is however sparing of precise references. The Dharma or Nirañjana of the Śûnya Purâna seems to be equivalent to Âdi-Buddha.

Sometimes the Âdi-Buddha is identified with Vajrasattva or Samantabhadra, although these beings are otherwise classified as Bodhisattvas. This appears analogous to the procedure common in Hinduism by which a devotee declares that his special deity is all the gods and the supreme spirit.

2 It would appear that some of the Tantras treat of five bodies, adding to the three here given others such as the Ânandakâya, Vajrakâya and Svabhâvakâya. For this doctrine see especially De la Vallée Poussin, *J.R.A.S.* 1906, pp. 943–997 and *Muséon*, 1913, pp. 257 ff. Jigs-med nam-mká, the historian of Tibetan Buddhism, describes four. See Huth, *Ges. d. Bud. in d. Mongolei*, vol. II. pp. 83–89. Hinduism also assigns to living beings three bodies, the Kâraṇa-śarîra, lingaś. and sthûlaś.

3 Translated into Chinese by Dharmaraksha between 397 and 439 A.D.

of enjoyment, that is to say the radiant and superhuman form in which Buddhas appear in their paradises or when otherwise manifesting themselves in celestial splendour. The third is the Nirmâna-kâya, or the body of transformation, that is to say the human form worn by Śâkyamuni or any other Buddha and regarded as a transformation of his true nature and almost a distortion, because it is so partial and inadequate an expression of it. Later theology regards Amitâbha, Amitâyus and Śâkyamuni as a series corresponding to the three bodies. Amitâbha does not really express the whole Dharma-kâya, which is incapable of personification, but when he is accurately distinguished from Amitâyus (and frequently they are regarded as synonyms) he is made the more remote and ethereal of the two. Amitâyus with his rich ornaments and his flask containing the water of eternal life is the ideal of a splendidly beneficent saviour and represents the Sambhoga-kâya[1]. Śâkyamuni is the same beneficent being shrunk into human form. But this is only one aspect, and not the most important, of the doctrine of the three bodies. We can easily understand the Sambhoga-kâya and Nirmâna-kâya: they correspond to a deity such as Vishnu and his incarnation Krishna, and they are puzzling in Buddhism simply because we think naturally of the older view (not entirely discarded by the Mahayana) which makes the human Buddha the crown and apex of a series of lives that find in him their fulfilment. But it is less easy to understand the Dharma-kâya.

The word should perhaps be translated as body of the law and the thought originally underlying it may have been that the essential nature of a Buddha, that which makes him a Buddha, is the law which he preaches. As we might say, the teacher lives in his teaching: while it survives, he is active and not dead.

The change from metaphor to theology is illustrated by Hsüan Chuang when he states[2] (no doubt quoting from his edition of the Pitakas) that Gotama when dying said to those around him "Say not that the Tathâgata is undergoing final

[1] The prototype of the Sambhoga-kâya is found in the Pali Canon, for the Buddha says (Mahâparinib. Sut. III. 22) that when he appears among the different classes of gods his form and voice are similar to theirs.

[2] Watters, vol. II. p. 38. "Spiritual essence" is Fa-shên in Chinese, *i.e.* Dharma-kâya. Another passage is quoted to the effect that "henceforth the observances of all my disciples constitute the Tathâgata's Fa-shên, eternal and imperishable."

extinction: his spiritual presence abides for ever unchangeable." This apparently corresponds to the passage in the Pali Canon[1], which runs "It may be that in some of you the thought may arise, the word of the Master is ended: we have no more a teacher. But it is not thus that you should regard it. The truths and the rules which I have set forth, let them, after I am gone, be the Teacher to you." But in Buddhist writings, including the oldest Pali texts, Dharma or Dhamma has another important meaning. It signifies phenomenon or mental state (the two being identical for an idealistic philosophy) and comprises both the external and the internal world. Now the Dharma-kâya is emphatically not a phenomenon but it may be regarded as the substratum or totality of phenomena or as that which gives phenomena whatever reality they possess and the double use of the word dharma rendered such divagations of meaning easier[2]. Hindus have a tendency to identify being and knowledge. According to the Vedânta philosophy he who knows Brahman, knows that he himself is Brahman and therefore he actually is Brahman. In the same way the true body of the Buddha is prajñâ or knowledge[3]. By this is meant a knowledge which transcends the distinction between subject and object and which sees that neither animate beings nor inanimate things have individuality or separate existence. Thus the Dharma-kâya being an intelligence which sees the illusory quality of the world and also how the illusion originates[4] may be regarded as the origin and ground of all phenomena. As such it is also called Tathâgata-garbha and Dharma-dhâtu, the matrix or storehouse of all phenomena. On the other hand, inasmuch as it is beyond them and implies their unreality, it may also be regarded as the annihilation of all phenomena, in other words as Nirvana. In fact the Dharma-kâya (or Bhûta-tathatâ) is sometimes[5] defined in words similar to those which the Pali Canon makes the Buddha use when asked if the Perfect Saint exists after death—"it is neither that which is existence nor that which is non-

[1] Mahâparinib. Sut. VI. i.

[2] Something similar might happen in English if think and thing were pronounced in the same way and a thing were believed to be that which we can think.

[3] See Ashṭasâhasrikâ Prajñâ-pâramitâ, chap. IV, near beginning.

[4] It is in this last point that no inferior intelligence can follow the thought of a Buddha.

[5] *The Awakening of Faith*, Teitaro Suzuki, p. 59.

existence, nor that which is at once existence and non-existence nor that which is neither existence nor non-existence." In more theological language it may be said that according to the general opinion of the Mahayanists a Buddha attains to Nirvana by the very act of becoming a Buddha and is therefore beyond everything which we call existence. Yet the compassion which he feels for mankind and the good Karma which he has accumulated cause a human image of him (Nirmâṇa-kâya) to appear among men for their instruction and a superhuman image, perceptible yet not material, to appear in Paradise.

CHAPTER XIX

MAHAYANIST METAPHYSICS

THUS the theory of the three bodies, especially of the Dharmakâya, is bound up with a theory of ontology. Metaphysics became a passion among the travellers of the Great Vehicle as psychology had been in earlier times. They may indeed be reproached with being bad Buddhists since they insisted on speculating on those questions which Gotama had declared to be unprofitable and incapable of an answer in human language. He refused to pronounce on the whence, the whither and the nature of things, but bade his disciples walk in the eightfold path and analyse the human mind, because such analysis conduces to spiritual progress. India was the last country in the world where such restrictions were likely to be observed. Much Mahayanist literature is not religious at all but simply metaphysics treated in an authoritative and ecclesiastical manner. The nature and origin of the world are discussed as freely as in the Vedânta and with similar results: the old ethics and psychology receive scant attention. Yet the difference is less than might be supposed. Anyone who reads these treatises and notices the number of apparently eternal beings and the talk about the universal mind is likely to think the old doctrine that nothing has an âtman or soul, has been forgotten. But this impression is not correct; the doctrine of *Nairâtmyam* is asserted so uncompromisingly that from one point of view it may be said that even Buddhas do not exist. The meaning of this doctrine is that no being or object contains an unchangeable permanent self, which lives unaltered in the same or in different bodies. On the contrary individual existences consist of nothing but a collection of skandhas or a *santâna*, a succession or series of mental phenomena. In the Pali books this doctrine is applied chiefly to the soul and psychological enquiries. The Mahayana applied it to the external world and proved by ingenious arguments that nothing at all exists. Similarly the doctrine of Karma is maintained, though it is seriously modified by the admission that merit can be transferred from one personality to another. The Mahayana continued to teach that an act once performed affects a particular series of mental states until its effect is exhausted, or in popular language that an individual enjoys or suffers through a series of births the consequences of previous acts. Even the instance of Amitâbha's paradise, though it strains the doctrine of Karma to the utmost, does not repudiate it. For the believer performs an act—to wit, the invocation of Amitâbha—to which has been attached the wonderful result that the performer is reborn in a blessed state. This is not essentially different from the idea found in the Pali Canon that attentions paid to a Buddha may be rewarded by a happy rebirth in heaven[1].

Mahayanist metaphysics, like all other departments of this theology, are beset by the difficulty that the authorities who treat of them are not always in accord and do not pretend to be in accord. The idea that variety is permissible in belief and conduct is deeply rooted in later Buddhism: there are many vehicles, some better than others no doubt and some very ramshackle, but all are capable of conveying their passengers to salvation. Nominally the Mahayana was divided into only two schools of philosophy: practically every important treatise propounds a system with features of its own. The two schools are the Yogâcâras and Mâdhyamikas[2]. Both are idealists and deny the reality of the external world, but whereas the Yogâcâras (also called Vijñânavâdins) admit that Vijñâna or consciousness and the series of states of which it consists are real, the Mâdhyamikas refuse the title of reality to both the subjective and the objective world and hence gained a reputation of being complete nihilists. Probably the Mâdhyamikas are the older school.

Both schools attach importance to the distinction between relative and absolute knowledge. Relative knowledge is true for human beings living in the world: that is to say it is not more false than the world of appearance in which they live. The Hinayanist doctrines are true in this sense. Absolute knowledge

[1] *E.g.* in Mahâparinib. Sut. IV. 57, the Buddha says "There has been laid up by Cunda the smith (who had given him his last meal) a karma redounding to length of life, to good fortune, to good fame, *to the inheritance of heaven*, and of sovereign power."

[2] Strictly speaking Madhyamaka is the name of the school Mâdhyamika of its adherents. Both forms are used, *e.g.* Madhyamakakârikâs and Mâdhyamikasûtra.

rises above the world of appearance and is altogether true but difficult to express in words. The Yogâcâra makes three divisions, dividing the inferior knowledge into two. It distinguishes first illusory knowledge (*parikalpita*) such as mistaking a piece of rope for a snake or belief in the existence of individual souls. Secondly knowledge which depends on the relations of things (*paratantra*) and which though not absolutely wrong is necessarily limited, such as belief in the real existence of ropes and snakes. And thirdly absolute knowledge (*parinishpanna*), which understands all things as the manifestation of an underlying principle. The Mâdhyamikas more simply divide knowledge into *samvṛiti-satya* and *paramârtha-satya*, that is the truth of everyday life and transcendental truth. The world and ordinary religion with its doctrines and injunctions about good works are real and true as *samvṛiti* but in absolute truth (*paramârtham*) we attain Nirvana and then the world with its human Buddhas and its gods exists no more. The word *śûnyam* or *śûnyatâ*, that is *void*, is often used as the equivalent of *paramârtham*. Void must be understood as meaning not an abyss of nothingness but that which is found to be devoid of all the attributes which we try to ascribe to it. The world of ordinary experience is not void, for a great number of statements can be made about it, but absolute truth is void, because nothing whatever can be predicated of it. Yet even this colourless designation is not perfectly accurate[1], because neither being nor not-being can be predicated of absolute truth. It is for this reason, namely that they admit neither being nor not-being but something between the two, that the followers of Nâgârjuna are known as the Mâdhyamikas or school of the middle doctrine, though the European reader is tempted to say that their theories are extreme to the point of being a *reductio ad absurdum* of the whole system. Yet though much of their logic seems late and useless sophistry, its affinity to early Buddhism cannot be denied. The fourfold proposition that the answer to certain questions cannot be any of the statements "is," "is not," "both is and is not," "neither is nor is not," is part of the earliest known stratum of Buddhism. The Buddha himself is represented as

[1] Nâgârjuna says Śûnyam iti na vaktavyam aśûnyam iti va bhavet Ubhayam nobhayam ceti prâjñâptyartham tu kathyate, "It cannot be called void or not void or both or neither but in order to somehow indicate it, it is called Śûnyatâ."

saying[1] that most people hold either to a belief in being or to a belief in not being. But neither belief is possible for one who considers the question with full knowledge. "That things have being is one extreme: that things have no being is the other extreme. These extremes have been avoided by the Tathâgata and it is a middle doctrine that he teaches," namely, dependent origination as explained in the chain of twelve links. The Mâdhyamika theory that objects have no absolute and independent existence but appear to exist in virtue of their relations is a restatement of this ancient dictum.

The Mahayanist doctors find an ethical meaning in their negations. If things possessed *svabhâva*, real, absolute, self-determined existence, then the four truths and especially the cessation of suffering and attainment of sanctity would be impossible. For if things were due not to causation but to their own self-determining nature (and the Hindus always seem to understand real existence in this sense) cessation of evil and attainment of the good would be alike impossible: the four Noble Truths imply a world which is in a state of constant becoming, that is a world which is not really existent.

But for all that the doctrine of *śûnyatâ* as stated in the Mâdhyamika aphorisms ascribed to Nâgârjuna leaves an impression of audacious and ingenious sophistry. After laying down that every object in the world exists only in relation to every other object and has no self-existence, the treatise proceeds to prove that rest and motion are alike impossible. We speak about the path along which we are passing but there is really no such thing, for if we divide the path accurately, it always proves separable into the part which has been passed over and the part which will be passed over. There is no part which is being passed over. This of course amounts to a denial of the existence of present time. Time consists of past and future separated by an indivisible and immeasurable instant. The minimum of time which has any meaning for us implies a change, and two elements, a former and a subsequent. The present minute or the present hour are fallacious expressions[2].

[1] Sam. Nik. XXII. 90. 16.

[2] Gotama, the founder of the Nyâya philosophy, also admitted the force of the arguments against the existence of present time but regarded them as a *reductio ad absurdum*. Shadworth Hodgson in his *Philosophy of Reflection*, vol. I. p. 253 also treats of the question.

Therefore no one ever *is passing* along a path. Again you cannot logically say that the passer is passing, for the sentence is redundant: the verb adds nothing to the noun and *vice versa*: but on the other hand you clearly cannot say that the non-passer is passing. Again if you say that the passer and the passing are identical, you overlook the distinction between the agent and the act and both become unreal. But you cannot maintain that the passer is different from the passing, for a passer as distinct from passing and passing as distinct from a passer have no meaning. "But how can two entities exist at all, if they exist neither as identical with one another nor as different from one another?"

The above, though much abridged, gives an idea of the logic of these sûtras. They proceed to show that all manner of things, such as the five skandhas, the elements, contact, attachment, fire and fuel, origination, continuation and extinction have no real existence. Similar reasoning is then applied to religious topics: the world of transmigration as well as bondage and liberation are declared non-existent. In reality no soul is in bondage and none is released[1]. Similarly Karma, the Buddha himself, the four truths, Nirvana and the twelve links in the chain of causation are all unreal. This is not a declaration of scepticism. It means that the Buddha as a human or celestial being and Nirvana as a state attainable in this world are conceivable only in connection with this world and therefore, like the world, unreal. No religious idea can enter into the unreal (that is the practical) life of the world unless it is itself unreal. This sounds a topsy turvy argument but it is really the same as the Advaita doctrine. The Vedânta is on the one hand a scheme of salvation for liberating souls which transmigrate unceasingly in a world ruled by a personal God. But when true knowledge is attained, the soul sees that it is identical with the Highest Brahman and that souls which are in bondage and God who rules the world are illusions like the world itself. But the Advaita has at least a verbal superiority over the Mâdhyamika philosophy, for in its terminology Brahman is the real and the existent contrasted with the world of illusion. The result of giving to what the Advaita calls the real and existent the name of śûnyatâ or

[1] The Sânkhya philosophy makes a similar statement, though for different reasons.

void is disconcerting. To say that everything without distinction is non-existent is much the same as saying that everything is existent. It only means that a wrong sense is habitually given to the word exist, as if it meant to be self-contained and without relation to other objects. Unless we can make a verbal contrast and assert that there is something which does exist, it seems futile to insist on the unreality of the world. Yet this mode of thought is not confined to text-books on logic. It invades the scriptures, and appears (for instance) in the Diamond Cutter[1] which is still one of the most venerated books of devotion in China and Japan. In this work the Buddha explains that a Bodhisattva must resolve to deliver all living beings and yet must understand that after he has thus delivered innumerable beings, no one has been delivered. And why? Because no one is to be called a Bodhisattva for whom there exists the idea of a being, or person. Similarly a saint does not think that he is a saint, for if he did so think, he would believe in a self, and a person. There occur continually in this work phrases cast in the following form: "what was preached as a store of merit, that was preached as no store of merit[2] by the Tathâgata and therefore it is called a store of merit. If there existed a store of merit, the Tathâgata would not have preached a store of merit." That is to say, if I understand this dark language rightly, accumulated merit is part of the world of illusion which we live in and by speaking of it as he did the Buddha implied that it, like everything else in the world, is really non-existent. Did it belong to the sphere of absolute truth, he would not have spoken of it as if it were one of the things commonly but erroneously supposed to exist. Finally we are told of the highest knowledge "Even the smallest thing is not known or perceived there; therefore it is called the highest perfect knowledge." That is to say perfect knowledge transcends all distinctions; it recognises the illusory nature of all individuality and the truth of sameness, the never-changing one behind the ever-changing many. In this sense it is said to perceive nothing and know nothing.

One might expect that a philosophy thus prone to use the

[1] Vajracchedikâ. See *S.B.E.* vol. XLIX. It was translated into Chinese by Kumârajîva (384–417 A.D.).

[2] Or in other repetitions of the same formula, beings, ideas, good things, signs, etc., etc.

language of extreme nihilism would slip into a destructive, or at least negative system. But Mahayanism was pulled equally strongly in the opposite direction by the popular and mythological elements which it contained and was on the whole inclined to theism and even polytheism quite as much as to atheism and acosmism. A modern Japanese writer[1] says that Dharma-kâya "may be considered to be equivalent to the Christian conception of the Godhead." This is excessive as a historical statement of the view current in India during the early centuries of our era, but it does seem true that Dharma-kâya was made the equivalent of the Hindu conception of Param Brahma and also that it is very nearly equivalent to the Chinese Tao[2].

The work called *Awakening of Faith*[3] and ascribed to Aśvaghosha is not extant in Sanskrit but was translated into Chinese in 553 A.D. Its doctrine is practically that of the Yogâcâra school and this makes the ascription doubtful, but it is a most important treatise. It is regarded as authoritative in China and Japan at the present day and it illustrates the triple tendency of the Mahayana towards metaphysics, mythology, and devotional piety. It declares that faith has four aspects. Three of these are the three Jewels, or Buddha, the Law and the Church, and cover between them the whole field of religion and morality as generally understood. The exposition is tinged with a fine unselfish emotion and tells the believer that though he should strive not for his own emancipation but for the salvation of others yet he himself receives unselfish and supernatural assistance. He is remembered and guarded by Buddhas and Bodhisattvas in all quarters of the Universe who are eternally trying to liberate mankind by various expedients (upâya). By expedient is meant a modified presentment of the truth, which is easier of comprehension and, if not the goal, at least on the road to it, such as the Paradise of Amitâbha[4].

[1] Soyen Shaku, *Sermons of a Buddhist Abbot*, p. 47.

[2] See for a simple and persuasive statement of these abstruse doctrines a charming little book called *Wu-Wei* by H. Borel.

[3] Translated from the Chinese by Teitaro Suzuki, 1900. The translation must be used with care, as its frequent use of the word *soul* may lead to misunderstanding.

[4] Asaṅga's work *Mahâyâna-sûtrâlankâra* (edited and translated by S. Lévi) which covers much of the same ground is extant in Sanskrit as well as in Chinese and Tibetan translations. It is a lucid and authoritative treatise but does not appear to have ever been popular, or to be read now in the Far East. For Yogâcâra see also *Muséon*, 1904, p. 370.

But the remaining aspect of faith, which is the one that the author puts first in his enumeration, and treats at great length, is "to believe in the fundamental truth, that is to think joyfully of suchness." By suchness (in Sanskrit *bhûta-tathatâ*, in Chinese *Chên ju*) is meant absolute truth as contrasted with the relative truth of ordinary experience[1]. The word is not illuminating nor likely to excite religious emotion and the most that can be said for it is that it is less dreary than the void of Nâgârjuna. Another and more positive synonym is *dharma-dhâtu*, the all-embracing totality of things. It is only through our ignorance and subjectivity that things appear distinct and individuate. Could we transcend this subjectivity, isolated objects would cease to exist. Things in their fundamental nature cannot be named or explained: they are beyond the range of language and perception: they have no signs of distinction but possess absolute sameness (samatâ). From this totality of things nothing can be excluded and to it nothing can be added. Yet it is also śûnyatâ, negation or the void, because it cannot be said to possess any of the attributes of the world we live in: neither existence nor non-existence, nor unity nor plurality can be predicted of it. According to the celebrated formula of Nâgârjuna known as the eight Nos there is in it "neither production (*utpâda*) nor destruction (*uccheda*) nor annihilation (*nirodha*) nor persistence (*sasvatâ*) nor unity (*ekârtha*) nor plurality (*nânârtha*) nor coming in (*âgamana*) nor going out (*nirgama*)." But when we perceive that both subject and object are unreal we also see that suchness is the one reality and from that point of view it may be regarded as the Dharma-kâya of all Buddhas. It is also called Tathâgata-garbha, the womb or store-house of the Buddha, from which all individual existences are evolved under the law of causation, but this aspect of it is already affected by ignorance, for in Bhûta-tathatâ as known in the light of the highest truth there is neither causation nor production. The Yogâcâra employs the word *śûnyatâ* (void), though not so much as its siste. school, but it makes special use of the term *âlaya-vijñâna*, the receptacle or store of consciousness. This in so far as it is superindividual is an aspect of suchness, but when it affirms and particularises itself it becomes *citta*, that is the human mind, or to be more

[1] The discussion of *tathatâ* in Kathâvatthu, XIX. 5 seems to record an early phase of these speculations.

accurate the substratum of the human mind from which is developed *manas*, or the principle of will, self-consciousness and self-affirmation. Similarly the Vedânta philosophy, though it has no term corresponding to *âlaya-vijñâna*, is familiar with the idea that Brahman is in one aspect immeasurable and all-embracing but in another is infinitesimal and dwells in the human heart: or that Brahman after creating the world entered into it. Again another aspect of suchness is enlightenment (*bodhi*), that is absolute knowledge free from the limitations of subject and object. This "is the universal Dharma-kâya of the Tathâgatas" and on account of this all Tathâgatas are spoken of as abiding in enlightenment *a priori*. This enlightenment may be negative (as *śûnyâta*) in the sense that it transcends all relations but it may also be affirmative and then "it transforms and unfolds itself, whenever conditions are favourable, in the form of a Tathâgata or some other form in order that all beings may be induced to bring their store of merit to maturity[1]."

It will be seen from the above that the absolute truth of the Mahayanists varies from a severely metaphysical conception, the indescribable thing in itself, to something very like an all-pervading benevolent essence which from time to time takes shape in a Buddha. And here we see how easy is the transition from the old Buddhism to a form of pantheism. For if we admit that the Buddha is a superhuman intelligence appearing from time to time according to a certain law, we add little to this statement by saying that the essence or spirit of the cosmos manifests itself from time to time as a Buddha. Only, such words as essence or spirit are not really correct. The world of individuals is the same as the highest truth, the same as the Dharma-kâya, the same as Nirvana. It is only through ignorance that it appears to be different and particularized. Ignorance, the essence of which consists in believing in the distinction between subject and object, is also called defilement and the highest truth passes through various stages of defilement ending with that where under the influence of egoism and passion the external world of particulars is believed to be everything. But the various stages may influence one another[2] so that under a higher influence the mind which is involved in subjectivity

[1] *Awakening of Faith*, Teitaro Suzuki, pp. 62 and 70.

[2] The process is generally called Vâsana or perfuming.

begins to long for Nirvana. Yet Nirvana is not something different from or beyond the world of experience; it does not really involve annihilation of the skandhas. Just as in the Advaita he who has the true knowledge sees that he himself and everything else is Brahman, so for the Mahayanist all things are seen *to be* Nirvana, *to be* the Dharma-kâya. It is sometimes[1] said that there are four kinds of Nirvana (*a*) absolute Nirvana, which is a synonym of the Dharma-kâya and in that sense universally present in all beings, (*b*) upadhiśesha-nirvâṇa, the state of enlightenment which can be attained during life, while the body with its limitations still remains, (*c*) anupadhiśesha-nirvâṇa, a higher degree of the same state attained after death when the hindrances of the body are removed, (*d*) Nirvana without abode or apratishṭhita-nirvâṇa. Those who attain to this understand that there is no real antithesis between Samsâra and Nirvana[2]: they do not seek for rest or emancipation but devote themselves to beneficent activity and to leading their fellows to salvation. Although these statements that Nirvana and Samsâra are the same are not at all in the manner of the older Buddhism, yet this ideal of disinterested activity combined with Nirvana is not inconsistent with the portrait of Gotama preserved in the Pali Canon.

The Mahayanist Buddhism of the Far East makes free use of such phrases as the Buddha in the heart, the Buddha mind and the Buddha nature. These seem to represent such Sanskrit terms as Buddhatva and Bodhicitta which can receive either an ethical or a metaphysical emphasis. The former line of thought is well shown in Śântideva[3] who treats Bodhicitta as the initial impulse and motive power of the religious life, combining intellectual illumination and unselfish devotion to the good of others. Thus regarded it is a guiding and stimulating principle somewhat analogous to the Holy Spirit in Christianity. But the Bodhicitta is also the essential quality of a Buddha (and the Holy Spirit too is a member of the Trinity) and in so far as a man has the Bodhicitta he is one with all Buddhas.

[1] Vijñânamâtra Śâstra. Chinese version quoted by Teitaro Suzuki, *Outlines of Mahâyâna Buddhism*, p. 343. Apparently both upâdhi and upadhi are used in Buddhist Sanskrit. Upâdi is the Pali form.

[2] So the Mâdhyamika Śâstra (xxv. 19) states that there is no difference between Samsâra and Nirvâna. Cf. Rabindranath Tagore, *Sadhana*, pp. 160–164.

[3] *E.g.* Bodhicaryâvatâra, chap. I, called praise of the Bodhicitta.

This conception is perhaps secondary in Buddhism but it is also as old as the Upanishads and only another form of the doctrine that the spirit in every man (antaryâmin) is identical with the Supreme Spirit. It is developed in many works still popular in the Far East[1] and was the fundamental thesis of Bodhidharma, the founder of the Zen school. But the practical character of the Chinese and Japanese has led them to attach more importance to the moral and intellectual side of this doctrine than to the metaphysical and pantheistic side.

[1] *E.g.* the P'u-t'i-hsin-li-hsiang-lun (Nanjio, 1304), translated from Nâgârjuna, and the Ta-Ch'êng-fa-chieh-wu-ch'a-pieh-lun, translated from Sthiramati (Nanjio, 1258).

CHAPTER XX

MAHAYANIST SCRIPTURES

In a previous chapter I have discussed the Pali Canon and I shall subsequently have something to say about the Chinese and Tibetan Canons, which are libraries of religious and edifying works rather than sacred books similar to the Vedas or the Bible. My present object is to speak of the Sanskrit literature, chiefly sutras, which appeared contemporaneously with the rise of Mahayanism in India.

The Mahayanist scriptures are the largest body of sacred writings extant in the world, but it is not easy either to define the limits of the Canon or to say when it was put together. According to a common tradition Kanishka played for the Church of the Great Vehicle much the same part as Asoka for the Theravâdins and summoned a Council which wrote commentaries on the Tripitaka. This may be reasonably held to include a recension of the text commented on but we do not know what that text was, and the brief and perplexing accounts of the Council which we possess indicate not that it gave its imprimatur to Mahayanist sutras but that it was specially concerned with the Abhidharma works of the Sarvâstivâdin school.

In any case no Canon formed in the time of Kanishka can have been equivalent to the collections of writings accepted today in China and Tibet, for they contain works later than any date which can be assigned to his reign, as do also the nine sacred books revered in Nepal. It was agreed among Indian Buddhists that the scriptures were divided among the three Pitakas or baskets, but we may surmise that there was no unanimity as to the precise contents of each basket. In India the need for unanimity in such matters is not felt. The Brahmans always recognized that the most holy and most jealously preserved scriptures could exist in various recensions and the Mahabharata shows how generations of respectful and uncritical hearers may allow adventitious matter of all sorts to be incorporated in a work. Something of the same kind happened with the Pitakas. We know that the Pali recension which we possess was not the only one, for fragments of a Sanskrit version have been discovered.

There was probably a large floating literature of sutras, often presenting several recensions of the same document worked up in different ways. Just as additions were made to the list of Upanishads up to the middle ages, although the character of the later works was different from that of the earlier, so new sutras, modern in date and in tone, were received in the capacious basket. And just as the Puranas were accepted as sacred books without undermining the authority of the Vedas, so new Buddhist scriptures superseded without condemning the old ones. Various Mahayanist schools had their own versions of the Vinaya which apparently contain the same rules as the Pali text but also much additional narrative, and Asanga quotes from works corresponding to the Pali Nikâyas, though his doctrine belongs to another age[1]. The Abhidharma section of the Pali Canon seems however to have been peculiar to the Theravâda school. The Sarvâstivâdin Pitaka of the same name was entirely different and, judging from the Chinese Canon, the Mahayanists gave the title to philosophic works by such authors as Asanga and Vasubandhu, some of which were described as revelations from Maitreya.

Specially characteristic of Mahayanist Buddhism are the Vaipulya[2] sutras, that is sutras of great extension or development. These works, of which the Lotus is an example, follow the same scheme as the older sutras but are of wider scope and on a much larger scale, for they often consist of twenty or more chapters. They usually attempt to give a general exposition of the whole Dharma, or at least of some aspect of it which is

[1] In the Mahâyâna-sûtrâlankâra he quotes frequently from the Samyukta and Ekottara Âgamas, corresponding to the Samyutta and Anguttara Nikâyas of the Pali.

[2] A reading Vaitulya has also been found in some manuscripts of the Lotus discovered at Kashgar and it is suggested that the word may refer to the sect of Vetullas or Vetulyakas mentioned in the Commentary on the Kathâvatthu as holding that the Buddha really remained in the Tushita heaven and sent a phantom to represent him in the world and that it was Ânanda, not the Buddha, who preached the law. See Kern, *Vers. en Med. der K. Ak. v. Wetenschappen, Letterk.*, R. 4 D. VIII. pp. 312–9, Amsterdam, 1907, and De la Vallée Poussin's notice of this article in *J.R.A.S.* 1907, pp. 434–6. But this interpretation does not seem very probable.

extolled as sufficient for the right conduct of life. The chief speaker is usually the Buddha, who is introduced as teaching on the Vulture Peak, or some other well-known locality, and surrounded by a great assemblage many of whom are superhuman beings. The occasion of the discourse is commonly signalized by his sending forth rays of light which illuminate the universe until the scene includes other worlds. As early as the Anguttara Nikâya[1] we find references to the danger of a taste for ornate and poetic sutras and these compositions seem to be the outcome of that taste. The literary ideas and methods which produced them are illustrated by the Sûtrâlankâra of Aśvaghosha, a collection of edifying tales, many of which use the materials supplied by the Pali Nikâyas and Vinaya but present them in a more effective and artistic form. It was thought a pious task to amplify and embellish the simple narratives handed down by tradition.

The Mahayanist scriptures are composed in Sanskrit not in Pali, but it is only rarely—for instance in the works of Aśvaghosha—that Buddhist Sanskrit conforms to the rules of the classical language. Usually the words deviate from this standard both in form and meaning and often suggest that the text as we have it is a sanskritized version of an older work in some popular dialect, brought into partial conformity with literary usage. In the poetical portions, this process of sanskritization encountered greater difficulties than in prose, because metre and prosody often refused to admit the changes required by grammar, so that this poetical dialect cannot be called either Sanskrit, Pali or Magadhi but remains a mixture of learned and popular speech. But Sanskrit did not become a sacred language for the Mahayanists like Latin for Roman Catholics. It is rather Pali which has assumed this position among the Hinayanists, for Burmese and Sinhalese translations of the Pitakas acquired no authority. But in the north the principle[2] that every man might read the Buddha's word in his own vernacular was usually respected: and the populations of Central Asia, the Chinese, the Tibetans, and the Mongols translated the scriptures into their

[1] IV. 160. 5.

[2] See Cullavagga, v. 33. The meaning evidently is that the Buddha's words are not to be enshrined in an artificial literary form which will prevent them from being popular.

own languages without attaching any superstitious importance to the original words, unless they were Dhâraṇîs or spells.

About the time of the Christian era or perhaps rather earlier, greater use began to be made of writing for religious purposes. The old practice of reciting the scriptures was not discontinued but no objection was made to preserving and reading them in written copies. According to tradition, the Pali scriptures were committed to writing in Ceylon during the reign of Vaṭṭagâmaṇi, that is according to the most recent chronology about 20 B.C., and Kanishka caused to be engraved on copper plates the commentaries composed by the council which he summoned. In Aśvaghosha[1] we find the story of a Brahman who casually taking up a book to pass the time lights on a copy of the Sutra of the Twelve Causes and is converted. But though the Buddhists remained on the whole true to the old view that the important thing was to understand and disseminate the substance of the Master's teaching and not merely to preserve the text as if it were a sacred formula, still we see growing up in Mahayanist works ideas about the sanctity and efficacy of scripture which are foreign to the Pali Canon. Many sutras (for instance the Diamond Cutter) extol themselves as all-sufficient for salvation: the Prajñâ-pâramitâ commences with a salutation addressed not as usual to the Buddha but to the work itself, as if it were a deity, and Hodgson states that the Buddhists of Nepal worship their nine sacred books. Nor was the idea excluded that certain words, especially formulæ or spells called Dhâraṇî, have in themselves a mysterious efficacy and potency[2]. Some of these are cited and recommended in the Lotus[3]. In so far as the repetition of sacred words or spells is regarded as an integral part of the religious life, the doctrine has no warrant in the earlier teaching. It obviously becomes more and more prominent in later works. But the idea itself is old, for it is clearly the same that produced a belief in the Brahmanic mantras, particularly the mantras of the Atharva Veda, and early Buddhism did not reject mantras in their proper place. Thus[4] the deities present themselves to the Buddha and offer to teach him a formula which will protect his disciples from the attacks of evil spirits. Hsüan Chuang even states that the council which

[1] Sûtrâlankâra, I. 2.

[2] See Waddell, "The Dhâraṇî cult" in *Ostasiat. Ztsft.* 1912, pp. 155 ff.

[3] Chap. XXI, which is however a later addition.

[4] Dig. Nik. 32.

sat at Râjagṛiha after the Buddha's death compiled five Pitakas, one of which consisted of Dhâraṇîs[1], and it may be that the collection of such texts was begun as early as the collection of discourses and rules. But for many centuries there is no evidence that they were in any way confounded with the Dharma.

The Mahayanist scriptures are so voluminous that not even the clergy were expected to master any considerable part of them[2]. Indeed they make no claim to be a connected whole. The theory was rather that there were many vehicles plying on the road to salvation and many guide books. No traveller thought of taking the whole library but only a few volumes which suited him. Most of the Chinese and Japanese sects avowedly base themselves upon three sutras, selected according to the taste of each school from the hundreds quoted in catalogues. Thus the T'ien-t'ai sect has for its scriptures the Lotus, the Nirvâṇa-sûtra and the Prajñâ-pâramitâ, while the Shin-shu sect admits only the three Amidist sutras.

The following are the names of some of the principal Mahayanist scriptures. Comparatively few of them have been published in Europe and some exist only in Chinese or Japanese translations.

1. Prajñâ-pâramitâ or transcendental knowledge[3] is a generic name given to a whole literature consisting of treatises on the doctrine of śûnyatâ, which vary greatly in length. They are classed as sutras, being described as discourses delivered by the Buddha on the Vulture Peak. At least ten are known, besides excerpts which are sometimes described as substantive works. The great collection translated into Chinese by Hsüan Chuang is said to consist of 200,000 verses and to comprise sixteen different sutras[4]. The earliest translation of one of these treatises into Chinese (Nanjio, 5) was made about 170 A.D. and

[1] Watters, *Yüan Chwang*, II. p. 160.

[2] The Mahâvyutpatti (65) gives a list of 105 sûtras.

[3] The word pâram-itâ means as an adjective *gone to the further shore* or *transcendent*. As a feminine substantive it means a transcendent virtue or perfection.

[4] See Walleser, *Prajñâpâramitâ* in *Quellen der Religionsgeschichte*, pp. 15 ff. *S.B.E.* XLIX. Nanjio, Catalogue Nos. 1–20 and Rajendralala Mitra's *Nepalese Buddhist Literature*, pp. 177 ff. Versions are mentioned consisting of 125,000 verses, 100,000 verses, 25,000 verses, 10,000 verses and 8000 verses respectively. (Similarly at the beginning of the Mahâbhârata we are told that the Epic consists of 8800 verses, of 24,000 and of 100,000.) Of these the last or Ashṭasâhasrikâ has been published in the *Bibliotheca Indica* and the second or Śatasâhasrikâ is in process

everything indicates that portions of the Prajñâ-pâramitâ are among the earliest Mahayanist works and date from about the first century of our era. Prajñâ not only means knowledge of the absolute truth, that is to say of śûnyatâ or the void, but is regarded as an ontological principle synonymous with Bodhi and Dharma-kâya. Thus Buddhas not only possess this knowledge in the ordinary sense but they *are* the knowledge manifest in human form, and Prajñâ is often personified as a goddess. All these works lay great stress on the doctrine of śûnyatâ, and the non-existence of the world of experience. The longest recension is said to contain a polemic against the Hinayana.

The Diamond Cutter is one of the best known of these transcendental treatises and the two short works called Heart of the Prajñâpâramitâ, which are widely read in Japan, appear to be brief abstracts of the essence of this teaching.

2. The Saddharma-puṇḍarîka, or Lotus of the Good Law[1], is one of the best known Mahayanist sutras and is highly esteemed in China and Japan. It purports to be a discourse delivered by Śâkyamuni on the Vulture Peak to an assemblage of Bodhisattvas. The Lotus clearly affirms the multiplicity of vehicles, or various ways of teaching the law, and also the eternity of the Buddha, but it does not emphasize, although it mentions, the doctrine of śûnyatâ. The work consists of two parts of which the second (chaps. XXI–XXVI) is a later addition. This second part contains spells and many mythological narratives, including one of an ancient Bodhisattva who burnt himself alive in honour of a former Buddha. Portions of the Lotus were translated into Chinese under the Western Tsin Dynasty 265–316 A.D. and it is quoted in the Mahâ-prajñâ-pâramitâ-sâstra ascribed to Nâgârjuna[2]. The first part is

of publication. It is in prose, so that the expression "verses" appears not to mean that the works are Gâthâs. A Khotanese version of the Vajracchedikâ is edited in Hoernle's *Manuscript Remains* by Sten Konow. The Sanskrit text was edited by Max Müller in *Anecdota Oxoniensia*.

[1] The Sanskrit text has been edited by Kern and Nanjio in *Bibliotheca Buddhica*; translated by Burnouf (*Le Lotus de la bonne Loi*), 1852 and by Kern (Saddharma-puṇḍarîka) in *S.B.E.* vol. XXI.

[2] There appears to have been an earlier Chinese version of 255 A.D. but it has been lost. See Nanjio, p. 390. One of the later Chinese versions alludes to the existence of two recensions (Nanjio, No. 139). See *B.E.F.E.O.* 1911, p. 453. Fragments of a shorter and apparently earlier recension of the Lotus have been discovered in E. Turkestan. See *J.R.A.S.* 1916, pp. 269–277.

probably not later than the first century A.D. The Lotus is unfortunately accessible to English readers only in a most unpoetic translation by the late Professor Kern, but it is a great religious poem which starting from humanity regards religion as cosmic and universal, rather than something mainly concerned with our earth. The discourses of Śâkyamuni are accompanied in it by stupendous miracles culminating in a grand cosmic phantasmagoria in which is evoked the stupa containing the body of a departed Buddha, that is a shrine containing the eternal truth.

3. The Lalita-vistara[1] is a life of Śâkyamuni up to the commencement of his mission. Though the setting of the story is miraculous and Buddhas and Bodhisattvas innumerable are freely spoken of, yet the work does not enunciate the characteristic Mahayanist doctrines so definitely as the other treatises here enumerated. It is said to have originally belonged to the school of the Sarvâstivâdins and to have been subsequently accepted by the Mahayanists, and though it is not an epic but a collection of ballads and legends, yet it often reads as if it were a preliminary study for Aśvaghosha's Buddhacarita. It contains Sanskrit versions of old legends, which are almost verbal renderings of the Pali text, but also new material and seems to be conscious of relating novelties which may arouse scepticism for it interrupts the narrative to anathematize those who do not believe in the miracles of the Nativity and to extol the merits of faith (*śraddhâ* not *bhakti*). It is probably coeval with the earlier Gandharan art but there are no facts to fix its date[2].

4. The Lankâvatâra[3] gives an account of the revelation of the good Law by Śâkyamuni when visiting Lanka. It is presumably subsequent to the period when Ceylon had become a

[1] Edited by Rajendralala Mitra in the *Bibliotheca Indica* and partially translated in the same series. A later critical edition by Lefmann, 1902–8.

[2] The early Chinese translations seem doubtful. One said to have been made under the later Han has been lost. See Nanjio, No. 159.

[3] See Burnouf, *Introduction*, pp. 458 ff. and *J.R.A.S.* 1905, pp. 831 ff. Rajendralala Mitra, *Nepalese Buddhist Literature*, p. 113. A brief analysis is given in *J.A.S.B.* June, 1905 according to which the sûtra professes to be the work of a human author, Jina of the clan of Kâtyâyana born at Campâ. An edition of the Sanskrit text published by the Buddhist Text Society is cited but I have not seen it. Chinese translations were made in 443 and 515 but the first is incomplete and does not correspond with our Sanskrit text.

centre of Buddhism, but the story is pure fancy and unconnected with history or with older legends. It relates how the Buddha alighted on Mt Malaya in Lanka. Ravana came to pay his respects and asked for definitions of virtue and vice which were given. The Bodhisattva Mahâmati (apparently Mañjuśrî) proceeded to propound a series of more abstruse questions which are answered at considerable length. The Lankâvatâra represents a mature phase of speculation and not only criticizes the Sânkhya, Pâsupata and other Hindu schools, but is conscious of the growing resemblance of Mahayanism to Brahmanic philosophy and tries to explain it. It contains a prophecy about Nâgârjuna and another which mentions the Guptas, and it appears to allude to the domination of the Huns. This allusion would make its date as late as the sixth century but a translation into Chinese which is said to correspond with the Sanskrit text was made in 513. If so the barbarians referred to cannot be the Huns. An earlier translation made in 443 does not agree with our Sanskrit text and perhaps the work existed in several recensions.

5. The Suvarṇa-prabhâsa or Glitter of Gold[1] is a Vaipulya sûtra in many ways resembling the Lotus. It insists on the supernatural character of the Buddha. He was never really born nor entered into Nirvana but is the Dharma-kâya. The scene is laid at Râjagṛiha and many Brahmanic deities are among the interlocutors. It was translated into Chinese about 420 A.D. and fragments of a translation into Uigur have been discovered in Turkestan[2]. The contents comprise philosophy, legends and spells.

6. Gaṇḍa-vyûha[3] or the Structure of the World, which is compared to a bubble. The name is not found in the catalogue of the Chinese Tripitaka but the work is said to be the same as the Avataṃsaka sûtra which is popular in the Far East under the name of Hua-yên in China or Ke-gon in Japan. The identity of the two books could not have been guessed from the extracts and analyses which have been published but is guaranteed by

[1] Abstract by Rajendralala Mitra, *Nepalese Buddhist Lit.* p. 241.

[2] See Nanjio, No. 127 and F. W. K. Muller in *Abhandl. der K. Preuss. Akad. der Wissenschaften*, 1908. The Uigur text is published in *Bibliotheca Buddhica*, 1914. Fragments of the Sanskrit text have also been found in Turkestan.

[3] Abstract by Raj. Mitra, *Nepalese Buddhist Lit.* pp. 90 ff. The Śikshâsamuccaya cites the Gaṇḍa-vyûha several times and does not mention the Avataṃsaka.

high authorities[1]. It is possible however that the Gaṇḍa-vyûha is only a portion of the larger work called Avataṃsaka. So far as can be judged from the extracts, this text preaches in a fully developed form, the doctrines of Śûnyatâ, Dharma-kâya, the omnipresence of the Buddha and the redemption of the world by the exertions of Bodhisattvas. Yet it seems to be early, for a portion of it was translated into Chinese about 170 A.D. (Nanjio, 102) and about 405 Kumârajîva translated a commentary on it ascribed to Nâgârjuna (Nanjio, 1180).

7. Tathâgata-guhyaka. This work is known by the analysis of Rajendralala Mitra from which it appears to be a Tantra of the worst class and probably late. Its proper title is said to be Śrîguhyasamaja. Watanabe states that the work catalogued by Nanjio under No. 1027 and translated into Chinese about 1000 A.D. is an expurgated version of it. The Śikshâsamuccaya cites the Tathâgata-guhya-sûtra several times. The relations of these works to one another are not quite clear.

8. Samâdhirâja[2] is a Vyâkaraṇa or narrative describing different forms of meditation of which the Samâdhirâja is the greatest and best. The scene is laid on the Vulture's Peak and the principal interlocutors are Śâkyamuni and Candraprabha, a rich man of Râjagṛiha. It appears to be the same as the Candrapradîpa-sûtra and is a complete and copious treatise, which not only expounds the topic from which it takes its name but incidentally enumerates the chief principles of Mahayanism. Watanabe[3] states that it is the Yüeh-têng-san-mei-ching (Nanjio, 191) translated about 450 and again in 557 A.D.

9. Daśabhûmîśvara[4]. An account of the ten stages in the career of a Bodhisattva before he can attain to Buddhahood. The scene is laid in the paradise of Indra where Śâkyamuni was temporarily sojourning and the principal interlocutor is a Bodhisattva named Vajragarbha. It is said to be the same as the Daśabhûmika-sûtra first translated into Chinese about 300 A.D.

[1] The statement was first made on the authority of Takakusu quoted by Winternitz in *Ges. Ind. Lit.* II. i. p. 242. Watanabe in *J.R.A.S.* 1911, 663 makes an equally definite statement as to the identity of the two works. The identity is confirmed by Pelliot in *J.A.* 1914, II. pp. 118–121.

[2] Abstract by Raj. Mitra, *Nepalese Buddhist Lit.* pp. 81 ff. Quoted in Śântideva's Bodhicaryâvatâra, VIII. 106.

[3] See *J.R.A.S.* 1911, 663.

[4] Abstract by Raj. Mitra, *Nepalese Buddhist Lit.* pp. 81 ff.

(Nanjio, 105 and 110) but this work appears to be merely a portion of the Gaṇḍa-vyûha or Avataṃsaka mentioned above.

These nine works are all extant in Sanskrit and are known in Nepal as the nine Dharmas, the word Dharma being an abbreviation for *Dharmaparyâya*, revolution or exposition of the law, a term frequently used in the works themselves to describe a comprehensive discourse delivered by the Buddha. They are all quoted in the Śikshâsamuccaya, supposed to have been written about 650 A.D. No similar collection of nine seems to be known in Tibet or the Far East and the origin of the selection is obscure. As however the list does not include the Svayambhû Purâṇa, the principal indigenous scripture of Nepal, it may go back to an Indian source and represent an old tradition.

Besides the nine Dharmas, numerous other sûtras exist in Sanskrit, Chinese, Tibetan and the languages of Central Asia. Few have been edited or translated and even when something is known of their character detailed information as to their contents is usually wanting. Among the better known are the following.

10. One of the sûtras most read in China and admired because its style has a literary quality unusual in Buddhist works is commonly known as the Lêng-yen-ching. The full title is Shou-lêng-yen-san-mei-ching which is the Chinese transliteration of Śûrangama Samâdhi[1]. This sutra is quoted by name in the Śikshâsamuccaya and fragments of the Sanskrit text have been found in Turkestan[2]. The Śûrangama-Samâdhi Sûtra has been conjectured to be the same as the Samâdhirâja, but the accounts of Rajendralala Mitra and Beal do not support this theory. Beal's translation leaves the impression that it resembles a Pali sutta. The scene is laid in the Jetavana with few miraculous accessories. The Buddha discusses with Ânanda the location of the soul and after confuting his theories expounds the doctrine of the Dharma-kâya. The fragments found in Turkestan recommend a particular form of meditation.

11. Târanâtha informs us that among the many Mahayanist works which appeared in the reign of Kanishka's son was the

[1] Translated in part by Beal, *Catena of Buddhist Scriptures*, pp. 286–369. See also Teitaro Suzuki, *Outlines of Mahâyâna*, p. 157. For notices of the text see Nanjio, Nos. 399, 446, 1588. Fa-Hsien, chap. XXIX. For the equivalence of Shou-lêng-yen and Śûrangama see Nanjio's note to No. 399 and Julien, *Méthode*, 1007 and Vasilief, p. 175.

[2] See Śikshâs, ed. Bendall, pp. 8, 91 and Hoernle, *Manuscript remains*, I. pp. 125 ff.

Ratna-kûṭa-dharma-paryâya in 1000 sections and the Ratnakûṭa is cited not only by the Śikshâsamuccaya but by Asanga[1]. The Tibetan and Chinese canons contain sections with this name comprising forty-eight or forty-nine items among which are the three important treatises about Amitâbha's paradise and many dialogues called Paripṛicchâ, that is, questions put by some personage, human or superhuman, and furnished with appropriate replies[2]. The Chinese Ratnakûṭa is said to have been compiled by Bodhiruchi (693–713 A.D.) but of course he is responsible only for the selection not for the composition of the works included. Section 14 of this Ratnakûṭa is said to be identical with chapters 11 and 12 of the Mûlasarvâstivâdin Vinaya[3].

12. The Guṇa-kâraṇḍa-vyûha and Kâraṇḍa-vyûha are said to be two recensions of the same work, the first in verse the second in prose. Both are devoted to the praise of Avalokita who is represented as the presiding deity of the universe. He has refused to enter Buddhahood himself until all living creatures attain to true knowledge and is specially occupied in procuring the release of those who suffer in hell. The Guṇa-kâraṇḍa-vyûha contains a remarkable account of the origin of the world which is said to be absent from the prose version. The primeval Buddha spirit, Âdi-Buddha or Svayambhû, produces Avalokita by meditation, and Avalokita produces the material world and the gods of Hinduism from his body, Śiva from his forehead, Nârâyaṇa from his heart and so on. As such doctrines are not known to have appeared in Indian Buddhism before the tenth century it seems probable that the versified edition is late. But a work with the title Ratna-kâraṇḍaka-vyûha-sûtra was translated into Chinese in 270 and the Kâraṇḍa-vyûha is said to have been the first work translated into Tibetan[4].

[1] Mahâyâna-sûtrâlankâra, XIX. 29.

[2] *E.g.* the Râshtra-pâla-paripṛicchâ edited in Sanskrit by Finot, *Biblioth. Buddhica*, 1901. The Sanskrit text seems to agree with the Chinese version. The real number of sûtras in the Ratnakûṭa seems to be 48, two being practically the same but represented as uttered on different occasions.

[3] There is another somewhat similar collection of sûtras in the Chinese Canon called Ta Tsi or Mahâsannipâta but unlike the Ratnakûṭa it seems to contain few well-known or popular works.

[4] I know of these works only by Raj. Mitra's abstracts, *Nepal. Bud. Lit.* pp. 95 and 101. The prose text is said to have been published in Sanskrit at Calcutta, 1873.

13. The Karuṇâ-puṇḍarîka[1] or Lotus of Compassion is mainly occupied with the description of an imaginary continent called Padmadhâtu, its Buddha and its many splendours. It exists in Sanskrit and was translated into Chinese about 400 A.D. (Nanjio, No. 142).

14. The Mahâvairocanâbhisambhodhi called in Chinese Ta-jih-ching or Great Sun sutra should perhaps be mentioned as it is the principal scripture of the Chên-yen (Japanese Shingon) school. It is a late work of unknown origin. It was translated into Chinese in 724 A.D. but the Sanskrit text has not been found.

There are a great number of other sutras which are important for the history of literature, although little attention is paid to them by Buddhists at the present day. Such are the Mahayanist version of the Mahâparinirvâṇa recounting the death and burial of the Buddha and the Mahâsannipâta-sûtra, which apparently includes the Sûryagarbha and Candragarbha sûtras. All these works were translated into Chinese about 420 A.D. and must therefore be of respectable antiquity.

Besides the sutras, there are many compositions styled Avadânas or pious legends[2]. These, though recognized by Mahayanists, do not as a rule contain expositions of the Ŝûnyatâ and Dharma-kâya and are not sharply distinguished from the more imaginative of the Hinayanist scriptures[3]. But they introduce a multiplicity of Buddhas and Bodhisattvas and represent Ŝâkyamuni as a superhuman worker of miracles.

They correspond in many respects to the Pali Vinaya but teach right conduct not so much by precept as by edifying stories and, like most Mahayanist works they lay less stress upon monastic discipline than on unselfish virtue exercised throughout successive existences. There are a dozen or more collections of Avadânas of which the most important are the Mahâvastu and the Divyâvadâna. The former[4] is an encyclopædic work which contains *inter alia* a life of Ŝâkyamuni. It describes itself as

[1] Raj. Mitra, *Nepalese Buddhist Lit.* pp. 285 ff. The Sanskrit text was published for the Buddhist Text Society, Calcutta, 1898.

[2] Avadâna is primarily a great and glorious act: hence an account of such an act.

[3] The Avadâna-śataka (Feer, *Annales du Musée Guimet*, XVIII) seems to be entirely Hinayanist.

[4] Edited by Senart, 3 vols. 1882–1897. Windisch, *Die Komposition des Mahâvastu*, 1909. Article "Mahâvastu" in *E.R.E.*

belonging to the Lokottaravâdins, a section of the Âryamahâsanghikas. The Lokottaravâdins were an ancient sect, precursors of the Mahayana rather than a branch of it, and much of the Mahâvastu is parallel to the Pali Canon and may have been composed a century or two before our era. But other parts seem to belong to the Gandharan period and the mention of Chinese and Hunnish writing points to a much later date[1]. If it was originally a Vinaya treatise, it has been distended out of all recognition by the addition of legends and anecdotes but it still retains a certain amount of matter found also in the Pali and Tibetan Vinayas. There were probably several recensions in which successive additions were made to the original nucleus. One interpolation is the lengthy and important section called Daśabhûmika, describing the career of a Bodhisattva. It is the only part of the Mahâvastu which can be called definitely Mahayanist. The rest of the work marks a transitional stage in doctrine, just as its language is neither Prakrit or Sanskrit but some ancient vernacular brought into partial conformity with Sanskrit grammar. No Chinese translation is known.

The Divyâvadâna[2] is a collection of legends, part of which is known as the Asokâvadâna and gives an edifying life of that pious monarch. This portion was translated into Chinese A.D. 317–420 and the work probably dates from the third century of our era. It is loosely constructed: considerable portions of it seem to be identical with the Vinaya of the Sarvâstivâdins and others with passages in the works of Aśvaghosha.

The Avadânas lie on the borderland between scripture and pious literature which uses human argument and refers to scripture for its authority. Of this literature the Mahayanist church has a goodly collection and the works ascribed to such doctors as Aśvaghosha, Nâgârjuna, Asanga and Vasubandhu hold a high place in general esteem. The Chinese Canon places many of them in the Pitakas (especially in the Abhidharma Pitaka) and not among the works of miscellaneous writers.

The Mahayanist scriptures are still a living force. In Nepal the nine Dharmas receive superstitious homage rather than

[1] So too do the words Horâpâthaka (astrologer), Ujjhebhaka (? Uzbek), Peliyaksha (? Felix). The word Yogâcâra (I. 120) may refer simply to the practice of Yoga and not to the school which bore this name.

[2] Edited by Cowell and Neil, 1886. See Nanjio, 1344.

intelligent study, but in Tibet and the Far East the Prajñâpâramitâ, the Lotus and the sutras about Amitâbha are in daily use for public worship and private reading. I have heard the first-named work as well as the Lêng-yen-ching expounded, that is, read aloud with an extempore paraphrase, to lay congregations in China, and the section of it called the Diamond Cutter is the book which is most commonly in the hands of religious Tibetans. The Lotus is the special scripture of the Nichiren sect in Japan but is universally respected. The twenty-fourth chapter which contains the praises of Avalokita is often printed separately. The Amitâbha sûtras take the place of the New Testament for the Jōdō and Shin sects and copies of them may also be found in almost every monastery throughout China and Annam. The Suvarṇaprabhâsa is said to be specially popular among the Mongols. I know Chinese Buddhists who read the Hua-yen (Avataṃsaka) every day. Modern Japanese writers quote frequently from the Lankâvatâra and Kâśyapa-parivarta but I have not met with any instance of these works being in popular use.

I have mentioned already the obscurity surrounding the history of the Mahayanist Canon in India and it may seem to throw doubt on the authenticity of these scriptures. Unauthentic they certainly are in the sense that European criticism is not likely to accept as historical the discourses which they attribute to the Buddha and others, but there is no reason to doubt that they are treatises composed in India early in our era and representing the doctrines then prevalent. The religious public of India has never felt any difficulty in accepting works of merit —and often only very moderate merit—as revelations, whether called Upanishads, Puranas, Sutras or what not. Only rarely have such works received any formal approbation, such as recognition by a council. Indeed it is rather in Ceylon, Burma, Tibet and China than in India itself that authoritative lists of scriptures have been compiled. The natural instinct of the Hindus was not to close the Canon but to leave it open for any additions which might be vouchsafed.

Two sketches of an elastic Mahayanist Canon of this kind are preserved, one in the Śikshâsamuccaya[1] attributed to Śântideva, who probably flourished in the seventh century, and

[1] Edited by Bendall in *Bibl. Buddhica.*

the other in a little work called the Duration of the Law, reporting a discourse by an otherwise unknown Nandimitra, said to have lived in Ceylon 800 years after the Buddha's death[1]. The former is a compendium of doctrine illustrated by quotations from what the author regarded as scripture. He cites about a hundred Mahayanist sutras, refers to the Vinaya and Divyâvadâna but not apparently to the Abhidharma. He mentions no Tantras[2] and not many Ḍhâraṇîs.

The second work was translated by Hsüan Chuang and was therefore probably written before 600 A.D.[3] Otherwise there is no external evidence for fixing its date. It represents Nandimitra as explaining on his deathbed the steps taken by the Buddha to protect the True Law and in what works that Law is to be found. Like the Chinese Tripitaka it recognizes both Mahayanist and Hinayanist works, but evidently prefers the former and styles them collectively Bodhisattva-Piṭaka. It enumerates about fifty sutras by name, beginning with the Prajñâ-pâramitâ, the Lotus and other well-known texts. Then comes a list of works with titles ending in Samâdhi, followed by others called Paripṛicchâ[4] or questions. A new category seems to be formed by the Buddhâvataṃsaka-sûtra with which the sutras about Amitâbha's Paradise are associated. Then comes the Mahâsannipâta-sûtra associated with works which may correspond to the Ratnakûṭa division of the Chinese Canon[5]. The writer adds that there are "hundreds of myriads of similar sutras classified in groups and categories." He mentions the Vinaya and Abhidharma without further particulars, whereas in describing the Hinayanist versions of these two Pitakas he gives many details.

The importance of this list lies in the fact that it is Indian rather than in its date, for the earliest catalogue of the Chinese Tripitaka compiled about[6] 510 is perhaps older and certainly

[1] Nanjio, No. 1466. For a learned discussion of this work see Lévi and Chavannes in *J.A.* 1916, Nos. I and II.

[2] It is not likely that the Tathâgatha-guhya-sûtra which it quotes is the same as the Tantra with a similar name analysed by Rajendralal Mitra.

[3] Watters, *J.R.A.S.* 1898, p. 331 says there seems to have been an earlier translation.

[4] Many works with this title will be found in Nanjio.

[5] But the Chinese title seems rather to represent Ratnarâsi.

[6] See Nanjio, pp. xiii–xvii.

ampler. But if the catalogue stood alone, it might be hard to say how far the selection of works in it was due to Chinese taste. But taking the Indian and Chinese evidence together, it is clear that in the sixth century Indian Mahayanists (*a*) tolerated Hinayanist scriptures while preferring their own, (*b*) made little use of the Vinaya or Abhidharma for argument or edification, though the former was very important as a code, (*c*) recognized extremely numerous sutras, grouped in various classes such as Mahâsannipâta and Buddhâvataṃsaka, (*d*) and did not use works called Tantras. Probably much the same is true of the fourth century and even earlier, for Asanga in one work[1] quotes both Maha- and Hinayanist scriptures and among the former cites by name seventeen sutras, including one called Paripṛicchâ or questions.

[1] Mahâyâna-sûtrâlankâra. See Lévi's introduction, p. 14. The "Questions" sutra is Brahma-paripṛicchâ.

CHAPTER XXI

CHRONOLOGY OF THE MAHAYANA

In the previous chapters I have enumerated some features of Mahayanism, such as the worship of Bodhisattvas leading to mythology, the deification of Buddhas, entailing a theology as complicated as the Christian creeds, the combination of metaphysics with religion, and the rise of new scriptures consecrating all these innovations. I will now essay the more difficult task of arranging these phenomena in some sort of chronological setting.

The voluminous Chinese literature concerning Buddhism offers valuable assistance, for the Chinese, unlike the Hindus, have a natural disposition to write simple narratives recording facts and dates. But they are diarists and chroniclers rather than historians. The Chinese pilgrims to India give a good account of their itinerary and experiences, but they have little idea of investigating and arranging past events and merely recount traditions connected with the places which they visited. In spite of this their statements have considerable historical value and on the whole harmonize with the literary and archæological data furnished by India.

The Tibetan Lama Târanâtha who completed his History of Indian Buddhism[1] in 1608 is a less satisfactory authority. He merits attention but also scepticism and caution. His work is a compilation but is not to be despised on that ground, for the Tibetan translations of Sanskrit works offer a rich mine of information about the history of the Mahayana. Unfortunately few of these works take the historical point of view and Târanâtha's own method is as uncritical as his materials. Dire confusion prevails as to chronology and even as to names[2], so

[1] Translated by Schiefner, 1869. Târanâtha informs us (p. 281) that his chief authorities were the history of Kshemendrabhadra, the Buddhapurâna of Indradatta and Bhaṭaghaṭî's history of the succession of the Acâryas.

[2] The Tibetans generally translate instead of transliterating Indian names. It is as if an English history of Greece were to speak of Leader of the People instead of Agesilaus.

that the work is almost useless as a connected account, though it contains many interesting details.

Two epochs are of special importance for the development of later Indian Buddhism, that of Kanishka and that of Vasubandhu and his brother Asanga. The reader may expect me to discuss at length the date of Kanishka's accession, but I do not propose to do so for it may be hoped that in the next few years archæological research in India or Central Asia will fix the chronology of the Kushans and meanwhile it is waste of time to argue about probabilities or at any rate it can be done profitably only in special articles. At present the majority of scholars place his accession at about 78 A.D., others put it back to 58 B.C. and arrange the Kushan kings in a different order[1], while still others[2] think that he did not come to the throne until the second century was well advanced. The evidence of art, particularly of numismatics, indicates that Kanishka reigned towards the end of his dynasty rather than at the beginning, but the use of Greek on his coins and his traditional connection with the beginnings of the Mahayana are arguments against a very late date. If the date 78 A.D. is accepted, the conversion of the Yüeh-chih to Buddhism and its diffusion in Central Asia cannot have been the work of Kanishka, for Buddhism began to reach China by land about the time of the Christian era[3]. There is however no reason to assume that they were his work. Kanishka, like Constantine, probably favoured a winning cause, and Buddhism may have been gradually making its way among the Kushans and their neighbours for a couple of centuries before his time. In any case, however important his reign may

[1] They place Kanishka, Vâsishka, Huvishka and Vasudeva before Kadphises I and Kadphises II.

[2] *E.g.* Staël Holstein who also thinks that Kanishka's tribe should be called Kusha not Kushan. Vincent Smith in his latest work (*Oxford History of India*, p. 130) gives 120 A.D. as the most probable date.

[3] My chief difficulty in accepting 78–123 A.D. as the reign of Kanishka is that the Chinese Annals record the doings of Pan Ch'ao between 73 and 102 in Central Asia, with which region Kanishka is believed to have had relations, and yet do not mention his name. This silence makes it *primâ facie* probable that he lived either before or after Pan Ch'ao's career.

The catalogues of the Chinese Tripitaka state that An-Shih-Kao (148–170 A.D.) translated the Mârgabhûmi-sûtra of Sangharaksha, who was the chaplain of Kanishka. But this unfortunately proves nothing except that Kanishka cannot have been very late. The work is not a scripture for whose recognition some lapse of time must be postulated. An-Shih-kao, who came from the west, may very well have translated a recent and popular treatise.

have been for the Buddhist Church, I do not think that the history of the Mahayana should be made to depend on his date. Chinese translations, supported by other evidence, indicate that the Mahayanist movement had begun about the time of our era. If it is proved that Kanishka lived considerably later, we should not argue that Mahayanism is later than was supposed but rather that his relation towards it has been misunderstood[1].

The date of Vasubandhu has also been much discussed and scholars have generally placed him in the fourth or fifth century but Péri[2] appears to have proved that he lived from about 280 to 360 A.D. and I shall adopt this view. This chronology makes a reasonable setting for the development of Buddhism. If Kanishka reigned from about 78 to 123 A.D. or even later, there is no difficulty in supposing that Aśvaghosha flourished in his reign and was followed by Nâgârjuna. The collapse of the Kushan Empire was probably accompanied by raids from Iranian tribes, for Persian influence appears to have been strong in India during the confused interval between the Kushans and Guptas (225–320). The latter inaugurated the revival of Hinduism but still showed favour to individual Buddhists, and we know from Fa-Hsien that Buddhism was fairly flourishing during his visit to India (399–415). There is nothing improbable in supposing that Vasubandhu, who is stated to have lived at Court, was patronized by the early Guptas. The blank in Buddhist history which follows his career can be explained first by the progress of Hinduism at the expense of Buddhism and secondly by the invasions of the Huns. The Chinese pilgrim Sung-Yün has left us an account of India in this distressful period and for the seventh century the works of Hsüan Chuang and I-Ching give copious information.

In investigating the beginnings of the Mahayana we may start from the epoch of Asoka, who is regarded by tradition as the patron and consolidator of the Hinayanist Church. And the tradition seems on the whole correct: the united evidence of

[1] In this connection we may remember Târanâtha's statement that Kanishka's Council put an end to dissentions which had lasted about a century. But he also states that it was after the Council that Mahayanist texts began to appear. If Kanishka flourished about 50 A.D. this would fit in with Târanâtha's statements and what we know of the history of Buddhism.

[2] *B.E.F.E.O.* 1911, 339–390. Satiśchandra Vidyâbhûshana arrived at the same conclusion in *J.A.S.B.* 1905, p. 227.

texts and inscriptions goes to show that the Buddhists of Asoka's time held the chief doctrines subsequently professed by the Sinhalese Church and did not hold the other set of doctrines known as Mahayanist. That these latter are posterior in time is practically admitted by the books that teach them, for they are constantly described as the crown and completion of a progressive revelation. Thus the Lotus[1] illustrates the evolution of doctrine by a story which curiously resembles the parable of the prodigal son except that the returned penitent does not recognize his father, who proceeds to reveal gradually his name and position, keeping back the full truth to the last. Similarly it is held in the Far East that there were five periods in Śâkyamuni's teaching which after passing through the stage of the Hinayana culminated in the Prajñâ-pâramitâ and Amitâbha sutras shortly before his death. Such statements admit the historical priority of the Hinayana: it is rudimentary (that is early) truth which needs completion and expansion. Many critics demur to the assumption that primitive Buddhism was a system of ethics purged of superstition and mythology. And in a way they are right. Could we get hold of a primitive Buddhist, we should probably find that miracles, magic, and superhuman beings played a large part in his mind and that the Buddha did not appear to him as what we call a human teacher. In that sense the germs of the Mahayana existed in the lifetime of Gotama. But the difference between early and later Buddhism lies in this, that the deities who surround the Buddha in the Pali Pitakas are mere accessories: his teaching would not be affected if they were all removed. But the Bodhisattvas in the Lotus or the Sutra of the Happy Land have a doctrinal significance.

Though in India old ideas persist with unusual vitality, still even there they can live only if they either develop or gather round them new accretions. As one of the religions of India, Buddhism was sensitive to the general movement of Indian thought, or rather it was a part of that movement. We see as clearly in Buddhist as in non-Buddhist India that there was a tendency to construct philosophic systems and another tendency to create deities satisfying to the emotions as well as to the intellect and yet another tendency to compose new scriptures. But apart

[1] Chap. IV.

from this parallel development, it becomes clear after the Christian era that Buddhism is becoming surrounded by Hinduism. The influence is not indeed one-sided: there is interdependence and interpenetration but the net result is that the general Indian features of each religious period overpower the specially Buddhist features and in the end we find that while Hinduism has only been profoundly modified Buddhism has vanished.

If we examine the Pali Pitakas, including the heresies mentioned in the Kathâvatthu, we find that they contain the germs of many Mahayanist ideas. Thus side by side with the human portrait of the Buddha there is the doctrine that he is one in a series of supernatural teachers, each with the same life-history, and this life is connected with the whole course of nature, as is shown by the sympathetic earthquakes which mark its crises. His birth is supernatural and had he willed it he could have lived until the end of the present Kalpa[1]. So, too, the nature of a Buddha when he is released from form, that is after death, is deep and unfathomable as the ocean[2]. The Kathâvatthu condemns the ideas (thus showing that they existed) that Buddhas are born in all quarters of the universe, that the Buddha was superhuman in the ordinary affairs of life, that he was not really born in the world of men and that he did not preach the Law himself. These last two heresies are attributed by the commentary to the Vetulyakas who are said to have believed that he remained in the Tushita heaven and sent a phantom to preach on earth. Here we have the rudiments of the doctrine afterwards systematized under the name of the three bodies of Buddha. Similarly though Nirvana is regarded as primarily an ethical state, the Pali Canon contains the expression Nirvâṇa-dhâtu and the idea[3] that Nirvana is a sphere or rêalm (*âyatanam*) which transcends the transitory world and in which such antitheses are coming and going, birth and death, cease to exist. This foreshadows the doctrine of Bhûta-tathatâ and we seem to hear a prelude to the dialectic of Nâgârjuna when the Kathâvatthu discusses whether Suññatâ or the void is predicable of the Skandhas and when it condemns the views that anything now existing existed in the past: and that knowledge of the present is possible (whereas the moment anything is known it

[1] Mahâparinib. Sut. III.

[2] Majj. Nik. 72.

[3] Udâna, VIII. 1–4.

is really past). The Kathâvatthu also condemns the proposition that a Bodhisattva can be reborn in realms of woe or fall into error, and this proposition hints that the career of a Bodhisattva was considered of general interest.

The Mahayana grows out of the Hinayana and in many respects the Hinayana passes into it and is preserved unchanged. It is true that in reading the Lotus we wonder how this marvellous cosmic vision can represent itself as the teaching of Gotama, but the Buddhacarita of Aśvaghosha, though embellished with literary mythology, hardly advances in doctrine beyond the Pali sutras describing the marvels of the Buddha's nativity[1] and the greater part of Nâgârjuna's Friendly Epistle, which purports to contain an epitome of the faith, is in phraseology as well as thought perfectly in harmony with the Pali Canon. Whence comes this difference of tone in works accepted by the same school? One difficulty of the historian who essays to account for the later phases of Buddhism is to apportion duly the influence of Indian and foreign elements. On the one hand, the Mahayana, whether we call it a development or perversion, is a product of Indian thought. To explain its trinities, its saviours, its doctrine of self sacrifice it is not necessary to seek abroad. New schools, anxious to claim continuity and antiquity, gladly retained as much of the old doctrine as they could. But on the other hand, Indian Buddhism came into contact with foreign, especially Iranian, ideas and undoubtedly assimilated some of them. From time to time I have drawn attention to such cases in this work, but as a rule the foreign ideas are so thoroughly mastered and indianized that they cease to be obvious. They merely open up to Indian thought a new path wherein it can move in its own way.

In the period following Asoka's death Buddhism suffered a temporary eclipse. Pushyamitra who in 184 B.C. overthrew the Mauryas and established the Sunga dynasty was a patron of the Brahmans. Târanâtha describes him[2] as a ferocious persecutor, and the Divyâvadâna supports the story. But the persecution, if it really occurred, was probably local and did not seriously check the spread of Buddhism, which before the time of Kanishka had extended northwards to Bactria and Kashmir. The latter territory became the special home of the Sarvâstivâdins. It was

[1] Accariyabbhutasuttam. Majj. Nik. 123.
[2] Chap. XVI.

in the reign of Pushyamitra that the Græco-Bactrian king Menander or Milinda invaded India (155–3 B.C.) and there were many other invasions and settlements of tribes coming from the north-west and variously described as Sakas, Pahlavas, Parthians and Yavanas, culminating in the conquests of the Kushans. The whole period was disturbed and confused but some general statements can be made with considerable confidence.

From about 300 B.C. to 100 A.D. we find inscriptions, buildings and statues testifying to the piety of Buddhist and Jain donors but hardly any indications of a similar liberality to Brahmans. In the second and third centuries A.D. grants of land to Brahmans and their temples begin to be recorded and in the fourth century (that is with the rise of the Gupta Dynasty) such grants become frequent. These facts can hardly be interpreted otherwise than as meaning that from 300 B.C. to 100 A.D. the upper classes of India favoured Buddhism and Jainism and did not favour the Brahmans in the same way or to the same extent. But it must be remembered that the religion of the Brahmans continued throughout this period and produced a copious literature, and also that the absence of works of art may be due to the fact that their worship was performed in sacrificial enclosures and that they had not yet begun to use temples and statues. After the first century A.D. we have first a gradual and then a rapid rise in Brahmanic influence. Inscriptions as well as books indicate that a linguistic change occurred in the same period. At first popular dialects were regarded as sufficiently dignified and current to be the medium for both scripture and official records. Sanskrit remained a thing apart—the peculiar possession of the Brahman literati. Then the popular language was sanskritized, the rules of Sanskrit grammar being accepted as the standard to which it ought to conform, though perfect conformity was impracticable. In much the same way the modern Greeks try to bring Romaic into line with classical Greek. Finally Sanskrit was recognized as the proper language for literature, government and religion. The earliest inscriptions[1] in correct Sanskrit seem to date from the second century A.D. Further, the invaders who entered India from the

[1] That of Rudradaman at Girnar, dated 72 in the Saka Era, has hitherto been considered the oldest, but it is now said that one discovered at Isapur near Muttra is older. See *J.R.A.S* 1912, p. 114.

north-west favoured Buddhism on the whole. Coins indicate that some of them worshipped Siva[1] but the number and beauty of Buddhist monuments erected under their rule can hardly be interpreted except as a sign of their patronage. And their conversion was natural for they had no strong religious convictions of their own and the Brahmans with their pride of caste shrank from foreigners. But Buddhism had no prejudice of race or class: it was animated by a missionary spirit and it was probably the stronger creed at this period. It not only met the invaders on their entry into India but it sent missionaries to them in Bactria and Afghanistan, so that to some extent they brought Buddhism with them. But it was a Buddhism combined with the most varied elements. Hellenic art and religion had made the figures of Apollo, Herakles and Helios familiar in Bactria, and both Bactria and northern India were in touch with Zoroastrians. The mixed cults of these borderlands readily professed allegiance to the Buddha but, not understanding Indian ideas, simply made him into a deity and having done this were not likely to repudiate other Indian deities. Thus in its outward form the Buddhism of the invaders tended to be a compound of Indian, Greek and Persian ideas in which Sun worship played a large part, for not only Indian myths, but Apollo and Helios and the Persian Mithra all entered into it. Persian influence in art is discernible as early as the architecture of Asoka: in doctrine it has something to do with such figures as Vairocana and Amitâbha. Græco-Roman influence also was powerful in art and through art affected religion. In Asoka's time likenesses of the Buddha were unknown and the adoration of images, if not entirely due to the art of Gandhara, was at least encouraged by it.

But though coins and sculpture bring clearly before us a medley of deities corresponding to a medley of human races, they do not help us much in tracing the growth of thought, phases of which are preserved in a literature sufficiently copious though the record sometimes fails at the points of transition where it would be of most interest. It is natural that sacred books should record accepted results rather than tentative innovations and even disguise the latter. But we can fix a few dates which enable us to judge what shape Buddhism was taking

[1] *E.g.* Kadphises II and Vasudeva.

about the time of the Christian era. The Tibetan historian Târanâtha is not of much help, for his chronology is most confused, but still he definitely connects the appearance of Mahayanist texts with the reign of Kanishka and the period immediately following it[1] and regards them as a new phenomenon. Greater assistance is furnished by the Chinese translators, whose dates are known with some exactitude. Thus the earliest Buddhist work rendered into Chinese is said to be the sutra of forty-two sections, translated by Kâśyapa Mâtanga in 67 A.D. It consists of extracts or resumés of the Buddha's teaching mostly prefaced by the words "The Buddha said," doubtless in imitation of the Confucian Analects where the introductory formula "The master said" plays a similar part. Its ideas and precepts are Hinayanist[2]: the Arhat is held up as the ideal and in a remarkable passage[3] where the degrees of sanctity are graded and compared no mention is made of Bodhisattvas. This first translation was followed by a long series of others, principally from the Sûtra-Piṭaka, for very little of the Vinaya was translated before the fifth century. A great number of Hinayanist sutras were translated before 300 A.D. but very few after 450. On the other hand portions of the sutra about Amîda's Paradise, of the Prajñâ-pâramitâ, and of the Avataṃsaka were translated about 150 A.D. and translations of the Lotus and Lalita-vistara appeared about 300.

Great caution is necessary in using these data and the circumstances of China as well as of India must be taken into account. If translations of the Vinaya and complete collections of sutras are late in appearing, it does not follow that the corresponding Indian texts are late, for the need of the Vinaya was not felt until monasteries began to spring up. Most of the translations made before the fifth century are extracts and of indifferent workmanship. Some are retained in the Chinese Tripitaka but are superseded by later versions. But however inaccurate and incomplete these older translations may be, if any of them can be identified with a part of an extant Sanskrit

[1] Chaps. XII, XIII.

[2] The last section (42) as translated by Teitaro Suzuki in the *Sermons of a Buddhist Abbot* may seem an exception, for it contains such statements as "I consider the doctrine of sameness as the absolute ground of reality." But the translation seems to me doubtful.

[3] Sec. 11.

work it follows that at least that part of the work and the doctrines contained in it were current in India or Central Asia some time before the translation was made. Applying this principle we may conclude that the Hinayana and Mahayana were flourishing side by side in India and Central Asia in the first century A.D. and that the Happy Land sutras and portions of the Prajñâ-pâramitâ already existed. From that time onwards Mahayanist literature as represented by Chinese translations steadily increases, and after 400 A.D. Hinayanist literature declines, with two exceptions, the Vinaya and the Abhidharma books of the Sarvâstivâdins. The Vinaya was evidently regarded as a rule of life independent of theology, but it is remarkable that Hsüan Chuang after his return from India in 645 should have thought it worth while to translate the philosophy of the Sarvâstivâdins.

Other considerations render this chronology probable. Two conspicuous features of the Mahayana are the worship of Bodhisattvas and idealist philosophy. These are obviously parallel to the worship of Śiva and Vishnu, and to the rise of the Vedanta. Now the worship of these deities was probably not prevalent before 300 B.C., for they are almost unknown to the Pali Pitakas, and it was fully developed about the time of the Bhagavad-gîtâ which perhaps assumed its present form a little before the Christian era. Not only is the combination of devotion and metaphysics found in this work similar to the tone of many Mahayanist sutras but the manifestation of Krishna in his divine form is like the transformation scenes of the Lotus[1]. The chief moral principle of the Bhagavad-gîtâ is substantially the same as that prescribed for Bodhisattvas. It teaches that action is superior to inaction, but that action should be wholly disinterested and not directed to any selfish object. This is precisely the attitude of the Bodhisattva who avoids the inaction of those who are engrossed in self-culture as much as the pursuit of wealth or pleasure. Both the Gîtâ and Mahayanist treatises lay stress on faith. He who thinks on Krishna when dying goes to Krishna[2] just as he who thinks on Amitâbha goes

[1] Just as all gods and worlds are seen within Krishna's body, so we are told in the Karaṇḍa-vyûha (which is however a later work) that in the pores of Avalokita's skin are woods and mountains where dwell saints and gods.

[2] Bhag. G. VIII. 5.

to the Happy Land and the idea is not unknown to the Pali texts, for it finds complete expression in the story of Maṭṭha-kuṇḍali[1].

The idea of a benevolent deity to be worshipped with devotion and faith and not with ceremonies is strange to old Buddhism and old Brahmanism alike. It was a popular idea which became so strong that neither priests nor Bhikshus could ignore it and in its ultimate result it is hard to say whether Buddhist or Brahmanic elements are more prominent. Both Avalokita and Krishṇa are Devas. The former has the beauty of holiness and the strength which it gives, but also the weakness of a somewhat abstract figure: the latter is very personal and springs from the heart of India but to those who are not Hindus seems wanting in purity and simplicity. The divine character of both figures is due to Brahmanism rather than Buddhism, but the new form of worship which laid stress on a frame of mind rather than on ceremonial and the idea of Avatâras or the periodic appearance of superhuman saviours and teachers indicate the influence of Buddhism on Brahmanism.

There is a similar parallel between the newer Buddhist philosophy and the Vedantist school represented by Śankara, and Indian critics detected it. Śankara was called a Pracchanna-bauddha or crypto-buddhist by his theological opponents[2] and the resemblance between the two systems in thought, if not in word, is striking. Both distinguish relative and absolute truth: for both the relative truth is practically theism, for both absolute truth is beyond description and whether it is called Brahman, Dharma-kâya or Śûnyatâ is not equivalent to God in the Christian or Mohammedan sense. Just as for the Vedantist there exist in the light of the highest knowledge neither a personal God nor an individual soul, so the Mâdhyamika Sûtra can declare that the Buddha does not really exist. The Mahayanist philosophers do not use the word Mâyâ but they state the same theory in a more subjective form by ascribing the appearance of the phenomenal world to ignorance, a nomen-

[1] *Commentary on Dhammapada*, P.T.S. edition, pp. 25 ff. especially p. 33.

[2] See Râmânuja, Śrîbhâshya, II. 2, 27 and Padma-Purâṇa uttarakanda 43 (quoted by Suhtankar in *Vienna Oriental Journ.* vol. XXII. 1908). Mâyâvâdam asacchâstrâm pracchannam bauddham ucyate. The Mâdhvas were specially bitter in their denunciation of Śankara.

clature which is derived from the Buddha's phrase, "From ignorance come the Sankhâras."

Here, as elsewhere, Buddhist and Brahmanic ideas acted and reacted in such complex interrelations that it is hard to say which has borrowed from the other. As to dates, the older Upanishads which contain the foundations but not the complete edifice of Vedantism, seem a little earlier than the Buddha. Now we know that within the Vedantist school there were divergences of opinion which later received classic expression in the hands of Śankara and Râmânuja. The latter rejected the doctrines of Mâyâ and of the difference between relative and absolute truth. The germs of both schools are to be found in the Upanishads but it seems probable that the ideas of Śankara were originally worked out among Buddhists rather than among Brahmans and were rightly described by their opponents as disguised Buddhism. As early as 520 A.D. Bodhidharma preached in China a doctrine which is practically the same as the Advaita.

The earliest known work in which the theory of Mâyâ and the Advaita philosophy are clearly formulated is the metrical treatise known as the Kârikâ of Gauḍapâda. This name was borne by the teacher of Śankara's teacher, who must have lived about 700 A.D., but the high position accorded to the work, which is usually printed with the Mâṇḍûkya Upanishad and is practically regarded as[1] a part of it, make an earlier date probable. Both in language and thought it bears a striking resemblance to Buddhist writings of the Mâdhyamika school and also contains many ideas and similes which reappear in the works of Śankara[2]. On the other hand the Lankâvatâra Sûtra which was translated into Chinese in 513 and therefore can hardly have been composed later than 450, is conscious that its doctrines resemble Brahmanic philosophy, for an interlocutor

[1] Or as itself forming four separate Upanishads. For other arguments in favour of an early date see Walleser, *Älterer Vedânta*, pp. 14 ff. He states that the Kârikâ is quoted in the Tibetan translations of Bhavaviveka's *Tārkajvālā*. Bhavaviveka was certainly anterior to the travels of Hsüan Chuang and perhaps was much earlier. But if he died about 600 A.D. a work quoted by him can hardly have been later than 550 and may be much earlier. But see also Jacobi in *J.A.O.S.* April, 1913, p. 51.

[2] For the resemblances to Nâgârjuna see *J.R.A.S.* 1910, pp. 136 ff. Especially remarkable are II. 32 na nirodho na cotpattir, etc., and IV. 59 and the whole argument that causation is impossible. Noticeable too is the use of Buddhist terms like upâya, nirvâṇa, buddha and âdibuddha, though not always in the Buddhist sense.

objects that the language used in it by the Buddha about the Tathâgatha-garbha is very like the Brahmanic doctrine of the Âtman. To which the Buddha replies that his language is a concession to those who cannot stomach the doctrine of the negation of reality in all its austerity. Some of the best known verses of Gauḍapâda compare the world of appearance to the apparent circle of fire produced by whirling a lighted torch. This striking image occurs first in the Maitrâyana Upanishad (VI. 24), which shows other indications of an acquaintance with Buddhism, and also in the Lankâvatâra Sûtra.

A real affinity unites the doctrine of Śankara to the teaching of Gotama himself. That teaching as presented in the Pali Pitakas is marked by its negative and deliberately circumscribed character. Its rule is silence when strict accuracy of expression is impossible, whereas later philosophy does not shrink from phrases which are suggestive, if not exact. Gotama refuses to admit that the human soul is a fixed entity or Âtman, but he does not condemn (though he also does not discuss) the idea that the whole world of change and becoming, including human souls, is the expression or disguise of some one ineffable principle. He teaches too that the human mind can grow until it develops new faculties and powers and becomes the Buddha mind, which sees the whole chain of births, the order of the world, and the reality of emancipation. As the object of the whole system is practical, Nirvana is always regarded as a *terminus ad quem* or an escape (nissaranam) from this transitory world, and this view is more accurate as well as more edifying than the view which treats Brahman or Śûnyatâ as the origin of the universe. When the Vedanta teaches that this changing troubled world is merely the disguise of that unchanging and untroubled state into which saints can pass, it is, I believe, following Gotama's thought, but giving it an expression which he would have considered imperfect.

CHAPTER XXII

FROM KANISHKA TO VASUBANDHU

Tradition, as mentioned above, connects the rise of the Mahayana with the reign of Kanishka. Materials for forming a picture of Indian life under his rule are not plentiful but it was clearly an age of fusion. His hereditary dominions were ample and he had no need to spend his reign in conquests, but he probably subdued Kashmir as well as Khotan, Yarkand and Kashgar[1]. Hostages from one of these states were sent to reside in India and all accounts agree that they were treated with generosity and that their sojourn improved the relations of Kaṇishka with the northern tribes. His capital was Purushapura or Peshawar, and the locality, like many other features of his reign, indicates a tendency to amalgamate India with Persia and Central Asia. It was embellished with masterpieces of Gandharan sculpture and its chief ornament was a great stûpa built by the king for the reception of the relics of the Buddha which he collected. This building is described by several Chinese pilgrims[2] and its proportions, though variously stated, were sufficient to render it celebrated in all the Buddhist world. It is said to have been several times burnt, and rebuilt, but so solid a structure can hardly have been totally destroyed by fire and the greater part of the monument discovered in 1908 probably dates from the time of Kanishka. The base is a square measuring 285 feet on each side, with massive towers at the corners, and on each of the four faces projections bearing stair-

[1] The uncertainty as to the date of Kanishka naturally makes it uncertain whether he was the hero of these conquests. Kashmir was certainly included in the dominions of the Kushans and was a favourite residence of Kanishka. About 90 A.D. a Kushan king attacked Central Asia but was repulsed by the Chinese general Pan-Ch'ao. Later, after the death of Pan-Ch'ao (perhaps about 103 A.D.), he renewed the attempt and conquered Kashgar, Yarkand and Khotan. See Vincent Smith, *Early History of India*, 3rd ed. pp. 253 ff.

[2] See Fa-Hsien, ed. Legge, p. 33, *B.E.F.E.O.* 1903 (Sung Yün), pp. 420 ff. Watters, *Yüan Chwang*, I. pp. 204 ff. *J.R.A.S.* 1909, p. 1056, 1912, p. 114. For the general structure of these stûpas see Foucher, *L'art Gréco-Bouddhique du Gandhara*, pp. 45 ff.

cases. The sides were ornamented with stucco figures of the Buddha and according to the Chinese pilgrims the superstructure was crowned with an iron pillar on which were set twenty-five gilded disks. Inside was found a metal casket, still containing the sacred bones, and bearing an inscription which presents two points of great interest. Firstly it mentions "Agiśala the overseer of works at Kanishka's vihâra," that is, probably Agesilaus, a foreigner in the king's service. Secondly it states that the casket was made "for the acceptance of the teachers of the Sarvâstivâdin sect[1]," and the idea that Kanishka was the special patron of the Mahayana must be reconsidered in the light of this statement.

Legends ascribe Kanishka's fervour for the Buddhist faith not to education but to conversion. His coinage, of which abundant specimens have been preserved, confirms this for it presents images of Greek, Persian, Indian and perhaps Babylonian deities showing how varied was the mythology which may have mingled with Gandharan Buddhism. The coins bearing figures of the Buddha are not numerous and, as he undoubtedly left behind him the reputation of a pious Buddhist, it is probable that they were struck late in his reign and represent his last religious phase[2]. Hsüan Chuang[3] repeats some legends which relate that he was originally anti-Buddhist, and that after his conversion he summoned a council and built a stupa.

The substance of these legends is probable. Kanishka as a barbarian but docile conqueror was likely to adopt Buddhism if he wished to keep abreast of the thought and civilisation of his subjects, for at that time it undoubtedly inspired the intellect and art of north-western India. Both as a statesman and as an enquirer after truth he would wish to promote harmony and stop sectarian squabbles. His action resembles that of Constantine who after his conversion to Christianity proceeded to summon the Council of Nicæa in order to stop the dissensions of the Church and settle what were the tenets of the religion which he had embraced, a point about which both he and

[1] *J.R.A.S.* 1909, p. 1058. "Acaryanam Sarvastivadinam pratigrahē."

[2] Similarly Harsha became a Buddhist late in life.

[3] Watters, vol. I. p. 203. He places Kanishka's accession 400 years after the death of the Buddha, which is one of the arguments for supposing Kanishka to have reigned about 50 B.C., but in another passage (Watters, I. 222, 224) he appears to place it 500 years after the death.

Kanishka seem to have felt some uncertainty. Our knowledge of Kanishka's Council depends chiefly on the traditions reported by Hsüan Chuang[1] which present many difficulties. He tells us that the king, acting in consultation with Parśva, issued summonses to all the learned doctors of his realm. They came in such crowds that a severe test was imposed and only 499 Arhats were selected. There was some discussion as to the place of meeting but finally Kashmir[2] was selected and the king built a monastery for the Brethren. When the Council met, there arose a question as to whether Vasumitra (who is not further described) should be admitted seeing that he was not an Arhat but aspired to the career of a Bodhisattva. But owing to the interposition of spirits he was not only admitted but made president.

The texts of the Tripitaka were collected and the Council "composed 100,000 stanzas of Upadeśa Śâstras explanatory of the canonical sûtras, 100,000 stanzas of Vinaya-vibhâshâ Śâstras explanatory of the Vinaya and 100,000 of Abhidharma-vibhâshâ Śâstras explanatory of the Abhidharma. For this exposition of the Tripitaka all learning from remote antiquity was thoroughly examined; the general sense and the terse language (of the Buddhist scriptures) was again and again made clear and distinct, and learning was widely diffused for the safe-guiding of disciples. King Kanishka caused the treatises when finished to be written out on copper plates and enclosed these in stone boxes which he deposited in a tope made for the purpose. He then ordered spirits to keep and guard the texts and not to allow any to be taken out of the country by heretics; those who wished to study them could do so in the country. When leaving to return to his own country, Kanishka renewed Asoka's gift of all Kashmir to the Buddhist Church[3]."

Paramârtha (499–569 A.D.) in his *Life of Vasubandhu*[4] gives an account of a council generally considered to be the same as

[1] Watters, vol. I. 270–1.

[2] But Târanâtha says some authorities held that it met at Jalandhara. Some Chinese works say it was held at Kandahar.

[3] Watters, *l.c.*

[4] Translated by Takakusu in *T'oung Pao*, 1904, pp. 269 ff. Paramârtha was a native of Ujjain who arrived at Nanking in 548 and made many translations, but it is quite possible that this life of Vasubandhu is not a translation but original notes of his own.

that described by Hsüan Chuang, though the differences in the two versions are considerable. He says that about five hundred years[1] after the Buddha's death (*i.e.* between 87 B.C. and 13 A.D. if the Buddha died 487 B.C.) an Indian Arhat called Katyâyanî-putra, who was a monk of the Sarvâstivâdin school, went to Kipin or Kashmir. There with 500 other Arhats and 500 Bodhi-sattvas he collected the Abhidharma of the Sarvâstivâdins and arranged it in eight books called Ka-lan-ta (Sanskrit *Grantha*) or Kan-tu (Pali *Gantho*). This compilation was also called Jñâna-prasthâna. He then made a proclamation inviting all who had heard the Buddha preach to communicate what they remembered. Many spirits responded and contributed their reminiscences which were examined by the Council and, when they did not contradict the sûtras and the Vinaya, were accepted, but otherwise were rejected. The selected pieces were grouped according to their subject-matter. Those about wisdom formed the Prajñâ Grantha, and those about meditation the Dhyâna Grantha and so on. After finishing the eight books they proceeded to the composition of a commentary or Vibhâshâ and invited the assistance of Aśvaghosha. When he came to Kashmir, Katyâyanî-putra expounded the eight books to him and Aśvaghosha put them into literary form. At the end of twelve years the composition of the commentary was finished. It consisted of 1,000,000 verses....Katyâyanî-putra set up a stone inscribed with this proclamation. "Those who hereafter learn this law must not go out of Kashmir. No sentence of the eight books, or of the Vibhâshâ must pass out of the land, lest other schools or the Mahayana should corrupt the true law." This proclamation was reported to the king who approved it. The sages of Kashmir had power over demons and set them to guard the entrance to the country, but we are told that anyone desirous of learning the law could come to Kashmir and was in no way interrupted.

There follows a story telling how, despite this prohibition, a native of Ayodhya succeeded in learning the law in Kashmir

[1] Chinese expressions like "in the five hundred years after the Buddha's death" probably mean the period 400–500 of the era commencing with the Buddha's death and not the period 500–600. The period 1–100 is "the one hundred years," 101–200 "the two hundred years" and so on. See *B.E.F.E.O.* 1911, 356. But it must be remembered that the date of the Buddha's death is not yet certain. The latest theory (Vincent Smith, 1919) places it in 554 B.C.

and subsequently teaching it in his native land. Paramârtha's account seems exaggerated, whereas the prohibition described by Hsüan Chuang is intelligible. It was forbidden to take the official copies of the law out of Kashmir, lest heretics should tamper with them.

Târanâtha[1] gives a singularly confused account of the meeting, which he expressly calls the third council, but makes some important statements about it. He says that it put an end to the dissensions which had been distracting the Buddhist Church *for nearly a century* and that it recognized all the eighteen sects as holding the true doctrine: that it put the Vinaya in writing as well as such parts of the Sûtrapiṭaka and Abhidharma as were still unwritten and corrected those which already existed as written texts: that all kinds of Mahayanist writings appeared at this time but that the Śrâvakas raised no opposition.

It is hard to say how much history can be extracted from these vague and discrepant stories. They seem to refer to one assembly regarded (at least in Tibet) as the third council of the Church and held under Kanishka four or five hundred years[2] after the Buddha's death. As to what happened at the council tradition seems to justify the following deductions, though as the tradition is certainly jumbled it may also be incorrect in details.

(*a*) The council is recognized only by the northern Church and is unknown to the Churches of Ceylon, Burma and Siam. It seems to have regarded Kashmir as sacred land outside which the true doctrine was exposed to danger. (*b*) But it was not a specially Mahayanist meeting but rather a conference of peace and compromise. Târanâtha says this clearly: in Hsüan Chuang's account an assembly of Arhats (which at this time must have meant Hinayanists) elect a president who was not an Arhat and according to Paramârtha the assembly consisted of 500 Arhats and 500 Bodhisattvas who were convened by a leader of the Sarvâstivâdin school and ended by requesting Aśvaghosha to revise their work. (*c*) The literary result of the council was the

[1] Chap. XII.

[2] See Watters, I. pp. 222, 224 and 270. It is worth noting that Hsüan Chuang says Asoka lived one hundred years after the Buddha's death. See Watters, I. p. 267. See also the note of S. Lévi in *J.R.A.S.* 1914, pp. 1016–1019, citing traditions to the effect that there were 300 years between Upagupta, the teacher of Asoka, and Kanishka, who is thus made to reign about 31 A.D. On the other hand Kanishka's chaplain Sangharaksha is said to have lived 700 years after the Buddha.

composition of commentaries on the three Pitakas. One of these, the Abhidharma-mahâvibhâshâ-śâstra, translated into Chinese in 437–9 and still extant, is said to be a work of encyclopædic character, hardly a commentary in the strict sense. Paramârtha perhaps made a confusion in saying that the Jñâna-prasthâna itself was composed at the council. The traditions indicate that the council to some extent sifted and revised the Tripitaka and perhaps it accepted the seven Abhidharma books of the Sarvâstivâdins[1]. But it is not stated or implied that it composed or sanctioned Mahayanist books. Târanâtha merely says that such books appeared at this time and that the Hinayanists raised no active objection.

But if the above is the gist of the traditions, the position described is not clear. The council is recognized by Mahayanists yet it appears to have resulted in the composition of a Sarvâstivâdin treatise, and the tradition connecting the Sarvâstivâdins with the council is not likely to be wrong, for they are recognized in the inscription on Kanishka's casket, and Gandhara and Kashmir were their headquarters. The decisions of councils are often politic rather than logical and it may be that the doctors summoned by Kanishka, while compiling Sarvâstivâdin treatises, admitted the principle that there is more than one vehicle which can take mankind to salvation. Perhaps some compromise based on geography was arranged, such as that Kashmir should be left to the Sarvâstivâdin school which had long flourished there, but that no opposition should be offered to the Mahayanists elsewhere.

The relations of the Sarvâstivâdins to Mahayanism are exceedingly difficult to define and there are hardly sufficient materials for a connected account of this once important sect, but I will state some facts about it which seem certain.

It is ancient, for the Kathâvatthu alludes to its doctrines[2]. It flourished in Gandhara, Kashmir and Central Asia, and Kanishka's casket shows that he patronized it[3]. But it appears

[1] See Takakusu in *J.P.T.S.* 1905, pp. 67 ff. For the Sarvâstivâdin Canon, see my chapter on the Chinese Tripitaka.

[2] See above, vol. I. p. 262. For an account of the doctrines see also Vasilief, 245 ff. Rockhill, *Life of the Buddha*, pp. 190 ff.

[3] Its connection with Gandhara and Kashmir is plainly indicated in its own scriptures. See Przyluski's article on "Le Nord-Ouest de l'Inde dans le Vinaya des Mûlasarvâstivâdins," *J.A.* 1914, II. pp. 493 ff. This Vinaya must have received considerable additions as time went on and in its present form is posterior to Kanishka.

to have been hardly known in Ceylon or Southern India. It was the principal northern form of Hinayanism, just as the Theravâda was the southern form. I-Ching however says that it prevailed in the Malay Archipelago.

Its doctrines, so far as known, were Hinayanist but it was distinguished from cognate schools by holding that the external world can be said to exist and is not merely a continual process of becoming. It had its own version of the Abhidharma and of the Vinaya. In the time of Fa-Hsien the latter was still preserved orally and was not written. The adherents of this school were also called Vaibhâshikas, and Vibhâshâ was a name given to their exegetical literature.

But the association of the Sarvâstivâdins with Mahayanists is clear from the council of Kanishka onwards. Many eminent Buddhists began by being Sarvâstivâdins and became Mahayanists, their earlier belief being regarded as preliminary rather than erroneous. Hsüan Chuang translated the Sarvâstivâdin scriptures in his old age and I-Ching belonged to the Mûlasarvâstivâdin school[1]; yet both authors write as if they were devout Mahayanists. The Tibetan Church is generally regarded as an extreme form of Mahayanism but its Vinaya is that of the Sarvâstivâdins.

Though the Sarvâstivâdins can hardly have accepted idealist metaphysics, yet the evidence of art and their own version of the Vinaya make it probable that they tolerated a moderate amount of mythology, and the Mahayanists, who like all philosophers were obliged to admit the provisional validity of the external world, may also have admitted their analysis of the same as provisionally valid. The strength of the Hinayanist schools lay in the Vinaya. The Mahayanists showed a tendency to replace it by legends and vague if noble aspirations. But a code of discipline was necessary for large monasteries and the code of the Sarvâstivâdins enjoyed general esteem in Central Asia and China.

Three stages in the history of Indian Buddhism are marked by the names of Aśvaghosha, Nâgârjuna and the two brothers

[1] The distinction between Sarvâstivâdin and Mûlasarvâstivâdin is not clear to me. I can only suggest that when a section of the school accepted the Mahâvibhâshâ and were known as Vaibhâshikas others who approved of the school chiefly on account of its excellent Vinaya called themselves Primitive Sarvâstivâdins.

Asanga and Vasubandhu. It would be easier to give a precise description of its development if we were sure which of the works ascribed to these worthies are authentic, but it seems that Aśvaghosha represents an ornate and transitional phase of the older schools leading to Mahayanism, whereas Nâgârjuna is connected with the Prajñâ-pâramitâ and the nihilistic philosophy described in the preceding chapter. Asanga was the founder of the later and more scholastic system called Yogâcâra and is also associated with a series of revelations said to have been made by Maitreya.

As mentioned above, tradition makes Aśvaghosha[1], one of the most brilliant among Sanskrit writers, live at the court of Kanishka[2] and according to some accounts he was given to the Kushans as part of a war indemnity. The tradition[3] is confirmed by the style and contents of his poems and it has been noted by Foucher that his treatment of legends is in remarkable accord with their artistic presentment in the Gandharan sculptures. Also fragmentary manuscripts of his dramas discovered in Central Asia appear to date from the Kushan epoch. Aśvaghosha's rank as a poet depends chiefly on his Buddhacarita, or life of the Buddha up to the time of his enlightenment. It is the earliest example of a Kâvya, usually translated as artificial epic, but here literary skill is subservient to the theme and does not, as too often in later works, overwhelm it. The Buddha is its hero, as Râma of the Râmâyana, and it sings the events of his earlier life in a fine flow of elaborate but impassioned language. Another of his poems[4], discovered only a few years ago, treats of the conversion of Nanda, the Buddha's half-brother.

[1] See Sylvain Lévi, *J.A.* 1908, XII. 57 ff., and Winternitz, *Ges. Ind. Lit.* II. i. pp. 201 ff.

[2] The only reason for doubting it is that two stories (Nos. 14 and 31) in the Sûtrâlankâra (which appears to be a genuine work) refer to Kanishka as if he had reigned in the past. This may be a poetic artifice or it may be that the stories are interpolations. See for the traditions Watters on *Yüan Chwang*, II. 102–4 and Takakusu in *J.R.A.S.* 1905, p. 53 who quotes the Chinese Samyukta-ratna-piṭaka-sûtra and the Record of Indian Patriarchs. The Chinese list of Patriarchs is compatible with the view that Aśvaghosha was alive about 125 A.D. for he was the twelfth Patriarch and Bodhidharma the twenty-eighth visited China in 520. This gives about 400 years for sixteen Patriarchs, which is possible, for these worthies were long-lived. But the list has little authority.

[3] The traditions are conveniently collected in the introduction to Teitaro Suzuki's translation of *The Awakening of Faith.*

[4] The Saundarânandakâvya.

Various other works are ascribed to Aśvaghosha and for the history of Buddhism it is of great interest to decide whether he was really the author of *The Awakening of Faith*. This skilful exposition of a difficult theme is worthy of the writer of the Buddhacarita but other reasons make his authorship doubtful, for the theology of the work may be described as the full-blown flower of Mahayanism untainted by Tantrism. It includes the doctrines of Bhûta-tathatâ, Âlayavijñâna, Tathâgatagarbha and the three bodies of Buddha. It would be dangerous to say that these ideas did not exist in the time of Kanishka, but what is known of the development of doctrine leads us to expect their full expression not then but a century or two later and other circumstances raise suspicions as to Aśvaghosha's authorship. His undoubted works were translated into Chinese about 400 A.D. but *The Awakening of Faith* a century and a half later[1]. Yet if this concise and authoritative compendium had existed in 400, it is strange that the earlier translators neglected it. It is also stated that an old Chinese catalogue of the Tripitaka does not name Aśvaghosha as the author[2].

The undoubted works of Aśvaghosha treat the Buddha with ornate but grave rhetoric as the hero of an epic. His progress is attended by miracles such as Indian taste demands, but they hardly exceed the marvels recounted in the Pali scriptures and there is no sign that the hero is identified, as in the Ramayana of Tulsi Das or the Gospel according to St John, with the divine spirit. The poet clearly feels personal devotion to a Saviour. He dwells on the duty of teaching others and not selfishly seeking one's own salvation, but he does not formulate dogmas.

The name most definitely connected with the early promulgation of Mahayanism is Nâgârjuna[3]. A preponderance of

[1] See Nanjio, Nos. 1182, 1351, 1250, 1299. It is noticeable that the translator Paramârtha shows a special interest in the life and works of Asanga and Vasubandhu.

[2] See Winternitz, *Ges. Ind. Lit.* II. i. p. 211. It is also noticeable that *The Awakening of Faith* appears to quote the Lankâvatâra sûtra which is not generally regarded as an early Mahayanist work.

[3] Nâgârjuna cannot have been the founder of the Mahayana for in his Mahâ-prajñâ-pâramitâ-śâstra (Nanjio, 1169, translation by Kumârajîva) he cites *inter alia* the Lotus, the Vimalakîrti-sûtra, and a work called Mahâyâna-śâstra. See *B.E.F.E.O.* 1911, p. 453. For Nâgârjuna see especially Grünwedel, *Mythologie*, pp. 29 ff. and the bibliography given in the notes. *Jour. Budd. Text. Soc.* v. part iv. pp. 7 ff. Watters, *Yüan Chwang*, pp. 200 ff. Târanâtha, chap. xv and Winternitz, *Ges. Ind. Lit.* II. i. pp. 250 ff.

Chinese tradition makes him the second patriarch after Aśvaghosha[1] and this agrees with the Kashmir chronicle which implies that he lived soon after Kanishka[2]. He probably flourished in the latter half of the second century. But his biographies extant in Chinese and Tibetan are almost wholly mythical, even crediting him with a life of several centuries, and the most that can be hoped is to extract a few grains of history from them. He is said to have been by birth a Brahman of Vidarbha (Berar) and to have had as teacher a Sudra named Saraha or Râhulabhadra. When the legend states that he visited the Nâgas in the depths of the sea and obtained books from them, it seems to admit that he preached new doctrines. It is noticeable that he is represented not only as a philosopher but as a great magician, builder, physician, and maker of images.

Many works are attributed to him but they have not the same authenticity as the poems of Aśvaghosha. Some schools make him the author of the Prajñâ-pâramitâ but it is more usually regarded as a revelation. The commentary on it known as Mahâ-prajñâ-pâramitâ-śâstra is generally accepted as his work. A consensus of tradition makes him the author of the Mâdhyamika[3] aphorisms of which some account has been given above. It is the principal authority of its school and is provided with a commentary attributed to the author himself and with a later one by Candrakîrti[4]. There is also ascribed to him a work called the Suhrillekha or friendly letter, a compendium of Buddhist doctrines, addressed to an Indian king[5]. This work

[1] He is omitted from the list of Buddhabhadra, giving the succession according to the Sarvâstivâdins, to which school he did not belong. I-Ching classes him with Aśvaghosha and Aryadeva as belonging to the early period.

[2] Râjataranginî, i. 173, 177.

[3] Edited in the *Bibliotheca Buddhica* by De la Vallée Poussin and (in part) in the *Journal of the Buddhist Text Soc.* See too Walleser, *Die Mittlere Lehre des Nâgârjuna nach der Tibetischen Version übertragen*, 1911: *nach der Chinesischen Version übertragen*, 1912.

[4] The ascription of these works to Nâgârjuna is probably correct for they were translated by Kumârajîva who was sufficiently near him in date to be in touch with good tradition.

[5] The name of this king, variously given as Udayana, Jetaka and Śâtavâhana, has not been identified with certainty from the various transcriptions and translations in the Chinese and Tibetan versions. See *J. Pali Text Soc.* for 1886 and I-Ching *Records of the Buddhist Religion* (trans. Takakusu), pp. 158 ff. The Ândhra kings who reigned from about 240 B.C. to 225 A.D. all claimed to belong to the Śâtavâhana dynasty. The stupa of Amarâvati in the Ândhra territory is surrounded by a stone railing ascribed to the period 160–200 A.D. and Nâgârjuna may have addressed a pious king living about that time.

is old for it was translated into Chinese in 434 A.D. and is a homily for laymen. It says nothing of the Mâdhyamika philosophy and most of it deals with the need of good conduct and the terrors of future punishment, quite in the manner of the Hinayana. But it also commends the use of images and incense in worship, it mentions Avalokita and Amitâbha and it holds up the ideal of attaining Buddhahood. Nâgârjuna's authorship is not beyond dispute but these ideas may well represent a type of popular Buddhism slightly posterior to Aśvaghosha[1].

In most lists of patriarchs Nâgârjuna is followed by Deva, also called Âryadeva, Kâṇadeva or Nîlanetra. I-Ching mentions him among the older teachers and a commentary on his principal work, the Śataśâstra, is attributed to Vasubandhu[2]. Little is known of his special teaching but he is regarded as an important doctor and his pupil Dharmatrâta is also important if not as an author at least as a compiler, for Sanskrit collections of verses corresponding to the Pali Dhammapada are ascribed to him. Âryadeva was a native of southern India[3].

The next epoch in the history of Buddhism is marked by the names of Asanga and Vasubandhu. The interval between them and Deva produced no teacher of importance, but Kumâralabdha, the founder of the Sautrântika school and perhaps identical with Kumârata the eighteenth Patriarch of the Chinese lists, may be mentioned. Hsüan Chuang says[4] that he was carried off in captivity by a king who reigned somewhere in the east of the Pamirs and that he, Aśvaghosha, Nâgârjuna and Deva were styled the four shining suns.

Asanga and Vasubandhu were brothers, sons of a Brahman who lived at Peshawar. They were both converted from the Sarvâstivâdin school to Mahayanism, but the third brother

[1] For other works attributed to Nâgârjuna see Nanjio, Nos. 1169, 1179, 1180, 1186 and Walleser's introduction to *Mittlere Lehre nach der Chinesischen Version* The Dharmasangraha, a Sanskrit theological glossary, is also attributed to Nâgârjuna as well as the tantric work Pancakrama. But it is not likely that the latter dates from his epoch.

[2] Nanjio, No. 1188.

[3] The very confused legends about him suggest a comparison with the Dravidian legend of a devotee who tore out one of his eyes and offered it to Śiva. See Grünwedel, *Mythologie*, p. 34 and notes. Polemics against various Hinayanist sects are ascribed to him. See Nanjio, Nos. 1259, 1260.

[4] Watters, *Yüan Chwang*, II. p. 286. Hsüan Chuang does not say that the four were contemporary but that in the time of Kumâralabdha they were called the four Suns.

Virincivatsa never changed his convictions. Tradition connects their career with Ayodhyā as well as with Peshawar and Vasubandhu enjoyed the confidence of the reigning monarch, who was probably Candragupta I. This identification depends on the hypothesis that Vasubandhu lived from about 280 to 360 A.D. which, as already mentioned, seems to me to have been proved by M. Péri[1]. The earlier Gupta kings though not Buddhists were tolerant, as is shown by the fact that the king of Ceylon[2] was allowed to erect a magnificent monastery at Nâlanda in the reign of Samudragupta (*c.* 330–375 A.D.).

Asanga founded the school known as Yogâcâra and many authorities ascribe to him the introduction of magical practices and Tantrism. But though he is a considerable figure in the history of Buddhism, I doubt if his importance or culpability is so great as this. For if tradition can be trusted, earlier teachers especially Nâgârjuna dealt in spells and invocations and the works of Asanga[3] known to us are characterized by a somewhat scholastic piety and are chiefly occupied in defining and describing the various stages in the spiritual development of a Bodhisattva. It is true that he admits the use of magical formulæ[4] as an aid in this evolution but they form only a slight part of his system and it does not appear that the Chên-yen or Shingon sect of the Far East (the Sanskrit Mantrayâṇa) traced its lineage back to him.

Our estimate of his position in the history of Buddhism must depend on our opinion as to the authorship of *The Awakening of Faith*. If this treatise was composed by Aśvaghosha then doctrines respecting the three bodies of Buddha, the Tathâgata-garbha and the Âlaya-vijñâna were not only known but scientifically formulated considerably before Asanga. The conclusion cannot be rejected as absurd—for Aśvaghosha might speak differently in poems and in philosophical treatises—but

[1] For Asanga and Vasubandhu see Péri in *B.E.F.E.O.* 1911, pp. 339–390. Vincent Smith in *Early History of India*, third edition, pp. 328–334. Winternitz, *Ges. Ind. Lit.* II. i. p. 256. Watters, *Yüan Chwang*, I. pp. 210, 355–359. Taranâtha, chap. XXII. Grünwedel, *Mythologie*, p. 35.

[2] Meghavarman. See V. Smith, *l.c.* 287.

[3] Two have been preserved in Sanskrit: the Mahâyâna-sûtrâlankâra (Ed. v. Transl., S. Lévi, 1907–1911) and the Bodhisattva-bhûmi (English summary in *Muséon*, 1905–6). A brief analysis of the literature of the Yogâcâra school according to Tibetan authorities is given by Stcherbatskoi in *Muséon*, 1905, pp. 144–155.

[4] Mahâyâna-sûtrâl. XVIII. 71–73. The ominous word *maithuna* also occurs in this work, XVIII. 46.

it is surprising, and it is probable that the treatise is not his. If so, Asanga may have been the first to elaborate systematically (though not to originate) the idea that thought is the one and only reality. Nâgârjuna's nihilism was probably the older theory. It sounds late and elaborate but still it follows easily if the dialectic of Gotama is applied uncompromisingly not only to our mental processes but to the external world. Yet even in India the result was felt to be fantastic and sophistical and it is not surprising if after the lapse of a few generations a new system of idealism became fashionable which, although none too intelligible, was abstruse rather than paradoxical.

Asanga was alleged to have received revelations from Maitreya and five of his works are attributed to this Bodhisattva who enjoyed considerable honour at this period. It may be that the veneration for the Buddha of the future, the Messiah who would reign over his saints in a pure land, owed something to Persian influence which was strong in India during the decadence of the Kushans[1]. Both Mithraism and Manichæism classified their adepts in various ranks, and the Yogâcâra doctors who delight in grading the progress of the Bodhisattva may have borrowed something from them[2]. Asanga's doctrine of defilement (kleśa) and purification may also owe something to Mani, as suggested by S. Lévi.

In spite of his literary merits Asanga remains a doctor rather than a saint or poet[3]. His speculations have little to do with either Gotama or Amitâbha and he was thus not in living touch with either the old or new schools. His brother Vasubandhu had perhaps a greater position. He is reckoned as the twentieth Patriarch and Tibetan tradition connects him with the worship of Amitâbha[4].

Paramârtha's life of Vasubandhu represents him as having frequented the court of Vikramâditya (to be identified with Candragupta I), who at first favoured the Sânkhya philosophy

[1] Vincent Smith, *l.c.* p. 275.

[2] But there are of course abundant Indian precedents, Brahmanical as well as Buddhist, for describing various degrees of sanctity or knowledge.

[3] The wooden statues of Asanga and Vasubandhu preserved in the Kōfukaji at Nara are masterpieces of art but can hardly claim to be other than works of imagination. They date from about 800 A.D. See for an excellent reproduction Tajima's *Select Relics*, II. x.

[4] See Eitel and Grünwedel, but I do not know in what texts this tradition is found. It is remarkable that Paramârtha's life (*T'oung Pao*, 1904, pp. 269–296) does not say either that he was twentieth patriarch or that he worshipped Amida.

but accorded some patronage to Buddhism. During this period Vasubandhu was a Sarvâstivâdin but of liberal views[1] and while in this phase wrote the Abhidharma-kośa, a general exposition of the Abhidharma, mainly according to the views of the Vaibhâshikas but not without criticism. This celebrated work is not well known in Europe[2] but is still a text-book amongst Japanese Buddhist students. It gained the esteem of all schools and we are given to understand that it presupposed the philosophy of the Vibhâshâ and of the Jñâna-prasthâna. According to Paramârtha the original work consisted of 600 aphorisms in verse which were sent by the author to the monks of Kashmir. They approved of the composition but, as the aphorisms were concise, asked for fuller explanations. Vasubandhu then expanded his verses into a prose commentary, but meanwhile his views had undergone a change and when he disapproved of any Vaibhâshika doctrine, he criticized it. This enlarged edition by no means pleased the brethren of Kashmir and called forth polemics. He also wrote a controversial work against the Sânkhya philosophy.

Late in life Vasubandhu, moved by the entreaties of his brother Asanga, became a devout Mahayanist and wrote in his old age Mahayanist treatises and commentaries[3].

[1] On receiving a large donation he built three monasteries, one for Hinayanists, one for Mahayanists and one for nuns.

[2] The work consists of 600 verses (Kârikâ) with a lengthy prose commentary (Bhâshya) by the author. The Sanskrit original is lost but translations have been preserved in Chinese (Nanjio, Nos. 1267, 1269, 1270) and Tibetan (see Cordier, *Cat. du Fonds tibétain de la Bib. Nat.* 1914, pp. 394, 499). But the commentary on the Bhâshya called Abhidharma-kósa-vyâkhyâ, or Sphuṭârtha, by Yásomitra has been preserved in Sanskrit in Nepal and frequently cites the verses as well as the Bhâshya in the original Sanskrit. A number of European savants are at present occupied with this literature and Sir Denison Ross (to whom I am indebted for much information) contemplates the publication of an Uighur text of Book I found in Central Asia. At present (1920), so far as I know, the only portion of the Abhidharma-kósa in print is De la Vallée Poussin's edition and translation of Book III, containing the Tibetan and Sanskrit texts but not the Chinese (De la Vallée Poussin—*Vasubandhu et Yaśomitra*, London, 1914–18). This chapter deals with such topics as the structure of the universe, the manner and place of rebirth, the chain of causation, the geography of the world, the duration and characteristics of Kalpas, and the appearance of Buddhas and Cakravartins.

[3] See Nanjio, pp. 371–2, for a list of his works translated into Chinese. Hsüan Chuang's account differs from the above (which is taken from Paramârtha) in details. He also tells a curious story that Vasubandhu promised to appear to his friends after death and ultimately did so, though he forgot his promise until people began to say he had gone to hell.

CHAPTER XXIII

INDIAN BUDDHISM AS SEEN BY THE CHINESE PILGRIMS

About the time of Vasubandhu there existed four schools of Indian Buddhism called Vaibhâshika, Sautrântika, Mâdhyamika and Yoga or Yogâcâra[1]. They were specially concerned with philosophy and apparently cut across the older division into eighteen sects, which at this period seem to have differed mainly on points of discipline. Though not of great practical importance, they long continued to play a certain part in controversial works both Buddhist and Brahmanic. The first two which were the older seem to have belonged to the Hinayana and the other two even more definitely to the Mahayana. I-Ching[2] is quite clear as to this. "There are but two kinds of the so-called Mahayana" he says, "first the Mâdhyamika, second the Yoga.... These two systems are perfectly in accordance with the noble doctrine. Can we say which of the two is right? Both equally conform to truth and lead us to Nirvana" and so on. But he does not say that the other two systems are also aspects of the truth. This is the more remarkable because he himself followed the Mûla-sarvâstivâdins. Apparently Sarvâstivâdin and Vaibhâshika were different names for the same school, the latter being applied to them because they identified themselves with the commentary (Vibhâshâ) already mentioned whereas the former and older designation came to be used chiefly with reference to their disciplinary rules. Also there were two groups of Sarvâṣtivâdins, those of Gandhara and those of Kashmir. The name of Vaibhâshika was applied chiefly to the latter who, if we may find a kernel of truth in legends which are certainly exaggerated, endeavoured to make Kashmir a holy land with a monopoly of the pure doctrine. Vasubandhu and Asanga appear to have broken up this isolation for they first preached

[1] See Vasilief, *Le Bouddhisme*, Troisième supplément, pp. 262 ff. Köppen, *Rel. des Buddha*, I. 151. Takakusu in *J. Pali Text Society*, 1905, pp. 67–146.

[2] *Records*, translated by Takakusu, p. 15.

the Vaibhâshika doctrines in a liberal and eclectic form outside Kashmir and then by a natural transition and development went over to the Mahayana. But the Vaibhâshikas did not disappear and were in existence even in the fourteenth century[1]. Their chief tenet was the real existence of external objects. In matters of doctrine they regarded their own Abhidharma as the highest authority[2]. They also held that Gotama had an ordinary human body and passed first into a preliminary form of Nirvana when he attained Buddhahood and secondly into complete Nirvana at his death. He was superhuman only in the sense that he had intuitive knowledge and no need to learn. Their contempt for sutras may have been due to the fact that many of them discountenance the Vaibhâshika views and also to a knowledge that new ones were continually being composed.

I-Ching, who ends his work by asserting that all his statements are according to the Ârya-mûla-sarvâstivâda-nikâya and no other, gives an interesting summary of doctrine.

"Again I say: the most important are only one or two out of eighty thousand doctrines of the Buddha: one should conform to the worldly path but inwardly strive to secure true wisdom. Now what is the worldly path? It is obeying prohibitive laws and avoiding any crime. What is the true wisdom? *It is to obliterate the distinction between subject and object*, to follow the excellent truth and to free oneself from worldly attachments: to do away with the trammels of the chain of causality: further to obtain merit by accumulating good works and *finally to realize the excellent meaning of perfect reality*."

Such a statement enables us to understand the remark which he makes elsewhere that the same school may belong to the Hinayana and Mahayana in different places, for, whatever may be meant by wisdom which aims at obliterating the difference between subject and object, it is clearly not out of sympathy with Yogâcâra doctrines. In another place where he describes the curriculum followed by monks he says that they learn the Yogâcârya-śâstra first and then eight compositions of Asanga and Vasubandhu. Among the works prescribed for logic is the Nyâyadvâra-śâstra attributed to Nâgârjuna. The monk

[1] They are mentioned in the Sarva-darśana-saṅgraha.

[2] Kern (*Indian Buddhism*, p. 126) says they rejected the authority of the Sûtras altogether but gives no reference.

should learn not only the Abhidharma of the Sarvâstivâdins but also the Âgamas, equivalent to the Sûtra-piṭaka. So the study of the sûtras and the works of Asanga and Vasubandhu is approved by a Sarvâstivâdin.

The Sautrântikas[1], though accounted Hinayanists, mark a step in the direction of the Mahayana. The founder of the school was Kumâralabdha, mentioned above. In their estimation of scripture they reversed the views of the Vaibhâshikas, for they rejected the Abhidharma and accepted only the sûtras, arguing that the Abhidharma was practically an extract from them. As literary criticism this is correct, if it means that the more ancient sûtras are older than the oldest Abhidharma books. But the indiscriminate acceptance of sûtras led to a creed in which the supernatural played a larger part. The Sautrântikas not only ascribed superhuman powers to the Buddha, but believed in the doctrine of three bodies. In philosophy, though they were realists, they held that external objects are not perceived directly but that their existence is inferred[2].

Something has already been said of the two other schools, both of which denied the reality of the external world. The differences between them were concerned with metaphysics rather than theology and led to no popular controversies.

Up to this point the history of Indian Buddhism has proved singularly nebulous. The most important dates are a matter of argument, the chief personages half mythical. But when the records of the Chinese pilgrims commence we are in touch with something more solid. They record dates and facts, though we must regret that they only repeat what they heard and make no attempt to criticize Indian traditions or even to weave them into a connected chronicle.

Fa-Hsien, the first of these interesting men, left China in 399 and resided in India from 405 to 411, spending three years at Pataliputra and two at Tamralipti. He visited the Panjab, Hindustan and Bengal and his narrative leaves the impression that all these were in the main Buddhist countries: of the Deccan which he did not visit he heard that its inhabitants were barbarous and not Buddhists, though it contained some

[1] See Vasilief, pp. 301 ff. and various notices in Hsüan Chuang and Watters. Also de la Vallée Poussin's article in E.R.E.

[2] Hsüan Chuang informs us that when he was in Śrughna he studied the Vibhâshâ of the Sautrântikas, but the precise significance of this term is not plain.

Buddhist shrines. Of the Middle Kingdom (which according to his reckoning begins with Muttra) he says that the people are free and happy and neither kill any living creature nor drink intoxicating liquor[1]. He does not hint at persecution though he once or twice mentions that the Brahmans were jealous of the Buddhists. Neither does he indicate that any strong animosity prevailed between Maha- and Hinayanists. But the two parties were distinct and he notes which prevailed in each locality. He left China by land and found the Hinayana prevalent at Shen-shen and Wu-i (apparently localities not far from Lob-Nor) but the Mahayana at Khotan. Nearer India, in countries apparently corresponding to parts of Kashmir and Gilgit, the monks were numerous and all Hinayanist. The same was the case in Udyana, and in Gandhara the Hinayanists were still in the majority. In the Panjab both schools were prevalent but the Hinayana evidently strong. In the district of Muttra the Law was still more flourishing, monasteries and topes were numerous and ample alms were given to the monks. He states that the professors of the Abhidharma and Vinaya made offerings to those works, and the Mahayanists to the book Prajñâ-pâramitâ, as well as to Manjuśrî and Kwan-shih-yin. He found the country in which are the sacred sites of Śrâvasti, Kapilavastu and Kusinârâ sparsely inhabited and desolate, but this seems to have been due to general causes, not specially to the decay of religion. He mentions that ninety-six[2] varieties of erroneous views are found among the Buddhists, which points to the existence of numerous but not acutely hostile sects and says that there still existed, apparently in Kośala, followers of Devadatta who recognized three previous Buddhas but not Śâkyamuni. He visited the birth-places of these three Buddhas which contained topes erected in their honour.

He found Magadha prosperous and pious. Of its capital, Patna, he says "by the side of the topes of Asoka has been made a Mahayana monastery very grand and beautiful, there is also a Hinayana one, the two together containing 600 or 700 monks." It is probable that this was typical of the religious condition of Magadha and Bengal. Both schools existed but the

[1] Fa-Hsien's *Travels*, chap. XVI.

[2] This figure is probably deduced from some artificial calculation of possible heresies like the 62 wrong views enumerated in the Brahma-Jala sûtra.

Mahayana was the more flourishing. Many of the old sites, such as Râjagṛiha and Gaya, were deserted but there were new towns near them and Bodh Gaya was a place of pilgrimage with three monasteries. In the district of Tamralipti (Tamluk) on the coast of Bengal were 22 monasteries. As his principal object was to obtain copies of the Vinaya, he stayed three years in Patna seeking and copying manuscripts. In this he found some difficulty, for the various schools of the Vinaya, which he says were divided by trivial differences only, handed down their respective versions orally. He found in the Mahayanist monastery one manuscript of the Mahâsânghika rules and considered it the most complete, but also took down the Sarvâstivâdin rules.

After the death of Vasubandhu few names of even moderate magnitude stand out in the history of Indian Buddhism. The changes which occurred were great but gradual and due not to the initiative of innovators but to the assimilative power of Hinduism and to the attractions of magical and emotional rites. But this tendency, though it doubtless existed, did not become conspicuous until about 700 A.D. The accounts of the Chinese pilgrims and the literature which has been preserved suggest that in the intervening centuries the monks were chiefly occupied with scholastic and exegetical work. The most distinguished successors of Asanga were logicians, among whom Diṅnâga was pre-eminent. Sthiramati[1] and Guṇamati appear to have belonged to the same school and perhaps Bhavaviveka[2] too. The statements as to his date are inconsistent but the interesting fact is recorded that he utilized the terminology of the Sânkhya for the purposes of the Mahayana.

Throughout the middle ages the study of logic was pursued but Buddhists and Jains rather than by Brahmans[3]. Vasubandhu composed some treatises dealing exclusively with logic but it was his disciple Diṅnâga who separated it definitely from philosophy and theology. As in idealist philosophy, so in pure logic there was a parallel movement in the Buddhist and Brahmanic schools, but if we may trust the statements of

[1] He must have lived in the fourth century as one of his works (Nanjio, 1243) was translated between 397 and 439.

[2] Watters, *Yüan Chwang*, II. 221–224. Nanjio, 1237. The works of Guṇamati also are said to show a deep knowledge of the Sânkhya philosophy.

[3] For the history of logic in India, see Vidyâbhusana's interesting work *Mediæval School of Indian Logic*, 1909. But I cannot accept all his dates.

Vâcaspatimiśra (about 1100 A.D.) Diṅnâga interpreted the aphorisms of the Nyâya philosophy in a heterodox or Buddhist sense. This traces the beginnings of Indian logic to a Brahmanic source but subsequently it flourished greatly in the hands of Buddhists, especially Diṅnâga and Dharmakîrti. The former appears to have been a native of Conjevaram and a contemporary of Kâlidâsa. Both the logician and the poet were probably alive in the reign of Kumâragupta (413–455). Diṅnâga spent much time in Nâlanda, and though the Sanskrit originals of his works are lost the Tibetan translations[1] are preserved.

The Buddhist schools of logic continued for many centuries. One flourished in Kashmir and another, founded by Candragomin, in Bengal. Both lasted almost until the Mohammedan conquest of the two countries.

From about 470 to 530 A.D. northern India groaned under the tyranny of the Huns. Their King Mihiragula is represented as a determined enemy of Buddhism and a systematic destroyer of monasteries. He is said to have been a worshipper of Śiva but his fury was probably inspired less by religious animosity than by love of pillage and slaughter.

About 530 A.D. he was defeated by a coalition of Indian princes and died ten years later amid storms and portents which were believed to signify the descent of his wicked soul into hell. It must have been about this time that Bodhidharma left India for he arrived in Canton about 520. According to the Chinese he was the son of a king of a country called Hsiang-Chih in southern India[2] and the twenty-eighth patriarch and he became an important figure in the religion and art of the Far East. But no allusion to him or to any of the Patriarchs after Vasubandhu has been found in Indian literature nor in the works of Hsüan Chuang and I-Ching. The inference is that he was of no importance in India and that his reputation in China was not great before the eighth century: also that the Chinese lists of patriarchs do not represent the traditions of northern India.

[1] Diṅnâga's principal works are the Pramâṇa-samuccaya and the Nyâya-praveśa. Hsüan Chuang calls him Ch'en-na. See Watters, II. 209. See Stcherbatskoï in *Muséon*, 1904, pp. 129–171 for Diṅnâga's influence on the development of the Naiyâyika and Vaiśeshika schools.

[2] His personal name is said to have been P'u-ti-to-lo and his surname Ch'a-ti-li. The latter is probably a corruption of Kshatriya. Hsiang-Chih possibly represents a name beginning with Gandha, but I can neither find nor suggest any identification.

Religious feeling often ran high in southern India. Buddhists, Jains and Hindus engaged in violent disputes, and persecution was more frequent than in the north. It is easy to suppose that Bodhidharma being the head of some heretical sect had to fly and followed the example of many monks in going to China. But if so, no record of his school is forthcoming from his native land, though the possibility that he was more than an individual thinker and represented some movement unknown to us cannot be denied. We might suppose too that since Nâgârjuna and Âryadeva were southerners, their peculiar doctrines were coloured by Dravidian ideas. But our available documents indicate that the Buddhism of southern India was almost entirely Hinayanist, analogous to that of Ceylon and not very sympathetic to the Tamils.

The pilgrims Sung-Yün and Hui-Shêng[1] visited Udyana and Gandhara during the time of the Hun domination (518–521). They found the king of the former a pious Buddhist but the latter was governed by an Ephthalite chieftain, perhaps Mihiragula himself, who was a worshipper of demons. Of the Yetha or Ephthalites they make the general observation that "their rules of politeness are very defective." But they also say that the population of Gandhara had a great respect for Buddhism and as they took back to China 170 volumes, "all standard works belonging to the Great Vehicle," the Ephthalite persecution cannot have destroyed the faith in north-western India. But the evil days of decay were beginning. Henceforward we have no more pictures of untroubled piety and prosperity. At best Buddhism receives royal patronage in company with other religions; sectarian conflicts increase and sometimes we hear of persecution. About 600 A.D. a king of Central Bengal named Saśâṅka who worshipped Śiva attempted to extirpate Buddhism in his dominions and destroyed the Bo tree at Bodh Gaya[2]. On the other hand we hear of the pious Pûrṇavarman, king of Magadha, who made amends for these sacrileges, and of Śîlâditya, king of the country called Mo-lo-po by the Chinese, who was so careful of animal life, that he even strained the water drunk by his horses and elephants, lest they should consume minute insects.

[1] See *B.E.F.E.O.* 1903, pp. 379 ff.

[2] His evil deeds are several times mentioned by Hsüan Chuang. It required a miracle to restore the Bo tree.

We know more of Indian Buddhism in the seventh century than in the periods which precede or follow it. The epoch was marked by the reign of the great king, or rather emperor, Harsha-Vardhana (606–648 A.D.), and the works written by Bâṇa, Bhartrihari and others who frequented his court have come down to us. Also we are fortunate in possessing the copious narrative of Hsüan Chuang, the greatest of the Chinese pilgrims, who spent sixteen years (629–645) in India as well as the work known as the "Record of the Buddhist religion as practised in India and the Malay Archipelago," composed by I-Ching who travelled in those countries from 671 to 695. I-Ching also wrote the lives of sixty Chinese pilgrims who visited India during the seventh century and probably there were many others of whom we have no record.

The reign of Harsha is thus illustrated by a number of contemporary dateable works unusual in India. The king himself wrote some Buddhist hymns[1], and three dramas are ascribed to him but were probably composed by some of the literary men whom he patronized. For all that, the religious ideas which they contain must have had his approval. The Ratnâvalî and Priyadarśikâ are secular pieces and so far as they have any religious atmosphere it is Brahmanic, but the Nâgânanda is a Buddhist religious drama which opens with an invocation of the Buddha and has a Jâtaka story for its plot[2]. Bâṇa was himself a devout Brahman but his historical romance Harshacarita and his novel called Kâdambarî both describe a mixture of religions founded on observation of contemporary life. In an interesting passage[3] he recounts the king's visit to a Buddhist ascetic. The influence of the holy man causes the more intelligent animals in his neighbourhood, such as parrots, to devote themselves to Buddhist lore, but he is surrounded by devotees of the most diverse sects, Jains, Bhâgavatas, Pâncarâtras, Lokâyatikas with followers of Kapila, Kaṇâda and many

[1] See Ettinghausen, *Harshavardhana*, Appendix III.

[2] The appearance of Gaurî as a *dea ex machina* at the end hardly shows that Harsha's Buddhism had a Śaktist tinge but it does show that Buddhists of that period turned naturally to Śivaite mythology.

[3] Harshacarita, chap. VIII. The parrots were expounding Vasubandhu's Abhidharmakośa. Bâṇa frequently describes troops of holy men apparently living in harmony but including followers of most diverse sects. See Kâdambarî, 193 and 394 : Harshacar. 67.

other teachers. Mayûra, another literary protégé of Harsha's, was like Bâṇa a Brahman, and Subandhu, who flourished a little before them, ignores Buddhism in his romance called Vâsavadattâ. But Bhartrihari, the still popular gnomic poet, was a Buddhist. It is true that he oscillated between the court and the cloister no less than seven times, but this vacillation seems to have been due to the weakness of the flesh, not to any change of convictions. For our purpose the gist of this literature is that Hinduism in many forms, some of them very unorthodox, was becoming the normal religion of India but that there were still many eminent Buddhists and that Buddhism had sufficient prestige to attract Harsha and sufficient life to respond to his patronage.

About 600 A.D. India was exhausted by her struggle with the Huns. After it there remained only a multitude of small states and obscure dynasties, but there was evidently a readiness to accept any form of unifying and tranquillizing rule and for nearly half a century this was provided by Harsha. He conquered northern India from the Panjab to Bengal but failed to subdue the Deccan. Though a great part of his reign was spent in war, learning and education flourished. Hsüan Chuang, who was his honoured guest, gives a good account of his administration but also makes it plain that brigandage prevailed and that travelling was dangerous.

After 643 Harsha, who was growing elderly, devoted much attention to religion and may be said to have become a Buddhist, while allowing himself a certain eclectic freedom. Several creeds were represented among his immediate relatives. Devotion to Śiva was traditional in the family: his father had been a zealous worshipper of the Sun and his brother and sister were Buddhists of the Sammitîya sect. Harsha by no means disowned Brahmanic worship, but in his latter years his proclivity to Buddhism became more marked and he endeavoured to emulate the piety of Asoka. He founded rest houses and hospitals, as well as monasteries and thousands of stupas. He prohibited the taking of life and the use of animal food, and of the three periods into which his day was divided two were devoted to religion and one to business. He also exercised a surveillance over the whole Buddhist order and advanced meritorious members.

Hsüan Chuang has left an interesting account of the religious fêtes and spectacles organized by Harsha. At Kanauj he attended a great assembly during which a solemn procession took place every day. A golden image of Buddha was borne on an elephant and Harsha, dressed as Indra, held a canopy over it, while his ally Raja Kumara[1], dressed as Brahmâ, waved a fly-whisk. It was subsequently washed by the king's own hands and in the evening his Majesty, who like Akbar had a taste for religious discussion, listened to the arguments of his Chinese guest. But the royal instructions that no one was to speak against the Master of the Law were so peremptory that even his biographer admits there was no real discussion. These edifying pageants were interrupted by disagreeable incidents which show that Harsha's tolerance had not produced complete harmony. A temporary monastery erected for the fêtes caught fire and a fanatic attempted to stab the king. He confessed under examination that he had been instigated to the crime by Brahmans who were jealous of the favours which the Buddhists received. It was also established that the incendiaries were Brahmans and, after the ringleaders had been punished, five hundred were exiled. Harsha then proceeded to Allahabad to superintend a quinquennial distribution of alms. It was his custom to let treasure accumulate for five years and then to divide it among holy men and the poor. The proceedings lasted seventy-five days and the concourse which collected to gaze and receive must have resembled the fair still held on the same spot. Buddhists, Brahmans and Jains all partook of the royal bounty and the images of Buddha, Sûrya and Śiva were worshipped on successive days, though greater honour was shown to the Buddha. The king gave away everything that he had, even his robes and jewels, and finally, arrayed in clothes borrowed from his sister, rejoiced saying "all I have has entered into incorruptible and imperishable treasuries." After this, adds Hsüan Chuang, the king's vassals offered him jewels and robes so that the treasury was replenished. This was the sixth quinquennial distribution which Harsha had held and the last, for he died in 648. He at first favoured the Hinayana but subsequently went over to the Mahayana, being moved in part by the exhortations of Hsüan Chuang.

[1] It is curious that Bâṇa (Harshacarita, VII.) says of this prince that from childhood he resolved never to worship anyone but Śiva.

Yet the substance of Hsüan Chuang's account is that though Buddhism was prospering in the Far East it was decaying in India. Against this can be set instances of royal piety like those described, the fame enjoyed by the shrines and schools of Magadha and the conversion of the king of Tibet in 638 A.D. This event was due to Chinese as well as Indian influence, but would hardly have occurred unless in north-eastern India Buddhism had been esteemed the religion of civilization. Still Hsüan Chuang's long catalogue of deserted monasteries[1] has an unmistakable significance. The decay was most pronounced in the north-west and south. In Gandhara there were only a few Buddhists: more than a thousand monasteries stood untenanted and the Buddha's sacred bowl had vanished. In Takshaśîla the monasteries were numerous but desolate: in Kashmir the people followed a mixed faith. Only in Udyâna was Buddhism held in high esteem. In Sind the monks were numerous but indolent.

No doubt this desolation was largely due to the depredations of Mihiragula. In the Deccan and the extreme south there was also a special cause, namely the prevalence of Jainism, which somewhat later became the state religion in several kingdoms. In Kalinga, Andhra and the kingdom of the Colas the pilgrim reports that Jains were very numerous but counts Buddhist monasteries only by tens and twenties. In Dravida there were also 10,000 monks of the Sthavira school but in Malakuta among many ruined monasteries only a few were still inhabited and here again Jains were numerous.

For all Central India and Bengal the pilgrim's statistics tell the same tale, namely that though Buddhism was represented both by monasteries and monks, the Deva-temples and unbelievers were also numerous. The most favourable accounts are those given of Kanauj, Ayodhya and Magadha where the sacred sites naturally caused the devout to congregate.

The statistics which he gives as to sects are interesting[2]. The total number of monks amounted to about 183,000. Of these only 32,000 belonged definitely to the Mahayana: more

[1] The Râshṭrapâlaparipṛicchâ (Ed. Finot, pp. ix–xi, 28–33) inveighs against the moral degeneration of the Buddhist clergy. This work was translated into Chinese between 589 and 618, so that demoralisation must have begun in the sixth century.

[2] See Rhys Davids in *J.R.A.S.* 1891, pp. 418 ff.

than 96,000 to the Hinayana, and 54,500 studied both systems or at any rate resided in monasteries which tolerated either course of study. Some writers speak as if after our era Mahayanism was predominant in India and the Hinayana banished to its extreme confines such as Ceylon and Kashmir. Yet about A.D. 640 this zealous Mahayanist[1] states that half the monks of India were definitely Hinayanist while less than a fifth had equally definite Mahayanist convictions. The Mahayana laid less stress on monasticism than the Hinayana and therefore its strength may have lain among the laity, but even so the admitted strength of the Hinayana is remarkable. Three Hinayanist schools are frequently mentioned, the Sthaviras, Sarvâstivâdins and Sammitîyas. The first are the well-known Sinhalese sect and were found chiefly in the south (Conjeevaram) and in East Bengal, besides the monks of the Sinhalese monastery at Gaya. The Sarvâstivâdins were found, as their history would lead us to expect, chiefly in the north and beyond the frontiers of India proper. But both were outnumbered by the Sammitîyas, who amounted to nearly 44,000 monks. The chief doctrine[2] of this sect is said to have been that individuals (puggalo) exist as such in the truest sense. This doctrine was supported by reference to the sutra known as the Burden and the Burden bearer[3]. It does not assert that there is a permanent and unchangeable soul (attâ) but it emphasizes the reality and importance of that personality which all accept as true for practical purposes. It is probable that in practice this belief differed little from the ordinary Brahmanic doctrine of metempsychosis and this may be one reason for the prevalence of the sect.

I-Ching, though he does not furnish statistics, gives a clear conspectus of Buddhist sects as they existed in his time. He starts from the ancient eighteen sects but divides them into four groups or Nikâyas. (*a*) The Ârya-Mahâsanghika-nikâya. This comprised seven subdivisions but was apparently the least influential school as it was not predominant anywhere, though

[1] Hsüan Chuang was not disposed to underrate the numbers of the Mahayana for he says that the monks of Ceylon were Mahayanists.

[2] See the beginning of the Kathâvatthu. The doctrine is formulated in the words Puggalo upalabbhati saccikaṭṭhaparamaṭṭhenâti, and there follows a discussion between a member of the orthodox school and a Puggalavâdin, that is one who believes in the existence of a person, soul or entity which transmigrates from this world to another.

[3] Sam. Nik. XXII. 221.

it coexisted with other schools in most parts. The Lokottaravâdins mentioned by Hsüan Chuang as existing at Bamiyan belonged to it. They held that the Buddha was not subject to the laws of nature. (*b*) Ârya-Sthavira-nikâya. This is the school to which our Pali Canon belongs. It was predominant in southern India and Ceylon and was also found in eastern Bengal. (*c*) The Ârya-Mûla-sarvâstivâda-nikâya with four subdivisions. Almost all belonged to this school in northern India and it was flourishing in Magadha. (*d*) The Ârya-Sammitîya-nikâya with four subdivisions flourished in Lâṭa and Sindhu. Thus the last three schools were preponderant in southern, northern and western India respectively. All were followed in Magadha, no doubt because the holy places and the University of Nâlandâ attracted all shades of opinion, and Bengal seems to have been similarly catholic. This is substantially the same as Hsüan Chuang's statement except that I-Ching takes a more favourable view of the position of the Sarvâstivâda, either because it was his own school or because its position had really improved.

It would seem that in the estimation of both pilgrims the Maha- and Hinayana are not schools but modes in which any school can be studied. The Nikâya[1] or school appears to have been chiefly, though not exclusively, concerned with the rule of discipline which naturally had more importance for Buddhist monks than it has for European scholars. The observances of each Nikâya were laid down in its own recension of the scriptures which was sometimes oral and sometimes in writing. Probably all the eighteen schools had separate Vinayas, and to some extent they had different editions of the other Pitakas, for the Sarvâstivâdins had an Abhidharma of their own. But there was no objection to combining the study of Sarvâstivâdin literature with the reading of treatises by Asanga and Vasu-

[1] This use of Nikâya must not be confused with its other use to denote a division of the Sûtra-Pitaka. It means a group or collection and hence can be used to denote either a body of men or a collection of treatises. These Nikâyas are also not the same as the four schools (Vaibhâshikas, etc.), mentioned above, which were speculative. Similarly in Europe a Presbyterian may be a Calvinist, but Presbyterianism has reference to Church government and Calvinism to doctrine.

There were in India at this time (1) two vehicles, Maha- and Hinayana, (2) four speculative schools, Vaibhâshikas, etc., (3) four disciplinary schools, Mûla-sarvâstivâdins, etc. These three classes are obviously not mutually exclusive. Thus I-Ching approved of (*a*) the Mahayana, (*b*) the Mâdhyamika and Yogâcâra, which he did not consider inconsistent and (*c*) the Mûla-sarvâstivâda.

bandhu[1] or sutras such as the Lotus, which I-Ching's master read once a day for sixty years. I-Ching himself seems to regard the two Vehicles as alternative forms of religion, both excellent in their way, much as a Catholic theologian might impartially explain the respective advantages of the active and contemplative lives. "With resolutions rightly formed" he says "we should look forward to meeting the coming Buddha Maitreya. If we wish to gain the lesser fruition (of the Hinayana) we may pursue it through the eight grades of sanctification. But if we learn to follow the course of the greater fruition (of the Mahayana) we must try to accomplish our work through long ages[2]."

I-Ching observes that both Vehicles agree in prescribing the same discipline, in prohibiting the same offences and enjoining the practice of the noble truths. His views, which are substantially those of Hsüan Chuang[3], must be those current in the seventh century when the Hinayana was allowing the Mahayana to overgrow it without resistance, but the relations of the two creeds are sometimes stated differently. For instance the Angulimâliya sutra[4], known only in a Tibetan translation, states that whereas for the Hinayana such formulæ as the four truths and the eightfold path are of cardinal importance, the Mahayana does not recognize them, and it is undoubtedly true that the Vaipulya sutras frequently ignore the familiar doctrines of early Buddhism and hint that they belong to a rudimentary stage of instruction.

I-Ching makes no mention of persecution but he deplores the decay of the faith. "The teaching of the Buddha is becoming less prevalent in the world from day to day" he says. "When I compare what I have witnessed in my younger days and what I see to-day in my old age, the state is altogether different and we are bearing witness to this and it is hoped we shall be more

[1] I-Ching, transl. Takakusu, p. 186.

[2] Three Asankhya Kalpas. I-Ching, Takakusu's transl. pp. 196–7. He seems to regard the Mahayana as the better way. He quotes Nâgârjuna's allusions to Avalokita and Amitâyus with apparent approval; he tells us how one of his teachers worshipped Amitâyus and strove to prepare himself for Sukhâvatî and how the Lotus was the favourite scripture of another. He further tells us that the Mâdhyamika and the Yoga systems are both perfectly correct.

[3] Hsüan Chuang speaks of Mahayanists belonging to the Sthavira school.

[4] Quoted by Rockhill, *Life of the Buddha*, pp. 196 ff.

attentive in future." Though he speaks regretfully of lax or incorrect discipline, he does not complain of the corruption of the faith by Tantrism and magical practices. He does however deprecate in an exceedingly curious passage the prevalence of religious suicide[1].

Except for progressive decay, the condition of Indian Buddhism as described by the two pilgrims is much the same. Meals were supplied to monks in the monasteries and it was no longer usual to beg for food in the streets, since the practice is mentioned by I-Ching as exceptional. On Upavasatha days it was the custom for the pious laity to entertain the monks and the meal was sometimes preceded by a religious service performed before an image and accompanied by music. I-Ching describes the musical services with devout enthusiasm. "The priests perform the ordinary service late in the afternoon or in the evening twilight. They come out of the monastery and walk three times round a stupa, offering incense and flowers. Then they all kneel down and one of them who sings well begins to chant hymns describing the virtues of the great Teacher and continues to sing ten or twenty ślokas. They then return to the place in the monastery where they usually assemble and, when all have sat down, a reciter mounting the lion-seat (which is near the head priest) reads a short sutra. Among the scriptures for such an occasion the 'Service in three parts' is often used. This is a selection of Aśvaghosha. The first part contains ten ślokas of a hymn. The second part is a selection from some scripture consisting of the Buddha's words. Then there is an additional hymn as the third part of the service, of more than ten ślokas, being prayers that express the wish to bring one's merits to maturity. After the singing the assembled Bhikshus exclaim Subhâshita or Sâdhu, that is well-said or bravo. The reader descends and the Bhikshus in order salute the lion-seat, the seats of Bodhisattvas and Arhats, and the superior of the monastery[2]."

[1] Chaps. XXXVIII and XXXIX. He seems to say that it is right for the laity to make an offering of their bodies by burning but not for Bhikshus. The practice is recognized and commended in the Lotus, chap. XXII, which however is a later addition to the original work.

[2] I-Ching, transl. Takakusu, pp. 153–4 somewhat abridged. I-Ching (pp. 156–7) speaks of Mâtricheta as the principal hymn writer and does not identify him with Aśvaghosha.

I-Ching also tells us of the ceremonial bathing of images and prefaces his description by the remark that "the meaning of the Truths is so profound that it is a matter beyond the comprehension of vulgar minds while the ablution of the holy images is practicable for all. Though the Great Teacher has entered Nirvana yet his image exists and we should worship it with zeal as though in his presence. Those who constantly offer incense and flowers to it are enabled to purify their thoughts and those who perpetually bathe his image are enabled to overcome the sins that involve them in darkness[1]." He appears to contemplate chiefly the veneration of images of Śâkyamuni but figures of Bodhisattvas were also conspicuous features in temples, as we know not only from archæology but from the biography of Hsüan Chuang, where it is said that worshippers used to throw flowers and silk scarves at the image of Avalokita and draw auguries from the way they fell.

Monasteries were liberally decorated with statues, carvings and pictures[2]. They often comprised several courts and temples. Hsüan Chuang says that a monastery in Magadha which he calls Ti-lo-shi-ka had "four courts with three storeyed halls, lofty terraces and a succession of open passages....At the head of the road through the middle gate were three temples with disks on the roof and hung with small bells; the bases were surrounded by balustrades, and doors, windows, beams, walls, and stairs were ornamented with gilt work in relief." In the three temples were large images representing the Buddha, Târâ and Avalokita.

The great centres of Buddhist learning and monastic life, mentioned by both pilgrims, were Valabhî or Balabhi in Gujarat and Nalanda. The former was a district rather than a single locality and contained 100 monasteries with 6000 monks of the Sammitîya school. Nalanda was in Magadha not far from Gaya. The date of its foundation is unknown but a great temple (though apparently not the first) was built about 485 A.D.[3]

[1] I believe the golden image in the Arakan Pagoda at Mandalay is still washed with a ceremonial resembling that described by I-Ching.

[2] I-Ching says that monasteries commonly had a statue of Mahâkâla as a guardian deity.

[3] By the Gupta king, Narasinha Gupta Bâlâditya. Much information about Nâlandâ will be found in Satis Chandra Vidyabhusana's *Mediæval School of Indian Logic*, pp. 145–147. Hsüan Chuang (*Life*, transl. Beal, p. 111) says that it was

Fa-Hsien mentions a village called Nala but without indicating that it was a seat of learning. Hence it is probable that the University was not then in existence or at least not celebrated. Hsüan Chuang describes it as containing six monasteries built by various kings and surrounded by an enclosing wall in which there was only one gate. I-Ching writing later says that the establishment owned 200 villages and contained eight halls with more than 3000 monks. In the neighbourhood of the monastery were a hundred sacred spots, several marked by temples and topes. It was a resort for Buddhists from all countries and an educational as well as a religious centre. I-Ching says that students spent two or three years there in learning and disputing after which they went to the king's court in search of a government appointment. Successful merit was rewarded not only by rank but by grants of land. Both pilgrims mention the names of several celebrities connected with Nalanda. But the worthies of the seventh century did not attain to more than scholastic eminence. The most important literary figure of the age is Ṡântideva of whose life nothing is known. His writings however prove that the Buddhism of this period was not a corrupt superstition, but could inspire and nourish some of the most beautiful thoughts which the creed has produced.

built 700 years before his time, that is, in the first century B.C. He dwells on the beauty of the buildings, ponds and flowers.

CHAPTER XXIV

DECADENCE OF BUDDHISM IN INDIA

THE theme of this chapter is sad for it is the decadence, degradation and ultimate disappearance of Buddhism in India. The other great religions offer no precise parallel to this phenomenon but they also do not offer a parallel to the circumstances of Buddhism at the time when it flourished in its native land. Mohammedanism has been able to maintain itself in comparative isolation: up to the present day Moslims and Christians share the same cities rather than the same thoughts, especially when (as often) they belong to different races. European Christianity after a few centuries of existence had to contend with no rival of approximately equal strength, for the struggle with Mohammedanism was chiefly military and hardly concerned the merits of the faiths. But Buddhism never had a similarly paramount and unchallenged position. It never attempted to extirpate its rivals. It coexisted with a mass of popular superstition which it only gently reprobated and with a powerful hereditary priesthood, both intellectual and pliant, tenacious of their own ideas and yet ready to countenance almost any other ideas as the price of ruling. Neither Islam nor Christianity had such an adversary, and both of them and even Judaism resemble Buddhism in having won greater success outside their native lands than in them. Jerusalem is not an altogether satisfactory spectacle to either Christians or Jews[1].

Still all this does not completely explain the disappearance of Buddhism from India. Before attempting to assign reasons, we shall do well to review some facts and dates relating to the period of decadence. If we take all India into consideration the period is long, but in many, indeed in most, districts the process of decay was rapid.

In the preceding chapter I have mentioned the accounts of Indian Buddhism which we owe to the Chinese travellers, Hsüan Chuang and I-Ching. The latter frankly deplores the decay of

[1] Written before the war.

the faith which he had witnessed in his own life (*i.e.* about 650–700 A.D.) but his travels in India were of relatively small extent and he gives less local information than previous pilgrims. Hsüan Chuang describing India in 629–645 A.D. is unwilling to admit the decay but his truthful narrative lets it be seen. It is only of Bengal and the present United Provinces that he can be said to give a favourable account, and the prosperity of Buddhism there was largely due to the personal influence of Harsha[1]. In central and southern India, he tells us of little but deserted monasteries. It is clear that Buddhism was dying out but it is not so clear that it had ever been the real religion of this region. In many parts it did not conquer the population but so to speak built fortresses and left garrisons. It is probable that the Buddhism of Andhra, Kalinga and the south was represented by little more than such outposts. They included Amarâvati, where portions of the ruins seem assignable to about 150 A.D., and Ajantâ, where some of the cave paintings are thought to be as late as the sixth century. But of neither site can we give any continuous history. In southern India the introduction of Buddhism took place under the auspices of Asoka himself, though his inscriptions have as yet been found only in northern Mysore and not in the Tamil country. The Tamil poems Manimêgalei and Silappadigaram, especially the former, represent it as prevalent and still preserving much of its ancient simplicity. Even in later times when it had almost completely disappeared from southern India, occasional Buddhist temples were founded. Rajaraja endowed one at Negapatam about 1000 A.D. In 1055 a monastery was erected at Belgami in Mysore and a Buddhist town named Kalavati is mentioned as existing in that state in 1533[2]. But in spite of such survivals, even in the sixth century Buddhism could not compete in southern India with either Jainism or Hinduism and there are no traces of its existence in the Deccan after 1150.

For the Konkan, Maharashtra and Gujarat, Hsüan Chuang's statistics are fairly satisfactory. But in all this region the Sammitîya sect which apparently was nearer to Hinduism than the others was the most important. In Ujjain Buddhism was

[1] Even at Kanauj, the scene of Harsha's pious festivities, there were 100 Buddhist monasteries but 200 Deva temples.

[2] Rice, *Mysore and Coorg from the Inscriptions*, p. 203.

almost extinct but in many of the western states it lingered on, perhaps only in isolated monasteries, until the twelfth century. Inscriptions found at Kanheri (843 and 851 A.D.), Dambal (1095 A.D.) and in Miraj (1110 A.D.) testify that grants were made to monasteries at these late dates[1]. But further north the faith had to endure the violence of strangers. Sind was conquered by the Arabs in 712; Gujarat and the surrounding country were invaded by northern tribes and such invasions were always inimical to the prosperity of monasteries.

This is even more true of the Panjab, the frontier provinces and Kashmir. The older invaders such as the Yüeh-chih had been favourably disposed to Buddhism, but those who came later, such as the Huns, were predaceous barbarians with little religion of any sort. In Hsüan Chuang's time it was only in Udyana that Buddhism could be said to be the religion of the people and the torrent of Mohammedan invasion which swept continuously through these countries during the middle ages overwhelmed all earlier religions, and even Hinduism had to yield. In Kashmir Buddhism soon became corrupt and according to the Râjataranginî[2] the monks began to marry as early as the sixth century. King Lâlitâditya (733–769) is credited with having built monasteries as well as temples to the Sun, but his successors were Śivaites.

Bengal, especially western Bengal and Bihar, was the stronghold of decadent Buddhism, though even here hostile influences were not absent. But about 730 A.D. a pious Buddhist named Gopâla founded the Pâla dynasty and extended his power over Magadha. The Pâlas ruled for about 450 years and supplied a long and devout line of defenders of the faith. But to the east of their dominions lay the principality of Kanauj, a state of varying size and fortunes and from the eighth century onwards a stronghold of Brahmanic learning.

The revolution in Hinduism which definitely defeated, though it did not annihilate, Buddhism is generally connected with the names of Kumârila Bhaṭṭa (*c.* 750) and Śaṅkara (*c.* 800). We know the doctrines of these teachers, for many of their works have come down to us, but when we enquire what was their political importance, or the scope and extent of the

[1] See the note by Bühler in *Journ. Pali Text Soc.* 1896, p. 108.
[2] Râjataranginî, III. 12.

movement which they championed we are conscious (as so often) of the extraordinary vagueness of Indian records even when the subject might appeal to religious and philosophic minds[1]. Kumârila is said to have been a Brahman of Bihar who abjured Buddhism for Hinduism and raged with the ardour of a proselyte against his ancient faith. Tradition[2] represents him as instigating King Sudhanvan to exterminate the Buddhists. But nothing is known of this king and he cannot have had the extensive empire with which he is credited.

Śaṅkara was a Brahman of the south who in a short life found time to write numerous works, to wander over India, to found a monastic order and build four monasteries. In doctrine and discipline he was more pliant than Kumârila and he assimilated many strong points of Buddhism. Both these teachers are depicted as the successful heroes of public disputations in which the interest at stake was considerable. The vanquished had to become a disciple of the vanquisher or to forfeit his life and, if he was the head of an institution, to surrender its property. These accounts, though exaggerated, are probably a florid version of what occurred and we may surmise that the popular faith of the day was generally victorious. What violence the rising tide of Hinduism may have wrought, it is hard to say. There is no evidence of any general persecution of Buddhism in the sense in which one Christian sect persecuted another in Europe. But at a rather later date we hear that Jains were persecuted and tortured by Śaiva princes both in southern India and Gujarat, and if there were any detailed account, epigraphic or literary, of such persecutions in the eighth and ninth centuries, there would be no reason for doubting it. But no details are forthcoming. Without resorting to massacre, an anti-Buddhist king had in his power many effective methods of hostility. He might confiscate or transfer monastic property, or forbid his subjects to support monks. Considering the state of Buddhism as represented by Hsüan Chuang and I-Ching it is probable that such measures would suffice to ensure the triumph of the Brahmans in most parts of India.

[1] See for the supposed persecution of Buddhism in India, *J.P.T.S.* 1896, pp. 87–92 and 107–111 and *J.R.A.S.* 1898, pp. 208–9.

[2] As contained in the Śaṅkara-dig-vijaya ascribed to Mâdhava and the Śaṅkara-vijaya ascribed to Ânandagiri.

After the epoch of Śaṅkara, the history of Indian Buddhism is confined to the Pâla kingdom. Elsewhere we hear only of isolated grants to monasteries and similar acts of piety, often striking but hardly worthy of mention in comparison with the enormous number of Brahmanic inscriptions. But in the Pâla kingdom[1] Buddhism, though corrupt, was flourishing so far as the number of its adherents and royal favour were concerned. Gopâla founded the monastery of Odontapuri or Udandapura, which according to some authorities was in the town of Bihar. Dharmapâla the second king of the dynasty (*c.* 800 A.D.) built on the north bank of the Ganges the even more celebrated University of Vikramaśila[2], where many commentaries were composed. It was a centre not only of tantric learning but of logic and grammar, and is interesting as showing the connection between Bengal and Tibet. Tibetans studied there and Sanskrit books were translated into Tibetan within its cloisters. Dharmapâla is said to have reigned sixty-four years and to have held his court at Patna, which had fallen into decay but now began to revive. According to Târanâtha his successor Devapâla built Somapuri, conquered Orissa and waged war with the unbelievers who had become numerous, no doubt as a result of the preaching of Śaṅkara. But as a rule the Pâlas, though they favoured Buddhism, did not actively discourage Hinduism. They even gave grants to Hindu temples and their prime ministers were generally Brahmans who[3] used to erect non-Buddhist images in Buddhist shrines. The dynasty continued through the eleventh century and in this period some information as to the condition of Indian Buddhism is afforded by the relations between Bengal and Tibet. After the persecution of the tenth century Tibetan Buddhism was revived by the preaching of monks from Bengal. Mahîpâla then occupied the throne (*c.* 978–1030) and during his reign various learned men accepted invita-

[1] Târanâtha in his twenty-eighth and following chapters gives an account, unfortunately very confused, of the condition of Buddhism under the Pâla dynasty. See also B. K. Sarkar, *Folklore Element in Hindu Culture*, chap. XII, in which there are many interesting statements but not sufficient references.

[2] See Vidyabhusana's *Mediæval School of Indian Logic*, p. 150, for an account of this monastery which was perhaps at the modern Pârthaghâta. I have found no account of what happened to Nalanda in this period but it seems to have disappeared as a seat of learning.

[3] See Târanâtha, chap. XXVIII.

tions to Tibet. More celebrated is the mission of Atîsa, a monk of the Vikramaśila monastery, which took place about 1038. That these two missions should have been invited and despatched shows that in the eleventh century Bengal was a centre of Buddhist learning. Probably the numerous Sanskrit works preserved in Tibetan translations then existed in its monasteries. But about the same time the power of the Pâla dynasty, and with it the influence of Buddhism, were curtailed by the establishment of the rival Sena dynasty in the eastern provinces. Still, under Râmapâla, who reigned about 1100, the great teacher Abhayakara was an ornament of the Mahayana. Târanâtha[1] says that he corrected the text of the scriptures and that in his time there were many Pandits and resident Bhikshus in the monasteries of Vikramasîla, Bodh-Gaya and Odontapuri.

There is thus every reason to suppose that in the twelfth century Buddhism still flourished in Bihar, that its clergy numbered several thousands and its learning was held in esteem. The blow which destroyed its power was struck by a Mohammedan invasion in 1193. In that year Ikhtiyar-ud-Din Muhammad[2], a general of Kutb-ud-Din, invaded Bihar with a band of only two hundred men and with amazing audacity seized the capital, which, consisting chiefly of palaces and monasteries, collapsed without a blow. The monks were massacred to a man, and when the victors, who appear not to have understood what manner of place they had captured, asked the meaning of the libraries which they saw, no one was found capable of reading the books[3]. It was in 1193 also that Benares was conquered by the Mohammedans. I have found no record of the sack of the monastery at Sarnath but the ruins are said to show traces of fire and other indications that it was overwhelmed by some sudden disaster.

The Mohammedans had no special animus against Buddhism. They were iconoclasts who saw merit in the destruction of images and the slaughter of idolaters. But whereas Hinduism was spread over the country, Buddhism was concentrated in

[1] Chap. XXXVI. It is interesting to notice that even at this late period he speaks of Hinayanists in Bengal.

[2] Often called Muhammad Bakhtyar but Bakhtyar seems to have been really his father's name.

[3] Raverty, *Tabat-i-Nasiri*, p. 552. "It was discovered that the whole of that fortress and city was a college and in the Hindi tongue they call a college Bihar."

the great monasteries and when these were destroyed there remained nothing outside them capable of withstanding either the violence of the Moslims or the assimilative influence of the Brahmans. Hence Buddhism suffered far more from these invasions than Hinduism but still vestiges of it lingered long[1] and exist even now in Orissa. Târanâtha says that the immediate result of the Moslim conquest was the dispersal of the surviving teachers and this may explain the sporadic occurrence of late Buddhist inscriptions in other parts of India. He also tells us that a king named Cangalarâja restored the ruined Buddhist temples of Bengal about 1450. Elsewhere[2] he gives a not discouraging picture of Buddhism in the Deccan, Gujarat and Rajputana after the Moslim conquest of Magadha but adds that the study of magic became more and more prevalent. In the life of Caitanya it is stated that when travelling in southern India (about 1510 A.D.) he argued with Buddhists and confuted them, apparently somewhere in Arcot[3]. Manuscripts preserved in Nepal indicate that as late as the fifteenth or sixteenth century Bengali copyists wrote out Buddhist works, and there is evidence that Bodh-Gaya continued to be a place of pilgrimage. In 1585 it was visited by a Nepalese named Abhaya Râjâ who on his return erected in Patan a monastery imitated from what he had seen in Bengal, and in 1777 the Tashi Lama sent an embassy. But such instances prove little as to the religion of the surrounding Hindu population, for at the present day numerous Buddhist pilgrims, especially Burmese, frequent the shrine. The control of the temple passed into the hands of the Brahmans and for the ordinary Bengali Buddha became a member of India's numerous pantheon. Pandit Haraprasad Sastri mentions a singular poem called Buddhacaritra, completed in 1711 and celebrating an incarnation of Buddha which apparently commenced in 1699 and was to end in the reappearance of the golden age. But the being called Buddha is a form of Vishṇu and the work is as strange a jumble of religion as it is

[1] Many of them have been collected by Pandit Haraprasad Sastri in *Jour. As. Soc.* Bengal, 1895, pp. 55 ff. and in his *Discovery of living Buddhism in Bengal*, Calcutta, 1897.

[2] Chap. XL *ad fin.* Is the Râmacandra whom he mentions the last Yadava King (about 1314)? Târanâtha speaks of his son.

[3] Caitanya-carit-amrita, chap. VII, transl. by Jadunath Sarkar, p. 85. This biography was written in 1582 by Krishṇadas. Caitanya died in 1533.

of languages, being written in "a curious medley of bad Sanskrit, bad Hindi and bad Bihari."

It is chiefly in Orissa that traces of Buddhism can still be found within the limits of India proper. The Saraks of Baramba, Tigaria and the adjoining parts of Cuttack describe themselves as Buddhists[1]. Their name is the modern equivalent of Śrâvaka and they apparently represent an ancient Buddhist community which has become a sectarian caste. They have little knowledge of their religion but meet once a year in the cave temples of Khandagiri, to worship a deity called Buddhadeva or Caturbhuja. All their ceremonies commence with the formula *Ahimsâ parama dharma* and they respect the temple of Puri, which is suspected of having a Buddhist origin.

Nagendranâth Vasu has published some interesting details as to the survival of Buddhist ideas in Orissa[2]. He traces the origin of this hardy though degraded form of Mahayanism to Râmâi Pandit[3], a tantric Acârya of Magadha who wrote a work called Śûnya Purâṇa which became popular. Orissa was one of the regions which offered the longest resistance to Islam, for it did not succumb until 1568. A period of Śivaism in the tenth and eleventh centuries is indicated by the temples of Bhubanesvar and other monuments. But in the twelfth and thirteenth centuries the reigning dynasty were worshippers of Vishnu and built the great temples at Puri and Konârak, dedicated to Jagannâtha and Sûrya-nârâyaṇa respectively. We do not however hear that they persecuted Buddhism and there are reasons for thinking that Jagannâtha is a form of the Buddha[4] and that the temple at Puri was originally a Buddhist site. It

[1] *Census of India*, 1901: vol. VI. Bengal, pp. 427–430.

[2] *The Archæological Survey of Mayurabhanj* (no date? 1911), vol. I. pp. cv–cclxiii. The part containing an account of Buddhism in Orissa is also printed separately with the title *Modern Buddhism*, 1911.

[3] For Râmâi Pandit see Dinesh Chandra Sen, *Hist. Bengali Language and Lit.* pp. 30–37, and also B. K. Sarkar, *Folklore Element in Hindu Culture*, p. 192, and elsewhere. He appears to have been born at the end of the tenth century and though the Śûnya Purâṇa has been re-edited and interpolated parts of it are said to be in very old Bengali.

[4] Nagendranâth Vasu quotes a couplet from the Mahâbhârata of the poet Saraladasa: "I pay my humble respects to the incarnation of Buddha who in the form of Buddha dwells in the Nîlâcala, *i.e.* Puri." The Imperial Gazetteer of India (s.v. Puri Town) states that in modern representations of Vishṇu's ten avatâras, the ninth, or Buddhâvatâra, is sometimes represented by Jagannâtha.

is said that it contains a gigantic statue of the Buddha before which a wall has been built and also that the image of Jagannâtha, which is little more than a log of wood, is really a case enclosing a Buddhist relic. King Pratâparudra († 1529) persecuted Buddhism, which implies that at this late date its adherents were sufficiently numerous to attract attention. Either at the beginning of his reign or before it there flourished a group of six poets of whom the principal were Acyutânanda Dâsa and Caitanya Dâsa[1]. Their works are nominally devoted to the celebration of Kṛishṇa's praises and form the chief vernacular scripture of the Vaishṇavas in Orissa but in them Kṛishṇa, or the highest form of the deity by whatever name he is called, is constantly identified with Śûnya or the Void, that favourite term of Mahayanist philosophy. Passages from them are also quoted stating that in the Kali age the followers of the Buddha must disguise themselves; that there are 3000 crypto-buddhists hidden in various parts of Orissa, that Hari has been incarnate in many Buddhas and that the Buddha will appear again on earth. The phrase "I take refuge in the Buddha, in Mâtâ Âdiśakti (= Dharma) and in the Sangha" is also quoted from these works and Caitanya Dâsa describes five Vishnus, who are apparently identical with the five Dhyâni Buddhas[2].

Târanâtha states that the last king of Orissa, Mukunda Deva, who was overthrown by the Mohammedans in 1568, was a Buddhist and founded some temples and monasteries. In the seventeenth century, there flourished a Buddhist poet named Mahâdevadâsa[3], and the Tibetan pilgrim Buddhagupta visited among other sites the old capital of Mayurabhanja and saw a stupa there. It is claimed that the tribe known as Bâthuris or Bâuris have always been crypto-buddhists and have preserved their ancient customs. They are however no credit to their religion, for one of their principal ceremonies is hook-swinging[4].

The doctrine of the Bâthuris is called Mahimâ Dharma and experienced an interesting revival in 1875[5]. A blind man named Bhîma Bhoi had a vision of the Buddha who restored his sight

[1] I give the dates or the authority of Narandra Nâth while thinking that they may be somewhat too early. The two authors named wrote the Śûnya Samhitâ and Nirguṇa Mâhâtmya respectively.

[2] *l.c.* clxxvi ff., ccxix–ccxxiii, ccxxxi.

[3] Author of a poem called Dharmagîtâ.

[4] *l.c.* cxvi ff. and ccxxxii.

[5] *l.c.* ccxxxiv ff.

and bade him preach the law. He attracted some thousands of adherents and led a band to Puri proclaiming that his mission was to bring to light the statue of Buddha concealed in the temple. The Raja resisted the attempt and the followers of Bhîma Bhoi were worsted in a sanguinary encounter. Since that time they have retired to the more remote districts of Orissa and are said to hold that the Buddha will appear again in a new incarnation. They are also called Kumbhipatias and according to the last census of India (1911) are hostile to Brahmans and probably number about 25,000.

Traces of Buddhism also survive in the worship of a deity called Dharma-Râjâ or Dharma-Thakur which still prevails in western and southern Bengal[1]. Priests of this worship are usually not Brahmans but of low caste, and Haraprasad thinks that the laity who follow it may number "several millions." Though Dharma has come to be associated with the goddess of small-pox and is believed even by his adorers to be a form of Vishnu or of Śiva, yet Dhyâna, or meditation, forms a part of his worship and the prayers and literature of the sect retain some traces of his origin. Thus he is said to be highly honoured in Ceylon and receives the epithet Śûnyamûrti.

A corrupt form of Buddhism still exists in Nepal[2]. This country when first heard of was in the hands of the Nevars who have preserved some traditions of a migration from the north and are akin to the Tibetans in race and language, though like many non-Aryan tribes they have endeavoured to invent for themselves a Hindu pedigree. Buddhism was introduced under Asoka. As Indian influence was strong and communication with Tirhut and Bengal easy, it is probable that Buddhism in Nepal reflected the phases which it underwent in Bengal. A Nepalese inscription of the seventh century gives a list of shrines of which seven are Śivaite, six Buddhist and four Vishnuite[3]. After that date it was more successful in main-

[1] See Haraprasad Sastri, *l.c.* He gives a curious account of one of his temples in Calcutta. See also B. K. Sarkar, *Folklore Element in Hindu Culture* for the decadence of Buddhism in Bengal and its survival in degenerate forms.

[2] See B. H. Hodgson, *Essays on the languages, literature and religion of Nepal and Tibet*, 1874. For the religion of Nepal see also Wright, *History of Nepal*, 1877: C. Bendall, *Journal of Literary and Archæological Research in Nepal*, 1886; Rajendralal Mitra, *Sanskrit Buddhist literature of Nepal*; and especially S. Lévi, *Le Népal*, 3 vols. 1905–8.

[3] S. Lévi in *J.A.* II. 1904, p. 225. He gives the date as 627.

taining itself, for it did not suffer from Mohammedan attacks and was less exposed to the assimilative influence of Brahmanism. That influence however, though operating in a foreign country and on people not bred among Brahmanic traditions, was nevertheless strong. In 1324 the king of Tirhut, being expelled thence by Mohammedans, seized the throne of Nepal and brought with him many learned Brahmans. His dynasty was not permanent but later in the fourteenth century a subsequent ruler, Jayasthiti, organized society and religion in consultation with the Brahman immigrants. The followers of the two religions were arranged in parallel divisions, a group of Buddhists classified according to occupation corresponding to each Hindu caste, and appropriate rules and ceremonies were prescribed for the different sections. The code then established is still in force in essentials and Nepal, being intellectually the pupil of India, has continued to receive such new ideas as appeared in the plains of Bengal. When these ascended to the mountain valleys they were adopted, with free modification of old and new material alike, by both Buddhists and Hindus, but as both sects were geographically isolated, each tended to resemble the other more than either resembled normal Buddhism or Hinduism. Naturally the new ideas were mainly Brahmanic and Buddhism had no chance of being fortified by an importation of even moderately orthodox doctrine. In the fourteenth century arose the community of wandering ascetics called Nâthas who were reverenced by Hindus and Buddhists alike. They rejected the observances of both creeds but often combined their doctrines and, though disavowed by the Brahmans, exercised a considerable influence among the lower castes. Some of the peculiar deities of Nepal, such as Matsyendranâth, have attributes traceable to these wanderers. In 1769 Nepal was conquered by the Gurkhas. This tribe seems related to the Tibetan stock, as are the Nevars, but it had long been hinduized and claimed a Rajput ancestry. Thus Gurkha rule has favoured and accelerated the hinduizing of Nepalese Buddhism.

Since the time of Hodgson the worship of the Âdi-Buddha, or an original divine Buddha practically equivalent to God, has been often described as characteristic of Nepalese religion and such a worship undoubtedly exists. But recent accounts indicate that it is not prominent and also that it can hardly be considered a distinct type of monotheistic Buddhism. The idea that the five Dhyâni-Buddhas are emanations or manifestations of a single primordial Buddha-spirit is a natural development of Mahayanist ideas, but no definite statement of it earlier than the Kâlacakra literature is forthcoming, though many earlier works point towards it[1]. In modern Nepal the chief temple of the Âdi-Buddha is on the hill of Svayambhû (the self-existent) near Katmandu. According to a legend preserved in the Svayambhû Purâṇa, a special divine manifestation occurred in ancient times on an adjoining lake; a miraculous lotus arose on its surface, bearing an image, over which a Caitya was subsequently erected. The shrine is greatly venerated but this Âdi-Buddha, or Svayambhû, does not differ essentially from other miraculous images in India which are said not to consist of ordinary matter but to embody in some special way the nature of a deity. The religion of Nepal is less remarkable for new developments of Buddhism than for the singular fusion of Buddhism with Hinduism which it presents and which helps us to understand what must have been the last phase in Bengal.

The Nepalese Brahmans tolerate Buddhism. The Nepâla-mâhâtmya says that to worship Buddha is to worship Śiva, and the Svayambhû Purâṇa returns the compliment by recommending the worship of Paśupati[2]. The official itinerary of the Hindu pilgrim includes Svayambhû, where he adores Buddha under that name. More often the two religions adore the same image under different names: what is Avalokita to the one is Mahâkâla to the other. Durgâ is explained as being the incarnation of the Prajñâ-pâramitâ and she is even identified with the Âdi-Buddha. The Nepalese pantheon like the Tibetan contains three elements, often united in modern legends: firstly aboriginal deities, such as Nagas and other nature spirits: secondly definitely Buddhist deities or Bodhisattvas of whom Manjuśrî receives the most honour: thirdly Hindu deities such as Gaṇeśa and Kṛishṇa. The popular deity Matsyendranath appears to combine all three elements in his own person.

Modern accounts of Nepal leave the impression that even

[1] The doctrine of the Âdi-Buddha is fully stated in the metrical version of the Kâraṇḍa-vyûha which appears to be a later paraphrase of the prose edition. See Winternitz, *Gesch. Ind. Lit.* II. i. 238.

[2] Compare the fusion of Śivaism and Buddhism in Java.

corrupt Buddhism is in a bad way, yet the number of religious establishments is considerable. Celibacy is not observed by their inmates, who are called banras (bandyas). On entering the order the novice takes the ancient vows but after four days he returns to his tutor, confesses that they are too hard for him and is absolved from his obligations. The classes known as Bhikshus and Gubhârjus officiate as priests, the latter being the higher order. The principal ceremony is the offering of melted butter. The more learned Gubhârjus receive the title of Vajrâcârya[1] and have the sole right of officiating at marriages and funerals.

There is little learning. The oldest scriptures in use are the so-called nine Dharmas[2]. Hodgson describes these works as much venerated and Rajendralal Mitra has analysed them, but Sylvain Lévi heard little of them in 1898, though he mentions the recitation of the Prajñâ-pâramitâ. The Svayambhû Purâṇa is an account of the manifestation of the Âdi-Buddha written in the style of those portions of the Brahmanic Purâṇas which treat of the glories of some sacred place. In its present form it can hardly be earlier than the sixteenth century A.D. The Nepâla-mâhâtmya is a similar work which, though of Brahmanic origin, puts Buddha, Vishnu and Śiva on the same footing and identifies the first with Krishna. The Vâgvatî-mâhâtmya[3] on the other hand is strictly Śivaite and ignores Buddha's claims to worship. The Vâmśâvali, or Chronicle of Nepal, written in the Gurkha language (Parbatiya) is also largely occupied with an account of sacred sites and buildings and exists in two versions, one Buddhist, the other Brahmanical.

But let us return to the decadence of Buddhism in India. It is plain that persecution was not its main cause nor even very important among the accessory causes. The available records contain clearer statements about the persecution of Jainism than of Buddhism but no doubt the latter came in for some rough handling, though not enough to annihilate a vigorous sect. Great numbers of monasteries in the north were demolished by the Huns and a similar catastrophe brought

[1] Or Vajrâcârya-arhat-bhikshu-buddha, which in itself shows what a medley Nepalese Buddhism has become.

[2] See above chap. xx. for some account of these works.

[3] Dedicated to the sacred river Vâgvatî or Bagmati.

about the collapse of the Church in Bihar. But this last incident cannot be called religious persecution, for Muhammad did not even know what he was destroying. Buddhism did not arouse more animosity than other Indian religions: the significant feature is that when its temples and monasteries were demolished it did not live on in the hearts of the people, as did Hinduism with all its faults.

The relation between the laity and the Church in Buddhism is curious and has had serious consequences for both good and evil. The layman "takes refuge" in the Buddha, his law and his church but does not swear exclusive allegiance: to follow supplementary observances is not treasonable, provided they are not in themselves objectionable. The Buddha prescribed no ceremonies for births, deaths and marriages and apparently expected the laity to continue in the observance of such rites as were in use. To-day in China and Japan the good layman is little more than one who pays more attention to Buddhism than to other faiths. This charitable pliancy had much to do with the victories of Buddhism in the Far East, where it had to struggle against strong prejudices and could hardly have made its way if it had been intolerant of local deities. But in India we see the disadvantages of the omission to make the laity members of a special corporation and the survival of the Jains, who do form such a corporation, is a clear object lesson. Social life in India tends to combine men in castes or in communities which if not castes in the technical sense have much the same character. Such communities have great vitality so long as they maintain their peculiar usages, but when they cease to do so they soon disintegrate and are reabsorbed. Buddhism from the first never took the form of a corporation. The special community which it instituted was the saṅgha or body of monks. Otherwise, it aimed not at founding a sect but at including all the world as lay believers on easy terms. This principle worked well so long as the faith was in the ascendent but its effect was disastrous when decline began. The line dividing Buddhist laymen from ordinary Hindus became less and less marked: distinctive teaching was found only in the monasteries: these became poorly recruited and as they were gradually deserted or destroyed by Mohammedans the religion of the Buddha disappeared from his native land.

Even in the monasteries the doctrine taught bore a closer resemblance to Hinduism than to the preaching of Gotama and it is this absence of the protestant spirit, this pliant adaptability to the ideas of each age, which caused Indian Buddhism to lose its individuality and separate existence. In some localities its disappearance and absorption were preceded by a monstrous phase, known as Tantrism or Śâktism, in which the worst elements of Hinduism, those which would have been most repulsive to Gotama, made an unnatural alliance with his church.

I treat of Tantrism and Śâktism in another chapter. The original meaning of Tantra as applied to literary compositions is a simplified manual[1]. Thus we hear of Vishnuite Tantras and in this sense there is a real similarity between Buddhist and tantric teaching, for both set aside Brahmanic tradition as needlessly complicated and both profess to preach a simple and practical road to salvation. But in Hinduism and Buddhism alike such words as Tantra and tantric acquire a special sense and imply the worship of the divine energy in a female form called by many names such as Kâlî in the former, Târâ in the latter. This worship which in my opinion should be called Śâktism rather than Tantrism combines many elements: ancient, savage superstitions as well as ingenious but fanciful speculation, but its essence is always magic. It attempts to attain by magical or sacramental formulæ and acts not only prosperity and power but salvation, nirvana and union with the supreme spirit. Some of its sects practise secret immoral rites. It is sad to confess that degenerate Buddhism did not remain uncorrupted by such abuses.

It is always a difficult and speculative task to trace the early stages of new movements in Indian religion, but it is clear that by the eighth century and perhaps earlier the Buddhism of Bihar and Bengal had fallen a prey to this influence. Apparently the public ritual in the Vihâras remained unchanged and the usual language about *nirvâna* and *śûnyatâ* was not discarded, but it

[1] Hardly any Buddhist Tantras have been edited in Europe. See Bendall, *Subhâshita-sangraha* for a collection of extracts (also published in *Muséon*, 1905), and De la Vallée Poussin, *Bouddhisme, Études et Matériaux*. *Id.* Pancakrama, 1896.

While this book was going through the press I received the Tibetan Tantra called Shrichakrasambhara (Avalon's Tantric Texts, vol. VII) with introduction by A. Avalon, but have not been able to make use of it.

was taught that those who followed a certain curriculum could obtain salvation by magical methods. To enter this curriculum it was necessary to have a qualified teacher and to receive from him initiation or baptism (abhisheka). Of the subsequent rites the most important is to evoke one of the many Buddhas or Bodhisattvas recognized by the Mahayana and identify oneself with him[1]. He who wishes to do this is often called a sâdhaka or magician but his achievements, like many Indian miracles, are due to self-hypnotization. He is directed to repair to a lonely place and offer worship there with flowers and prayers. To this office succeed prolonged exercises in meditation which do not depart much from the ancient canon since they include the four Brahmâ-vihâras. Their object is to suppress thought and leave the mind empty. Then the sâdhaka fills this void with the image of some Bodhisattva, for instance Avalokita. This he does by uttering mystic syllables called bîja or seed, because they are supposed to germinate and grow into the figures which he wishes to produce. In this way he imagines that he sees the emblems of the Bodhisattva spring up round him one by one and finally he himself assumes the shape of Avalokita and becomes one with him. Something similar still exists in Tibet where every Lama chooses a tutelary deity or Yi-dam whom he summons in visible form after meditation and fasting[2]. Though this procedure when set forth methodically in a mediæval manual seems an absurd travesty of Buddhism, yet it has links with the early faith. It is admitted in the Pitakas that certain forms of meditation[3] lead to union with Brahmâ and it is no great change to make them lead to union with other supernatural beings. Still we are not here breathing the atmosphere of the Pitakas. The object is not to share Brahmâ's heaven but to become temporarily identified with a deity, and this is not a byway of religion but the high road.

But there is a further stage of degradation. I have already mentioned that various Bodhisattvas are represented as accompanied by a female deity, particularly Avalokita by Târâ. The

[1] See Foucher, *Iconographie bouddhique*, pp. 8 ff. De la Vallée Poussin, *Bouddhisme, Études et Matériaux*, pp. 213 ff. For Japanese tantric ceremonies see the Si-Do-In-Dzon in the *Annales du Musée Guimet*, vol. VIII.

[2] In ancient Egypt also the Kher ḥeb or magician-priest claimed the power of becoming various gods. See Budge, *Osiris*, II. 170 and Wiedemann, *Magic im alten Aegypten*, 13 ff.

[3] The Brahmâ-vihâras. *E.g.* Dig. Nik. XIII.

mythological and metaphysical ideas which have grown up round Śiva and Durgâ also attached themselves to these couples. The Buddha or Bodhisattva is represented as enjoying nirvana because he is united to his spouse, and to the three bodies already enumerated is added a fourth, the body of perfect bliss[1]. Sometimes this idea merely leads to further developments of the practices described above. Thus the devotee may imagine that he enters into Târâ as an embryo and is born of her as a Buddha[2]. More often the argument is that since the bliss of the Buddha consists in union with Târâ, nirvana can be obtained by sexual union here, and we find many of the tantric wizards represented as accompanied by female companions. The adept should avoid all action but he is beyond good and evil and the dangerous doctrine that he can do evil with impunity, which the more respectable sects repudiate, is expressly taught. The sage is not defiled by passion but conquers passion by passion: he should commit every infamy: he should rob, lie and kill Buddhas[3]. These crazy precepts are probably little more than a speculative application to the moral sphere of the doctrine that all things are non-existent and hence equivalent. But though tantrists did not go about robbing and murdering so freely as their principles allowed, there is some evidence that in the period of decadence the morality of the Bhikshus had fallen into great discredit. Thus in the allegorical Vishnuite drama called Prabodhacandrodaya and written at Kalanjar near the end of the eleventh century Buddhists and Jains are represented as succumbing to the temptations of inebriety and voluptuousness.

It is necessary to mention this phase of decadence but no good purpose would be served by dwelling further on the absurd and often disgusting prescriptions of such works as the Tathâgata-guhyaka. If the European reader is inclined to condemn unreservedly a religion which even in decrepitude could find place for such monstrosities, he should remember that the aberrations of Indian religion are due not to its

[1] Mahâsukhakâya or vajrakâya.

[2] De la Vallée Poussin, *Bouddhisme, Études et Matériaux*, p. 153.

[3] See *Subhâshita-saṅgraha* edited by Bendall. Part II. pp. 29 ff. especially p. 41. Parasvaharaṇam kâryam paradârânishevaṇam Vaktavyam cânṛitam nityam sarvabuddhâṃśca ghâtayet. See also Tathâgata-guhyaka in Rajendralal Mitra's *Sanskrit Literature in Nepal*, pp. 261–264.

inherent depravity, but to its universality. In Europe those who follow disreputable occupations rarely suppose that they have anything to do with the Church. In India, robbers, murderers, gamblers, prostitutes, and maniacs all have their appropriate gods, and had the Marquis de Sade been a Hindu he would probably have founded a new tantric sect. But though the details of Śâktism are an unprofitable study, it is of some importance to ascertain when it first invaded Buddhism and to what extent it superseded older ideas.

Some critics[1] seem to imply—for their statements are not very explicit—that Śâktism formed part if not of the teaching of the Buddha, at least of the medley of beliefs held by his disciples. But I see no proof that Śâktist beliefs—that is to say erotic mysticism founded on the worship of goddesses—were prevalent in Magadha or Kosala before the Christian era. Although Siri, the goddess of luck, is mentioned in the Pitakas, the popular deities whom they bring on the scene are almost exclusively masculine[2]. And though in the older Brahmanic books there are passages which might easily become tantric, yet the transition is not made and the important truths of religion are kept distinct from unclean rites and thoughts. The Bṛihad-âraṇyaka contains a chapter which hardly admits of translation but the object of the practices inculcated is simply to ensure the birth of a son. The same work (not without analogies in the ecstatic utterances of Christian saints) boldly compares union with the Âtman to the bliss of one who is embraced by a beloved wife, but this is a mere illustration and there is no hint of the doctrine that the goal of the religious life is obtainable by *maithuna*. Still such passages, though innocent in themselves, make it easy to see how degrading superstitions found an easy entrance into the noblest edifices of Indian thought and possibly some heresies condemned in the Kathâvatthu[3] indicate that even at this early date the Buddhist Church was contaminated by erotic fancies. But, if so, there is no evidence that such malpractices were widespread. The

[1] For instance De la Vallée Poussin in his *Bouddhisme, Études et Matériaux*, 1896. In his later work, *Bouddhisme, Opinions sur l'histoire de la dogmatique*, he modifies his earlier views.

[2] See Dig. Nik. XX. and XXXII.

[3] Kathâv. XXIII. 1 and 2.

appendices to the Lotus[1] show that the worship of a many-named goddess, invoked as a defender of the faith, was beginning to be a recognized feature of Buddhism. But they contain no indications of left-handed Tantrism and the best proof that it did not become prevalent until much later is afforded by the narratives of the three Chinese pilgrims who all describe the condition of religion in India and notice anything which they thought singular or reprehensible. Fa-Hsien does not mention the worship of any female deity[2], nor does the Life of Vasubandhu, but Asanga appears to allude to Śâktism in one passage[3]. Hsüan Chuang mentions images of Târâ but without hinting at tantric ritual, nor does I-Ching allude to it, nor does the evidence of art and inscriptions attest its existence. It may have been known as a form of popular superstition and even have been practised by individual Bhikshus, but the silence of I-Ching makes it improbable that it was then countenanced in the schools of Magadha. He complains[4] of those who neglect the Vinaya and "devote their whole attention to the doctrine of nothingness," but he says not a word about tantric abuses[5].

The change probably occurred in the next half century[6] for Padma-Sambhava, the founder of Lamaism who is said to have resided in Gaya and Nalanda and to have arrived in Tibet in 747 A.D., is represented by tradition as a tantric wizard, and about the same time translations of Tantras begin to appear in Chinese. The translations of the sixth and seventh centuries, including those of I-Ching, comprise a considerable though not preponderant number of Dhâraṇîs. After the seventh century

[1] These appendices are later additions to the original text but they were translated into Chinese in the third century. Among the oldest Sanskrit MSS. from Japan is the Ushṇisha-vijaya-dhâraṇî and there is a goddess with a similar name. But the Dhâraṇî is not Śâktist. See text in Anec. Oxon. Aryan series.

[2] He speaks of Kwan-shih-yin but this is probably the male Avalokita.

[3] Mahâyâna-sûtrâlankâra, IX. 46. Of course there may be many other allusions in yet unedited works of Asanga but it is noticeable that this allusion to *maithuna* is only made in passing and is not connected with the essence of his teaching.

[4] Transl. Takakusu, p. 51.

[5] Târanâtha, chap. XXII seems also to assign a late origin to the Tantras though his remarks are neither clear nor consistent with what he says in other passages. He is doubtless right in suggesting that tantric rites were practised surreptitiously before they were recognized openly.

[6] It is about this time too that we hear of Tantrism in Hinduism. In the drama Mâlatî and Mâdhava (*c.* 730 A.D.) the heroine is kidnapped and is about to be sacrificed to the goddess Candâ when she is rescued.

these became very numerous and several Tantras were also translated[1]. The inference seems to be that early in the eighth century Indian Buddhists officially recognized Tantrism.

Tantric Buddhism was due to the mixture of Mahayanist teaching with aboriginal superstitions absorbed through the medium of Hinduism, though in some cases there may have been direct contact and mutual influence between Mahayanism and aboriginal beliefs. But as a rule what happened was that aboriginal deities were identified with Hindu deities and Buddhism had not sufficient independence to keep its own pantheon distinct, so that Vairocana and Târâ received most of the attributes, brahmanic or barbarous, given to Śiva or Kâli. The worship of the goddesses, described in their hinduized form as Durgâ, Kâlî, etc., though found in most parts of India was specially prevalent in the sub-himalayan districts both east and west. Now Padma-Sambhava was a native of Udyâna or Swat and Târanâtha represents the chief Tantrists[2] as coming from there or visiting it. Hsüan Chuang[3] tells us that the inhabitants were devout Mahayanists but specially expert in magic and exorcism. He also describes no less than four sacred places in it where the Buddha in previous births gave his flesh, blood or bones for the good of others. Have we here in a Buddhist form some ancient legend of dismemberment like that told of Satî in Assam? Of Kashmir he says that its religion was a mixture of Buddhism with other beliefs[4]. These are precisely the conditions most favourable to the growth of Tantrism and though

[1] See the latter part of Appendix II in Nanjio's Catalogue.

[2] *E.g.* Lalitavajra, Lîlâvajra, Buddhaśânti, Ratnavajra. Târanâtha also (tr. Schiefner, p. 264) speaks of Tantras "Welche aus Udyana gebracht und nie in Indien gewesen sind." It is also noticeable, as Grünwedel has pointed out, that many of the siddhas or sorcerers bear names which have no meaning in Aryan languages: Bir-va-pa, Na-ro-pa, Lui-pa, etc. A curious late tradition represents Śâktism as coming from China. See a quotation from the Mahâcînatantra in the *Archæological Survey of Mayurabhanj*, p. xiv. Either China is here used loosely for some country north of the Himalayas or the story is pure fancy, for with rare exceptions (for instance the Lamaism of the Yüan dynasty) the Chinese seem to have rejected Śâktist works or even to have expurgated them, *e.g.* the Tathâgata-guhyaka.

[3] His account of Udyâna and Kashmir will be found in Watters, chapters VII and VIII.

[4] Traces of Buddhism still exist, for according to Bühler the Nilamata Purâṇa orders the image of Buddha to be worshipped on Vaisakha 15 to the accompaniment of recitations by Buddhist ascetics.

the bulk of the population are now Mohammedans, witchcraft and sorcery are still rampant. Among the Hindu Kashmîris[1] the most prevalent religion has always been the worship of Śiva, especially in the form representing him as half male, half female. This cult is not far from Śâktism and many allusions[2] in the Râjataranginî indicate that left-hand worship was known, though the author satirizes it as a corruption. He also several times mentions[3] Mâtri-cakras, that is circles sacred to the Mothers or tantric goddesses. In Nepal and Tibet tantric Buddhism is fully developed but these countries have received so much from India that they exhibit not a parallel growth, but late Indian Tantrism as imported ready-made from Bengal. It is here that we come nearest to the origins of Tantrism, for though the same beliefs may have flourished in Udyâna and Kashmir they did not spread much in the Panjab or Hindustan, where their progress was hindered at first by a healthy and vigorous Hinduism and subsequently by Mohammedan invasions. But from 700 to 1197 A.D. Bengal was remote alike from the main currents of Indian religion and from foreign raids: little Aryan thought or learning leavened the local superstitions which were infecting and stifling decadent Buddhism. Hsüan Chuang informs us that Bhaskaravarma king of Kâmarûpa[4] attended the fêtes celebrated by Harsha in 644 A.D. and inscriptions found at Tezpur indicate that kings with Hindu names reigned in Assam about 800 A.D. This is agreeable to the supposition that an amalgamation of Śivaism and aboriginal religion may have been in formation about 700 A.D. and have influenced Buddhism.

In Bihar from the eighth century onwards the influence of Tantrism was powerful and disastrous. The best information about this epoch is still to be found in Târanâtha, in spite of his defects.

He makes the interesting statement that in the reign of Gopâla who was a Buddhist, although his ministers were not (730–740 A.D.), the Buddhists wished their religious buildings to

[1] For notices of Kashmirian religion see Stein's translation of the Râjataranginî and Bühler, *Tour in Search of Sanskrit manuscripts. J. Bomb. A.S.* 1877.

[2] VI. 11–13, VII. 278–280, 295, 523.

[3] I. 122, 335, 348 : III. 99, V. 55.

[4] Also called Kumâra.

be kept separate from Hindu temples but that, in spite of protests, life-sized images of Hindu deities were erected in them[1]. The ritual too was affected, for we hear several times of burnt offerings[2] and how Bodhibhadra, one of the later professors of Vikramaśila, was learned in the mystic lore of both Buddhists and Brahmans. Nalanda and the other viharas continued to be seats of learning and not merely monasteries, and for some time there was a regular succession of teachers. Târanâtha gives us to understand that there were many students and authors but that sorcery occupied an increasingly important position. Of most teachers we are told that they saw some deity, such as Avalokita or Târâ. The deity was summoned by the rites already described[3] and the object of the performer was to obtain magical powers or siddhi. The successful sorcerer was known as siddha, and we hear of 84 mahâsiddhas, still celebrated in Tibet, who extend from Rahulabhadra Nâgârjuna to the thirteenth century. Many of them bear names which appear not to be Indian.

The topics treated of in the Tantras are divided into Kriyâ (ritual), Caryâ (apparently corresponding to Vinaya), Yoga, and Anuttara-yoga. Sometimes the first three are contrasted with the fourth and sometimes the first two are described as lower, the third and fourth as higher. But the Anuttara-yoga is always considered the highest and most mysterious[4]. Târanâtha says[5] that the Tantras began to appear simultaneously with the Mahayana sûtras but adds that the Anuttara-yoga tantras appeared gradually[6]. He also observes that the Âcârya Ânandagarbha[7] did much to spread them in Magadha. It is not until

[1] Similarly statues of Mahâdevî are found in Jain temples now, *i.e.* in Gujarat.

[2] This very unbuddhist practice seems to have penetrated even to Japan. Burnt offerings form part of the ritual in the temple of Narita.

[3] See for instance the account of how Kamalarakshita summoned Yamâri.

[4] So too the Saṃhitâs of the Vaishṇavas and the Âgamas of the Śaivas are said to consist of four quarters teaching Jñâna, Yoga, Kriyâ and Caryâ respectively. See Schrader, *Introd. to Pancaratra*, p. 22. Sometimes five classes of Tantras are enumerated which are perhaps all subdivisions of the Anuttara-yoga, namely Guhyasamâja, Mâyâjâla, Buddhasammâyoga, Candraguhyatilaka, Manjuśrîkrodha. See Târanâtha (Schiefner), p. 221.

[5] Chap. XLIII. But this seems hardly consistent with his other statements.

[6] The Lamas in Tibet have a similar theory of progressive tantric revelation. See Waddell, *Buddhism of Tibet*, pp. 56, 57.

[7] In the reign of Mahîpâla, 978–1030 A.D.

a late period of the Pâla dynasty that he mentions the Kâlacakra which is the most extravagant form of Buddhist Tantrism.

This accords with other statements to the effect that the Kâlacakra tantra was introduced in 965 A.D. from Śambhala, a mysterious country in Central Asia. This system is said to be Vishnuite rather than Śivaite. It specially patronizes the cult of the mystic Buddhas such as Kâlacakra and Heruka, all of whom appear to be regarded as forms of Âdi-Buddha or the primordial Buddha essence. The Siddha named Pito is also described as the author of this doctrine[1], which had less importance in India than in Tibet.

On the other hand Târanâtha gives us the names of several doctors of the Vinaya who flourished under the Pâla dynasty. Even as late as the reign of Râmapâla (? 1080–1120) we hear that the Hinayanists were numerous. In the reign of Dharmapâla (*c.* 800 A.D.) some of them broke up the great silver image of Heruka at Bodh-Gaya and burnt the books of Mantras[2]. These instances show that the older Buddhism was not entirely overwhelmed by Tantrism[3] though perhaps it was kept alive more by pilgrims than by local sentiment. Thus the Chinese inscriptions of Bodh-Gaya though they speak at length of the three bodies of Buddha show no signs of Tantrism. It would appear that the worship celebrated in the holy places of Magadha preserved a respectable side until the end. In the same way although Tantrism is strong in the literature of the Lamas, none of the many descriptions of Tibet indicate that there is anything scandalous in the externals of religion. Probably in Tibet, Nepal and mediæval Magadha alike the existence of disgraceful tantric literature does not indicate such widespread depravity as might be supposed. But of its putrefying influence in corrupting the minds of those who ought to have preserved

[1] Târanâtha, p. 275. For the whole subject see Grünwedel, *Mythologie des Buddhismus*, pp. 41–2 and my chapters on Tibet below.

[2] Schiefner (transl. Târanâtha, p. 221) describes these Śrâvakas or Hinayanists as "Saindhavas welche Çrâvakas aus Simhala u.s.w. waren." They are apparently the same as the Saindhava-çrâvakas often mentioned by Târanâtha. Are they Hinayanists from Sindh where the Sammitiya school was prevalent? See also Pag Sam Jon Zang, pp. cxix, 114 and 134 where Sarat Chandra Das explains Sendha-pa as a brahmanical sect.

[3] The curious story (Târanâtha, p. 206) in which a Buddhist at first refuses on religious grounds to take part in the evocation of a demon seems also to hint at a disapproval of magic.

the pure faith there can be no doubt. More than any other form of mixed belief it obliterated essential differences, for Buddhist Tantrism and Śivaite Tantrism are merely two varieties of Tantrism.

What is happening at Bodh-Gaya at present[1] illustrates how Buddhism disappeared from India. The abbot of a neighbouring Śivaite monastery who claims the temple and grounds does not wish, as a Mohammedan might, to destroy the building or even to efface Buddhist emblems. He wishes to supervise the whole establishment and the visits of pilgrims, as well as to place on the images of Buddha Hindu sectarian marks and other ornaments. Hindu pilgrims are still taken by their guides to venerate the Bodhi tree and, but for the presence of foreign pilgrims, no casual observer would suppose the spot to be anything but a Hindu temple of unusual construction. The same process went a step further in many shrines which had not the same celebrity and effaced all traces and memory of Buddhism.

At the present day the Buddha is recognized by the Brahmans as an incarnation of Vishnu[2], though the recognition is often qualified by the statement that Vishnu assumed this form in order to mislead the wicked who threatened to become too powerful if they knew the true method of attaining superhuman powers. But he is rarely worshipped *in propriâ personâ*[3]. As a rule Buddhist images and emblems are ascribed to Vishnu or Śiva, according to sectarian preferences, but in spite of fusion some lingering sense of original animosity prevents Gotama from receiving even such respect as is accorded to incarnations like Paraśurâma. At Bodh-Gaya I have been told that Hindu pilgrims are taken by their guides to venerate the Bodhi-tree but not the images of Buddha.

Yet in reviewing the disappearance of Buddhism from India we must remember that it was absorbed not expelled. The result of the mixture is justly called Hinduism, yet both in

[1] This passage was written about 1910. In the curious temple at Gaya called Bishnupad the chief object of veneration is a foot-like mark. Such impressions are venerated in many parts of the world as Buddha's feet and it seems probable, considering the locality, that this footprint was attributed to Buddha before it was transferred to Vishnu.

[2] There are no very early references to this Avatâra. It is mentioned in some of the Puranas (*e.g.* Bhâgavata and Agni) and by Kshemendra.

[3] But see the instances quoted above from Kashmir and Nepal.

usages and beliefs it has taken over much that is Buddhist and without Buddhism it would never have assumed its present shape. To Buddhist influence are due for instance the rejection by most sects of animal sacrifices: the doctrine of the sanctity of animal life: monastic institutions and the ecclesiastical discipline found in the Dravidian regions. We may trace the same influence with more or less certainty in the philosophy of Śaṅkara and outside the purely religious sphere in the development of Indian logic. These and similar points are dealt with in more detail in other parts of this work and I need not dwell on them here.

BOOK V

HINDUISM

BOOK V

THE present book deals with Hinduism and includes the period just treated in Book IV. In many epochs the same mythological and metaphysical ideas appear in a double form, Brahmanic and Buddhist, and it is hard to say which form is the earlier.

Any work which like the present adopts a geographical and historical treatment is bound to make Buddhism seem more important than Hinduism and rightly, for the conversion and transformation of China, Japan and many other countries are a series of exploits of great moment for the history not merely of religion but of civilization. Yet when I think of the antiquity, variety and vitality of Hinduism in India—no small sphere—the nine chapters which follow seem very inadequate. I can only urge that though it would be easy to fill an encyclopædia with accounts of Indian beliefs and practices, yet there is often great similarity under superficial differences: the main lines of thought are less numerous than they seem to be at first sight and they tend to converge.

CHAPTER XXV

SIVA AND VISHṆU

1

THE striking difference between the earlier and later phases of Indian religious belief, between the Vedic hymns, Brâhmaṇas, Upanishads and their accessory treatises on the one hand, and the epics, Purâṇas, Tantras and later literature on the other, is due chiefly to the predominance in the latter of the great gods Śiva and Vishṇu, with the attendant features of sectarian worship and personal devotion to a particular deity. The difference is not wholly chronological, for late writers sometimes take the Vedic standpoint and ignore the worship of these deities, but still their prominence in literature, and probably in popular mythology, is posterior to the Vedic period. The change created by their appearance is not merely the addition of two imposing figures to an already ample pantheon; it is a revolution which might be described as the introduction of a new religion, except that it does not come as the enemy or destroyer of the old. The worship of the new deities grows up peacefully in the midst of the ancient rites; they receive the homage of the same population and the ministrations of the same priests. The transition is obscured but also was facilitated by the strength of Buddhism during the period when it occurred. The Brahmans, confronted by this formidable adversary, were disposed to favour any popular religious movement which they could adapt to their interests.

When the Hindu revival sets in under the Guptas, and Buddhism begins to decline, we find that a change has taken place which must have begun several centuries before, though our imperfect chronology does not permit us to date it. Whereas the Vedic sacrificers propitiated all the gods impartially and regarded ritual as a sacred science giving power over nature, the worshipper of the later deities is generally sectarian and often emotional. He selects one for his adoration, and this selected deity becomes not merely a great god among others but a gigantic cosmical figure in whom centre the philosophy, poetry and passion of his devotees. He is almost God in the European sense, but still Indian deities, though they may have a monopoly of adoration in their own sects, are never entirely similar to Jehovah or Allah. They are at once more mythical, more human and more philosophical, since they are conceived of not as creators and rulers external to the world, but as forces manifesting themselves in nature. An exuberant mythology bestows on them monstrous forms, celestial residences, wives and offspring: they make occasional appearances in this world as men and animals; they act under the influence of passions which if titanic, are but human feelings magnified. The philosopher accommodates them to his system by saying that Vishṇu or Śiva is the form which the Supreme Spirit assumes as Lord of the visible universe, a form which is real only in the same sense that the visible world itself is real.

Vishṇu and Rudra are known even to the Ṛig Veda but as deities of no special eminence. It is only after the Vedic age that they became, each for his own worshippers, undisputed Lords of the Universe. A limiting date to the antiquity of Śivaism and Vishnuism, as their cults may be called, is furnished by Buddhist literature, at any rate for north-eastern India. The Pali Piṭakas frequently[1] introduce popular deities, but give no prominence to Vishṇu and Śiva. They are apparently mentioned under the names of Veṇhu and Isâna, but are not differentiated from a host of spirits now forgotten. The Piṭakas have no prejudices in the matter of deities and their object is to represent the most powerful of them as admitting their inferiority to the Buddha. If Śiva and Vishṇu are not put forward in the same way as Brahmâ and Indra, the inference seems clear: it had not occurred to anyone that they were particularly important.

The suttas of the Dîgha Nikâya in which these lists of deities occur were perhaps composed before 300 B.C.[2] About that date Megasthenes, the Greek envoy at Pataliputra, describes two Indian deities under the names of Dionysus and Herakles. They are generally identified with Kṛishṇa and Śiva. It might be difficult to deduce this identity from an analysis of each

[1] See especially Dig. Nik. XX. and XXXII.

[2] But the lists may be pieces of folk-lore older than the suttas in which they are incorporated.

description and different authorities have identified both Śiva and Kṛishṇa with Dionysus, but the fact remains that a somewhat superficial foreign observer was impressed with the idea that the Hindus worshipped two great gods. He would hardly have derived this idea from the Vedic pantheon, and it is not clear to what gods he can refer if not to Śiva and Vishṇu. It thus seems probable that these two cults took shape about the fourth century B.C. Their apparently sudden appearance is due to their popular character and to the absence of any record in art. The statuary and carving of the Asokan period and immediately succeeding centuries is exclusively Buddhist. No temples or images remain to illustrate the first growth of Hinduism (as the later form of Indian religion is commonly styled) out of the earlier Brahmanism. Literature (on which we are dependent for our information) takes little account of the early career of popular gods before they win the recognition of the priesthood and aristocracy, but when that recognition is once obtained they appear in all their majesty and without any hint that their honours are recent.

As already mentioned, we have evidence that in the fifth or sixth century before Christ the Vedic or Brahmanic religion was not the only form of worship and philosophy in India. There were popular deities and rites to which the Brahmans were not opposed and which they countenanced when it suited them. What takes place in India to-day took place then. When some aboriginal deity becomes important owing to the prosperity of the tribe or locality with which he is connected, he is recognized by the Brahmans and admitted to their pantheon, perhaps as the son or incarnation of some personage more generally accepted as divine. The prestige of the Brahmans is sufficient to make such recognition an honour, but it is also their interest and millennial habit to secure control of every important religious movement and to incorporate rather than suppress. And this incorporation is more than mere recognition: the parvenu god borrows something from the manners and attributes of the olympian society to which he is introduced. The greater he grows, the more considerable is the process of fusion and borrowing. Hindu philosophy ever seeks for the one amongst the many and popular thought, in a more confused way, pursues the same goal. It combines and identifies its deities, feeling dimly that taken singly they are too partial to be truly divine, or it piles attributes upon them striving to make each an adequate divine whole.

Among the processes which have contributed to form Vishṇu and Śiva we must reckon the invasions which entered India from the north-west[1]. In Bactria and Sogdiana there met and were combined the art and religious ideas of Greece and Persia, and whatever elements were imported by the Yüeh-chih and other tribes who came from the Chinese frontier. The personalities of Vishṇu and Śiva need not be ascribed to foreign influence. The ruder invaders took kindly to the worship of Śiva, but there is no proof that they introduced it. But Persian and Græco-Bactrian influence favoured the creation of more definite deities, more personal and more pictorial. The gods of the Vedic hymns are vague and indistinct: the Supreme Being of the Upanishads altogether impersonal, but Mithra and Apollo, though divine in their majesty, are human in their persons and in the appeal they make to humanity. The influence of these foreign conceptions and especially of their representation in art is best seen in Indian Buddhism. Hinduism has not so ancient an artistic record and therefore the Græco-Bactrian influence on it is less obvious, for the sculpture of the Gupta period does not seem due to this inspiration. Neither in outward form nor in character do Vishṇu and Śiva show much more resemblance to Apollo and Mithra than to the Vedic gods. Their exuberant, fantastic shapes, their many heads and arms, are a symbol of their complex and multiple attributes. They are not restricted by the limits of personality but are great polymorphic forces, not to be indicated by the limits of one human shape[2].

[1] The Dionysus of Megasthenes is a deity who comes from the west with an army that suffers from the heat of the plains. If we could be certain that he meant Śiva by Dionysus this would be valuable evidence. But he clearly misunderstood many things in Indian religion. Greek legends connected Dionysus with India and the East.

[2] Macdonell seems to me correct in saying (*J.R.A.S.* 1915, p. 125) that one reason why Indian deities have many arms is that they may be able to carry the various symbols by which they are characterized. Another reason is that worship is usually accompanied by dhyâna, that is forming a mental image of the deity as described in a particular text. *E.g.* the worshipper repeats a mantra which describes a deity in language which was originally metaphorical as having many heads and arms and at the same time he ought to make a mental image of such a figure.

2

Though alike in their grandeur and multiplicity, Vishṇu and Śiva are not otherwise similar. In their completely developed forms they represent two ways of looking at the world. The main ideas of the Vaishṇavas are human and emotional. The deity saves and loves: he asks for a worship of love. He appears in human incarnations and is known as well or better by these incarnations than in his original form. But in Śivaism the main current of thought is scientific and philosophic rather than emotional[1]. This statement may seem strange if one thinks of the wild rites and legends connected with Śiva and his spouse. Nevertheless the fundamental conception of Śivaism, the cosmic force which changes and in changing both destroys and reproduces, is strictly scientific and contrasts with the human, pathetic, loving sentiments of Vishnuism. And scandalous as the worship of the generative principle may become, the potency of this impulse in the world scheme cannot be denied. Agreeably to his character of a force rather than an emotion Śiva does not become incarnate[2] as a popular hero and saviour like Râma or Kṛishṇa, but he assumes various supernatural forms for special purposes. Both worships, despite their differences, show characteristics which are common to most phases of Indian religion. Both seek for deliverance from transmigration and are penetrated with a sense of the sorrow inherent in human and animal life: both develop or adopt philosophical doctrines which rise high above the level usually attained by popular beliefs, and both

[1] But some forms of Śivaism in southern India come even nearer to emotional Christianity than does Vishnuism.

[2] I cannot discover that any alleged avatâra of Śiva has now or has had formerly any importance, but the Vâyu, Liṅga and Kûrma Purâna give lists of such incarnations, as does also the Catechism of the Shaiva religion translated by Foulkes. But Indian sects have a strong tendency to ascribe all possible achievements and attributes to their gods. The mere fact that Vishṇu becomes incarnate incites the ardent Śivaite to say that his god can do the same. A curious instance of this rivalry is found in the story that Śiva manifested himself as Śarabha-mûrti in order to curb the ferocity of Vishṇu when incarnate in the Man Lion (see Gopinâtha Rao, *Hindu Icon.* p. 45). Śiva often appears in a special form, not necessarily human, for a special purpose (*e.g.* Vîrabhadra) and some tantric Buddhas seem to be imitations of these apparitions. There is a strong element of Śivaism borrowed from Bengal in the mythology of Tibet and Mongolia, where such personages as Hevajra, Saṃvara, and Mahâkâla have a considerable importance under the strange title of Buddhas.

have erotic aspects in which they fall below the standard of morality usually professed by important sects whether in Asia or Europe.

The name Śiva is euphemistic. It means propitious and, like Eumenides, is used as a deprecating and complimentary title for the god of terrors. It is not his earliest designation and does not occur as a proper name in the Ṛig Veda where he is known as Rudra, a word of disputed derivation, but probably meaning the roarer. Comparatively few hymns are addressed to Rudra, but he is clearly distinguished from the other Vedic gods. Whereas they are cheerful and benevolent figures, he is maleficent and terrible: they are gods of the heaven but he is a god of the earth. He is the "man-slayer" and the sender of disease, but if he restrains these activities he can give safety and health. "Slay us not, for thou art gracious," and so the Destroyer comes to be the Gracious One[1]. It has been suggested that the name Śiva is connected with the Tamil word *çivappu* red and also that Rudra means not the roarer but the red or shining one. These etymologies seem to me possible but not proved. But Rudra is different in character from the other gods of the Ṛig Veda. It would be rash to say that the Aryan invaders of India brought with them no god of this sort but it is probable that this element in their pantheon increased as they gradually united in blood and ideas with the Dravidian population. But we know nothing of the beliefs of the Dravidians at this remote period. We only know that in later ages emotional religion, finding expression as so-called devil-dancing in its lower and as mystical poetry in its higher phases, was prevalent among them.

The White Yajur Veda[2] contains a celebrated prayer known as the Śatarudrîya addressed to Rudra or the Rudras, for the power invoked seems to be now many and now one. This deity, who is described by a long string of epithets, receives the name of Śaṅkara (afterwards a well-known epithet of Śiva) and is blue-necked. He is begged to be *śiva* or propitious, but the word is an epithet, not a proper name. He haunts mountains and deserted, uncanny places: he is the patron of violent and lawless men, of soldiers and robbers (the two are evidently

[1] The passage from one epithet to the other is very plain in *R.V.* I. 114.

[2] Book XVI.

considered much the same), of thieves, cheats and pilferers[1], but also of craftsmen and huntsmen and is himself "an observant merchant": he is the lord of hosts of spirits, "ill-formed and of all forms." But he is also a great cosmic force who "dwells in flowing streams and in billows and in tranquil waters and in rivers and on islands...and at the roots of trees...": who "exists in incantations, in punishments, in prosperity, in the soil, in the threshing-floor...in the woods and in the bushes, in sound and in echo...in young grass and in foam...in gravel and in streams...in green things and in dry things...Reverence to the leaf and to him who is in the fall of the leaf, the threatener, the slayer, the vexer and the afflicter." Here we see how an evil and disreputable god, the patron of low castes and violent occupations, becomes associated with the uncanny forces of nature and is on the way to become an All-God[2].

Rudra is frequently mentioned in the Atharva Veda. He is conceived much as in the Śatarudrîya, and is the lord of spirits and of animals. "For thee the beasts of the wood, the deer, swans and various winged birds are placed in the forest: thy living creatures exist in the waters: for thee the celestial waters flow. Thou shootest at the monsters of the ocean, and there is to thee nothing far or near[3]."

These passages show that the main conceptions out of which the character of the later Śiva is built existed in Vedic times. The Rudra of the Yajur and Atharva Vedas is not Brahmanic: he is not the god of priests and orderly ritual, but of wild people and places. But he is not a petty provincial demon who afflicts rustics and their cattle. Though there is some hesitation between one Rudra and many Rudras, the destructive forces are unified in thought and the destroyer is not opposed to creation as a devil or as the principle of evil, but with profounder insight is recognized as the Lord and Law of all living things.

But though the outline of Śiva is found in Vedic writings, later centuries added new features to his cult. Chief among these is the worship of a column known as the Linga, the emblem under which he is now most commonly adored. It is a phallic

[1] In the play Mricchakaṭikâ or The Clay Cart (probably of the sixth century A.D.) a burglar invokes Kârtikeya, the son of Śiva, who is said to have taught different styles of house-breaking.

[2] A similarly strange collocation of attributes is found in Daksha's hymn to Śiva. Mahâbhârata, XII. Sec. 285.

[3] Atharva, V. xi. 2. 24.

symbol though usually decent in appearance. The Vedas do not countenance this worship and it is not clear that it was even known to them[1]. It is first enjoined in the Mahâbhârata and there only in two passages[2] which appear to be late additions. The inference seems to be that it was accepted as part of Hinduism just about the time that our edition of the Mahâbhârata was compiled[3]. The old theory that it was borrowed from aboriginal and especially from Dravidian tribes[4] is now discredited. In the first place the instances cited of phallic worship among aboriginal tribes are not particularly numerous or striking. Secondly, linga worship, though prevalent in the south, is not confined to it, but flourishes in all parts of India, even in Assam and Nepal. Thirdly, it is not connected with low castes, with orgies, with obscene or bloodthirsty rites or with anything which can be called un-Aryan. It forms part of the private devotions of the strictest Brahmans, and despite the significance of the emblem, the worship offered to it is perfectly decorous[5]. The evidence thus suggests that this cultus grew up among Brahmanical Hindus in the early centuries of our era. The idea that there was something divine in virility and generation already existed. The choice of the symbol—the stone pillar—may have been influenced by two circumstances. Firstly, the Buddhist veneration of stûpas, especially miniature stûpas, must have made familiar the idea that a cone or column is a religious emblem[6], and secondly the linga may be compared to

[1] It is not certain if the Śiśnadevâḥ whom Indra is asked to destroy in Ṛig. V. VII. 21. 5 and X. 99. 3 are priapic demons or worshippers of the phallus.

[2] VII. secs. 202, 203, and XIII. sec. 14.

[3] The inscriptions of Camboja and Champa seem to be the best proof of the antiquity of Linga worship. A Cambojan inscription of about 550 A.D. records the dedication of a linga and the worship must have taken some time to reach Camboja from India. Some lingas discovered in India are said to be anterior to the Christian era.

[4] See F. Kittel, *Ueber den Ursprung der Linga Kultus*, and Barth, *Religions of India*, p. 261.

[5] As is also its appearance, as a rule. But there are exceptions to this. Some Hindus deny that the Linga is a phallic emblem. It is hardly possible to maintain this thesis in view of such passages as Mahâbh. XIII. 14 and the innumerable figures in which there are both a linga and a Yoni. But it is true that in its later forms the worship is purged of all grossness and that in its earlier forms the symbol adored was often a stûpa-like column or a pillar with figures on it.

[6] Such scenes as the relief from Amarâvati figured in Grünwedel, *Buddhist art in India*, p. 29, fig. 8, might easily be supposed to represent the worship of the linga, and some of Aśoka's pillars have been worshipped as lingas in later times.

the carved pillars or stone standards erected in honour of Vishṇu. Some lingas are carved and bear one or four faces, thus entirely losing any phallic appearance. The wide extension of this cult, though its origin seems late, is remarkable. Something similar may be seen in the worship of Gaṇeśa: the first records of it are even later, but it is now universal in India.

It may seem strange that a religion whose outward ceremonies though unassuming and modest consist chiefly of the worship of the linga, should draw its adherents largely from the educated classes and be under no moral or social stigma. Yet as an idea, as a philosophy, Śivaism possesses truth and force. It gives the best picture which humanity has drawn of the Lord of this world, not indeed of the ideal to which the saint aspires, nor of the fancies with which hope and emotion people the spheres behind the veil, but of the force which rules the Universe as it is, which reproduces and destroys, and in performing one of these acts necessarily performs the other, seeing that both are but aspects of change. For all animal and human existence[1] is the product of sexual desire: it is but the temporary and transitory form of a force having neither beginning nor end but continually manifesting itself in individuals who must have a beginning and an end. This force, to which European taste bids us refer with such reticence, is the true creator of the world. Not only is it unceasingly performing the central miracle of producing new lives but it accompanies it by unnumbered accessory miracles, which provide the new born child with nourishment and make lowly organisms care for their young as if they were gifted with human intelligence. But the Creator is also the Destroyer, not in anger but by the very nature of his activity. When the series of changes culminates in a crisis and an individual breaks up, we see death and destruction, but in reality they occur throughout the process of growth. The egg is destroyed when the chicken is hatched: the embryo ceases to exist when the child is born; when the man comes into being, the child is no more. And for change, improvement and progress death is as necessary as birth. A world of immortals would be a static world.

When once the figure of Śiva has taken definite shape,

[1] But not of course the soul which, according to the general Indian idea, exists before and continues after the life of the body.

attributes and epithets are lavished on it in profusion. He is the great ascetic, for asceticism in India means power, and Śiva is the personification of the powers of nature. He may alternate strangely between austerities and wild debauch, but the sentimentality of some Kṛishṇaite sects is alien to him. He is a magician, the lord of troops of spirits, and thus draws into his circle all the old animistic worship. But he is also identified with Time (Mahâkâla) and Death (Mṛityu) and as presiding over procreation he is Ardhanareśvara, half man, half woman. Stories are invented or adapted to account for his various attributes, and he is provided with a divine family. He dwells on Mount Kailâsa: he has three eyes: above the central one is the crescent of the moon and the stream of the Ganges descends from his braided hair: his throat is blue and encircled by a serpent and a necklace of skulls. In his hands he carries a three-pronged trident and a drum. But the effigy or description varies, for Śiva is adored under many forms. He is Mahâdeva, the Great God, Hara the Seizer, Bhairava the terrible one, Paśupati, the Lord of cattle, that is of human souls who are compared to beasts. Local gods and heroes are identified with him. Thus Gor Bâba[1], said to be a deified ghost of the aboriginal races, reappears as Goreśvara and is counted a form of Śiva, as is also Khandoba or Khande Rao, a deity connected with dogs. Ganeśa, "the Lord of Hosts," the God who removes obstacles and is represented with an elephant's head and accompanied by a rat, is recognized as Śiva's son. Another son is Skanda or Kârtikeya, the God of War, a great deity in Ceylon and southern India. But more important both for the absorption of aboriginal cults and for its influence on speculation and morality is the part played by Śiva's wife or female counterpart.

The worship of goddesses, though found in many sects, is specially connected with Śivaism. A figure analogous to the Madonna, the kind and compassionate goddess who helps and pities all, appears in later Buddhism but for some reason this train of thought has not been usual in India. Lakshmî, Sarasvatî and Sîtâ are benevolent, but they hold no great position in popular esteem[2], and the being who attracts millions of wor-

[1] Crooke, *Popular Religion and Folklore of Northern India*, I. 84; II. 219.

[2] They are however of some importance in Vishnuite theology. For instance according to the school of Râmânuja it is the Śakti (Śrî) who reveals the true doctrine to mankind. Vishṇu is often said to have three consorts, Śrî, Bhû and Lîlâ.

shippers under such names as Kâlî, Dûrgâ, or Mahâdevî, though she has many forms and aspects, is most commonly represented as a terrible goddess who demands offerings of blood. The worship of this goddess or goddesses, for it is hard to say if she is one or many, is treated of in a separate chapter. Though in shrines dedicated to Śiva his female counterpart or energy (Śakti) also receives recognition, yet she is revered as the spouse of her lord to whom honour is primarily due. But in Śâktist worship adoration is offered to the Śakti as being the form in which his power is made manifest or even as the essential Godhead.

3

Let us now pass on to Vishṇu. Though not one of the great gods of the Veda, he is mentioned fairly often and with respect. Indian commentators and comparative mythologists agree that he is a solar deity. His chief exploit is that he took (or perhaps in the earlier version habitually takes) three strides. This was originally a description of the sun's progress across the firmament but grew into a myth which relates that when the earth was conquered by demons, Vishṇu became incarnate as a dwarf and induced the demon king to promise him as much space as he could measure in three steps. Then, appearing in his true form, he strode across earth and heaven and recovered the world for mankind. His special character as the Preserver is already outlined in the Veda. He is always benevolent: he took his three steps for the good of men: he established and preserves the heavens and earth. But he is not the principal solar deity of the Ṛig Veda: Sûrya, Savitri and Pushan receive more invocations. Though one hymn says that no one knows the limits of his greatness, other passages show that he has no pre-eminence, and even in the Mahâbhârata and the Vishṇu-Purâṇa itself he is numbered among the Âdityas or sons of Aditi. In the Brâhmaṇas, he is somewhat more important than in the Ṛig Veda[1], though he has not yet attained to any position like that which he afterwards occupies.

Just as for Śiva, so for Vishṇu we have no clear record of the steps by which he advanced from a modest rank to the

[1] *E.g.* Śat. Brâh. I. 2. 5. See also the strange legend *ib.* XI. 1. 1 where Vishṇu is described as the best of the gods but is eaten by Indra. He is frequently (e.g. in the Śata Brâh) stated to be identical with the sacrifice, and this was probably one of the reasons for his becoming prominent.

position of having but one rival in the popular esteem. But the lines on which the change took place are clear. Even in his own Church, Vishṇu himself claims comparatively little attention. He is not a force like Śiva that makes and mars, but a benevolent and retiring personality who keeps things as they are. His worship, as distinguished from that of his incarnations, is not conspicuous in modern India, especially in the north. In the south he is less overshadowed by Kṛishṇa, and many great temples have been erected in his honour. In Travancore, which is formally dedicated to him as his special domain, he is adored under the name of Padmanabha. But his real claim to reverence, his appeal to the Indian heart, is due to the fact that certain deified human heroes, particularly Râma and Kṛishṇa, are identified with him.

Deification is common in India[1]. It exists to the present day and even defunct Europeans do not escape its operation. In modern times, when the idea of reincarnation had become familiar, eminent men like Caitanya or Vallabhâcârya were declared after their death to be embodiments of Kṛishṇa without more ado, but in earlier ages the process was probably double. First of all the departed hero became a powerful ghost or deity in his own right, and then this deity was identified with a Brahmanic god. Many examples prove that a remarkable man receives worship after death quite apart from any idea of incarnation.

The incarnations of Vishṇu are most commonly given as ten[2] but are not all of the same character. The first five, namely, the Fish, Tortoise, Boar, Man-Lion and Dwarf, are mythical, and due to his identification with supernatural creatures playing a benevolent rôle in legends with which he had originally no connection. The sixth, however, Paraśu-râma or Râma with the axe, may contain historical elements. He is represented as a militant Brahman who in the second age of the world extermin-

[1] See many modern examples in Crooke, *Popular Religion and Folk Lore of Northern India*, chap. IV. and *Census of India*, 1901, vol. VI. *Bengal*, pp. 196–8, where are described various deified heroes who are adored in Bengal, such as Goveiyâ (a bandit), Sailesh, Karikh, Lárik, Amar Singh, and Gobind Raut (a slayer of tigers). Compare too the worship of Gopi Nath and Zinda Kaliana in the Panjâb as described in *Census of India*, 1901, vol. XVII. pp. 118–9.

[2] The Bhâgavata Purâna (I. iii.) and the Bhaktamâla (see *J.R.A.S.* 1909, pp. 621 ff.) give longer lists of 22 and 26, and the Pancarâtra gives 39. See Ahirbudhnya Saṃhitâ, v. 50–55.

ated the Kshatriyas, and after reclaiming Malabar from the sea, settled it with Brahmans. This legend clearly refers to a struggle for supremacy between the two upper castes, though we may doubt if the triumphs attributed to the priestly champion have any foundation in fact. The Râmâyaṇa[1] contains a singular account of a contest between this Râma and the greater hero of the same name in which Paraśu-râma admits the other's superiority. That is to say an epic edited under priestly supervision relates how the hero-god of the warriors vanquishes the hero-god of the priests, and this hero-god of the warriors is then worshipped by common consent as the greater divinity, but under priestly patronage. The tenacity and vitality of the Brahmans enabled them ultimately to lead the conqueror captive, and Râma-candra became a champion of Brahmanism as much as Paraśu-râma.

Very interesting too is the ninth avatâra (to leave for a moment the strict numerical order) or Buddha[2]. The reason assigned in Brahmanic literature for Vishṇu's appearance in this character is that he wished to mislead the enemies of the gods by false teaching, or that out of compassion for animals he preached the abolition of Vedic sacrifices. Neither explanation is very plausible and it is pretty clear that in the period when degenerate Buddhism offered no objection to deification and mythology, the Brahmans sanctioned the worship of the Buddha under their auspices. But they did so only in a half-hearted way. The Buddha was so important a personage that he had to be explained by the intervention, kindly or hostile, of a deity[3].

In his tenth incarnation or Kalkî[4], which has yet to take

[1] Book I, cantos 74–76.

[2] A parallel phenomenon is the belief found in Bali, that Buddha is Śiva's brother.

[3] For Brahmanic ideas about Buddha see Vishṇu Purâṇa, III. 18. The Bhâgavata Purâṇa, I. 3. 24 seems to make the Buddha incarnation future. It also counts Kapila and Ṛishabha, apparently identical with the founder of the Sânkhya and the first Jain saint, as incarnations. The Padma Purâṇa seems to ascribe not only Buddhism but the Mâyâ doctrine of Śankara to delusions deliberately inspired by gods. I have not been able to find the passage in the printed edition of the Purâṇa but it is quoted in Sanskrit by Aufrecht, *Cat. Cod. Bib. Bodl.* p. 14, and Muir, *Original Sanskrit Texts*, p. 198.

[4] See Norman in *Trans. Third Int. Congress of Religions*, II. p. 85. In the *Ind. Ant.* 1918, p. 145 Jayaswal tries to prove that Kalkî is a historical personage and identical with King Yaśodharman of Central India (about A.D. 500) and that the idea of

place, Vishṇu will appear as a Messiah, a conception possibly influenced by Persian ideas. Here, where we are in the realm of pure imagination, we see clearly what the signs of his avatâras are supposed to be. His mission is to sweep away the wicked and to ensure the triumph of the pious, but he comes as a warrior and a horseman, not as a teacher, and if he protects the good he does so by destroying evil. He has thus all the attributes of a Kshatriya hero, and that is as a matter of fact the real character of the two most important avatâras to which we now turn, Râma and Kṛishṇa.

Râma, often distinguished as Râma-candra, is usually treated as the seventh incarnation and anterior to Kṛishṇa, for he was born in the second age of this rapidly deteriorating world, whereas Kṛishṇa did not appear until the third. But his deification is later than that of Kṛishṇa and probably an imitation of it. He was the son of Daśaratha, King of Ayodhyâ or Oudh, but was driven into banishment by a palace intrigue. He married Sîtâ, daughter of the King of Mithilâ. She was carried off by Râvana, the demon tyrant of Ceylon, and Râma re-captured her with the aid of Hanuman, King of the Monkeys, and his hosts[1]. Is there any kernel of history in this story? An examination of Hindu legends suggests that they usually preserve names and genealogies correctly but distort facts, and fantastically combine independent narratives. Râma was a semi-divine hero in the tales of ancient Oudh, based on a real personality, and Ceylon was colonized by Indians of Aryan speech[2]. But can we assume that a king of Oudh really led an expedition to the far south, with the aid of ape-like aborigines?

his being a *future* saviour is late. This theory offers difficulties, for firstly there is no proof that the passages of the Mahabharata which mention Kalkî (III. 190, 13101; III. 191, 13111; XII. 340, 12968) are additions later than Yaśodharman and secondly if Kalkî was first a historical figure and then projected into the future we should expect to hear that he will *come again*, but such language is not quoted. On the other hand it seems quite likely (1) that there was an old tradition about a future saviour called Kalkî, (2) that Yaśodharman after defeating the Huns assumed the rôle, (3) and that when it was found that the golden age had not recommenced he was forgotten (as many pseudo-Messiahs have been) and Kalkî again became a hope for the future. Vincent Smith (*Hist. of India*, ed. III. p. 320) intimates that Yaśodharman performed considerable exploits but was inordinately boastful.

[1] Another version of the story which omits the expedition to Laṅka and makes Sîtâ the sister of Râma is found in the Dasaratha Jâtaka (641).

[2] But this colonization is attributed by tradition to Vijaya, not Râma.

It is doubtful, and the narrative of the Râmâyaṇa reads like poetic invention rather than distorted history. And yet, what can have prompted the legend except the occurrence of some such expedition? In Râma's wife Sîtâ, seem to be combined an agricultural goddess and a heroine of ancient romance, embodying the Hindu ideal of the true wife.

We have no record of the steps by which Râma and Kṛishṇa were deified, although in different parts of the epic they are presented in very different aspects, sometimes as little more than human, sometimes as nothing less than the Supreme Deity. But it can hardly be doubted that this deification owes something to the example of Buddhism. It may be said that the development of both Buddhism and Hinduism in the centuries immediately preceding and following our era gives parallel manifestations of the same popular tendency to deify great men. This is true, but the non-Buddhist forms of Indian religion while not objecting to deification did not particularly encourage it. But in this period, Buddhism and Jainism were powerful: both of them sanctioned the veneration of great teachers and, as they did not recognize sacrifice or adoration of gods, this veneration became the basis of their ceremonies and easily passed into worship. The Buddhists are not responsible for the introduction of deification, but the fact that it was to some extent the basis of their public ceremonies must have gone far to make the worship of Râma and Kṛishṇa seem natural.

It is commonly said that whereas the whole divine nature of Vishṇu was embodied in Kṛishṇa, Râma was only a partial incarnation. Half the god's essence took human form in him, the other half being distributed among his brothers. Kṛishṇa is a greater figure in popular esteem and receives the exclusive devotion of more worshippers. The name of Râma commands the reverence of most Hindus, and has a place in their prayers, but his figure has not been invested with the attributes (often of dubious moral value) which most attract sectarian devotion. His worship combines easily with the adoration of other deities. The great temple of Ramesvaram on Adam's Bridge is dedicated not to Râma himself but to the linga which he erected there, and Tulsi Das, the author of the Hindi Râmâyaṇa, while invoking Râma as the Supreme Lord and redeemer of the world, emphatically states[1] that his worship is not antagonistic to that of Śiva.

No inscriptions nor ancient references testify to the worship of Râma before our era and in the subsequent centuries two phases can be distinguished. First, Râma is a great hero, an incarnation of Vishṇu for a particular purpose and analogous to the Vâmana or any other avatâra: deserving as such of all respect but still not the object of any special cult. This is the view taken of Râma in the Mahâbhârata, the Purâṇas, the Raghuvaṃsa, and those parts of the Râmâyaṇa which go beyond it are probably late additions[2]. But secondly Râma becomes for his worshippers the supreme deity. Râmânuja (on the Vedânta sûtras, II. 42) mentions him and Kṛishṇa as two great incarnations in which the supreme being became manifest, and since Kṛishṇa was certainly worshipped at this period as identical with the All-God, it would appear that Râma held the same position. Yet it was not until the fourteenth or fifteenth century that he became for many sects the central and ultimate divine figure.

In the more liberal sects the worship of Râma passes easily into theism and it is the direct parent of the Kabirpanth and Sikhism, but unlike Kṛishṇaism it does not lead to erotic excess. Râma personifies the ideal of chivalry, Sîtâ of chastity. Less edifying forms of worship may attract more attention, but it must not be supposed that Râma is relegated to the penumbra of philosophic thought. If anything so multiplex as Hinduism can be said to have a watchword, it is the cry, Râm, Râm. The story of his adventures has travelled even further than the hero himself, and is known not only from Kashmir to Cape Comorin but from Bombay to Java and Indo-China where it is a common subject of art. In India the Râmâyaṇa is a favourite recitation among all classes, and dramatized versions of various episodes are performed as religious plays. Though two late Upanishads, the Râmapûrvatâpanîya and Râma-uttaratâpanîya extol Râma as the Supreme Being, there is no Râmapurâṇa. The fact is significant, as showing that his worship did not possess precisely those features of priestly sectarianism which mark the Purâṇas and perhaps that it is later than the

[1] See especially book VI. p. 67, in Growse's *Translation*.

[2] See Muir's *Sanskrit Texts*, vol. IV. especially pp. 441–491

Purâṇas. But it has inspired a large literature, more truly popular than anything that the Purâṇas contain. Thus we have the Sanskrit Râmâyaṇa itself, the Hindi Râmâyaṇa, the Tamil Râmâyaṇa of Kamban, and works like the Adhyâtma-Râmâyaṇa and Yoga-Vasiṣṭha-Râmâyaṇa[1]. Of all these, the Râmâyaṇa of Tulsi Das is specially remarkable and I shall speak of it later at some length.

4

Kṛishṇa, the other great incarnation of Vishṇu, is one of the most conspicuous figures in the Indian pantheon, but his historical origin remains obscure. The word which means black or dark blue occurs in the Ṛig Veda as the name of an otherwise unknown person. In the Chândogya Upanishad[2], Kṛishṇa, the son of Devakî, is mentioned as having been instructed by the sage Ghora of the Âṅgirasa clan, and it is probably implied that Kṛishṇa too belonged to that clan[3]. Later sectarian writers never quote this verse, but their silence may be due to the fact that the Upanishad does not refer to Kṛishṇa as if he were a deity, and merely says that he received from Ghora instruction after which he never thirsted again. The purport of it was that the sacrifice may be performed without rites, the various parts being typified by ordinary human actions, such as hunger, eating, laughter, liberality, righteousness, etc. This doctrine has some resemblance to Buddhist language[4] and if this Kṛishṇa is really the ancient hero out of whom the later deity was evolved, there may be an allusion to some simple form of worship which rejected ceremonial and was practised by the tribes to whom Kṛishṇa belonged. I shall recur to the question of these tribes

[1] Ekanâtha, who lived in the sixteenth century, calls the Adhyâtma R. a modern work. See Bhandarkar, *Vaishn. and Saivism*, page 48. The Yoga-Vasishṭha R. purports to be instruction given by Vasishṭha to Râma who wishes to abandon the world. Its date is uncertain but it is quoted by authors of the fourteenth century. It is very popular, especially in south India, where an abridgment in Tamil called Jñâna-Vasishṭha is much read. Its doctrine appears to be Vedântist with a good deal of Buddhist philosophy. Salvation is never to think that pleasures and pains are "mine."

[2] Chând. Up. III. 17. 6.

[3] The Kaush. Brâhm. says that Kṛishṇa was an Âṅgirasa XXX. g. The Anukramanî says that the Kṛishṇa of Ṛig Veda, VIII. 74 was an Âṅgirasa. For Ghora Âṅgirasa "the dread descendent of the Angirases" see Macdonell and Keith, *Vedic Index*, s.v.

[4] *E.g.* Dig. Nik. v. The Pâncarâtra expressly states that Yoga is worship of the heart and self-sacrifice, being thus a counterpart of the external sacrifice (bâhya-yâga).

and the Bhâgavata sect below, but in this section I am concerned with the personality of Kṛishṇa.

Vâsudeva is a well-known name of Kṛishṇa and a sûtra of Pâṇini[1], especially if taken in conjunction with the comment of Patañjali, appears to assert that it is not a clan name but the name of a god. If so Vâsudeva must have been recognized as a god in the fourth century B.C. He is mentioned in inscriptions which appear to date from about the second century B.C.[2] and in the last book of the Taittirîya Âraṇyaka[3], which however is a later addition of uncertain date.

The name Kṛishṇa occurs in Buddhist writings in the form Kaṇha, phonetically equivalent to Kṛishṇa. In the Dîgha Nikâya[4] we hear of the clan of the Kaṇhâyanas (= Kârshṇâyanas) and of one Kaṇha who became a great sage. This person may be the Kṛishṇa of the Ṛig Veda, but there is no proof that he is the same as our Kṛishṇa.

The Ghata-Jâtaka (No. 454) gives an account of Kṛishṇa's childhood and subsequent exploits which in many points corresponds with the Brahmanic legends of his life and contains several familar incidents and names, such as Vâsudeva, Baladeva, Kaṃsa. Yet it presents many peculiarities and is either an independent version or a misrepresentation of a popular story that had wandered far from its home. Jain tradition also shows that these tales were popular and were worked up into different forms, for the Jains have an elaborate system of ancient patriarchs which includes Vâsudevas and Baladevas. Kṛishṇa is the ninth of the Black Vâsudevas[5] and is connected with Dvâravatî or Dvârakâ. He will become the twelfth tîrthankara of the next world-period and a similar position will be attained by Devakî, Rohinî, Baladeva and Javakumâra, all members of his family. This is a striking proof of the popularity of the Kṛishṇa legend outside the Brahmanic religion.

[1] Pâṇ. IV. 3. 98, *Vâsudevârjunâbhyâm vun.* See Bhandarkar, *Vaishnavism and Śaivism*, p. 3 and *J.R.A.S.* 1910, p. 168. Sûtra 95, just above, appears to point to *bhakti*, faith or devotion, felt for this Vâsudeva.

[2] Especially the Besnagar column. See Rapson, *Ancient India*, p. 156 and various articles in *J.R.A.S.* 1909–10.

[3] X. i. vi.

[4] III. i. 23, Ulâro so Kaṇho isi ahosi. But this may refer to the Rishi mentioned in *R.V.* VIII. 74 who has not necessarily anything to do with the god Kṛishṇa.

[5] See Hemacandra Abhidhânacintâmani, Ed. Boehtlingk and Rien, p. 128, and Barnett's translation of the *Antagada Dasão*, pp. 13–15 and 67–82.

No references to Kṛishṇa except the above have been found in the earlier Upanishads and Sûtras. He is not mentioned in Manu but in one aspect or another he is the principal figure in the Mahâbhârata, yet not exactly the hero. The Râmâyaṇa would have no plot without Râma, but the story of the Mahâbhârata would not lose its unity if Kṛishṇa were omitted. He takes the side of the Pâṇḍavas, and is sometimes a chief sometimes a god but he is not essential to the action of the epic.

The legend represents him as the son of Vasudeva, who belonged to the Sâttvata sept[1] of the Yâdava tribe, and of his wife Devakî. It had been predicted to Kaṃsa, king of Mathura (Muttra), that one of her sons would kill him. He therefore slew her first six children: the seventh, Balarâma, who is often counted as an incarnation of Vishṇu, was transferred by divine intervention to the womb of Rohinî. Kṛishṇa, the eighth, escaped by more natural methods. His father was able to give him into the charge of Nanda, a herdsman, and his wife Yâsodâ who brought him up at Gokula and Vrindâvana. Here his youth was passed in sporting with the Gopîs or milkmaids, of whom he is said to have married a thousand. He had time, however, to perform acts of heroism, and after killing Kaṃsa, he transported the inhabitants of Mathura to the city of Dvârakâ which he had built on the coast of Gujarat. He became king of the Yâdavas and continued his mission of clearing the earth of tyrants and monsters. In the struggle between the Pâṇḍavas and the sons of Dhṛitarâshṭra he championed the cause of the former, and after the conclusion of the war retired to Dvârakâ. Internecine conflict broke out among the Yâdavas and annihilated the race. Kṛishṇa himself withdrew to the forest and was killed by a hunter called Jaras (old age) who shot him supposing him to be a deer.

In the Mahâbhârata and several Purâṇas this bare outline is distended with a plethora of miraculous incident remarkable even in Indian literature, and almost all possible forms of divine and human activity are attributed to this many-sided figure. We may indeed suspect that his personality is dual even in the simplest form of the legend for the scene changes from Mathurâ to Dvârakâ, and his character is not quite the same in the two regions. It is probable that an ancient military hero of the west

[1] Apparently the same as the Vṛishṇis.

has been combined with a deity or perhaps more than one deity. The pile of story, sentiment and theology which ages have heaped up round Kṛishṇa's name, represents him in three principal aspects. Firstly, he is a warrior who destroys the powers of evil. Secondly, he is associated with love in all its forms, ranging from amorous sport to the love of God in the most spiritual and mystical sense. Thirdly, he is not only a deity, but he actually becomes God in the European and also in the pantheistic acceptation of the word, and is the centre of a philosophic theology.

The first of these aspects is clearly the oldest and it is here, if anywhere, that we may hope to find some fragments of history. But the embellishments of poets and story-tellers have been so many that we can only point to features which may indicate a substratum of fact. In the legend, Kṛishṇa assists the Pâṇḍavas against the Kauravas. Now many think that the Pâṇḍavas represent a second and later immigration of Aryans into India, composed of tribes who had halted in the Himalayas and perhaps acquired some of the customs of the inhabitants, including polyandry, for the five Pâṇḍavas had one wife in common between them. Also, the meaning of the name Kṛishṇa, black, suggests that he was a chief of some non-Aryan tribe. It is, therefore, possible that one source of the Kṛishṇa myth is that a body of invading Aryans, described in the legend as the Pâṇḍavas, who had not exactly the same laws and beliefs as those already established in Hindustan, were aided by a powerful aboriginal chief, just as the Sisodias in Rajputana were aided by the Bhîls. It is possible too that Kṛishṇa's tribe may have come from Kabul or other mountainous districts of the north west, although one of the most definite points in the legend is his connection with the coast town of Dvârakâ. The fortifications of this town and the fruitless efforts of the demon king, Salva, to conquer it by seige are described in the Mahâbhârata[1], but the narrative is surrounded by an atmosphere of magic and miracle rather than of history[2].

[1] III. xv.

[2] It would seem that the temple of Dvârakâ was built between the composition of the narrative in the Mahâbhârata and of the Vishṇu Purâṇa, for while the former says the whole town was destroyed by the sea, the latter excepts the temple and says that whoever visits it is freed from all his sins. See Wilson, *Vishṇu Purâṇa*, v. p. 155.

Though it would not be reasonable to pick out the less fantastic parts of the Kṛishṇa legend and interpret them as history, yet we may fairly attach significance to the fact that many episodes represent him as in conflict with Brahmanic institutions and hardly maintaining the position of Vishṇu incarnate[1]. Thus he plunders Indra's garden and defeats the gods who attempt to resist him. He fights with Śiva and Skanda. He burns Benares and all its inhabitants. Yet he is called Upendra, which, whatever other explanations sectarian ingenuity may invent, can hardly mean anything but the Lesser Indra, and he fills the humble post of Arjuna's charioteer. His kinsmen seem to have been of little repute, for part of his mission was to destroy his own clan and after presiding over its annihilation in internecine strife, he was slain himself. In all this we see dimly the figure of some aboriginal hero who, though ultimately canonized, represented a force not in complete harmony with Brahmanic civilization. The figure has also many solar attributes but these need not mean that its origin is to be sought in a sun myth, but rather that, as many early deities were forms of the sun, solar attributes came to be a natural part of divinity and were ascribed to the deified Kṛishṇa just as they were to the deified Buddha[2].

Some authors hold that the historical Kṛishṇa was a teacher, similar to Zarathustra, and that though of the military class he was chiefly occupied in founding or supporting what was afterwards known as the religion of the Bhâgavatas, a theistic system inculcating the worship of one God, called Bhagavat, and perhaps identical with the Sun. It is probable that Kṛishṇa

[1] A most curious chapter of the Vishṇu Purâṇa (IV. 13) contains a vindication of Kṛishṇa's character and a picture of old tribal life.

[2] Neither can I agree with some scholars that Kṛishṇa is mainly and primarily a deity of vegetation. All Indian ideas about the Universe and God emphasize the interaction of life and death, growth and decay, spring and winter. Kṛishṇa is undoubtedly associated with life, growth and generation, but so is Śiva the destroyer, or rather the transmuter. The account in the Mahâbhâshya (on Pâṇ. III. 1. 26) of the masque representing the slaughter of Kaṃsa by Kṛishṇa is surely a slight foundation for the theory that Kṛishṇa was a nature god. It might be easily argued that Christ is a vegetation spirit, for not only is Easter a spring festival but there are numerous allusions to sowing and harvest in the Gospels and Paul illustrates the resurrection by the germination of corn. It is a mistake to seek for uniformity in the history of religion. There were in ancient times different types of mind which invented different kinds of gods, just as now professors invent different theories about gods.

the hero was connected with the worship of a special deity, but I see no evidence that he was primarily a teacher[1]. In the earlier legends he is a man of arms: in the later he is not one who devotes his life to teaching but a forceful personage who explains the nature of God and the universe at the most unexpected moments. Now the founders of religions such as Mahâvîra and Buddha preserve their character as teachers even in legend and do not accumulate miscellaneous heroic exploits. Similarly modern founders of sects, like Caitanya, though revered as incarnations, still retain their historical attributes. But on the other hand many men of action have been deified not because they taught anything but because they seemed to be more than human forces. Râma is a classical example of such deification and many local deities can be shown to be warriors, bandits and hunters whose powers inspired respect. It is said that there is a disposition in the Bombay Presidency to deify the Maratha leader Śivaji[2].

In his second aspect, Kṛishṇa is a pastoral deity, sporting among nymphs and cattle. It is possible that this Kṛishṇa is in his origin distinct from the violent and tragic hero of Dvârakâ. The two characters have little in common, except their lawlessness, and the date and locality of the two cycles of legend are different. But the death of Kaṃsa which is one of the oldest incidents in the story (for it is mentioned in the Mahâbhâshya[3]) belongs to both and Kaṃsa is consistently connected with Muttra. The Mahâbhârata is mainly concerned with Kṛishṇa the warrior: the few allusions in it to the freaks of the pastoral Kṛishṇa occur in passages suspected of being late interpolations and, even if they are genuine, show that little attention was paid to his youth. But in later works, the relative importance is reversed and the figure of the amorous herdsman almost banishes the warrior. We can trace the growth of this figure in the sculptures of the sixth century, in the Vishṇu and Bhâgavata Purâṇas and the Gîtâ-govinda (written about 1170). Even later is the worship of Râdhâ, Kṛishṇa's mistress, as a portion of the

[1] The Kṛishṇa of the Chândogya Upanishad *receives* instruction but it is not said that he was himself a teacher.

[2] Hopkins, *India Old and New*, p. 105.

[3] Bhandarkar. Allusions to Kṛishṇa in Mahâbhâshya, *Ind. Ant.* 1874, p. 14. For the pastoral Kṛishṇa see Bhandarkar, *Vaishṇavism and Śaivism*, chap. IX.

deity, who is supposed to have divided himself into male and female halves[1]. The birth and adventures of the pastoral Kṛishṇa are located in the land of Braj, the district round Muttra and among the tribe of the Âbhîras, but the warlike Kṛishṇa is connected with the west, although his exploits extend to the Ganges valley[2]. The Âbhîras, now called Ahirs, were nomadic herdsmen who came from the west and their movements between Kathiawar and Muttra may have something to do with the double location of the Kṛishṇa legend.

Both archæology and historical notices tell us something of the history of Muttra. It was a great Buddhist and Jain centre, as the statues and vihâras found there attest. Ptolemy calls it the city of the gods. Fa-Hsien (400 A.D.) describes it as Buddhist, but that faith was declining at the time of Hsüan Chuang's visit (*c.* 630 A.D.). The sculptural remains also indicate the presence of Græco-Bactrian influence. We need not therefore feel surprise if we find in the religious thought of Muttra elements traceable to Greece, Persia or Central Asia. Some claim that Christianity should be reckoned among these elements and I shall discuss the question elsewhere. Here I will only say that such ideas as were common to Christianity and to the religions of Greece and western Asia probably did penetrate to India by the northern route, but of specifically Christian ideas I see no proof. It is true that the pastoral Kṛishṇa is unlike all earlier Indian deities, but then no close parallel to him can be adduced from elsewhere, and, take him as a whole, he is a decidedly un-Christian figure. The resemblance to Christianity consists in the worship of a divine child, together with his mother. But this feature is absent in the New Testament and seems to have been borrowed from paganism by Christianity.

The legends of Muttra show even clearer traces than those already quoted of hostility between Kṛishṇa and Brahmanism. He forbids the worship of Indra[3], and when Indra in anger sends down a deluge of rain, he protects the country by holding

[1] The divinity of Râdhâ is taught specially in the Brahmavaivarta Purâṇa and the Nârada pañcarâtra, also called Jñânâmṛitasara. She is also described in the Gopâla-tâpanîya Upanishad of unknown date.

[2] But Kaṃsa appears in both series of legends, *i.e.*, in the Ghata-Jâtaka which contains no hint of the pastoral legends but is a variant of the story of the warlike Kṛishṇa.

[3] Vishṇu Purâṇa, v. 10, 11 from which the quotations in the text are taken. Much of it is repeated in the Harivamsa. See for instance H. 3808.

up over it the hill of Goburdhan, which is still one of the great centres of pilgrimage[1]. The language which the Vishṇu Purâṇa attributes to him is extremely remarkable. He interrupts a sacrifice which his fosterfather is offering to Indra and says, "We have neither fields nor houses: we wander about happily wherever we list, travelling in our waggons. What have we to do with Indra? Cattle and mountains are (our) gods. Brahmans offer worship with prayer: cultivators of the earth adore their landmarks but we who tend our herds in the forests and mountains should worship them and our kine."

This passage suggests that Kṛishṇa represents a tribe of highland nomads who worshipped mountains and cattle and came to terms with the Brahmanic ritual only after a struggle. The worship of mountain spirits is common in Central Asia, but I do not know of any evidence for cattle-worship in those regions. Clemens of Alexandria[2], writing at the end of the second century A.D., tells us that the Indians worshipped Herakles and Pan. The pastoral Kṛishṇa has considerable resemblance to Pan or a Faun, but no representations of such beings are recorded from Græco-Indian sculptures. Several Bacchic groups have however been discovered in Gandhara and also at Muttra[3] and Megasthenes recognized Dionysus in some Indian deity. Though the Bacchic revels and mysteries do not explain the pastoral element in the Kṛishṇa legend, they offer a parallel to some of its other features, such as the dancing and the crowd of women, and I am inclined to think that such Greek ideas may have germinated and proved fruitful in Muttra. The Greek king Menander is said to have occupied the city (*c.* 155 B.C.), and the sculptures found there indicate that Greek artistic forms were used to express Indian ideas. There may have been a similar fusion in religion.

In any case, Buddhism was predominant in Muttra for several centuries. It no doubt forbade the animal sacrifices of

[1] The Muttra cycle of legends cannot be very late for the inscription of Glai Lomor in Champa (811 A.D.) speaks of Nârâyana holding up Goburdhan and a Cambojan inscription of Prea Eynkosey (970 A.D.) speaks of the banks of the Yamunâ where Kṛishṇa sported. These legends must have been prevalent in India some time before they travelled so far. Some of them are depicted on a pillar found at Mandor and possibly referable to the fourth century A.D. See *Arch. Survey Ind.* 1905–1906, p. 135.

[2] Strom. III. 194. See M'Crindle, *Ancient India*, p. 183.

[3] Vincent Smith, *Fine Art in India*, pp. 134–138.

the Brahmans and favoured milder rites. It may even offer some explanation for the frivolous character of much in the Kṛishṇa legend[1]. Most Brahmanic deities, extraordinary as their conduct often is, are serious and imposing. But Buddhism claimed for itself the serious side of religion and while it tolerated local godlings treated them as fairies or elves. It was perhaps while Kṛishṇa was a humble rustic deity of this sort, with no claim to represent the Almighty, that there first gathered round him the cycle of light love-stories which has clung to him ever since. In the hands of the Brahmans his worship has undergone the strangest variations which touch the highest and lowest planes of Hinduism, but the Muttra legend still retains its special note of pastoral romance, and exhibits Kṛishṇa in two principal characters, as the divine child and as the divine lover. The mysteries of birth and of sexual union are congenial topics to Hindu theology, but in the cult of Muttra we are not concerned with reproduction as a world force, but simply with childhood and love as emotional manifestations of the deity. The same ideas occur in Christianity, and even in the Gospels Christ is compared to a bridegroom, but the Kṛishṇa legend is far more gross and naïve.

The infant Kṛishṇa is commonly adored in the form known as Makhan Chor or the Butter Thief[2]. This represents him as a crawling child holding out one hand full of curds or butter which he has stolen. We speak of idolizing a child, and when Hindu women worship this image they are unconsciously generalizing the process and worshipping childhood, its wayward pranks as well as its loveable simplicity, and though it is hard for a man to think of the freaks of the butter thief as a manifestation of divinity, yet clearly there is an analogy between these childish escapades and the caprices of mature deities, which are respectfully described as mysteries. If one admits the worship of the Bambino, it is not unreasonable to include in it admiration of his rogueries, and the tender playfulness which is permitted to enter into this cult appeals profoundly to

[1] In the Sutta-nipâta Mâra, the Evil One is called Kaṇha, the phonetic equivalent of Kṛishṇa in Prâkrit. Can it be that Mâra and his daughters have anything to do with Kṛishṇa and the Gopîs?

[2] Compare the Greek stories of the infant Hermes who steals Apollo's cattle and invents the lyre. Compare too, as having a general resemblance to fantastic Indian legends, the story of young Hephæstus.

Indian women. Images of the Makhan Chor are sold by thousands in the streets of Muttra.

Even more popular is the image known as Kanhaya, which represents the god as a young man playing the flute as he stands in a careless attitude, which has something of Hellenic grace. Kṛishṇa in this form is the beloved of the Gopîs, or milk-maids, of the land of Braj, and the spouse of Râdhâ, though she had no monopoly of him. The stories of his frolics with these damsels and the rites instituted in memory thereof have brought his worship into merited discredit. Krishnaism offers the most extensive manifestation to be found in the world of what W. James calls the theopathic condition as illustrated by nuns like Marguérite Marie Alacoque, Saint Gertrude and the more distinguished Saint Theresa. "To be loved by God and loved by him to distraction (jusqu'à la folie), Margaret melted away with love at the thought of such a thing....She said to God, 'Hold back, O my God, these torrents which overwhelm me or else enlarge my capacity for their reception'[1]." These are not the words of the Gîtâ-govinda or the Prem Sagar, as might be supposed, but of a Catholic Bishop describing the transports of Sister Marguérite Marie, and they illustrate the temper of Kṛishṇa's worshippers. But the verses of the Marathi poet, Tukaram, who lived about 1600 A.D. and sang the praises of Kṛishṇa, rise above this sentimentality though he uses the language of love. In a letter to Sivaji, who desired to see him, he wrote, "As a chaste wife longs only to see her lord, such am I to Viṭṭhala[2]. All the world is to me Viṭṭhala and nothing else: thee also I behold in him." He also wrote elsewhere, "he that taketh the unprotected to his heart and doeth to a servant the same kindness as to his own children, is assuredly the image of God." More recently Râmakṛishṇa, whose sayings breathe a wide intelligence as well as a wide charity, has given this religion of love an expression which, if somewhat too sexual to be perfectly in accordance with western taste, is nearly related to emotional Christianity. "A true lover sees his god as his nearest and dearest relative" he writes, "just as the shepherd women of

[1] Mgr. Bongard, *Histoire de la Bienheureuse Marguérite Marie.* Quoted by W. James, *Varieties of Religious Experience*, p. 343.

[2] Viṭṭhal or Viṭṭoba is a local deity of Pandharpur in the Deccan (perhaps a deified Brahman of the place) now identified with Kṛishṇa.

Vṛindâvana saw in Kṛishṇa not the Lord of the Universe but their own beloved....The knowledge of God may be likened to a man, while the love of God is like a woman. Knowledge has entry only up to the outer rooms of God, and no one can enter into the inner mysteries of God save a lover....Knowledge and love of God are ultimately one and the same. There is no difference between pure knowledge and pure love[1]."

These extracts show how Kṛishṇa as the object of the soul's desire assumes the place of the Supreme Being or God. But this surprising transformation[2] is not specially connected with the pastoral and erotic Kṛishṇa: the best known and most thorough-going exposition of his divinity is found in the Bhagavad-gîtâ, which represents him as being in his human aspect, a warrior and the charioteer of Arjuna. Probably some seventy-five millions to-day worship Kṛishṇa, especially under the name of Hari, as God in the pantheistic sense and naturally the more his identity with the supreme spirit is emphasized, the dimmer grow the legendary features which mark the hero of Muttra and Dvârakâ, and the human element in him is reduced to this very important point that the tie uniting him to his worshippers is one of sentiment and affection.

In the following chapters I shall treat of this worship when describing the various sects which practise it. A question of some importance for the history of Kṛishṇa's deification is the meaning of the name Vâsudeva. One explanation makes it a patronymic, son of Vasudeva, and supposes that when this prince Vâsudeva was deified his name, like Râma, was transferred to the deity. The other regards Vâsudeva as a name for the deity used by the Sâttvata clan and supposes that when Kṛishṇa was deified this already well-known divine name was bestowed on him. There is much to be said for this latter theory. As we have seen the Jains give the title Vâsudeva to a series of supermen, and a remarkable legend states[3] that a king called

[1] *Life and Sayings of Râmakṛishna.* Trans. F. Max Müller, pp. 137–8. The English poet Crashaw makes free use of religious metaphors drawn from love and even Francis Thompson represents God as the lover of the Soul, *e.g.* in his poem *Any Saint.*

[2] Though surprising, it can be paralleled in modern times for Kabir (*c.* 1400) was identified by his later followers with the supreme spirit.

[3] Mahâbhâr. Sabhâp. XIV. Vishṇu Pur. v. xxxiv. The name also occurs in the Taittirîya Âraṇyaka (i. 31) a work of moderate if not great antiquity Nâzâyaṇâya vidmahe Vasudevâya dhîmahi.

Paundraka who pretended to be a deity used the title Vâsudeva and ordered Kṛishṇa to cease using it, for which impertinence he was slain. This clearly implies that the title was something which could be detached from Kṛishṇa and not a mere patronymic. Indian writings countenance both etymologies of the word. As the name of the deity they derive it from *vas* to dwell, he in whom all things abide and who abides in all[1].

5

Śiva and Vishṇu are not in their nature different from other Indian ideas, high or low. They are the offspring of philosophic and poetic minds playing with a luxuriant popular mythology. But even in the epics they have already become fixed points in a flux of changing fancies and serve as receptacles in which the most diverse notions are collected and stored. Nearly all philosophy and superstition finds its place in Hinduism by being connected with one or both of them. The two worships are not characteristic of different periods: they coexist when they first become known to us as they do at the present day and in essential doctrines they are much alike. We have no name for this curious double theism in which each party describes its own deity as the supreme god or All-god, yet without denying the god of the other. Something similar might be produced in Christianity if different Churches were avowedly to worship different persons of the Trinity.

Śiva and Vishṇu are sometimes contrasted and occasionally their worshippers quarrel[2]. But the general inclination is rather

[1] See Vishṇu Pur. VI. v. See also Wilson, *Vishṇu Purâṇa*, I. pp. 2 and 17.

[2] Thus the Saura Purâṇa inveighs against the Mâdhva sect (XXXVIII.–XL.) and calls Vishṇu the servant of Śiva: a Purâṇic legal work called the Vriddha-Harita-Samhitâ is said to contain a polemic against Śiva. Occasionally we hear of collisions between the followers of Vishṇu and Śiva or the desecration of temples by hostile fanatics. But such conflicts take place most often not between widely different sects but between subdivisions of the same sect, *e.g.*, Ten-galais and Vada-galais. It would seem too that at present most Hindus of the higher castes avoid ostentatious membership of the modern sects, and though they may practise special devotion to either Vishṇu or Śiva, yet they visit the temples of both deities when they go on pilgrimages. Jogendra Nath Bhattacharya in his *Hindu Castes and Sects* says (p. 364) that aristocratic Brahmans usually keep in their private chapels both a salâgram representing Vishṇu and emblems representing Śiva and his spouse. Hence different observers vary in their estimates of the importance of sectarian divisions, some holding that sect is the essence of modern Hinduism and others that most educated Hindus do not worship a sectarian deity. The Kûrma Purâṇa, Part I. chap. XXII. contains some curious rules as to what deities should be worshipped by the various classes of men and spirits.

to make the two figures approximate by bestowing the same attributes on both. A deity must be able to satisfy emotional devotion: hence the Tamil Śivaite says of Śiva the destroyer, "one should worship in supreme love him who does kindness to the soul." But then the feature in the world which most impresses the Hindu is the constant change and destruction, and this must find a place in the All-god. Hence the sportive kindly Kṛishṇa comes to be declared the destroyer of the worlds[1]. It is as if in some vast Dravidian temple one wandered through two corridors differently ornamented and assigned to the priests of different rites but both leading to the same image. Hence it is not surprising to find that there is actually a deity—if indeed the term is suitable, but European vocabularies hardly provide one which meets the case—called Harihara (or Śankara-Nârâyaṇa), that is Śiva and Vishṇu combined. The Harivaṁsa contains a hymn addressed to him: fairly ancient sculptures attest the prevalence of his worship in the Deccan, especially at Badâmi, he was once the chief deity of Camboja and he is still popular in south India. Here besides being worshipped under his own name he has undergone a singular transformation and has probably been amalgamated with some aboriginal deity. Under the designation of Ayenâr (said to be a corruption of Harihara) he is extensively worshipped as a village god and reputed to be the son of Śiva and Vishṇu, the latter having kindly assumed the form of a woman to effect his birth.

Another form of this inclination to combine and unite the various manifestations of the Divine is the tendency to worship groups of gods, a practice as old as the Vedas. Thus many temples are dedicated to a group of five, namely, Śiva, Vishṇu, Dûrgâ, Gaṇeśa and the Sun and it is stated that every Hindu worships these five deities in his daily prayers[2]. The Trimûrti, or figure of Brahmâ, Śiva and Vishṇu, illustrates the worship of groups. Its importance has sometimes been over-estimated by Europeans from an idea that it corresponded to the Christian Trinity, but in reality this triad is late and has little significance. No stress is laid on the idea of three in one and the number of persons can be increased. The Brahma-vaivarta Purâṇa for instance adds Kṛishṇa to Brahmâ, Śiva and Vishṇu. The union

[1] Bhag.-gîtâ, XI. 23–34.

[2] See Srisa Chandra Vasu, *Daily practice of the Hindus*, p. 118.

of three personalities is merely a way of summing up the chief attributes of the All-God. Thus the Vishṇu Purâṇa[1] extols Vishṇu as being "Hiraṇyagarbha, Hari and Śaṅkara (*i.e.* Brahmâ, Vishṇu and Śiva), the creator, preserver and destroyer," but in another passage as him who is "Brahma, Îśvara and spirit (Puṁs), who with the three Guṇas (qualities of matter) is the cause of creation, preservation and destruction...." The origin of the triad, so far as it has any doctrinal or philosophical meaning, is probably to be sought in the personification of the three Guṇas[2].

[1] II. 1 and I. 1.

[2] See Maitrâyaṇa Up. v. 2. It is highly probable that the celebrated image at Elephanta is not a Trimûrti at all but a Maheśamûrti of Śiva. See Gopinâtha Rao, *Hindu Iconog.* II. 382.

CHAPTER XXVI

FEATURES OF HINDUISM: RITUAL, CASTE, SECT, FAITH

1

In the last chapter I traced the growth of the great gods Śiva and Vishṇu. The prominence of these figures is one of the marks which distinguish the later phase of Indian religion from the earlier. But it is also distinguished by various practices, institutions and beliefs, which are more or less connected with the new deities. Such are a new ritual, the elaboration of the caste system, the growth of sects, and the tendency to make devotion to a particular deity the essence of religion. In the present chapter I shall say something of these phenomena.

Hinduism has often and justly been compared to a jungle. As in the jungle every particle of soil seems to put forth its spirit in vegetable life and plants grow on plants, creepers and parasites on their more stalwart brethren, so in India art, commerce, warfare and crime, every human interest and aspiration seek for a manifestation in religion, and since men and women of all classes and occupations, all stages of education and civilization, have contributed to Hinduism, much of it seems low, foolish and even immoral. The jungle is not a park or garden. Whatever can grow in it, does grow. The Brahmans are not gardeners but forest officers. To attempt a history or description of Indian creeds seems an enterprise as vast, hopeless and pathless as a general account of European politics. As for many centuries the life of Europe has expressed itself in politics, so for even longer ages the life of India, which has more inhabitants than western Europe[1], has found expression in religion, speculation and philosophy, and has left of all this thought a voluminous record, mighty in bulk if wanting in dates and events. And why should it chronicle them? The truly religious mind does not care for the history of religion,

[1] The population of India (about 315 millions) is larger than that of Europe without Russia.

just as among us the scientific mind does not dwell on the history of science.

Yet in spite of their exuberance Hinduism and the jungle have considerable uniformity. Here and there in a tropical forest some well-grown tree or brilliant flower attracts attention, but the general impression left on the traveller by the vegetation as he passes through it mile after mile is infinite repetition as well as infinite luxuriance. And so in Hinduism. A monograph on one god or one teacher is an interesting study. But if we continue the experiment, different gods and different teachers are found to be much the same. We can write about Vishnuism and Śivaism as if they were different religions and this, though incomplete, is not incorrect. But in their higher phases both show much the same excellences and when degraded both lead to much the same abuses, except that the worship of Vishṇu does not allow animal sacrifices. This is true even of externals. In the temples of Madura, Poona and Benares, the deities, the rites, the doctrines, the race of the worshippers and the architecture are all different, yet the impression of uniformity is strong. In spite of divergences the religion is the same in all three places: is smacks of the soil and nothing like it can be found outside India.

Hinduism is an unusual combination of animism and pantheism, which are commonly regarded as the extremes of savage and of philosophic belief. In India both may be found separately but frequently they are combined in startling juxtaposition. The same person who worships Vishṇu as identical with the universe also worships him in the form of a pebble or plant[1]. The average Hindu, who cannot live permanently in the altitudes of pantheistic thought, regards his gods as great natural forces, akin to the mighty rivers which he also worships, irresistible and often beneficent but also capricious and destructive. Whereas Judaism, Christianity and Islam all identify the moral law with the will and conduct of the deity, in Hinduism this is not completely admitted in practice, though a library might be filled

[1] But compare the English poet

"Flower in the crannied wall,
I pluck you out of the crannies,
......but if I could understand
What you are, root and all, and all in all
I should know what God and man is."

with the beautiful things that have been said about man and God. The outward forms of Indian religion are pagan after the fashion of the ancient world, a fashion which has in most lands passed away. But whereas in the fourth century A.D. European paganism, despite the efforts of anti-christian eclectics, proved inelastic and incapable of satisfying new religious cravings, this did not happen in India. The bottles of Hinduism have always proved capable of holding all the wine poured into them. When a new sentiment takes possession of men's souls, such as love, repentance, or the sense of sin, some deity of many shapes and sympathies straightway adapts himself to the needs of his worshippers. And yet in so doing the deity, though he enlarges himself, does not change, and the result is that we often meet with strange anachronisms, as if Jephthah should listen appreciatively to the Sermon on the Mount and then sacrifice his daughter to Christ. Many Hindu temples are served by dancing girls who are admittedly prostitutes[1], an institution which takes us back to the cultus of Corinth and Babylon and is without parallel in any nation on approximately the same level of civilization. Only British law prevents widows from being burned with their dead husbands, though even in the Vedic age the custom had been discontinued as barbarous[2]. But for the same legislation, human sacrifice would probably be common. What the gods do and what their worshippers do in their service cannot according to Hindu opinion be judged by ordinary laws of right and wrong. The god is supra-moral: the worshipper when he enters the temple leaves conventionality outside.

Yet it is unfair to represent Hinduism as characterized by licence and cruelty. Such tendencies are counterbalanced by the strength and prevalence of ideas based on renunciation and self-effacement. All desire, all attachment to the world is an evil; all self-assertion is wrong. Hinduism is constantly in extremes: sometimes it exults in the dances of Kṛishṇa or the destructive fury of Kâlî: more often it struggles for release from the transitory and for union with the permanent and real by

[1] Efforts are now being made by Hindus to suppress this institution.

[2] In the Vedic funeral ceremonies the wife lies down by her dead husband and is called back to the world of the living which points to an earlier form of the rite where she died with him. But even at this period, those who did not follow the Vedic customs may have killed widows with their husbands (see too Ath. Veda, XII. 3), and later, the invaders from Central Asia probably reinforced the usage. The much-abused Tantras forbid it.

self-denial or rather self-negation, which aims at the total suppression of both pleasure and pain. This is on the whole its dominant note.

In the records accessible to us the transition from Brahmanism—that is, the religion of the Vedas and Brâhmaṇas—to Hinduism does not appear as direct but as masked by Buddhism. We see Buddhism grow at the expense of Brahmanism. We are then conscious that it becomes profoundly modified under the influence of new ideas. We see it decay and the religion of the Brahmans emerge victorious. But that religion is not what it was when Buddhism first arose, and is henceforth generally known as Hinduism. The materials for studying the period in which the change occurred—say 400 B.C. to 400 A.D.—are not scanty, but they do not facilitate chronological investigation. Art and architecture are mainly Buddhist until the Gupta period (*c.* 320 A.D.) and literature, though plentiful, is undated. The Mahâbhârata and Râmâyaṇa must have been edited in the course of these 800 years, but they consist of different strata and it is not easy to separate and arrange them without assuming what we want to prove. From 400 B.C. (if not from an earlier date) onwards there grew up a great volume of epic poetry, founded on popular ballads, telling the stories of Râma and the Pâṇḍavas[1]. It was distinct from the canonical literatures of both Brahmans and Buddhists, but though it was not in its essential character religious, yet so general in India is the interest in religion that whole theological treatises were incorporated in these stories without loss, in Indian opinion, to the interest of the narrative. If at the present day a congregation is seen in

[1] For the history of the Râmâyaṇa and Mahâbhârata and the dates assignable to the different periods of growth, see Winternitz, *Gesch. Ind. Lit.* vol. I. p. 403 and p. 439. Also Hopkins' *Great Epic of India*, p. 397. The two poems had assumed something like their present form in the second and fourth centuries A.D. respectively. These are probably the latest dates for any substantial additions or alterations and there is considerable evidence that poems called Bhârata and Râmâyaṇa were well known early in the Christian era. Thus in Aśvaghosha's Sûtrâlankâra (story XXIV) they are mentioned as warlike poems inculcating unbuddhist views. The Râmâyaṇa is mentioned in the Mahâvibhâshâ and was known to Vasubandhu (*J.R.A.S.* 1907, p. 99). A Cambojan inscription dating from the first years of the seventh century records arrangements made for the recitation of the Râmâyaṇa, Purâṇa and complete (aśesha) Bhârata, which implies that they were known in India considerably earlier. See Barth, *Inscrip. Sanscrites de Cambodge*, pp. 29–31. The Mahabharata itself admits that it is the result of gradual growth for in the opening section it says that the Bhârata consists of 8800 verses, 24,000 verses and 100,000 verses.

a Hindu temple listening to a recitation, the text which is being chanted will often prove to be part of the Mahâbhârata. Such a ceremony is not due to forgetfulness of the Veda but is a repetition of what happened long before our era when rhapsodists strung together popular narratives and popular theology. Such theology cannot be rigidly separated from Brahmanism and Buddhism. It grew up under their influence and accepted their simpler ideas. But it brought with it popular beliefs which did not strictly speaking belong to either system. By attacking the main Brahmanic doctrines the Buddhists gave the popular religion its opportunity. For instance, they condemned animal sacrifices and derided the idea that trained priests and complicated rites are necessary. This did not destroy the influence of the Brahmans but it disposed them to admit that the Vedic sacrifices are not the only means of salvation and to authorize other rites and beliefs. It was about this time, too, that a series of invasions began to pour into India from the north-west. It may be hard to distinguish between the foreign beliefs which they introduced and the Indian beliefs which they accepted and modified. But it is clear that their general effect was to upset traditional ideas associated with a ritual and learning which required lifelong study.

2

It has been well said[1] that Buddhism did not waste away in India until rival sects had appropriated from it everything they could make use of. Perhaps Hinduism had an even stronger doctrinal influence on Buddhism. The deification of the Buddha, the invention of Bodhisattvas who are equivalent to gods and the extraordinary alliance between late Buddhism and Śivaism, are all instances of the general Indian view overcoming the special Buddhist view. But Buddhism is closely connected with the theory of incarnations and the development of the Advaita philosophy, and in the externals of religion, in rites, ceremonies and institutions, its influence was great and lasting. We may take first the doctrine of Ahiṃsâ, non-injury, or in other words the sanctity of animal life. This beautiful doctrine, the glory of India, if not invented by the Buddha at least arose in schools which were not Brahmanic and were related to the Jain and

[1] Hardy, *Indische Religionsgeschichte*, p. 101.

Buddhist movements. It formed no part of the Vedic religion in which sacrifice often meant butchery. But in Hinduism, it meets with extensive though not universal acceptance. With the Vaishṇavas it is an article of faith nor do the worshippers of Śiva usually propitiate him with animal sacrifices, though these are offered by the Śâktas and also by the small class of Brahmans who still preserve the Vedic ritual[1]. Hardly any Hindus habitually eat meat and most abhor it, especially beef. Yet beef-eating seems to have been permitted in Vedic times and even when parts of the Mahâbhârata were composed.

Apart from animal sacrifices Buddhism was the main agent in effecting a mighty revolution in worship and ritual. One is tempted to regard the change as total and complete, but such wide assertions are rarely true in India: customs and institutions are not swept away by reformers but are cut down like the grass and like the grass grow up again. They sometimes die out but they are rarely destroyed. The Vedic sacrifices are still occasionally offered[2], but for many centuries have been almost entirely superseded by another form of worship associated with temples and the veneration of images. This must have become the dominant form of Hindu cultus in the first few centuries of our era and probably earlier. It is one of the ironies of fate that the Buddha and his followers should be responsible for the growth of image worship, but it seems to be true. He laughed at sacrifices and left to his disciples only two forms of religious exercise, sermons and meditation. For Indian monks, this was perhaps sufficient, but the laity craved for some outward form of worship. This was soon found in the respect shown to the memory of the Buddha and the relics of his body, although Hinduism never took kindly to relic worship. We hear too of Cetiyas. In the Piṭakas this word means a popular shrine unconnected with either Buddhist or Brahmanic ceremonial, sometimes

[1] But some of these latter sacrifice images made of dough instead of living animals.

[2] It is said that the Agnishtoma was performed in Benares in 1898, and in the last few years I am told that one or two Vedic sacrifices have been offered annually in various parts of southern India. I have myself seen the sites where such sacrifices were offered in 1908–9 in Mysore city and in Chidambaram, and in 1912 at Wei near Poona. The most usual form of sacrifice now-a-days is said to be the Vâjapeya. Much Vedic ritual is still preserved in the domestic life of the Nambathiri and other Brahmans of southern India. See Cochin, *Tribes and Castes*, and Thurston, *Castes and Tribes of southern India.*

perhaps merely a sacred tree or stone, probably honoured by such simple rites as decorating it with paint or flowers. A little later, in Buddhist times, the Cetiya became a cenotaph or reliquary, generally located near a monastery and surrounded by a passage for reverential circumambulation.

Allusions in the Piṭakas also indicate that then as now there were fairs. The early Buddhists thought that though such gatherings were not edifying they might be made so. They erected sacred buildings near a monastery, and held festivals so that people might collect together, visit a holy place, and hear sermons. In the earliest known sanctuaries, the funeral monument (for we can scarcely doubt that this is the origin of the stûpa)[1] has already assumed the conventional form known as Dagoba, consisting of a dome and chest of relics, with a spire at the top, the whole surrounded by railings or a colonnade, but though the carving is lavish, no figure of the Buddha himself is to be seen. He is represented by a symbol such as a footprint, wheel, or tree. But in the later school of sculpture known as Gandhara or Græco-Buddhist he is frequently shown in a full length portrait. This difference is remarkable. It is easy to say that in the older school the Buddha was not depicted out of reverence, but less easy to see why such delineation should have shocked an Indian. But at any rate there is no difficulty in understanding that Greeks or artists influenced by Greeks would think it obvious and proper to make an effigy of their principal hero.

In these shrines we have if not the origin of the Hindu temple, at any rate a parallel development more nearly allied to it than anything in the Vedic religion[2]. For the Buddhist shrine was a monument built over a receptacle containing relics and the essential feature of Hindu temples is a cell containing an image or emblem and generally surmounted by a tower. The surrounding courts and corridors may assume gigantic proportions, but the central shrine is never large. Images had no place

[1] The outline of a stûpa may be due to imitation of houses constructed with curved bamboos as Vincent Smith contends (*History of Fine Art*, p. 17). But this is compatible with the view that stone buildings with this curved outline had come to be used specially as funeral monuments before Buddhism popularized in India and all Eastern Asia the architectural form called stûpa.

[2] The temple of Aihole near Badami seems to be a connecting link between a Buddhist stûpa with a pradakshiṇa path and a Hindu shrine.

in the Vedic sacrifices and those now worshipped in temples are generally small and rude, and sometimes (as at Bhuvaneshwar and Srirangam) the deity is represented by a block or carved stone which cannot be moved, and may have been honoured as a sacred rock long before the name of Vishṇu or Śiva was known in those regions[1]. The conspicuous statues often found outside the shrine are not generally worshipped and are merely ornaments. Buddhism did not create the type of ritual now used in Hindu temples, yet it contributed towards it, for it attacked the old Brahmanic sacrifices, it countenanced the idea that particular places and objects are holy, and it encouraged the use of images. It is strange that these wide-spread ideas should find no place in the Vedic religion, but even now-a-days whenever the old Vedic sacrifices are celebrated they are uncontaminated by the temple ceremonial. More than this, the priests or Pujâris who officiate in temples are not always Brahmans and they rarely enjoy much consideration[2]. This curious and marked feature may be connected with the inveterate Indian feeling that, though it is well to multiply rites and rules for neophytes, no great respect is due to men occupied with mere ceremonial. But it also testifies to a dim consciousness that modern temples and their ceremonies have little to do with the thoughts and mode of life which made the Brahmans a force in India. In many ways the Brahmans dissociate themselves from popular religion. Those of good family will not perform religious rites for Śûdras and treat the Brahmans who do so as inferiors[3].

The simplest ceremonial in use at the present day is that employed in some Śivaite temples. It consists in placing leaves on the linga and pouring holy water over it. These rites, which may be descended from prehistoric stone worship, are generally

[1] In most temples (at least in southern India) there are two images: the *mûla-vigraha* which is of stone and fixed in the sanctuary, and the *utsava-vigraha* which is smaller, made of metal and carried in processions.

[2] Thus Bhaṭṭâchârya (*Hindu Castes and Sects*, p. 127) enumerates eleven classes of Brahmans, who "have a very low status on account of their being connected with the great public shrines," and adds that mere residence in a place of pilgrimage for a few generations tends to lower the status of a Brahmanic family.

[3] Thus in Bengal there is a special class, the Barna Brahmans, who perform religious rites for the lower castes, and are divided into six classes according to the castes to whom they minister. Other Brahmans will not eat or intermarry with them or even take water from them.

accompanied by the reading of a Purâṇa. But the commonest form of temple ritual consists in treating the image or symbol as an honoured human being[1]. It is awakened, bathed, dressed and put to bed at the close of day. Meals are served to it at the usual hours. The food thus offered is called *prasâd* (or favour) and is eaten by the devout. Once or twice a day the god holds a levee and on festivals he is carried in procession. These ceremonies are specially characteristic of the worship of Kṛishṇa whose images receive all the endearments lavished on a pet child. But they are also used in the temples of Śiva and Parvatî, and no less than twenty-two of them are performed in the course of the day at the temple of Bhuvaneshwar in Orissa. It is clear that the spirit of these rites is very different from that which inspires public worship in other civilized countries at the present day. They are not congregational or didactic, though if any of the faithful are in the temple at the time of the god's levee it is proper for them to enter and salute him. Neither do they recall the magical ceremonies of the Vedic sacrifices[2]. The waving of lights (arati) before the god and the burning of incense are almost the only acts suggestive of ecclesiastical ritual. The rest consists in treating a symbol or image as if it were a living thing capable of enjoying simple physical pleasures. Here there are two strata. We have really ancient rites, such as the anointing or ornamenting of stones and offerings of food in sacred places. In this class too we may reckon the sacrifice of goats (and formerly of human beings) to Kâlî[3]. But on the other hand the growing idea of Bhakti, that is faith or devotion, imported a sentimental element and the worshipper endeavoured to pet, caress and amuse the deity.

It is hard to see anything either healthy or artistic in this

[1] This is extraordinarily like the temple ritual of the ancient Egyptians. For some account of the construction and ritual of south Indian temples see Richards in *J. of Mythic Soc.* 1919, pp. 158–167.

[2] But Vedic mantras are used in these ceremonies. The libations of water or other liquids are said to be accompanied by the mantras recited at the Soma sacrifice.

[3] At these sacrifices there is no elaborate ritual or suggestion of symbolism. The animal is beheaded and the inference is that Kâlî likes it. Similarly simple is the offering of coco-nuts to Kâlî. The worshipper gives a nut to the pujâri who splits it in two with an axe, spills the milk and hands back half the nut to the worshipper. This is the sort of primitive offering that might be made to an African fetish.

emotional ritual. The low and foolish character of many temple ceremonies disgusts even appreciative foreigners, but these services are not the whole of Hindu worship. All Hindus perform in the course of the day numerous acts of private devotion varying according to sect, and a pious man is not dependent on the temple like a catholic on his church. Indian life is largely occupied with these private, intimate, individual observances, hardly noticeable as ceremonies and concerned with such things as dressing, ablution and the preparation of food.

The monastic institutions of India seem due to Buddhism. There were wandering monks before the Buddha's time, but the practice of founding establishments where they could reside permanently, originated in his order. There appears to be no record of Hindu (as opposed to Buddhist) monasteries before the time of Śaṅkara in the ninth century, though there must have been places where the learned congregated or where wandering ascetics could lodge. Śaṅkara perceived the advantage of the cenobitic life for organizing religion and founded a number of maṭhs or colleges. Subsequent religious leaders imitated him. At the present day these institutions are common, yet it is clear that the wandering spirit is strong in Hindus and that they do not take to monastic discipline and fixed residence as readily as Tibetans and Burmese. A maṭh is not so much a convent as the abode of a teacher. His pupils frequent it and may become semi-resident: aged pilgrims may make it their last home, but the inmates are not a permanent body following a fixed rule like the monks of a Vihâra. The Sattras of Assam, however, are true monasteries (though even there vows and monastic costume are unknown) and so are the establishments of the Swâminârâyaṇa sect at Ahmedabad and Wartâl.

3

The vast and complicated organization of caste is mainly a post-Vedic growth and in the Buddha's time was only in the making[1]. His order was open to all classes alike, but this does not imply that he was adverse to caste, so far as it then pre-

[1] See especially the Ambaṭṭha Sûtta (Dig. Nik. 3) and Rhys Davids's introduction.

vailed, or denied that men are divided into categories determined by their deeds in other births. But on the whole the influence of Buddhism was unfavourable to caste, especially to the pretensions of the Brahmans, and an extant polemic against caste is ascribed (though doubtfully) to Aśvaghosha[1]. On the other hand, though caste is in its origin the expression of a social rather than of a religious tendency, the whole institution and mechanism have long been supported and exploited by the Brahmans. Few of them would dispute the proposition that a man cannot be a Hindu unless he belongs to a caste. The reason of this support is undisguised, namely, that they are the first and chief caste. They make their own position a matter of religion and claim the power of purifying and rehabilitating those who have lost caste but they do not usually interfere with the rules of other castes or excommunicate those who break them[2]. That is the business of the Pancayat or caste council.

Sometimes religion and caste are in opposition, for many modern religious leaders have begun by declaring that among believers there are no social distinctions. This is true not only of teachers whose orthodoxy is dubious, such as Nânak, the founder of the Sikhs, and Basava, the founder of the Lingâyats[3], but also of Vallabhâcârya and Caitanya. But in nearly all cases caste reasserts itself. The religious teachers of the sect receive extravagant respect and form a body apart. This phenomenon, which recurs in nearly all communities, shows how the Brahmans established their position. At the same time social distinctions make themselves felt among the laity, and those who claim to be of good position dissociate themselves from those of lower birth. The sect ends by observing caste on ordinary occasions, and it is only in some temples (such as that of Jagannath at Puri)[4] that the worshippers mix and eat a sacred meal together. Sometimes, however, the sect which renounces caste becomes

[1] See Weber, *Die Vajrasuchi* and Nanjio, Catal. No. 1303. In Ceylon at the present day only members of the higher castes can become Bhikkhus.

[2] But it is said that in Southern India serious questions of caste are reported to the abbot of the Sringeri monastery for his decision.

[3] The modern Lingâyats demur to the statement that their founder rejected caste.

[4] So too in the cakras of the Śâktists all castes are equal during the performance of the ceremony.

itself a caste. Thus, the Sikhs have become almost a nation and other modern castes arising out of sects are the Atiths, who are Śivaites, the Saraks, who appear to have been originally Buddhists, and the Baishnabs (Vaishnavas), a name commonly given in Bengal to those followers of Caitanya who persist in the original rule of disregarding caste regulations within the sect, and hence now form a separate community. But as a rule sect and caste are not co-extensive and the caste is not a religious corporation. Thus the different subdivisions of the Baniyas belong to different sects and even in the same subdivision there is no religious uniformity[1].

Caste in its later developments is so complex and irregular, that it is impossible to summarize it in a formula or explain it as the development of one principle. In the earliest form known two principles are already in operation. We have first racial distinction. The three upper castes represent the invading Aryans, the fourth the races whom they found in India. In the modern system of caste, race is not a strong factor. Many who claim to be Brahmans and Kshatriyas have no Aryan blood, but still the Aryan element is strongest in the highest castes and decreases as we descend the social scale and also decreases in the higher castes in proportion as we move from the north-west to the east and south. But secondly in the three upper castes the dividing principle, as reported in the earliest accounts, is not race but occupation. We find in most Aryan countries a division into nobles and people, but in India these two classes become three, the priests having been able to assume a prominence unknown elsewhere and to stamp on literature their claim to the highest rank. This claim was probably never admitted in practice so completely as the priests desired. It was certainly disputed in Buddhist times and I have myself heard a young Rajput say that the Brahmans falsified the Epics so as to give themselves the first place.

It is not necessary for our purpose to describe the details of the modern caste system. Its effect on Indian religion has been considerable, for it created the social atmosphere in which the

[1] Some (Khandelwals, Dasa Srimalis and Palliwals) include both Jains and Vaishnavas: the Agarwals are mostly Vaishnavas but some of them are Jains and some worship Śiva and Kâlî. Jogendra Nath Bhattacharya, *Hindu Castes and Sects*, pp. 205 ff.

various beliefs grew up and it has furnished the Brahmans with the means of establishing their authority. But many religious reformers preached that in religion caste does not exist—that there is neither Jew nor Gentile in the language of another creed —and though the application of this theory is never complete, the imperfection is the result not of religious opposition but of social pressure. Hindu life is permeated by the instinct that society must be divided into communities having some common interest and refusing to intermarry or eat with other communities. The long list of modern castes hardly bears even a theoretical relation to the four classes of Vedic times[1]. Numerous subdivisions with exclusive rules as to intermarriage and eating have arisen among the Brahmans and the strength of this fissiparous instinct is seen among the Mohammedans who nominally have no caste but yet are divided into groups with much the same restrictions.

This remarkable tendency to form exclusive corporations is perhaps correlated with the absence of political life in India. Such ideas as nationality, citizenship, allegiance to a certain prince, patriotic feelings for a certain territory are rarer and vaguer than elsewhere, and yet the Hindu is dependent on his fellows and does not like to stand alone. So finding little satisfaction in the city or state he clings the more tenaciously to smaller corporations. These have no one character: they are not founded on any one logical principle but merely on the need felt by people who have something in common to associate together. Many are based on tribal divisions; some, such as the Marathas and Newars, may be said to be nationalities. In many the bond of union is occupation, in a few it is sectarian religion. We can still observe how members of a caste who migrate from their original residence tend to form an entirely new caste, and how intertribal marriages among the aborigines create new tribes.

[1] The names used are not the same. The four Vedic castes are called *Varṇa*: the hundreds of modern castes are called *Jâti*.

4

Sect[1] must not be confounded with caste. Hindu sects are of many kinds; some, if not militant, are at least exceedingly self-confident. Others are so gentle in stating their views that they might be called schools rather than sects, were the word not too intellectual. The notion that any creed or code can be *quod semper, quod ubique, quod ab omnibus*, is less prevalent than in Europe and even the Veda, though it is the eternal word, is admitted to exist in several recensions. Hinduism is possible as a creed only to those who select. In its literal sense it means simply all the beliefs and rites recognized in India, too multifarious and inconsistent for the most hospitable and addled brain to hold. But the Hindus, who are as loth to abolish queer beliefs and practices as they are to take animal life, are also the most determined seekers after a satisfying form of religion. Brahmanic ritual and Buddhist monasticism demand the dedication of a life. Not every one can afford that, but the sect is open to all. It attempts to sort out of the chaos of mythology and superstition something which all can understand and all may find useful. It selects some aspect of Hinduism and makes the best of it. Sects usually start by preaching theism and equality in the sight of God, but in a few generations mythology and social distinctions creep in. Hence though the prevalence of sect is undoubtedly a feature of modern Hinduism it is also intelligible that some observers should assert that most Hindus belong to the same general religion and that only the minority are definitely sectarian. The sectarian tendency is stronger in Vishnuism than in Śivaism. The latter has produced some definite sects, as, for instance, Lingâyats, but is not like Vishnuism split up into a number of Churches each founded by a human teacher and provided by him with a special creed.

Most Indian sects are in their origin theistic, that is to say, they take a particular deity and identify him with the Supreme Being. But the pantheistic tendency does not disappear. Popular religion naturally desires a personal deity. But it is significant that the personal deity frequently assumes pantheistic attributes and is declared to be both the world and the

[1] Sampradâya seems to be the ordinary Sanskrit word for sectarian doctrine It means traditional teaching transmitted from one teacher to another.

human soul. The best known sects arose after Islam had entered India and some of them, such as the Sikhs, show a blending of Hindu and Moslem ideas. But if Mohammedan influence favoured the formation of corporations pledged to worship one particular deity, it acted less by introducing something new than by quickening a line of thought already existing. The Bhagavad-gîtâ is as complete an exposition of sectarian pantheism as any utterances posterior to Mohammedanism.

The characteristic doctrine of sectarian Hinduism is *bhakti*, faith or devotion. The older word *śraddhâ*, which is found in the Vedas, is less emotional for it means simply belief in the existence of a deity, whereas *bhakti* can often be rendered by love. It is passionate, self-oblivious devotion to a deity who in return (though many would say there is no bartering) bestows his grace (*prasâda* or *anugraha*). St Augustine in defining faith says: "Quid est credere in Deum? credendo amare, credendo diligere, credendo in eum ire, et ejus membris incorporari[1]." This is an excellent paraphrase of *bhakti* and the words have an oriental ring which is not quite that of the New Testament. Though the doctrine of *bhakti* marks the beginning of a new epoch in Hinduism it is not necessary to regard it as an importation or due to Christianity. About the time of the Christian era there was felt in many countries a craving for a gentler and more emotional worship and though the history of Bhaktism is obscure, Indian literature shows plainly how it may be a development of native ideas. Its first great textbook is the Bhagavad-gîtâ, but it is also mentioned in the last verse of the Śvetâśvatara Upanishad and Pâṇini appears to allude to *bhakti* felt for[2] Vâsudeva. The Kaṭhâ Upanishad[3] contains the following passage:

"That Âtman cannot be gained by the Veda, nor by understanding nor by much learning. He whom the Âtman chooses, by him the Âtman can be gained. The Âtman chooses him as his own." Here we have not the idea of faith or love, but we have the negative statement that the Âtman is not won by knowledge and the positive statement that this Âtman chooses

[1] I am discussing elsewhere the possible debt which Christianity and Hinduism may owe to one another.

[2] Pâṇini, IV. 3. 95–98.

[3] Kaṭhâ Up. I. 1. 2, 23.

his own. In the Ṛig Veda[1] there is a poem put into the mouth of Vac or speech, containing such sentiments as "I give wealth to him who gives sacrifice....I am that through which one eats, breathes, sees, and hears....Him that I love I make strong, to be a priest, a seer, a sage." This reads like an ancient preliminary study for the Bhagavad-gîtâ. Like Kṛishṇa the deity claims to be in all and, like him, to reward her votaries. It is true that the "Come unto me" is not distinctly expressed, but it is surely struggling for expression[2]. Again, in the Kaushîtaki Upanishad (III. 1 and 2) Indra says to Pratardana, who had asked him for a boon, "Know me only: that is, what I deem most beneficial to man, that he should know me....He who meditates on me as life and immortality gains his full life in this world and in heaven immortality." Here the relation of the devotee to the deity is purely intellectual not emotional, but the idea that intellectual devotion directed to a particular deity will be rewarded is clearly present. In the Ṛig Veda this same Indra is called a deliverer and advocate; a friend, a brother and a father; even a father and mother in one. Here the worshipper does not talk of *bhakti* because he does not analyze his feelings, but clearly these phrases are inspired by affectionate devotion.

Nor is the spirit of *bhakti* absent from Buddhism. The severe doctrine of the older schools declares that the Buddha is simply a teacher and that every man must save himself. But since the teacher is the source of the knowledge which saves, it is natural to feel for him grateful and affectionate devotion. This sentiment permeates the two books of poems called Thera and Therîgâthâ and sometimes finds clear expression[3]. In the commentary on the Dhammapada[4] the doctrine of salvation by devotion is affirmed in its extreme form, namely that a dying man who has faith in the Buddha will be reborn in heaven. But this commentary is not of early date and the doctrine quoted is probably an instance of the Hinayana borrowing the attractive features of the Mahayana. The sutras about Amitâbha's paradise, which were composed about the time of the Christian era and owe something to Persian though not to Christian

[1] R.V. x. 125.

[2] Compare too the hymns of the R.V. to Varuṇa as a rudimentary expression of Bhakti from the worshipper's point of view.

[3] *E.g.* Theragâthâ, 818–841 and 1231–1245.

[4] I. 2.

influence, preach faith in Amitâbha as the whole of religion. They who believe in him and call on his name will go to heaven.

When bhakti was once accepted as a part of Indian religion, it was erected into a principle, analogous or superior to knowledge and was defined in Sûtras[1] similar to those of the Sâṅkhya and Vedânta. But its importance in philosophy is small, whereas its power as an impulse in popular religion has been enormous. To estimate its moral and intellectual value is difficult, for like so much in Hinduism it offers the sharpest contrasts. Its obvious manifestations may seem to be acts of devotion which cannot be commended ethically and belief in puerile stories: yet we find that this offensive trash continually turns into gems of religious thought unsurpassed in the annals of Buddhism and Christianity.

The doctrine of bhakti is common to both Vishnuites and Śivaites. It is perhaps in general estimation associated with the former more than with the latter, but this is because the Bhagavad-gîtâ and various forms of devotion to Kṛishṇa are well known, whereas the Tamil literature of Dravidian Śivaism is ignored by many European scholars. One might be inclined to suppose that the emotional faith sprang up first in the worship of Vishṇu, for the milder god seems a natural object for love, whereas Śiva has to undergo a certain transformation before he can evoke such feelings. But there is no evidence that this is the historical development of the bhakti sentiment, and if the Bhagavad-gîtâ is emphatic in enjoining the worship of Kṛishṇa only, the Śvetâśvatara and Maitrâyanîya Upanishads favour Śiva, and he is abundantly extolled in many parts of the Mahâbhârata. Here, as so often, exact chronology fails us in the early history of these sects, but it is clear that the practice of worshipping Śiva and Vishṇu, as being each by himself all-sufficient, cannot have begun much later than the Christian era and may have begun considerably earlier, even though people did not call themselves Śaivas or Vaishṇavas.

[1] They are called the Śâṇdilya Sûtras and appear to be not older than about the twelfth century A.D., but the tradition which connects them with the School of Śâṇdilya may be just, for the teaching of this sage (Chāndog. Up. III. 14) lays stress on will and belief. Râmânuja (Śrîbhâshya, II. 2. 43) refers to Śâṇdilya as the alleged author of the Pañcarâtra. There are other Bhakti sûtras called Nâradîya and ascribed to Nârada, published and translated in *The Sacred Books of the Hindus*, No. 23. They consist of 84 short aphorisms. Raj. Mitra in his notices of Sanskrit MSS. describes a great number of modern works dealing with Bhakti.

Bhakti is often associated with the doctrine of the playfulness of God. This idea—so strange to Europe[1]—may have its roots partly in the odd non-moral attributes of some early deities. Thus the Rudra of the Śatarudrîya hymn is a queer character and a trickster. But it soon takes a philosophical tinge and is used to explain the creation and working of the universe which is regarded not as an example of capricious, ironical, inscrutable action, but rather as manifesting easy, joyous movement and the exuberant rhythm of a dance executed for its own sake. The European can hardly imagine a sensible person doing anything without an object: he thinks it almost profane to ascribe motiveless action to the Creator: he racks his brain to discover any purpose in creation which is morally worthy and moderately in accord with the facts of experience. But he can find none. The Hindu, on the contrary, argues that God being complete and perfect cannot be actuated by aims or motives, for all such impulses imply a desire to obtain something, whereas a perfect and complete being is one which by its very definition needs neither change nor addition. Therefore, whatever activity is ascribed to the creator must not be thought of as calculating, purposeful endeavour, but as spontaneous, exultant movement, needing and admitting no explanation, and analogous to sport and play rather than to the proceedings of prudent people. This view of the divine activity is expounded by so serious a writer as Śaṅkara in his commentary on the Vedânta Sûtras, and it also finds mythological expression in numerous popular legends. The Tamil Purâṇas describe the sixty-four miracles of Śiva as his amusements: his laughter and joyous movements brighten all things, and the street minstrels sing "He sports in the world, He sports in the soul[2]." He is supposed to dance in the Golden Hall of the temple at Chidambaram and something of the old legends of the Śatarudriya

[1] Yet it is found in Francis Thompson's poem called *Any Saint*

So best
God loves to jest
With children small, a freak
Of heavenly hide and seek
Fit
For thy wayward wit.

[2] Pope, *The History of Manikka-Vaçagar*, p. 23. For the 64 sports of Śiva see Siddhanta Dipika, vol. IX.

hangs about such popular titles as the Deceiver and the Maniac (*Kalvar*) and the stories of his going about disguised and visiting his worshippers in the form of a mendicant. The idea of sport and playfulness is also prominent in Vishnuism. It is a striking feature in the cultus of both the infant and the youthful Kṛishṇa, but I have not found it recorded in the severer worship of Râma.

Another feature of Hindu sects is the extravagant respect paid to Gurus or teachers. The sanctity of the Guru is an old conviction in India. By common consent he is entitled to absolute obedience and offences against him are heinous crimes. But in sectarian literature there appears a new claim, namely, that the Guru in some way is or represents the god whose worship he teaches. If the deity is thought of primarily as a saviour, the Guru is said to deliver from suffering and hell: if he requires surrender and sacrifice, then person and possessions must be dedicated to the Guru. Membership of a sect can be attained only by initiation at the hands of a Guru who can teach a special mantra or formula of which each sect has its own. In some of the more modern sects the Guru need not be a Brahman, but if he cannot be venerated for his caste, the deficiency is compensated by the respect which he receives as a repository of oral teaching. The scriptural basis of many sects is dubious and even when it exists, many of the devout (especially women) have not the inclination or ability to read and therefore take their religion from the lips of the Guru, who thus becomes an oracle and source of truth. In Bengal, the family Guru is a regular institution in respectable castes. In many sects the founder or other prominent saint is described as an incarnation and receives veneration after death[1].

This veneration or deification of the Guru is found in most sects and assumes as extreme a form among the Śaivas as among the Vaishṇavas. The Śaiva Siddhânta teaches that divine instruction can be received only from one who is both god and man, and that the true Guru is an incarnation of Śiva. Thus the works of Mâṇikka-Vâçagar and Umâpati speak of Śiva coming to his devotees in the form of the Guru. In the sects that worship Kṛishṇa the Gurus are frequently called Gosain

[1] *E.g.* Râmânuja, Nammâṛvâr, Basava.

(Goswami)[1]. Sometimes they are members of a particular family, as among the Vallabhâcâryas. In other sects there is no hereditary principle and even a Sudra is eligible as Guru.

One other feature of Sectarian Hinduism must be mentioned. It may be described as Tantrism or, in one of its aspects, as the later Yoga and is a combination of practices and theories which have their roots in the old literature and began to form a connected doctrine at least as early as the eighth century A.D. Some of its principal ideas are as follows: (i) Letters and syllables (and also their written forms and diagrams) have a potent influence both for the human organism and for the universe. This idea is found in the early Upanishads[2] and is fully developed in the later Sectarian Upanishads. (ii) The human organism is a miniature copy of the universe[3]. It contains many lines or channels (nâḍî) along which the nerve force moves and also nervous centres distributed from the hips to the head. (iii) In the lowest centre resides a force identical with the force which creates the universe[4]. When by processes which are partly physical it is roused and made to ascend to the highest centre, emancipation and bliss are obtained. (iv) There is a mysterious connection between the process of cosmic evolution and sound, especially the sacred sound *Om*.

These ideas are developed most thoroughly in Śâktist works, but are by no means peculiar to them. They are found in the Pancarâtra and the later Puranas and have influenced almost all modern sects, although those which are based on emotional devotion are naturally less inclined to favour physical and magical means of obtaining salvation.

[1] Apparently meaning "possessor of cows," and originally a title of the youthful Kṛishṇa. It is also interpreted as meaning Lord of the Vedas or Lord of his own senses.

[2] *E.g.* the beginning of the Chând. Up. about the syllable *Om*. See too the last section of the Aitareya Âran. The Yoga Upanishads analyse and explain *Om* and some Vishnuite Upanishads (Nṛisiṃha- and Râmatâ-panîya) enlarge on the subject of letters and diagrams.

[3] The same idea pervades the old literature in a slightly different form. The parts of the sacrifice are constantly identified with parts of the universe or of the human body.

[4] The cakras are mentioned in Act v of Mâlatî and Mâdhava written early in the eighth century. The doctrine of the nâḍîs occurs in the older Upanishads (*e.g.* Chând. and Maitrâyaṇa) in a rudimentary form.

CHAPTER XXVII

THE EVOLUTION OF HINDUISM. BHÂGAVATAS AND PÂŚUPATAS

1

INDIA is a literary country and naturally so great a change as the transformation of the old religion into theistic sects preaching salvation by devotion to a particular deity found expression in a long and copious literature. This literature supplements and supersedes the Vedic treatises but without impairing their theoretical authority, and, since it cannot compare with them in antiquity and has not the same historic interest, it has received little attention from Indianists until the present century. But in spite of its defects it is of the highest importance for an understanding of medieval and contemporary Hinduism. Much of it is avowedly based on the principle that in this degenerate age the Veda is difficult to understand[1], and that therefore God in His mercy has revealed other texts containing a clear compendium of doctrine. Thus the great Vishnuite doctor Râmânuja states authoritatively "The incontrovertible fact then is as follows: The Lord who is known from the Vedânta texts...recognising that the Vedas are difficult to fathom by all beings other than himself...with a view to enable his devotees to grasp the true meaning of the Vedas, himself composed the Pancarâtra-Śâstra[2]."

This later sectarian literature falls into several divisions.

A. Certain episodes of the Mahâbhârata. The most celebrated of these is the Bhagavad-gîtâ, which is probably anterior to the Christian era. Though it is incorporated in the Epic it is frequently spoken of as an independent work. Later and less celebrated but greatly esteemed by Vishnuites is the latter part

[1] An attempt was made to adapt the Veda to modern ideas by composing new Upanishads. The inspiration of such works is not denied but they have not the same influence as the literature mentioned below.

[2] Śri Bhâshya, II. 2. 43. So too the Vishṇu Purâṇa, I. 1 describes itself as equal in sanctity to the Vedas. Śankara on Brah. Sûtras, I. 3. 33 says that the Purâṇas are authoritative.

of book XII, commonly known as Nârâyaṇîya[1]. Both these episodes and others[2] are closely analogous to metrical Upanishads. The Mahâbhârata even styles itself (I. 261) the Veda of Kṛishṇa (Kârshṇa).

The Râmâyaṇa does not contain religious episodes comparable to those mentioned but the story has more than once been re-written in a religious and philosophic form. Of such versions the Adhyâtmarâmâyaṇa[3] and Yoga-vaśishṭha-râmâyaṇa are very popular.

B. Though the Purâṇas[4] are not at all alike, most of them show clear affinity both as literature and as religious thought to the various strata of the Mahâbhârata, and to the Law Books, especially the metrical code of Manu. These all represent a form of orthodoxy which while admitting much that is not found in the Veda is still Brahmanic and traditionalist. The older Purâṇas (*e.g.* Matsya, Vâyu, Mârkaṇḍeya, Vishṇu), or at least the older parts of them, are the literary expression of that Hindu reaction which gained political power with the accession of the Gupta dynasty. They are less definitely sectarian than later works such as the Nârada and Liṅga Purânas, yet all are more or less sectarian.

The most influential Purâṇa is the Bhâgavata, one of the great scriptures for all sects which worship Kṛishṇa. It is said to have been translated into every language of India and forty versions in Bengali alone are mentioned[5]. It was probably com-

[1] See Grierson in *Ind. Ant.* 1908, p. 251 and p. 373.

[2] *E.g.* the Sanatsujatîya and Anugîtâ (both in *S.B.E.* VIII.). See Deussen, *Vier philosophische Texte des Mahâbhâratam.*

[3] Forming part of the Brahmâṇḍa Purâṇa.

[4] See for a summary of them Winternitz, *Gesch. Ind. Lit.* I. pp. 450–483. For the dates see Pargiter Dynasties of the Kali age. He holds that the historical portions of the older Purânas were compiled in Prakrit about 250 A.D. and re-edited in Sanskrit about 350. See also Vincent Smith, *Early History*, p. 21 and, against Pargiter, Keith in *J.R.A.S.* 1914, p. 1021. Alberuni (who wrote in 1030) mentions eighteen Purânas and gives two lists of them. Bâṇa (*c.* 620 A.D.) mentions the recitation of the Vâyu Purâṇa. The commentary on the Śvetaśvatara Upan. ascribed to Śaṅkara quotes the Brahma P., Linga P. and Vishṇu P. as authorities as well as Puranic texts described as Vishṇudharma and Śivadharmottara. But the authorship of this commentary is doubtful. The Puranic literature as we know it probably began with the Gupta dynasty or a century before it, but the word Purâṇa in the sense of an ancient legend which ought to be learnt occurs as early as the Śatapatha Brâhmaṇa (XI. 5. 6. 8) and even in A.V. XI. 7. 24.

[5] See Dinesh Chandra Sen, *Hist. Bengali Language and Lit.* pp. 220–225.

posed in the eighth or ninth century[1]. A free translation of the tenth book into Hindi, called the Prem Sagar or Ocean of Love, is greatly revered in northern India[2]. Other sectarian Purâṇas are frequently read at temple services. Besides the eighteen great Purâṇas there are many others, and in south India at any rate they were sometimes composed in the vernacular, as for instance the Periya Purâṇa (*c.* 1100 A.D.). These vernacular Purâṇas seem to be collections of strangely fantastic fairy tales.

C. The word Tantra originally meant a manual giving the essentials of a subject but later usage tends to restrict it to works, whether Hindu or Buddhist, inculcating the worship of Śiva's spouse. But there are exceptions to this restriction: the Panca-tantra is a collection of stories and the Lakshmî-tantra is a Vishnuite work[3].

The fact is that a whole class of Sanskrit religious literature is described by the titles Tantra, Âgama and Saṃhitâ[4], which taken in a wide sense are practically synonymous, though usage is inclined to apply the first specially to Śâktist works, the second to Śivaite and the third to Vishnuite. The common character of all these productions is that they do not attempt to combine Vedic rites and ideas with sectarian worship, but boldly state that, since the prescriptions of the Veda are too hard for this age, some generous deity has revealed an easier teaching. This teaching naturally varies in detail, but it usually comprises devotion to some special form of the godhead and also a special ceremonial, which commences with initiation and includes the use of mystic formulæ, letters and diagrams.

[1] Pargiter, *l.c.* pp. xvii, xxviii. It does not belong to the latest class of Purâṇas for it seems to contemplate the performance of Smârta rites not temple ceremonial, but it is not quoted by Râmânuja (twelfth century) though he cites the Vishṇu Purâṇa. Probably he disapproved of it.

[2] It was made as late as 1803 by Lallû Jî Lâl, but is a rendering into Hindi of a version in the Braj dialect, probably made in the sixteenth century.

[3] Another Vishnuite work is cited indifferently as Pâdma-tantra or Pâdma-samhîtâ, and the Bhâgavata Purâṇa (I. 3. 8) speaks of the Sâttvatam Tantram, which is apparently the Sâttvata-saṃhitâ. The work edited by Schrader is described as the *Ahirbudhnya Saṃhitâ of the Pâncarâtra Âgama.*

[4] See for some notices of these works A. Avalon's various publications about Tantra. Srinivasa Iyengar, *Outlines of Indian Philosophy*, 118–191. Govindacarya Svâmi on the Vaishnava Samhitâs, *J.R.A.S.* 1911, pp. 935 ff. Schomerus, *Çaiva-Siddhânta*, pp. 7 ff. and Schrader's *Introduction to the Pâncarâtra.* Whereas these works claim to be independent of the Veda, the Sectarian Upanishads (see vol. I. p. 76) are an attempt to connect post-Vedic sects with the Veda.

Tantras, Âgamas and Saṃhitâs all treat of their subject-matter in four divisions[1] the first of which relates to the great problems of philosophy, the second to the discipline necessary for uniting the self and God; the third and fourth to ceremonial.

These works have another feature in common, namely that they are little known except to those Hindus who use them for religious purposes and are probably not very anxious to see them published. Though they are numerous, few of them have been printed and those few have not been much studied by European scholars. I shall say something more about them below in treating of the various sects. Some are of respectable antiquity but it is also clear that modern texts pass under ancient names. The Pancarâtram and Pâśupatam which are Vishnuite and Śivaite Saṃhitâs are mentioned in the Mahâbhârata, and some extant Vishnuite Saṃhitâs were perhaps composed in the fourth century A.D.[2] Râmânuja as quoted above states that the Pancarâtra-śâstra (apparently the same as the Pancarâtra-tantra which he also mentions) was composed by Vâsudeva himself and also cites as scripture the Śâttvata, Paushkara and Parama Saṃhitâs. In the same context he speaks of the Mahâbhârata as Bhârata-Saṃhitâ and the whole passage is interesting as being a statement by a high authority of the reasons for accepting a non-Vedic work like the Pancarâtra as revealed scripture.

As already indicated European usage makes the words Tantra, Tantrism and tantric refer to the worship of goddesses. It would be better to describe this literature and worship as Sâktism and to use Tantrism for a tendency in doctrine and ceremonial which otherwise has no special name. I have been informed by Tamil Pandits that at the present day the ritual in some temples is smârta or according to Smriti, but in the majority according to the Âgamas or tantric. The former which is followed by many well-known shrines (for instance in Benares and in the great temples of south India) conforms to the pre-

[1] Jñâna, Yoga, Caryâ, Kriyâ. The same names are used of Buddhist Tantras, except that Anuttara replaces Jñâna.

[2] See Schrader, *Introd. to the Pâncarâtra*, p. 98. In the Raghuvaṃsa, x. 27. Âgamas are not only mentioned but said to be extremely numerous. But in such passages it is hard to say whether Âgama means the books now so-called or merely tradition. Alberuni seems not to have known of this literature and a Tantra for him is merely a minor treatise on astronomy. He evidently regards the Vedas, Purâṇas, philosophical Darśanas and Epics as constituting the religious literature of India.

cepts of the Purâṇas, especially on festival days. The officiants require no special initiation and burnt offerings are presented. But the Agamic ritual can be performed only by priests who have received initiation, burnt offerings rarely form part of the ceremony and vernacular hymns are freely used[1].

Such hymns however as well as processions and other forms of worship which appeal directly to the religious emotions are certainly not tantric. Tantrism is a species of religious magic, differing from the Vedic sacrifices in method rather than principle[2]. For all that, it sets aside the old rites and announces itself as the new dispensation for this age. Among its principal features are the following. The Tantras are a scripture for all, and lay little stress on caste: the texts and the ritual which they teach can be understood only after initiation and with the aid of a teacher: the ritual consists largely in the correct use of spells, magical or sacramental syllables and letters, diagrams and gestures: its object is less to beseech than to compel the god to come to the worshipper: another object is to unite the worshipper to the god and in fact transform him into the god: man is a microcosm corresponding to the macrocosm or universe: the spheres and currents of the universe are copied in miniature in the human body and the same powers rule the same parts in the greater and the lesser scheme. Such ideas are widely disseminated in almost all modern sects[3], though without

[1] Râjagopala Chariar (*Vaishnavite Reformers*, p. 4) says that in Vishnu temples two rituals are used called Pâncarâtra and Vaikhânasa. The latter is apparently consistent with Smârta usage whereas the Pâncarâtra is not. From Gopinâtha Rao's *Elements of Hindu Iconography*, pp. 56, 77, 78 it appears that there is a Vaikhânasâgama parallel to the Pancarâtrâgama. It is frequently quoted by this author, though as yet unpublished. It seems to be the ritual of those Bhâgavatas who worship both Śiva and Vishṇu. It is said to exist in two recensions, prose and metrical, of which the former is perhaps the oldest of the Vaishṇava Âgamas. The Vaikhânasa ritual was once followed at Śrirangam but Râmânuja substituted the Pâncarâtra for it.

[2] Avalon, *Principles of Tantra*, p. xxvii describes it as "that development of the Vaidika Karmakâṇḍa which under the name of the Tantra Shâstra is the scripture of the Kali age." This seems to me a correct statement of the tantric heory.

[3] Thus the Gautamîya Tantra which is held in high estimation by Vishnuite householders in Bengal, though not by ascetics, is a complete application of Śâkta worship to the cult of Kṛishṇa. The Vârâhi Tantra is also Vishnuite. See Raj. Mitra, *Sanskrit MSS. of Bikaner*, p. 583 and *Notices of Sk. MSS.* III. (1876), p. 99, and I. cclxxxvii. See too the usages of the Nambuthiri Brahmans as described in

forming their essential doctrine, but I must repeat that to say all sects are tantric does not mean that they are all Śâktist. But Śâktist sects are fundamentally and thoroughly tantric in their theory and practice.

D. Besides the Sanskrit books mentioned above numerous vernacular works, especially collections of hymns, are accepted as authoritative by various sects, and almost every language has scriptures of its own. In the south two Tamil hymnals, the Devaram of the Śivaites and Nâlâyira Prabandham of the Vishnuites, are recited in temples and are boldly stated to be revelations equivalent to the Veda. In northern India may be mentioned the Hindi Ramayana of Tulsi Das, which is almost universally venerated, the Bhakta-mâlâ of Nâbhâ Das[1], the Sur-sagar of Surdas and the Prem Sagar. In Assam the Nam Gosha of Madhab Deb is honoured with the same homage as a sacred image. The awkwardness of admitting direct inspiration in late times is avoided by the theory of spiritual descent, that is to say of doctrinal transmission from teacher to teacher, the divine revelation having been made to the original teacher at a discreetly remote epoch.

2

In considering the evolution of modern Hinduism out of the old Vedic religion, three of the many factors responsible for this huge and complicated result deserve special attention. The first is the unusual intensity and prevalence of the religious temperament. This has a double effect, both conservative and alterative: ancient customs receive an unreasonable respect: they are not abolished for their immorality or absurdity; but since real interest implies some measure of constructive power, there is a constant growth of new ideas and reinterpretations resulting in inconsistent combinations. The second is the absence of hierarchy and discipline. The guiding principle of the Brahmans has always been not so much that they have a particular creed to enforce, as that whatever is the creed of India they must be its ministers. Naturally every priest is the champion of his own god or rite, and such zeal may lead to occasional conflicts. But

Cochin Tribes and Castes, II. pp. 229–233. In many ways the Nambuthiris preserve the ancient Vedic practices.

[1] See Grierson's articles Gleanings from the Bhaktamala in *J.R.A.S.* 1909–1910.

though the antithesis between the ritualism of the older Brahmanism and the faith or philosophy of Śivaism and Vishnuism may remind us of the differences between the Catholic Church and Protestant reformers, yet historically there is no resemblance in the development of the antithesis. To some extent Hinduism showed a united front against Buddhism, but the older Brahmanism had no organization which enabled it to stand as a separate Church in opposition to movements which it disliked. The third factor is the deeply rooted idea, which reappears at frequent intervals from the time of the Upanishads until to-day, that rules and rites and even creeds are somehow part of the lower and temporal order of things which the soul should transcend and leave behind. This idea tinges the whole of Indian philosophy and continually crops up in practice. The founder of a strange sect who declares that nothing is necessary but faith in a particular deity and that all ceremonies and caste observances are superfluous is not in the popular esteem a subverter of Hinduism.

The history of both Śivaism and Vishnuism illustrates these features. Śiva begins as a wild deity of non-moral attributes. As the religious sense develops he is not rejected like the less reputable deities of the Jews and Arabs but remains and collects round himself other strange wild ideas which in time are made philosophical but not ethical. The rites of the new religion are, if not antagonistic, at least alternative to the ancient sacrifices, yet far from being forbidden they are performed by Brahmans and modern Indian writers describe Śiva as peculiarly the Brahman's god. Finally the Śivaite schools of the Tamil country reject in successive stages the grosser and more formal elements until there remains nothing but an ecstatic and mystical monotheism. Similarly among the Vishnuites Kṛishṇa is the centre of legends which have even less of conventional morality. Yet out of them arises a doctrine that the love of God is the one thing needful so similar to Christian teaching that many have supposed it must be borrowed.

The first clear accounts of the worship of Śiva and Vishṇu are contained in the epics and indicate the existence of sectarian religion, that is to say of exclusive devotion to one or other deity. But there is also a tendency to find a place for both, a tendency which culminates in the composite deity Śaṅkara-

Nârâyaṇa already mentioned. Many of the Purâṇas[1] reflect this view and praise the two deities impartially. The Mahâbhârata not unfrequently does the same but the general impression left by this poem is that the various parts of which it consists have been composed or revised in a sectarian spirit. The body of the work is a narrative of exploits in which the hero Kṛishṇa plays a great part but revised so as to make him appear often as a deity and sometimes as the Supreme Spirit. But much of the didactic matter which has been added, particularly books xii and xiii, breathes an equally distinct Śivaite spirit and in the parts where Kṛishṇa is treated as a mere hero, the principal god appears to be not Vishṇu but Śiva.

The Mahabharata and Puranas contain legends which, though obscure, refer to conflicts of the worshippers of Śiva with those who offered Vedic sacrifices as well as with the votaries of Vishṇu, and to a subsequent reconciliation and blending of the various cults. Among these is the well-known story of Daksha's sacrifice to which Śiva was not invited. Enraged at the omission he violently breaks up the sacrifice either in person or through a being whom he creates for the purpose, assaults the officiants and the gods who are present, and is pacified by receiving a share. Similarly we hear[2] that he once seized a victim at a sacrifice and that the gods in fear allotted to him the choicest portion of the offerings. These stories indicate that at one time Brahmans did not countenance his worship and he is even represented as saying to his wife that according to rule (dharmataḥ) he has no share in the sacrifice[3]. Possibly human victims were immolated in his honour, as they were in Kâlî's until recently, for in the Mahabharata[4] it is related how Kṛishṇa expostulated with Jarâsandha who pro-

[1] *E.g.* Mârkaṇḍeya, Vâmana and Varâha. Also the Skanda Upanishad.

[2] Mahâbh. Vanaparvan, 11001 ff. The Bhâgavata Purâṇa, Book iv. sec. 2-7 emphasizes more clearly the objections of the Rishis to Śiva as an enemy of Vedic sacrifices and a patron of unhallowed rites.

[3] Mahâbh. xii. sec. 283. In the same way the worship of Dionysus was once a novelty in Greece and not countenanced by the more conservative and respectable party. See Eur. Bacchae, 45. The Varâha-Purâna relates that the Śivaite scriptures were revealed for the benefit of certain Brahmans whose sins had rendered them incapable of performing Vedic rites. There is probably some truth in this legend in so far as it means that Brahmans who were excommunicated for some fault were disposed to become the ministers of non-Vedic cults.

[4] Mahâbh. ii. secs. 16, 22 ff.

posed to offer to Śiva a sacrifice of captive kings. In the Vishṇu-Purâṇa, Kṛishṇa fights with Śiva and burns Benares. But by the time that the Mahabharata was put together these quarrels were not in an acute stage. In several passages[1] Kṛishṇa is made to worship Śiva as the Supreme Spirit and in others[2] vice versa Śiva celebrates the glory of Kṛishṇa. Vishnuites do not disbelieve in Śiva but they regard him as a god of this world, whereas their own deity is cosmic and universal. Many Vishnuite works[3] are said to be revealed by Śiva who acts as an intermediary between us and higher spheres.

3

In the following sections I shall endeavour to relate the beginnings of sectarianism. The sects which are now most important are relatively modern and arose in the twelfth century or later, but the sectarian spirit can be traced back several centuries before our era. By sectarians I mean worshippers of Śiva or Vishṇu who were neither in complete sympathy with the ancient Brahmanism nor yet excommunicated by it and who had new texts and rites to replace or at least supplement the Vedas and the Vedic sacrifices. It is probable that the different types of early Indian religion had originally different geographical spheres. Brahmanism flourished in what we call the United Provinces: Buddhism arose in the regions to the east of this district and both Vishnuism and Śivaism are first heard of in the west.

The earliest sect of which we have any record is that of the Bhâgavatas, who were or became Vishnuite. At a date which it is impossible to fix but considerably before the epoch of Pâṇini, a tribe named the Yâdavas occupied the country between Muttra and the shores of Gujarat. Septs of this tribe were called Vṛishṇi and Sâttvata. The latter name has passed into theology. Kṛishṇa belonged to this sept and it is probable that this name Vâsudeva was not originally a patronymic but the name of a deity worshipped by it. The hero Kṛishṇa was identified with this god and subsequently when the Brahmans wished to bring this powerful sect within the pale of orthodoxy

[1] Droṇa-p., 2862 ff. Anusâsana-p., 590 ff.
[2] *E.g.* Anusâsana-p., 6806 ff.
[3] *E.g.* the Ahirbudhnya Saṃhitâ and Adhyâtma Râmâyaṇa.

both were identified with Vishṇu. In the Mahabharata[1] the rule or ritual (vidhi) of the Sâttvatas is treated as equivalent to that of the Bhâgavatas and a work called the Sâttvata Saṃhitâ is still extant. Bhâgavata appears to be the most general name of the sect or sects and means simply *of the Lord* (Bhagavat), that is worshippers of the one Lord[2]. Their religion is also called Ekântika dharma, or the religion with one object, that is monotheism[3].

A considerable literature grew up in this school and the principal treatise is often spoken of as Pâncarâtra because it was revealed by Nârâyaṇa during five nights[4]. The name however appears to be strictly speaking applicable to a system or body of doctrine and the usual term for the books in which this system is expounded is Saṃhitâ. All previous discussions and speculations about these works, of which little was known until recently, are superseded by Schrader's publication of the Ahirbudhnya Saṃhitâ, which appears to be representative of its class[5]. The names of over two hundred are cited and of these more than thirty are known to be extant in MS.[6] The majority were composed in north-western India but the Pâncarâtra doctrine spread to the Dravidian countries and new Saṃhitâs were produced there, the chief of which, the Îśvara Saṃhitâ, can hardly be later than 800 A.D.[7] Of the older works Schrader

[1] Śântipar. cccxxxvii, 12711 ff. In the Bhagavad-gîtâ Kṛishṇa says that he is Vâsudeva of the Vṛishṇis, XI. 37.

[2] Cf. the title Bhâgavata Purâṇa.

[3] Ekâyana is mentioned several times in the Chândogya Up. (VII. 1, 2 and afterwards) as a branch of religious or literary knowledge and in connection with Nârada. But it is not represented as the highest or satisfying knowledge.

[4] Even in the Śatapatha Br. Nârâyaṇa is mentioned in connection with a sacrifice lasting five days, XIII. 6. 1.

[5] The Saṃhitâs hitherto best known to orientalists appear to be late and spurious. The Bṛihadbrahma Saṃhitâ published by the Anandasrama Press mentions Râmânuja. The work printed in the *Bibliotheca Indica* as Nârada pancarâtra (although its proper title apparently is Jñânâmritasâra) has been analyzed by Roussel in *Mélanges Harlez* and is apparently a late liturgical compilation of little originality. Schrader's work was published by the Adyar Library in Madras, 1916. Apparently the two forms Pâñcarâtra and Pañcarâtra are both found, but that with the long vowel is the more usual. Govindâcârya's article in *J.R.A.S.* 1911, p. 951 may also be consulted.

[6] The oldest are apparently the Paushkara, Vârâha, Brâhma, Sâttvata, Jaya and Ahirbudhnya Saṃhitâs, all quoted as authoritative by either Râmânuja or Vedânta Deśika.

[7] It is quoted as equal to the Vedas by Yâmunâcârya, so it must then have been in existence some centuries.

thinks that the Ahirbudhnya was written in Kashmir[1] between 300 and 800 A.D. and perhaps as early as the fourth century. It mentions the Śâttvata and Jayâkhya, which must therefore be older.

The most remarkable feature of this literature is its elaborate doctrine of evolution and emanation from the Deity, the world process being conceived in the usual Hindu fashion as an alternation of production and destruction. A distinction is drawn between pure and gross creation. What we commonly call the Universe is bounded by the shell of the cosmic egg and there are innumerable such eggs, each with its own heavens and its own tutelary deities such as Brahmâ and Śiva who are sharply distinguished from Vishṇu. But beyond this multitude of worlds are more mysterious and spiritual spheres, the highest heaven or Vaikuṇṭha wherein dwells God in his highest form (Para) with his Śaktis[2], certain archangels and liberated souls. Evolution commences when at the end of the cosmic night the Śakti of Vishṇu[3] is differentiated from her Lord and assumes the two forms of Force and Matter[4]. He as differentiated from her is Vâsudeva a personal deity with six attributes[5] and is the first emanation, or Vyûha, of the ineffable godhead. From him proceeds Sankarshaṇa, from Sankarshaṇa Pradyumna, and from Pradyumna Aniruddha. These three Vyûhas take part in creation but also correspond to or preside over certain aspects of human personality, namely Ṣankarshaṇa to the soul that animates all beings, Pradyumna to intelligence and Aniruddha to individuality. Strange to say these seem to be the names of distinguished personages in the Śâttvata or Vṛishṇi clan[6]. Mere deification occurs in many countries but the transformation of heroes into metaphysical or psychological terms could hardly have happened outside India. Next to the Vyûhas come twelve

[1] The story of Śvetadvîpa or White Island in the Śântiparvan of the Mahâbhârata states definitely that Nârada received the Pancarâtra there.

[2] There is much diversity of statement as to whether there are one or many Śaktis.

[3] Vishṇu is the name of God in all his aspects, but especially God as the absolute. Vâsudeva is used both of God as the absolute and also as the first emanation (Vyûha).

[4] Kriyâśakti and Bhûtiśakti.

[5] Jñâna, aiśvarya, śakti, bala, vîrya, tejas. These are called guṇas but are not to be confounded with the three ordinary guṇas.

[6] The words seem to have been originally proper names. See the articles in the *Petersburg Lexicon*.

sub-Vyûhas, among whom is Nârâyaṇa[1], and thirty-nine Avatâras. All these beings are outside the cosmic eggs and our gross creation. As a prelude to this last there takes place the evolution of the aggregates or sources from which individual souls and matter are drawn, of space and of time, and finally of the elements, the process as described seeming to follow an older form of the Sânkhya philosophy than that known to us. The task of human souls is to attain liberation, but though the language of the Saṃhitâs is not entirely consistent, the older view is that they become like to God, not that they are absorbed in him[2].

Thus it is not incorrect to say that the Bhâgavata religion is monotheistic and recognizes a creator of souls. Indeed Śankara[3] condemns it on the very ground that it makes individual souls originate from Vâsudeva, in which case since they have an origin they must also have an end. But Râmânuja in replying to this criticism seems to depart from the older view, for he says that the Supreme Being voluntarily abides in four forms which include the soul, mind and the principle of individuality. This, if not Pantheism, is very different from European monotheism[4].

The history of these Bhâgavatas, Pâncarâtras or worshippers of Vishṇu must have begun several centuries before our era, for there are allusions to them in Pâṇini and the Niddesa[5]. The names of Vâsudeva and Sankarshaṇa occur in old inscriptions[6] and the Greek Heliodoros calls himself a Bhâgavata on the column found at Besnagar and supposed to date from the first part of the second century B.C.

The Pâncarâtra was not Brahmanic in origin[7] and the form

[1] Nârâyaṇa like Vishṇu is used to designate more than one aspect of God. Sometimes it denotes the Absolute.

[2] The above brief sketch is based on Schrader's *Int. to the Pâncarâtra* where the reader can find full details.

[3] Comment on Vedânta sûtras, II. 2. 42.

[4] And, as Schrader observes, the evolutionary system of the Pâncarâtra is practically concerned with only one force, the Śakti, which under the name Bhûti is manifested as the Universe and as Kriyâ vitalizes and governs it (p. 31).

[5] On Sutta-nipâta, 790, 792. The doctrine of the Vyûhas is expounded in the Mahâbhârata Śântip. CCCXL. 36 ff., 70 ff.; CCCXLI. 26 ff.

[6] Lüder's List of Brahmi inscriptions, No. 6, supposed not to be later than 200 B.C. and No. 1112 supposed to be of the first century B.C. Sankarshaṇa is also mentioned in the Kauṭilîya Arthaśâstra, XIII. 3.

[7] Some Saṃhitâs emphasize the distinction between the followers of the Veda and the enlightened ones who worship the Lord. See Schrader, *Pâncarâtra*, p. 97.

of the Sânkhya philosophy from which it borrowed was also un-Brahmanic. It seems to have grown up in north-western India in the centuries when Iranian influence was strong and may owe to Zoroastrianism the doctrine of the Vyûhas which finds a parallel in the relation of Ahura Mazda to Spenta Mainyu, his Holy Spirit, and in the Fravashis. It is also remarkable that God is credited with six attributes comparable with the six Amesha Spentas. In other ways the Pâncarâtra seems to have some connection with late Buddhism. Though it lays little stress on the worship of goddesses, yet all the Vyûhas and Avatâras are provided with Śaktis, like the Buddhas and Bodhisattvas of tantric Buddhism, and in the period of quiescence which follows on the dissolution of the Universe Vishṇu is described under the name of Śûnya or the void. It attaches great importance to the *Cakra*, the wheel or discus which denotes Vishṇu's will to be[1], to evolve and maintain the universe, and it may have contributed some ideas to the very late form of Buddhism called Kâlacakra. This very word is used in the Ahirbudhnya Saṃhitâ as the name of one of the many wheels engaged in the work of evolution.

Though the Pâncarâtra is connected with Kṛishṇa in its origin, it gives no prominence to devotion to him under that name as do modern sects and it knows nothing of the pastoral Kṛishṇa[2]. It recommends the worship of the four Vyûhas[3] presiding over the four quarters in much the same way that late Buddhism adores the four Jinas depicted in somewhat similar forms. Similarly the Śivaites say that Śiva has five faces, namely Îśâna or Sadâśiva (the highest, undifferentiated form of the deity) at the top and below Vâmadeva, Aghora, Tatpurusha and Sadyojâta, presiding respectively over the north, south, east and west. It is thus clear that in the early centuries of our era (or perhaps even before it) there was a tendency in Vishnuism, Śivaism and Mahayanist Buddhism alike to represent the ineffable godhead as manifested in four aspects somewhat more intelligible to human minds and producing in their turn many inferior manifestations. Possibly the

[1] Syâm iti Sankalpa, Ahirbudh. Sam. II. 7. In some late Upanishads (*e.g.* Nâradaparivrâjaka and Bṛihatsannyâsa) Cakrî is used as a synonym for a Pâñcarâtra.

[2] The same is true of Râmânuja, who never quotes the Bhâgavata Purâna.

[3] See the quotations from the Sâttvata Saṃhitâ in Schrader, pp. 150–154. As in the Pâncarâtra there is the Para above the four Vyûhas, so some late forms of Buddhism regard Vairocana as the source of four Jinas.

theory originated among the Vishnuites[1], but as often happened in India it was adopted by their opponents. None of these theories are of much importance as living beliefs at the present day but their influence can be seen in iconography.

As a sect the Pâncarâtras seem to have been a subdivision of the Bhâgavatas and probably at the present day many Vishnuites would accept the second name but not the first. The Pañcarâtra is studied at only a few places in southern India but its doctrines permeate the popular work called Bhaktamâlâ and in view of the express approbation of Râmânuja and other authorities it can hardly be repudiated by the Śrî-Vaishṇavas. Bhâgavata is sometimes used in the south as a name for Smârtas who practise Vedic rites and worship both Śiva and Vishnu[2].

4

In these early times there were strenuous theological struggles now forgotten, though they have left their traces in the legends which tell how the title of Kṛishṇa and others to divine honours was challenged. Amalgamation was the usual method of conciliation. Several gods grew sufficiently important to become in the eyes of their worshippers the supreme spirit and at least four were united in the deity of the Bhâgavatas, namely, Vâsudeva, Kṛishṇa, Vishṇu and Nârâyaṇa. Of the first three I have spoken already. Nârâyaṇa never became like Vishṇu and Kṛishṇa a great mythological figure, but in the late Vedic period he is a personification of the primæval waters from which all things sprang or of the spirit which moved in them[3]. From this he easily became the supreme spirit who animates all the universe and the name was probably acceptable to those who desired a purer and simpler worship because it was connected with comparatively few legends. But there is some confusion in its use, for it is applied not only to the supreme being but to a double incarnation of him called Nara-Nârâyaṇa, and images of the pair may still be seen in Vishnuite temples.

[1] The Manicheans also had groups of five deities (see Chavannes and Pelliot in *J.A.* 1913, I. pp. 333–338) but they are just as likely to have borrowed from Buddhism as *vice versâ*.

[2] See Bhattacharya, *Hindu Castes and Sects*, p. 565.

[3] Manu, I. 10–11, identifies him with Brahmâ and says. "The waters are called Nârah because they are produced from Nara, and he is called Nârâyaṇa because they were his place of movement (ayana)." The same statement occurs in the Nârâyaṇîya.

They are said to have revealed the true doctrine to Nârada and are invoked at the beginning of each book of the Mahâbhârata[1]. One of the main theses of the Nârâyaṇîya[2] is the identity of Nârâyaṇa and Vâsudeva, the former being a Brahmanic, the latter a non-Brahmanic name for the Deity.

The celebrated Bhagavad-gîtâ[3] which is still held in such respect that, like the New Testament or Koran, it is used in law courts for the administration of oaths, is an early scripture of the Bhâgavata sect. In it the doctrines of Kṛishṇa's divinity, the power of faith and the efficacy of grace are fully established. It is declared to be too hard for flesh and blood to find by meditation their way to the eternal imperceptible spirit, whereas Kṛishṇa comes straightway to those who make him their sole desire. "Set thy heart on me, become my devotee, sacrifice to me and worship thou me. Then shalt thou come to me. Truly I declare to thee thou art dear to me. Leave all (other) religious duties and come to me as thy sole refuge. I will deliver thee from thy sins. Sorrow not." But the evolution of Saṅkarshaṇa, etc., is not mentioned. The poem has perhaps been re-edited

[1] They are said to have been the sons of Dharma (religion or righteousness) and Ahiṃsâ (not-injuring). This is obvious allegory indicating that the Bhâgavata religion rejected animal sacrifices. At the beginning of the Nârâyaṇîya (Śântip. cccxxxv.) it is said that Nârâyaṇa the soul of the universe took birth in a quadruple form as the offspring of Dharma, viz. Nara, Nârâyaṇa, Hari and Kṛishṇa. Nara and Nârâyaṇa are often identified with Arjuna and Vâsudeva. *E.g.* Udyogap. xxlx. 19.

[2] Mahâbhâr. XII.

[3] It is an episode in Mahâbhâr. VI. and in its present form was doubtless elaborated apart from the rest. But we may surmise that the incident of Kṛishṇa's removing Arjuna's scruples by a discourse appeared in the early versions of the story and also that the discourse was longer and profounder than would seem appropriate to the European reader of a tale of battles. But as the Vedânta philosophy and the doctrine of Kṛishṇa's godhead developed, the discourse may have been amplified and made to include later theological views. Garbe in his German translation attempts to distinguish the different strata and his explanation of the inconsistencies as due to successive redactions and additions may contain some truth. But these inconsistencies in theology are common to all sectarian writings and I think the main cause for them must be sought not so much in the alteration and combination of documents, as in a mixed and eclectic mode of thought. Even in European books of the first rank inconsistencies are not unknown and they need not cause surprise in works which were not written down but committed to memory. A poet composing a long religious poem in this way and feeling, as many Hindus feel, both that God is everything and also that he is a very present personal help, may very well express himself differently in different parts. On the other hand the editors of such poems are undoubtedly tempted to insert in them later popular doctrines.

and interpolated several times but the strata can hardly be distinguished, for the whole work, if not exactly paradoxical, is eclectic and continually argues that what is apparently highest is not best for a particular person. The Hindus generally regard the contemplative life as the highest, but the Bhagavad-gîtâ is insistent in enjoining unselfish action: it admits that the supreme reality cannot be grasped by the mind or expressed in speech, but it recommends the worship of a personal deity. Even the older parts of the poem appear to be considerably later than Buddhism. But its mythology, if not Vedic, is also hardly Puranic and it knows nothing of the legends about the pastoral Kṛishṇa. It presupposes the Sâṅkhya and Yoga, though in what stage of development it is hard to say, and in many respects its style resembles the later Upanishads. I should suppose that it assumed its present form about the time of the Christian era, rather before than after, and I do not think it owes anything to direct Christian influence. In its original form it may have been considerably older.

The Bhagavad-gîtâ identifies Kṛishṇa with Vâsudeva and with Vishṇu but does not mention Nârâyaṇa and from its general style I should imagine the Nârâyaṇîya to be a later poem. If so, the evolution of Bhâgavata theology will be that Kṛishṇa, a great hero in a tribe lying outside the sphere of Brahmanism, is first identified with Vâsudeva, the god of that tribe, and then both of them with Vishṇu. At this stage the Bhagavad-gîtâ was composed. A later current of speculation added Nârâyaṇa to the already complex figure, and a still later one, not accepted by all sects, brought the pastoral and amorous legends of Kṛishṇa. Thus the history of the Bhâgavatas illustrates the Indian disposition to combine gods and to see in each of them only an aspect of the one. But until a later period the types of divinity known as Vishṇu and Śiva resisted combination. The worshippers of Śiva have in all periods shown less inclination than the Vishnuites to form distinct and separate bodies and the earliest Śivaite sect of which we know anything, the Pâśupatas[1], arose slightly later than the Bhâgavatas.

[1] The name appears not to be in common use now, but the Pâśupata school is reviewed in the Sarva-darśana-saṅgraha (*c.* 1330).

5

Patañjali the grammarian (*c.* 150 B.C.) mentions devotees of Śiva[1] and also images of Śiva and Skanda. There is thus no reason to doubt that worshippers of Śiva were recognized as a sect from at least 200 B.C. onwards. Further it seems probable that the founder or an early teacher of the sect was an ascetic called Lakulin or Lakulîśa, the club-bearer. The Vâyu Purâṇa[2] makes Śiva say that he will enter an unowned corpse and become incarnate in this form at Kâyârohana, which has been identified with Kârvân in Baroda. Now the Vâyu is believed to be the oldest of the Purâṇas, and it is probable that this Lakulin whom it mentions lived before rather than after our era and was especially connected with the Pâśupata sect. This word is derived from Paśupati, the Lord of cattle, an old title of Rudra afterwards explained to mean the Lord of human souls. In the Śântiparvan[3] five systems of knowledge are mentioned. Sâṅkhya, Yoga, the Vedas, Pâśupatam and Pancarâtram, promulgated respectively by Kapila, Hiraṇyagarbha, Apântaratamas, Śiva the Lord of spirits and son of Brahmâ, and "The Lord (Bhagavân) himself." The author of these verses, who evidently supported the Pâncarâtra, considered that these five names represented the chief existing or permissible varieties of religious thought. The omission of the Vedânta is remarkable but perhaps it is included under Veda. Hence we may conclude that when this passage was written (that is probably before 400 A.D. and perhaps about the beginning of our era) there were two popular religions ranking in public

[1] Śivabhâgavata, see his comment on Pâṇiṇi, v. 3. 99 and v. 2. 76. The name is remarkable and suggests that the Śivaites may have imitated the Bhâgavatas.

[2] I. xxiii. 209. The *Bibliotheca Ind.* edition reads Nakulî. Aufrecht (*Bodl. MSS.*) has Lakulî. The same story is found in Linga P. chap. XXIV. Lakulî is said to have had four pupils who founded four branches. Lakulin does not play an important part in modern Śivaism but is mentioned in inscriptions from the tenth till the thirteenth centuries. The Sarva-darśana-saṅgraha describes the Nakulîśa-Pâśupata system and quotes Nakulîsa who is clearly the same as Lakulin. The figures on Kushan coins representing Śiva as holding a club may be meant for Lakulin but also may be influenced by Greek figures of Herakles. See for Lakulin Fleet in *J.R.A.S.* 1907, pp. 419 ff. and Bhandarkar *Vaishṇavism and Śaivism*, pp. 115 ff. The coins of Wema Kadphises bear the title Mahiśvara, apparently meaning worshipper of the Great Lord. Temples in south India seem to have been named after Kâyârohana in the seventh century A.D. See Gopinâtha Rao, *Hindu Iconography*, II. p. 19.

[3] Mahâbhâr. XII.

esteem with the philosophic and ritual doctrines of the Brahmans. The Mahâbhârata contains a hymn[1] which praises Śiva under 1008 names and is not without resemblance to the Bhagavad-gîtâ. It contains a larger number of strange epithets, but Śiva is also extolled as the All-God, who asks for devotion and grants grace. At the close of the hymn Śiva says that he has introduced the Pâśupata religion which partly contradicts and partly agrees with the institutions of caste and the Âśramas, but is blamed by fools[2].

These last words hint that the Pâśupatas laid themselves open to criticism by their extravagant practices, such as strange sounds and gestures[3]. But in such matters they were outdone by other sects called Kâpâlikas or Kâlâmukhas. These carried skulls and ate the flesh of corpses, and were the fore-runners of the filthy Aghoris, who were frequent in northern India especially near Mount Abu and Girnar a century ago and perhaps are not yet quite extinct. The biographers of Śankara[4] represent him as contending with these demoniac fanatics not merely with the weapons of controversy but as urging the princes who favoured him to exterminate them.

Hindu authorities treat the Pâśupatas as distinct from the Śaivas, or Śivaites, and the distinction was kept up in Camboja in the fourteenth century. The Śaivas appear to be simply worshippers of Śiva, who practice a sane ritual. In different parts of India they have peculiarities of their own but whereas the Vaishṇavas have split up into many sects each revering its own founder and his teaching, the Śaivas, if not a united body, present few well-marked divisions. Such as exist I shall notice below in their geographical or historical connection[5]. Most of them accept a system of theology or philosophy[6] which starts

[1] Mahâbhâr. XII. 13702 ff. It is recited by Daksha when he recognizes the might of Śiva after the unfortunate incident of his sacrifice.

[2] Śânti-parvan, section cclxxxv especially line 10, 470 ff.

[3] See Sarva-darśana-saṅgraha, chap. VI. and the comments of Râmânuja and Śankara on Vedânta Sûtras, II. 2. 36.

[4] *E.g.* Śaṅkara-dig-vijaya. The first notice of these sects appears to be an inscription at Igatpuri in the Nâsik district of about 620 A.D. recording a grant for the worship of Kapaleśvara and the maintenance of Mahâvrâtins (=Kâpâlikâs) in his temple. But doubtless the sects are much older.

[5] The principal are, the Pâśupatas, the Śaivasiddhântam of southern India and the Śivaism of Kashmir.

[6] The Sarva-darśana-saṅgraha, chap. VII. gives a summary of it.

with three principles, all without beginning or end. These are Pati or the Lord, that is Śiva: Paśu, or the individual soul: Pâśa or the fetter, that is matter or Karma[1]. The task of the soul is to get free of its fetters and attain to the state of Śiva. But this final deliverance is not quite the same as the identity with Brahman taught by the Vedânta: the soul becomes a Śiva, equal to the deity in power and knowledge but still dependent on him rather than identical with him[2].

Peculiar to Śaiva theology is the doctrine of the five kañcukas[3] or envelopes which limit the soul. Spirit in itself is free: it is timeless and knows no restrictions of space, enjoyment, knowledge and power. But when spirit is contracted to individual experience, it can apprehend the universe only as a series of changes in time and place: its enjoyment, knowledge and power are cramped and curtailed by the limits of personality. The terminology of the Śaivas is original but the theory appears to be an elaboration of the Pâncarâtra thesis that the soul is surrounded by the sheath of Mâyâ.

The early literature of the worshippers of Śiva (corresponding to the Saṃhitâs of the Pâncarâtras) appears to have consisted of twenty-eight works composed in Sanskrit and called Âgamas[4]. There is fairly good evidence for their antiquity. Tirumular, one of the earliest Tamil poets who is believed to have lived in the first centuries of our era, speaks of them with enthusiasm and the Buddhist Sanskrit works called Âgamas (corresponding to

[1] The Pâśupatas seem to attach less importance to this triad, though as they speak of Pati, Paśu and the impurities of the soul there is not much difference. In their views of causation and free will they differed slightly from the Śaivas, since they held that Śiva is the universal and absolute cause, the actions of individuals being effective only in so far as they are in conformity with the will of Śiva. The Śaiva siddhânta however holds that Śiva's will is not irrespective of individual Karma, although his independence is not thereby diminished. He is like a man holding a magnet and directing the movements of needles.

[2] There is some difference of language and perhaps of doctrine on this point in various Śivaite works. Both Śivaites and Pañcarâtrins sometimes employ the language of the Advaita. But see Schrader, *Int. to Pañcarâtra*, pp. 91 ff.

[3] The five Kañcukas (or six including Mâyâ) are strictly speaking tattvas of which the Śaivas enumerate 36 and are kâla, niyati, râga, vidyâ and kalâ contrasted with nityatva, vyâpakatva, pûrṇatva, sarvajnatva, sarvakartṛitva which are qualities of spirit. See Chatterji, *Kashmir Śaivism*, 75 ff., 160, where he points out that the Kañcukas are essentially equivalent to Kant's "forms of perception and conception." See too Schrader, *Int. to Pancarâtra*, 64, 90, 115.

[4] See for names and other details Schomerus, *Der Śaiva-Siddhânta*, pp. 7, 23: also many articles in the *Siddhânta-Dipika*.

the Pali Nikâyas) cannot be later than that period. It is highly probable that the same word was in use among both Hindus and Buddhists at the same time. And since the Mahâbhârata mentions the Pâśupatam, there is no difficulty in supposing that expositions of Śivaite doctrine were current in the first century A.D. or even B.C. But unless more texts of the Âgamas come to light the question of their age has little practical importance, for it is said by native scholars that of the twenty-eight primary books there survive only fragments of twenty, which treat of ritual, besides the verses which form the text expounded at length in the Śivañânabotham[1]. There are also said to be 120 Upâgamas of which only two or three have been preserved entire. Of these two have been printed in part, the Mṛigendra and Paushkara[2]. The former is cited in the Sarva-darśana-saṅgraha (about 1330) but does not show any signs of great antiquity. It is thus clear that the Âgamas are not much studied by modern Śivaites but it is unhesitatingly stated that they are a revelation direct from Śiva and equal to the Veda[3] and this affirmation is important, even though the texts so praised are little known, for it testifies to the general feeling that there are other revelations than the Veda. But the Vedas, and the Vedânta Sûtras are not ignored. The latter are read in the light of Nîlakaṇṭha's[4] commentary which is considered by south Indian Pandits to be prior to Śankara.

[1] They are taken from the Âgama called Raurava. The Śivaites of Kashmir appear to have regarded the extant Śiva-sûtras as an Âgama.

[2] The Sanskrit text and translation of the Mṛigendra are published in the *Siddhânta-Dipika*, vol. IV. 1901 ff. It is sometimes described as an Upâgama and sometimes as the Jñânapâda of the Kâmika Âgama.

[3] So Tirumûlar. Nîlakaṇṭha in his commentary on the Vedânta Sûtras says: "I see no difference between the Veda and the Śaivâgama."

[4] Or Śrîkaṇṭha. The commentary is translated in *Siddhânta-Dipika*, vol. I. ff. In spite of sectarian views as to its early date, it seems to be influenced by the views and language of Râmânuja.

CHAPTER XXVIII

ŚANKARA. ŚIVAISM IN SOUTHERN INDIA. KASHMIR. LINGÂYATS

1

ABOUT the sixth century A.D. the decadence of Buddhism and the invigoration of Brahmanism were both well advanced. The Mahabharata existed as a great collection of epic and religious poetry and the older Puranas were already composed. Even at the present day authorities differ as to whether Śiva or Vishṇu commands the allegiance of the majority and naturally it is hard to describe the distribution of sects in earlier times. The monuments of the Guptas (for instance the ruins at Eran) suggest that they were Vishnuites but a little later the cult of Śiva becomes more prominent. The Emperor Harsha (612–648) and his family were eclectic, honouring Śiva, the Sun and the Buddha, but it is not recorded that they worshipped Vishṇu. Bâṇa who lived at his court indicates[1] that Śivaism was the predominant form of worship, but also mentions Buddhists and Bhâgavatas. Hsüan Chuang on the other hand holds him up as a devout Buddhist. Great Śivaite shrines in different parts of India such as the temple of Bhuvaneshwar in Orissa and the Kailas at Ellora were probably constructed in the seventh century and it is likely that in the defeat of Buddhism the worshippers of Śiva played an active part.

This conflict is connected with the names of Kumârila Bhaṭṭa (*c.* 725 A.D.) and Śaṅkara Âcârya (*c.* 800 A.D.). It clearly represents forces which cannot be restricted to the character of individuals or the span of human lives. The elements which compose Hinduism had been vigorous long before the eighth century and Buddhism, though decadent, continued to exist in India later. But probably the careers of these two men are the best record of the decisive turn of the tide. It is often said that they revived Hinduism, but however much they insisted on the

[1] In various allusions to be found in the Kâdambarî and Harshacarita.

authority of ancient tradition, the real result of their labours was not to re-establish the order of things which prevailed before the rise of Buddhism, but to give authority and solidity to the mixture of Brahmanism, Buddhism and popular beliefs which had grown up. Kumârila is said to have been a Brahman of Bihar who was a Buddhist monk but became a worshipper of Śiva and so zealous a persecutor of his former faith that he persuaded a king of his time named Sudhanvan to exterminate it from the Himalaya to Cape Comorin. This is a monstrous exaggeration but he was doubtless a determined enemy of the Buddhists, as can be seen from his philosophical works[1]. He taught little about metaphysics or the nature of God, but he insisted on the necessity and efficacy of Vedic rites.

More important both as a thinker and an organizer was Śankara. There is some discrepancy in the traditions of his birth, but he was probably born about 788 A.D.[2] in a family of Nambutiri Brahmans at Kaladi[3] in the Cochin state. Kaladi occupies a healthy position at some height above the sea level and the neighbourhood is now used as a sanatorium. The cocoanut trees and towered temples which mark many south Indian landscapes are absent, and paddy fields alternate with a jungle of flowering plants studded with clumps of bamboos. A broad river broken by sandbanks winds through the district and near the villages there are often beautiful avenues of great trees. Not far distant is Trichur which possesses a Vedic college and a large temple, forbidden to Europeans but like most edifices in Malabar modest in architecture. This is not the land of giant gopurams and multitudinous sculpture, but of lives dedicated

[1] The best known of these is the Tantravârttika, a commentary on the Pûrva-mîmâmsâ.

[2] This is the generally accepted date and does not appear to conflict with anything else that is at present known of Śankara. An alternative suggestion is some date between 590 and 650 (see Telang, *I.A.* XIII. 1884, p. 95 and Fleet, *I.A.* XVI. 1887, p. 41). But in this case, it is very strange that I-Ching does not mention so conspicuous an enemy of the Buddhists. It does not seem to me that the use of Pûrnavarman's name by Śankara in an illustration (*Comm. on Vedanta Sut.* II. i. 17) necessarily implies they were contemporaries, but it does prove that he cannot have lived before Pûrnavarman.

[3] Another tradition says he was born at Chidambaram, but the temple at Badrinath in the Himalayas said to have been founded by him has always been served by Nambutiri Brahmans from Malabar. In 1910 a great temple erected in his honour was consecrated at Kaladi.

to the acquisition of traditional learning and the daily performance of complicated but inconspicuous rites.

The accounts of Śankara's life are little but a collection of legends, in which, however, the following facts stand out. He was the pupil of Govinda, who was himself the pupil of Gauḍapâda and this connection would be important could we be certain that this Gauḍapâda was the author of the metrical treatise on philosophy bearing his name. He wrote popular hymns as well as commentaries on the Upanishads, Vedânta Sutras and Bhagavad-gîtâ, thus recognizing both Vedic and post-Vedic literature: he resided for some time on the Narbudda and at Benares, and in the course of the journeys in which like Paul he gave vent to his activity, he founded four maṭhs or monasteries, at Sringeri, Puri, Dwârakâ and Badrinath in the Himalaya. Near the latter he died before he was an old man. On his deathbed he is said to have asked forgiveness for going on pilgrimages and frequenting temples, because by so doing he had seemed to forget that God is everywhere.

It is clear that his work both as an author and organizer was considerable and permanent, and that much of his career was spent outside Dravidian lands. His greatest achievement was his exposition of the Vedânta, of which I treat elsewhere. He based his arguments unreservedly on the Vedic texts and aimed at being merely conservative, but those texts and even the ancient commentaries are obscure and inconsistent, and it was reserved for his genius to produce from them a system which in consistency, thoroughness and profundity holds the first place in Indian philosophy. His work did not consist, as he himself supposed, in harmonizing the Upanishads. In this department of interpretation he is as uncritical as other orthodox commentators, but he took the most profound thoughts of the old literature and boldly constructed with them a great edifice of speculation. Since his time the Vedânta has been regarded as the principal philosophy of India—a position which it does not seem to have held before—and his interpretation of it, though often contested and not suited to popular religion, still commands the respect and to some extent the adherence of most educated Hindus.

In practical religion he clearly felt, as every Indian reformer still must feel, the want of discipline and a common standard,

Though the Buddhism of his day had ceased to satisfy the needs of India, he saw that its strength lay in its morality, its relative freedom from superstition and its ecclesiastical organization. Accordingly he denounced extravagant sects[1] and forbade such practices as branding. He also instituted an order of ascetics[2]. In doing this he was not only trying to obtain for Hinduism the disciplinary advantages of the Buddhist church but also to break through the rule prescribing that a Brahman must first be a householder and only late in life devote himself entirely to religion. This rule did the Brahmans good service in insuring the continuity and respectability of their class but it tended to drive enthusiasts to other creeds.

It does not seem that any sect can plausibly claim Śaṅkara as founder or adherent. His real religion was Vedântism and this, though not incompatible with sectarian worship, is predisposed to be impartial. The legend says that when summoned to his mother's deathbed, he spoke to her first of the Vedânta philosophy. But she bade him give her some consolation which she could understand. So he recited a hymn to Śiva, but when the attendants of that god appeared she was frightened. Śaṅkara then recited a hymn to Vishṇu and when his gentler messengers came to her bedside, she gave her son her blessing and allowed them to take her willing soul.

This story implies that he was ready to sanction any form of reputable worship with a slight bias towards Vishnuism[3]. At the present day the Smârtas, who consider themselves his followers, have a preference for the worship of Śiva. But the basis of their faith is not Śivaism but the recognition of the

[1] His conflicts with them are described in works called Śankara-vijaya of which at least four are extant.

[2] They are called Daśanâmis which merely means that each ascetic bears one or other of ten surnames (Sarswati, Bharati, Tirtha, etc.). See for a further account of them Jogendra Nath Bhattacharya, *Hindu Castes and Sects*, pp. 374–379.

The order in all its branches seems to have strong pantheistic inclinations. They mutter the formula Sivo'ham, I am Śiva.

[3] I have been told by south Indian Pandits that they think Śaṅkara was born in a Bhâgavata family and that there is some evidence his kinsmen were trustees of a temple of Kṛishṇa. The Śâktas also claim him, but the tradition that he opposed the Śâktas is strong and probable. Many hymns addressed to Vishṇu, Śiva and various forms of Durgâ are attributed to him. I have not been able to discover what is the external evidence for their authenticity but hymns must have been popular in south India before the time of Śaṅkara and it is eminently probable that he did not neglect this important branch of composition.

great body of Indian traditions known as Smriti. And that, next to Vedântism, was the essence of Śaṅkara's teaching: he wished to regard tradition as a coherent whole, based on the eternal Veda but including authoritative Smriti to be interpreted in the light of the Veda, and thus he hoped to correct extravagant and partial views and to lead to those heights whence it is seen that all is one, "without difference."

The results of Śaṅkara's labours may still be seen in the organization of southern Hinduism which is more complete than in the north. It is even said that the head of the Śringeri monastery in Mysore exercises an authority over Smârta Brahmans similar to that of the Pope[1]. This is probably an exaggeration but his decision is accepted as settling caste disputes, and even to-day the Śringeri maṭh[2] is one of the most important religious institutions in India. The abbot, who is known as Jagadguru, is head of the Smârta Brahmans. The present occupant is said to be thirty-third in succession from Śaṅkara and numbers among his predecessors Sâyanâcârya, the celebrated Vedic commentator who lived in the fourteenth century. The continued prosperity of this establishment and of other religious corporations in the Dravidian country, whereas the Mohammedans destroyed all monasteries whether Hindu or Buddhist in the north, is one of the reasons for certain differences in northern and southern Hinduism. For instance in northern India any Brahman, whatever his avocation may be, is allowed to perform religious ceremonies, whereas in the Deccan and south India Brahmans are divided into Laukikas or secular and Bhikshus or religious. The latter are householders, the name having lost its monastic sense, but they have the exclusive right of officiating and acting as Gurus and thus form a married clergy.

[1] See Bhattacharya, *Hindu Castes and Sects*, p. 16.

[2] This maṭh has an endowment of about £5000 a year, instituted by the kings of Vijayanagar. The Guru is treated with great respect. His palankin is carried crossways to prevent anyone from passing him and he wears a jewelled head-dress, not unlike a papal tiara, and wooden shoes covered with silver. See an interesting account of Śringeri in *J. Mythic Society* (Bangalore), vol. VIII. pp. 18–33.

Schrader in his catalogue of the Sanskrit MSS. in the Adyar Library, 1908, notices an Upanishad called Mahâmâyopanishad, ascribed to Śaṅkara himself, which deals with the special qualities of the four maṭhs. Each is described as possessing one Veda, one Mahâvâkyam, etc. The second part deals with the three ideal maṭhs, Sumeru, Paramâtman and Śâstrâthajnâna.

It is possible that the influence of Śaṅkara may have had a puritanical side which partly accounts for the degeneration of later Indian art. His higher teaching inculcated a spiritual creed which needed no shrines, while for those who required rites he recommended the old Brahmanic ritual rather than the modern temple cultus. The result of this may have been that piety and learning were diverted from art, so that architecture and sculpture ceased to be in touch with the best religious intelligence.

The debt of Śaṅkara to Buddhism is an interesting question. He indited polemics against it and contributed materially to its downfall, but yet if the success of creeds is to be measured by the permanence of ideas, there is some reason for thinking that the vanquished led the conqueror captive. Śaṅkara's approval both in theory and in practice of the monastic life is Buddhistic rather than Brahmanical[1]. The doctrines of Mâyâ and the distinction between higher and lower truth, which are of cardinal importance in his philosophy, receive only dubious support from the Upanishads and from Bâdarâyaṇa, but are practically identical with the teachings of the Mâdhyamika School of Buddhism and it was towards this line of thought rather than towards the theism of the Pâśupatas or Bhâgavatas that he was drawn. The affinity was recognized in India, for Śaṅkara and his school were stigmatized by their opponents as Buddhists in disguise[2].

2

The reader will perhaps have noticed that up to the career of Śaṅkara we have been concerned exclusively with northern India, and even Śaṅkara, though a native of the south, lived much in the north and it was the traditional sacred lore of the north which he desired to establish as orthodoxy. Not only the older literature, Brahmanic as well as Buddhist, but most of the Purâṇas ignore the great stretch of Dravidian country which forms the southern portion of the peninsula and if the Râmâyaṇa sings of Râma's bridge and the conquest of Laṅka this is clearly an excursion into the realms of fancy. Yet the Dravidian dis-

[1] There is some reason to suppose that the Maṭh of Sringeri was founded on the site of a Buddhist monastery. See *Journal of Mythic Society*, Bangalore, 1916, p. 151.

[2] Pracchanna-bauddha. See for further details Book IV. chap. XXI. *ad fin.*

tricts are ample in extent, their monuments are remarkable, their languages are cultivated, and Tamil literature possesses considerable interest, antiquity and originality. Unfortunately in dealing with these countries we experience in an unusually acute form the difficulties which beset every attempt to trace the history of ideas in India, namely, the absence of chronology. Before 1000 A.D. materials for a connected history are hardly accessible. There are, however, many inscriptions and a mass of literature (itself of disputable date) containing historical allusions, and from these may be put together not so much a skeleton or framework as pictures of ancient life and thought which may be arranged in a plausible order.

It may be said that where everything is so vague, it would be better to dismiss the whole subject of southern India and its religion, pending the acquisition of more certain information, and this is what many writers have done. But such wide regions, so many centuries, such important phases of literature and thought are involved, that it is better to run the risk of presenting them in false sequence than to ignore them. Briefly it may be regarded as certain that in the early centuries of our era Buddhism, Jainism and Brahmanism all flourished in Dravidian lands. The first two gradually decayed and made way for the last, although Jainism remained powerful until the tenth century. At a fairly early date there were influential Śivaite and Vishnuite sects, each with a devotional literature in the vernacular. Somewhat later this literature takes a more philosophic and ecclesiastical tinge and both sects produce a succession of teachers. Tamil Śivaism, though important for the south, has not spread much beyond its own province, but the Vishnuism associated with such eminent names as Râmânuja and Râmânand has influenced all India, and the latter teacher is the spiritual ancestor of the Kabirpanthis, Sikhs and various unorthodox sects. Political circumstances too tended to increase the importance of the south in religion, for when nearly all the north was in Moslim hands the kingdom of Vijayanagar was for more than two centuries (*c.* 1330–1565) the bulwark of Hinduism. But in filling up this outline the possibilities of error must be remembered. The poems of Manikka-Vaçagar have such individuality of thought and style that one would suppose them to mark a conspicuous religious movement. Yet some authorities refer them to the third century and others to the eleventh, nor has any standard been formulated for distinguishing earlier and later varieties of Tamil.

I have already mentioned the view that the worship of Śiva and the Linga is Dravidian in origin and borrowed by the Aryans. There is no proof that this worship had its first home in the south and spread northwards, for the Vedic and epic literature provides a sufficient pedigree for Śiva. But this deity always collected round himself attributes and epithets which are not those of the Vedic gods but correspond with what we know of non-Aryan Indian mythology. It is possible that these un-Aryan cults attained in Dravidian lands fuller and more independent development than in the countries colonized by the Aryans, so that the portrait of Śiva, especially as drawn by Tamil writers, does retain the features of some old Dravidian deity, a deity who dances, who sports among men and bewilders them by his puzzling disguises and transformations[1]. But it is not proved that Śiva was the chief god of the early Tamils. An ancient poem, the Purra-Poruḷ Veṇbâ-Mâlai[2], which contains hardly any allusions to him mentions as the principal objects of worship the goddess Koṭṭavai (Victorious) and her son Muruvan. Popular legends[3] clearly indicate a former struggle between the old religion and Hinduism ending as usual in the recognition by the Brahmans of the ancient gods in a slightly modified form.

We have no records whatever of the introduction of Brahmanism into southern India but it may reasonably be supposed to have made its appearance there several centuries before our era, though in what form or with what strength we cannot say. Tradition credits Agastya and Paraśu-Râma with having established colonies of Brahmans in the south at undated but remote epochs. But whatever colonization occurred was not on a large scale. An inscription found in Mysore[4] states that Mukkaṇṇa Kadamba (who probably lived in the third century A.D.) imported a number of Brahman families from the north,

[1] The old folklore of Bengal gives a picture of Śiva, the peasant's god, which is neither Vedic nor Dravidian. See Dinesh Chandra Sen, *Bengali Lang. and Lit.* pp. 68 ff. and 239 ff.

[2] *J.R.A.S.* 1899, p. 242.

[3] See some curious examples in Whitehead's *Village Gods of South India.*

[4] Rice, *Mysore and Coorg from the Inscriptions*, pp. 27 and 204.

because he could find none in the south. Though this language may be exaggerated, it is evidence that Brahmans cannot have been numerous at that time and it is probable that Buddhism and Jainism were better represented. Three of Asoka's inscriptions have been found in Mysore and in his last edict describing his missionary efforts he includes "the kings of the Pândyas and Colas in the south" among the conquests of Buddhism. Mahinda founded a monastery in the Tanjore district and probably established Buddhism at various points of the Tamil country on his way to Ceylon[1]. There is therefore no reason to be doubtful of Buddhist activity, literary or other, if evidence for it is forthcoming. Hsüan Chuang in 640 A.D. deplores the decay of Buddhism and speaks of the ruins of many old monasteries.

According to Jain tradition, which some think is supported by inscriptions at Śravana-Beḷgoḷa[2], Bhadrabâhu accompanied by Candra Gupta (identified with the Maurya king of that name) led a migration of Jains from the north to Mysore about 300 B.C. The authenticity of this tradition has been much criticized but it can hardly be disputed that Jainism came to southern India about the same time as Buddhism and had there an equally vigorous and even longer existence.

Most Tamil scholars are agreed in referring the oldest Tamil literature to the first three centuries of our era and I see nothing improbable in this. We know that Asoka introduced Buddhism into south India. About the time of the Christian era there are many indications that it was a civilized country[3] which maintained commercial relations with Rome and it is reasonable to suppose that it had a literature. According to native tradition there were three successive Sanghams, or Academies, at Madura. The two earlier appear to be mythical, but the third has some historical basis, although it is probable that poems belonging to several centuries have been associated with it. Among those which have been plausibly referred to the second century A.D. are the two narrative poems Śilappadhikaram and Mani-

[1] The early Brahmi inscriptions of southern India are said to be written in a Dravidian language with an admixture not of Sanskrit but of Pali words. See *Arch. Survey India,* 1911–12, Part I. p. 23.

[2] See Rice, *Mysore and Coorg,* pp. 3–5 and Fleet's criticisms, *I.A.* XXI. 1892, p. 287.

[3] The various notices in European classical authors as well as in the Sinhalese chronicles prove this.

mêkhalai as well as the celebrated collection of didactic verses known as the Kural. The first two poems, especially the Manimêkhalai, are Buddhist in tone. The Kural is ethical rather than religious, it hardly mentions the deity[1], shows no interest in Brahmanic philosophy or ritual and extols a householder's life above an ascetic's. The Nâladiyâr is an anthology of somewhat similar Jain poems which as a collection is said to date from the eighth century, though verses in it may be older. This Jain and Buddhist literature does not appear to have attained any religious importance or to have been regarded as even quasi-canonical, but the Dravidian Hindus produced two large collections of sacred works, one Śivaite the other Vishnuite, which in popular esteem rival the sanctity of the Vedas. Both consist of hymns, attributed to a succession of saints and still sung in the temple worship, and in both sects the saints are followed by a series of teachers and philosophers. We will take the Śivaites first.

3

Their collection of hymns is known as Tirumurai, and was compiled by Nambi-Andar-Nambi said to have lived under King Râjarâja (*c.* 1000 A.D.). The first portion of it, known as Devâram, contains the hymns of Sambandha, Appar and Sundara. These persons are the most eminent of the sixty-three saints[2] of the southern Śivaites and are credited with many miracles. Tamil scholars[3] consider that Sambandha cannot have lived later than the beginning of the seventh century. He was an adversary of the Jains and Appar is said to have been persecuted by the Buddhists. Of the other works comprised in the Tirumurai the most important is the Tiruvâçagam of Mâṇikka-Vâçagar[4], one of the finest devotional poems which India can show. It is not, like the Bhagavad-gîtâ, an exposition *by* the deity, but an outpouring of the soul *to* the deity. It only incidentally explains the poet's views: its main purpose is to tell of his emotions, experiences and aspirations. This character-

[1] Except in the first chapter.

[2] A complete list of them is given in Foulkes, *Catechism of the Shaiva religion*, 1863, p. 21.

[3] *Tamilian Antiquary*, 3, 1909, pp. 1–65.

[4] Edited and translated by Pope, 1900.

istic seems not to be personal but to mark the whole school of Tamil Śaiva writers.

This school, which is often called the Siddhânta[1], though perhaps that term is better restricted to later philosophical writers, is clearly akin to the Pâśupata but alike in thought, sentiment and ritual far more refined. It is in fact one of the most powerful and interesting forms which Hinduism has assumed and it has even attracted the sympathetic interest of Christians. The fervour of its utterances, the appeals to God as a loving father, seem due to the temperament of the Tamils, since such sentiments do not find so clear an expression in other parts of India. But still the whole system, though heated in the furnace of Dravidian emotion, has not been recast in a new mould. Its dogmas are those common to Śivaism in other parts and it accepts as its ultimate authority the twenty-eight Śaiva Âgamas. This however does not detract from the beauty of the special note and tone which sound in its Tamil hymns and prayers.

Whatever the teaching of the little known Âgamas may be, the Śaiva-Siddhânta is closely allied to the Yoga and theistic forms of the Sânkhya. It accepts the three ultimates, Pati the Lord, Paśu his flock or souls, and Pâśa the fetter or matter. So high is the first of these three entities exalted, so earnestly supplicated, that he seems to attain a position like that of Allah in Mohammedanism, as Creator and Disposer. But in spite of occasional phrases, the view of the Yoga that all three—God, souls and matter—are eternal is maintained[2]. Between the world periods there are pauses of quiescence and at the end of these Śiva evolves the universe and souls. That he may act in them he also evolves from himself his energy or Paraçatti (Sk. Śakti). But this does not prevent the god himself in a personal and often visible form from being for his devotees the one central and living reality. The Śakti, often called Umâ, is merely Śiva's reflex and hardly an independent existence.

[1] Established opinion or doctrine. Used by the Jains as a name for their canon.

[2] Thus the catechism of the Śaiva religion by Sabhapati Mudaliyar (transl. Foulkes, 1863) after stating emphatically that the world is created also says that the soul and the world are both eternal. Also just as in the Bhagavad-gîtâ the ideas of the Vedanta and Sâṅkhya are incongruously combined, so in the Tiruvaçagam (*e.g.* Pope's edition, pp. 49 and 138) Śiva is occasionally pantheized. He is the body and the soul, existence and non-existence, the false and the true, the bond and the release.

The remarkable feature of this religion, best seen in the Tiruvaçagam, is the personal tie which connects the soul with God. In no literature with which I am acquainted has the individual religious life—its struggles and dejection, its hopes and fears, its confidence and its triumph—received a delineation more frank and more profound. Despite the strangely exotic colouring of much in the picture, not only its outline but its details strikingly resemble the records of devout Christian lives in Europe. Śiva is addressed not only as Lord but as Father. He loves and desires human souls. "Hard though it is for Brahmâ and Vishṇu to reach thee, yet thou did'st desire me." What the soul desires is deliverance from matter and life with Śiva, and this he grants by bestowing grace (Arul). "With mother love he came in grace and made me his"; "O thou who art to thy true servants true"; "To thee, O Father, may I attain, may I yet dwell with thee." Sometimes[1] the poet feels that his sins have shut him off from communion with God. He lies "like a worm in the midst of ants, gnawed by the senses and troubled sore" ejaculating in utter misery "Thou hast forsaken me." But more often he seems on the point of expressing a thought commoner in Christianity than in Indian religion, namely that the troubles of this life are only a preparation for future beatitude. The idea that matter and suffering are not altogether evil is found in the later Sânkhya where Prakriti (which in some respects corresponds to Śakti) is represented as a generous female power working in the interests of the soul.

Among the many beauties of the Tiruvâçagam is one which reminds us of the works of St Francis and other Christian poetry, namely the love of nature and animals, especially birds and insects. There are constant allusions to plants and flowers; the refrain of one poem calls on a dragon fly to sing the praises of God and another bids the bird known as Kuyil call him to come. In another ode the poet says he looks for the grace of God like a patient heron watching night and day.

The first perusal of these poems impresses on the reader their resemblance to Christian literature. They seem to be a tropical version of Hymns Ancient and Modern and to ascribe to the deity and his worshippers precisely those sentiments

[1] *E.g.* Hymn vi.

which missionaries tell us are wanting among pagans—fatherly love, yearning devotion and the bliss of assured salvation. It is not surprising if many have seen in this tone the result of Christian influence. Yet I do not think that the hypothesis is probable. For striking as is the likeness the contrast is often equally striking. The deity described in words which almost literally render "Sun of my soul, Thou Saviour dear" is also the spouse of Umâ with the white breasts and curled locks; he dances in the halls of Tillai; and the line "Bid thou in grace my fears begone" is followed by two others indicated by dots as being "not translateable[1]." Nor can we say that emotional religion here uses the language of a mythology which it has outgrown. The emotion itself while charged with the love of god, the sense of sin and contrition, has in it another strain which jars on Europeans. Śiva sports with the world and his worshippers treat him with an affectionate intimacy which may be paralleled in the religion of Kṛishṇa but hardly in Christianity[2]. Thus several hymns have reference to a game, such as tossing about a ball (hymn vii), battledore and shuttlecock (xiv) or some form of wrestling in which the opponents place their hands on each other's shoulders (xv). The worshipper can even scold the deity. "If thou forsake me, I will make people smile at thee. I shall abuse thee sore: madman clad in elephant skin: madman that ate the poison: madman, who chose even me as thy own[3]."

Again, though in part the tone of these poems is Christian, yet they contain little that suggests Christian doctrine. There is nothing about redemption or a suffering god[4], and many ideas common to Christianity and Hinduism—such as the incarnation[5], the Trinity, and the divine child and his mother—are absent. It is possible that in some of the later works of the Sittars

[1] Pope's *Tiruvaçagam*, p. 257.

[2] Yet I have read that American revivalists describe how you play base ball (an American game) with Jesus.

[3] Pope's *Tiruvaçagam*, p. 101.

[4] It does not seem to me that the legend of Śiva's drinking the hala-hala poison is really parallel to the sufferings of the Christian redeemer. At the most it is a benevolent exploit like many performed by Vishṇu.

[5] Although Śiva is said to have been many times incarnate (see for instance *Catechism of the Shaiva religion*, p. 20) he seems to have merely appeared in human form on special occasions and not to have been like Christ or Kṛishṇa a god living as a man from birth to death.

Christian influence[1] may have supervened but most of this Tamil poetry is explicable as the development of the ideas expressed in the Bhagavad-gîtâ and the Śvetâśvatara Upanishad. Chronologically Christian influence is not impossible and there is a tradition that Mâṇikka-Vâçagar reconverted to Hinduism some natives of Malabar who had become Christians[2] but the uncertainty of his date makes it hard to fix his place in the history of doctrine. Recent Hindu scholars are disposed to assign him to the second or third century[3]. In support of this, it is plausibly urged that he was an active adversary of the Buddhists, that tradition is unanimous in regarding him as earlier than the writers of the Devâram[4] who make references (not however indisputable) to his poem, and that Perisiriyar, who commented on it, lived about 700 A.D. I confess that the tone and sentiments of the poem seem to me what one would expect in the eleventh rather than in the third century: it has something of the same emotional quality as the Gîtâ-govinda and the Bhâgavata-purâṇa, though it differs from them in doctrine and in its more masculine devotion. But the Dravidians are not of the same race as the northern Hindus and since this ecstatic monotheism is clearly characteristic of their literature, it may have made its appearance in the south earlier than elsewhere.

The Tiruvaçagam is not unorthodox but it deals direct with God and is somewhat heedless of priests. This feature becomes more noticeable in other authors such as Paṭṭaṇaṭṭu Piḷḷai, Kapilar and the Telugu poet Vêmana. The first named appears to have lived in the tenth century. The other two are legendary figures to whom anthologies of popular gnomic verses are ascribed and some of those attributed to Kapilar are probably ancient. In all this poetry there rings out a note of almost defiant monotheism, iconoclasm and antisacerdotalism. It may

[1] The lines which seem most clearly to reflect Christian influence are those quoted by Caldwell from the Nana nuru in the introduction to his *Comparative Grammar of the Dravidian languages*, p. 127, but neither the date of the work nor the original of the quotation is given. This part of the introduction is omitted in the third edition.

[2] *Tamilian Antiquary*, 4, 1909, pp. 57–82.

[3] *Ib.* pp. 1–57; Sesha Aiyar gives 275 A.D. as the probable date, and 375 as the latest date.

[4] The Śaiva catechism translated by Foulkes says (p. 27) that Śiva revealed the Tiruvaçagam twice, first to Manikka-Vaçagar and later to Tiru-Kovaiyar.

be partly explained by the fact that in the south Brahmanism was preceded, or at least from early times accompanied, by Buddhism and Jainism. These creeds did not make a conquest, for the Dravidian temperament obviously needed a god who could receive and reward passionate devotion, but they cleared the air and spread such ideas as the superiority of good deeds to rites and the uselessness of priests. Even now verses expressing these thoughts are popular in the Madras Presidency, but the sect which produced them, known as the Sittars[1], is entirely extinct. Caldwell attributes its literature to the seventeenth century, but the evidence available is small and it is clear that this theistic anti-brahmanic school had a long life. As in other cases, the Brahmans did not suppress so much as adapt it. The collection which goes by the name of Śiva-vâkyam contains poems of different ages and styles. Some are orthodox, others have no trace of Brahmanism except the use of Śiva as the name of the deity. Yet it would seem that the anthology as a whole has not fallen under sacerdotal censure[2].

The important sect of the Lingâyats should perhaps be regarded as an offshoot of this anti-brahmanic school, but before describing it, it may be well briefly to review the history of orthodox Śivaism in the south.

By this phrase is not meant the sect or school which had the support of Śankara but that which developed out of the poems mentioned above without parting company with Brahmanism. Śankara disapproved of their doctrine that the Lord is the efficient cause of the world, nor would the substitution of vernacular for Sanskrit literature and temple ceremonies for Vedic sacrifices have found favour with him. But these were evidently strong tendencies in popular religion. An important portion of the Devâram and the Kanda Purâṇa of Kachiyappar, a Tamil adaptation of the Skanda Purâṇa, were probably written between 600 and 750 A.D.[3] About 1000 A.D. the Tirumurai (including the Devâram) was arranged as a collection in eleven parts, and about a century later Sekkilar composed the Periya Purâṇa, a poetical hagiology, giving the legends of

[1] Sanskrit, *Siddha*.

[2] Space forbids me to quote the Śiva-vâkyam and Paṭṭaṇaṭṭu Piḷḷai, interesting as they are. The reader is referred to Gover, *Folk-Songs of southern India*, 1871, a work which is well worth reading.

[3] The date of the Skanda Purâṇa creates no difficulty for Bendall considered a MS. of it found in Nepal to be anterior to 659 A.D.

Śivaite saints and shrines. Many important temples were dedicated to Śiva during the eleventh and twelfth centuries.

There followed a period of scholasticism in which the body of doctrine called the Śaiva Siddhânta was elaborated by four Âcâryas, namely Mey-Kaṇḍa-Devar[1] (1223), Aruṇandi, Marai-ñâna-Sambandhar and Umâpati (1313). It will thus be seen that the foundation of Śivaite philosophy in Tamil is later than Râmânuja and the first Vishnuite movements, and perhaps it was influenced by them but the methodical exposition of the Śaiva-Siddhântam[2] does not differ materially from the more poetic utterances of the Tiruvaçagam. It recognizes the three entities, the Lord, the soul and matter as separate, but it shows a tendency (doubtless due to the influence of the Vedânta) both to explain away the existence of matter and to identify the soul with the Lord more closely than its original formulæ allow. Matter is described as Mâyâ and is potentially contained in the Lord who manifests it in the creative process which begins each kalpa. The Lord is also said to be one with our souls and yet other. The soul is by nature ignorant, in bondage to the illusion of Mâyâ and of Karma, but by the grace of the Lord it attains to union (not identity) with him, in which it sees that its actions are his actions.

In modern times Śaiva theology is represented among Dravidians by the works of Śivañânar (1785) and his disciple Kachiyappar: also by the poems of Râma-linga. Śivaism in Madras and other parts of southern India is still a vigorous and progressive Church which does not neglect European methods. Its principal organ is an interesting magazine called Siddhanta-Dipika or the Light of Truth. In northern India the Śivaites are less distinct as a body and have less organization, but temples to Śiva are numerous and perhaps the majority of Brahmans and ascetics regard him as their special deity and read Śivaite rather than Vishnuite texts. But it is probably also true that they are not sectarian in the same sense as the worshippers of Kṛishṇa.

It is not easy to estimate the relative numbers of Śivaites and Vishnuites in south India, and good authorities hold

[1] One of his maxims was *adu adu âdal*, that is the mind becomes that (spiritual or material) with which it identifies itself most completely.

[2] It is contained in fourteen śâstras, most of which are attributed to the four teachers mentioned above.

opposite views. The Śivaites are more united than the Vishnuites (whose many divisions and conspicuous sectarian marks attract attention) and are found chiefly among the upper classes and among ascetics, but perhaps there is much truth in an opinion which I once heard expressed by a Tamil Brahman, that the real division is not between the worshippers of Śiva and of Vishṇu, but between Smârtas, those who follow more or less strictly the ancient ritual observances and those who seek for salvation by devotion and in practice neglect the Sanskrit scriptures. There is little hostility. The worship of both gods is sometimes performed in the same building as at Chidambaram or in neighbouring shrines, as at Śrirangam. In south Kanara and Travancore it is generally held that the two deities are of equal greatness and in many places are found images representing them united in one figure. But the great temples at Madura, Tinnevelly and Tanjore are all dedicated to Śiva or members of his family. If in the philosophical literature of the Siddhânta the purity of the theism taught is noticeable, in these buildings it is rather the rich symbolism surrounding the god which attracts attention. In his company are worshipped Parvatî, Gaṇeśa, Subrahmaṇya, the bull Nandi and minor attendants: he is shown leaping in the ecstacy of the dance and on temple walls are often depicted his sixty-four sports or miracles (lîlâ). For the imagination of the Dravidians he is a great rhythmic force, throbbing and exulting in all the works of nature and exhibiting in kindly playfulness a thousand antics and a thousand shapes.

4

Another school of Śivaite philosophy flourished in Kashmir[1] from the ninth century onwards and is not yet extinct among Pandits. It bases itself on the Âgamas and includes among them the still extant Śiva-sûtras said to have been discovered as revelation by Vasugupta. He lived about 800 A.D. and abandoned Buddhism for Śivaism. The school produced a dis-

[1] For the Kashmir school see Barnett in *Muséon*, 1909, pp. 271–277. *J.R.A.S.* 1910, pp. 707–747. Kashmir Sanskrit series, particularly vol. II. entitled *Kashmir Śaivism.* The Śiva sûtras and the commentary Vimar'sinî translated in *Indian Thought*, 1911–12. Also Srînivasa Iyengar, *Outlines of Indian Philosophy*, pp. 168–175 and *Sarva-darśana-saṅgraha*, chap. VIII.

tinguished line of literary men who flourished from the ninth to the eleventh centuries[1].

The most recent authorities state that the Kashmir school is one and that there is no real opposition between the Spanda and Pratyabhijñâ sections[2]. The word Spanda, equivalent to the godhead and ultimate reality, is interesting for it means vibration accompanied by consciousness or, so to speak, self-conscious ether. The term Pratyabhijñâ or recognition is more frequent in the later writings. Its meaning is as follows. Śiva is the only reality and the soul is Śiva, but Mâyâ[3] forces on the soul a continuous stream of sensations. By the practice of meditation it is possible to interrupt the stream and in those moments light illuminates the darkness of the soul and it recognizes that it is Śiva, which it had forgotten. Also the world is wholly unreal apart from Śiva. It exists by his will and in his mind. What seems to the soul to be cognition is really recognition, for the soul (which is identical with the divine mind but blinded and obstructed) recognizes that which exists only in the divine mind.

It has been held that Kashmirian Śivaism is the parent of the Dravidian Śaiva Siddhânta and spread from Kashmir southwards by way of Kalyan in the eleventh century, and this hypothesis certainly receives support from the mention of Kashmiri Brahmans in south Indian inscriptions of the fourteenth century[4]. Yet I doubt if it is necessary to assume that south Indian Śivaism was *derived* from Kashmir, for the worship of Śiva must have been general long before the eleventh century[5] and Kashmiri Brahmans, far from introducing Śivaism to the south, are more likely to have gone thither because they were sure of a good reception, whereas they were exposed to Moslim

[1] Among them may be mentioned Kallata, author of the *Spanda Kârikâs* and Somânanda of the Śivadṛishti, who both flourished about 850–900. Utpala, who composed the Pratyabhijñâ-kârikâs, lived some fifty years later, and in the eleventh century Abhinava Gupta and Kshemarâja composed numerous commentaries.

[2] Kashmirian Śaivism is often called Trika, that is tripartite, because, like other varieties, it treats of three ultimates *Śiva, Śakti, Anu* or *Pati, Paśu, Pâśa.* But it has a decided tendency towards monism.

[3] Also called the Śakti or Mâtrikâ.

[4] See *Epig. Carn.* VII. Sk. 114. 19, 20 and *Jour. Mythic Society*, 1917, pp. 176, 180.

[5] To say nothing of Śivaite temples like the Kailas at Ellora, the chief doctrines and even the terminology of Śivaite philosophy are mentioned by Śankara on Ved. Sutras, II. 2. 37.

persecution in their own country. Also the forms which Śivaism assumed in these two outlying provinces present differences: in Kashmir it was chiefly philosophic, in the Dravidian countries chiefly religious. In the south it calls on God to help the sinner out of the mire, whereas the school of Kashmir, especially in its later developments, resembles the doctrine of Śankara, though its terminology is its own.

Before the advent of Islam, Kashmir was a secluded but cultured land. Its pleasant climate and beautiful scenery, said to have been praised by Gotama himself[1], attracted and stimulated thinkers and it had some importance in the history of Buddhism and of the Pancarâtra as well as for Śivaism. It is connected with the Buddhist sect called Sarvâstivâdins and in this case the circumstances seem clear. The sect did not originate in Kashmir but its adherents settled there after attending the Council of Kanishka and made it into a holy land. Subsequently, first Vishnuism and then Śivaism[2] entered the mountain valleys and flourished there. Kashmirian thinkers may have left an individual impress on either system but they dealt with questions which had already been treated of by others and their contributions, though interesting, do not seem to have touched the foundations of belief or to have inspired popular movements. The essential similarity of all Śivaite schools is so great that coincidences even in details do not prove descent or borrowing and the special terms of Kashmirian philosophy, such as *spanda* and *pratyabhijña*, seem not to be used in the south.

The Śiva-sûtras consist of three sections, describing three methods of attaining *svacchanda* or independence. One (the gist of which has been given above) displays some though not great originality: the second is Śâktist, the third follows the ordinary prescriptions of the Yoga. All Śivaite philosophy is really based on this last and teaches the existence of matter, souls and a deity, manifested in a series of phases. The relations of these three ultimates are variously defined, and they may be identified with one another, for the Sânkhya-Yoga doctrine may be com-

[1] In the Samyuktavastu, chap. XL. (transl. in *J.A.* 1914, II. pp. 534, etc.) the Buddha is represented as saying that Kashmir is the best land for meditation and leading a religious life.

[2] Chatterji, *Kashmir Śaivism*, p. 11, thinks that Abhinava Gupta's *Paramârtha-sâra*, published by Barnett, was an adaptation of older verses current in India and called the Âdhâra Kârikâs.

bined (though not very consistently) with the teaching of the Vedânta. In Kashmirian Śivaism Vedântist influences seem strong and it even calls itself Advaita. It is noteworthy that Vasugupta, who *discovered* the Śiva-sûtras, also wrote a commentary on the Bhagavad-gîtâ.

The gist of the matter is that, since a taste for speculation is far more prevalent in India than in Europe, there exist many systems of popular philosophy which, being a mixture of religion and metaphysics, involve two mental attitudes. The ordinary worshipper implores the Lord to deliver him from the bondage of sin and matter: the philosopher and saint wish to show that thought is one and such ideas as sin and matter partial and illusory. The originality of the Śaiva Siddhânta lies less in its dogmas than in its devotional character: in the feeling that the soul is immersed in darkness and struggles upwards by the grace of the Lord, so that the whole process of Karma and Mâyâ is really beneficent.

5

As already mentioned Śivaism has an important though unorthodox offshoot in the Lingâyats[1] or Lingavants. It appears that they originated at Kalyan (now in the Nizam's dominions) at the time when a usurper named Bijjala (1156–1167) had seized the throne of the Chalukyas. Their founder was Basava (the vernacular form of Vrishabha) assisted by his nephew Channabasava[2], whose exploits and miracles are recorded in two Purâṇas composed in Kanarese and bearing their respective names. According to one story Bijjala, who was a Jain, persecuted the Lingâyats and was assassinated by them. But there are other versions and the early legends of the sect merit little credence. The Lingâyats are Puritans. They reject caste, the supremacy of the Brahmans, sacrifices and other rites, and all the later Brahmanic literature. In theory they reverence the Vedas but practically the two Purâṇas mentioned are their

[1] See Thurston, *Castes and Tribes of southern India*, s.v. vol. IV. pp. 236–291 and *Gazetteer of the Bombay Presidency*, vol. XXIII. article Bijapur, pp. 219–1884.

[2] An inscription found at Ablur in Dharwar also mentions Ramayya as a champion of Śivaite monotheism. He is perhaps the same as Channabasava. The Lingâyats maintain that Basava merely revived the old true religion of Śiva and founded nothing new.

sacred books[1]. They are strict vegetarians and teetotallers: they do not insist on child marriages nor object to the remarriage of widows. Their only object of worship is Śiva in the form of a lingam and they always carry one suspended round the neck or arm. It is remarkable that an exceptionally severe and puritanical sect should choose this emblem as its object of worship, but, as already observed, the lingam is merely a symbol of the creative force and its worship is not accomplished by indecent rites[2]. They hold that true Lingâyats are not liable to be defiled by births or deaths, that they cannot be injured by sorcery and that when they die their souls do not transmigrate but go straight to Śiva. No prayers for the dead are needed.

Though trustworthy details about the rise of the Lingâyats are scarce, we can trace their spiritual ancestry. They present in an organized form the creed which inspired Paṭṭanaṭṭu Piḷḷai in the tenth century. About a hundred years later came Râmânuja who founded a great Vishnuite Church and it is not surprising if the Śivaites followed this example, nor if the least orthodox party became the most definitely sectarian.

The sectarian impulse which is conspicuous after the eleventh century was perhaps stimulated by the example of Mohammedanism. There was little direct doctrinal influence, but a religious people like the Hindus can hardly have failed to notice the strength possessed by an association worshipping one god of its own and united by one discipline. Syrian Christianity also might have helped to familiarize the Lingâyats with the idea of a god not to be represented by images or propitiated by sacrifices, but there is no proof that it was prevalent in the part of the Deccan where they first appeared.

The Lingâyats spread rapidly after Basava's death[3]. They still number about two millions and are to be found in most Karanese-speaking districts. They are easily recognizable for all carry the lingam, which is commonly enclosed in a red scarf

[1] They have also a book called *Prabhuling-lila*, which is said to teach that the deity ought to live in the believer's soul as he lives in the lingam, and collections of early Kanarese sermons which are said to date from the thirteenth century.

[2] The use of the Linga by this sect supports the view that even in its origin the symbol is not exclusively phallic.

[3] Their creed is said to have been the state religion of the Wodeyars of Mysore (1399–1600) and of the Nayaks of Keladi, Ikken or Bednur (1550–1763).

worn round the neck or among the richer classes in a silver-box. It is made of grey soapstone and a Lingâyat must on no account part with it for a moment. They are divided into the laity and the Jangams or priests. Some of these marry but others are itinerant ascetics who wander over India frequenting especially the five Simhâsanas or Lingâyat sees[1]. They are treated with extreme respect by the laity and sometimes wear fantastic costumes such as plates resembling armour or little bells which announce their approach as they walk.

In doctrine the Lingâyats remain faithful to their original tenets and do not worship any god or goddess except Śiva in the form of the Lingam, though they show respect to Gaṇeśa, and other deities as also to the founder of their sect. But in social matters it is agreed by all observers that they show a tendency to reintroduce caste and to minimize the differences separating them from more orthodox sects. According to Basava's teaching all members of the community both men and women are equal. But though converts from all castes are still accepted, it was found at the last census that well-to-do Lingâyats were anxious to be entered under the name of Vîraśaiva Brahmans, Kshatriyas, etc., and did not admit that caste distinctions are obliterated among them. Similarly though the remarriage of widows is not forbidden there is a growing tendency to look at it askance.

[1] At Kadur, Ujjeni, Benares, Śrîsailam and Kedarnâth in the Himalayas. In every Lingâyat village there is a monastery affiliated to one of these five establishments. The great importance attached to monastic institutions is perhaps due to Jain influence.

CHAPTER XXIX

VISHNUISM IN SOUTH INDIA

1

THOUGH Śivaism can boast of an imposing array of temples, teachers and scriptures in the north as well as in the south, yet Vishnuism was equally strong and after 1000 A.D. perhaps stronger. Thus Alberuni writing about north-western India in 1030 A.D. mentions Śiva and Durgâ several times incidentally but devotes separate chapters to Nârâyaṇa and Vâsudeva; he quotes copiously from Vishnuite works[1] but not from sectarian Śivaite books. He mentions that the worshippers of Vishṇu are called Bhâgavatas and he frequently refers to Râma. It is clear that in giving an account of Vishnuism he considered that he had for all practical purposes described the religion of the parts of India which he knew.

In their main outlines the histories of Vishnuism and Śivaism are the same. Both faiths first assumed a definite form in northern India, but both flourished exceedingly when transplanted to the south and produced first a school of emotional hymn writers and then in a maturer stage a goodly array of theologians and philosophers as well as offshoots in the form of eccentric sects which broke loose from Brahmanism altogether. But Vishnuism having first spread from the north to the south returned from the south to the north in great force, whereas the history of Śivaism shows no such reflux[2]. Śivaism remained comparatively homogeneous, but Vishnuism gave birth from the eleventh century onwards to a series of sects or Churches still extant and forming exclusive though not mutually hostile associations. The chief Churches or Sampradâyas bear the names of Sanakâdi, Śrî, Brahmâ and Rudra. The first three were founded by Nimbâditya, Râmânuja and Madhva respectively.

[1] Such as the Vishṇu Purâṇa, Vishṇu Dharma, said to be a section of the Garuda Purâṇa and the Bhagavad-gîtâ.

[2] The Hindus are well aware that the doctrine of Bhakti spread from the south to the north. See the allegory quoted in *J.R.A.S.* 1911, p. 800.

The Rudra-sampradâya was rendered celebrated by Vallabha, though he was not its founder.

The belief and practice of all Vishnuite sects alike is a modified monotheism, the worship of the Supreme Being under some such name as Râma or Vâsudeva. But the monotheism is not perfect. On the one hand it passes into pantheism: on the other it is not completely disengaged from mythology and in all sects the consort and attendants of the deity receive great respect, even if this respect is theoretically distinguished from adoration. Nearly all sects reject sacrifice *in toto* and make the basis of salvation emotional—namely devotion to the deity, and as a counterpart to this the chief characteristic of the deity is loving condescension or grace. The theological philosophy of each sect is nearly always, whatever name it may bear, a variety of the system known as Viśishṭâdvaita, or qualified monism, which is not unlike the Sâṅkhya-Yoga[1]. For Vishnuites as for Śivaites there exist God, the soul and matter, but most sects shrink from regarding them as entirely separate and bridge over the differences with various theories of emanations and successive manifestations of the deity. But for practical religion the soul is entangled in matter and, with the help of God, struggles towards union with him. The precise nature and intimacy of this union has given rise to as many subtle theories and phrases as the sacraments in Europe. Vishnuite sects in all parts of India show a tendency to recognize vernacular works as their scriptures, but they also attach great importance to the Upanishads, the Bhagavad-gîtâ, the Nârâyaṇîya and the Vedânta Sûtras. Each has a special interpretation of these last which becomes to some extent its motto.

But these books belong to the relatively older literature. Many Vishnuite, or rather Krishnaite, works composed from the eighth century onwards differ from them in tone and give prominence to the god's amorous adventures with the Gopis and (still later) to the personality of Râdhâ. This ecstatic and sentimental theology, though found in all parts of India, is more prevalent in the north than in the south. Its great textbook is the Bhâgavata Purâṇa. The same spirit is found in

[1] Thus Râmânuja says (Śrî Bhâshya, II. 2. 43) that the Vedânta Sûtras do not refute the Sâṅkhya and Yoga but merely certain erroneous views as to Brahman not being the self.

Jayadeva's Gîtâ-govinda, apparently composed in Bengal about 1170 A.D. and reproducing in a polished form the religious dramas or Yâtras in which the life of Kṛishṇa is still represented.

2

The sect[1] founded by Nimbârka or Nimbâditya has some connection with this poem. Its chief doctrine is known as dvaitâdvaitamata, or dualistic non-duality, which is explained as meaning that, though the soul and matter are distinct from God, they are yet as intimately connected with him as waves with water or the coils of a rope with the rope itself. This doctrine is referred to in the religious drama called Prabodhacandrodaya, probably composed at the end of the eleventh century. The Nimâvats, as the adherents of the sect are called, are found near Muttra and in Bengal. It is noticeable that this sect, which had its origin in northern India, is said to have been persecuted by the Jains[2] and to have been subsequently revived by a teacher called Nivâsa. This may explain why in the twelfth century Vishnuism flourished in the south rather than in the north[3]. Less is known of the Nimbârkas than of the other sects. They worship Kṛishṇa and Râdhâ and faith in Kṛishṇa is said to be the only way to salvation. Kṛishṇa was the deity of the earliest bhakti-sects. Then in the fourteenth and fifteenth centuries there was a reaction in favour of Râma as a more spiritual deity, but subsequently Vallabha and Caitanya again made the worship of Kṛishṇa popular. Nimbârka expressed his views in a short commentary on the Vedânta Sûtras and also in ten verses containing a compendium of doctrine[4].

[1] It has been described as the earliest of the Vishnuite Churches and it would be so if we could be sure that the existence of the doctrine called Dvaitâdvaita was equivalent to the existence of the sect. But Bhandarkar has shown some reason for thinking that Nimbâditya lived after Râmânuja. It must be admitted that the worship of Râdhâ and the doctrine of self-surrender or prapatti, both found in the Daśaśloki, are probably late.

[2] See Grierson in *E.R.E.* vol. II. p. 457.

[3] The Church of the Nimavats is also called Sanakâdi-sampradâya because it professes to derive its doctrine from Sanaka and his brethren who taught Nârada, who taught Nimbârka. At least one sub-sect founded by Harivamsa (born 1559) adopts a doctrine analogous to Saktism and worships Râdhâ as the manifestation of Kṛishṇa's energy.

[4] Called the Daśaśloki. It is translated in Bhandarkar's *Vaishṇ. and Śaivism*, pp. 63–5.

3

As among the Śivaites, so among the Vishnuites of the south, history begins with poet-saints. They are called the twelve Âr̤vârs[1]. For the three earliest no historical basis has been found, but the later ones seem to be real personalities. The most revered of them is Namm'âr̤vâr also called Sathagopa, whose images and pictures may be seen everywhere in south India and receive the same reverence as figures of the gods[2]. He may have lived in the seventh or eighth century A.D.[3]

The chronology of the Âr̤vârs is exceedingly vague but if the praises of Śiva were sung by poet-saints in the seventh century, it is probable that the Vishṇu worshippers were not behindhand. Two circumstances argue a fairly early date. First Nâthamuni is said to have arranged the hymns of the Âr̤vârs and he probably lived about 1000 A.D. Therefore the Âr̤vârs must have become classics by this date. Secondly the Bhâgavata Purâṇa[4] says that in the Kali age the worshippers of Nârâyaṇa will be numerous in the Dravidian country, though in other parts found only here and there, and that those who drink the water of the Kaveri and other southern rivers will mostly be devotees of Vâsudeva. This passage must have been written after a Vishnuite movement had begun in the Dravidian country[5].

The hymns attributed to the Âr̤vârs are commonly known by the name of Prabandham or Nâlâyiram and are accepted by the Tengalai Vishnuites as their canonical scriptures. The whole collection contains 4000 verses arranged in four parts[6] and an

[1] Also spelt Alvar and Azhvar. The Tamil pronunciation of this difficult letter varies in different districts. The word apparently means one who is drowned or immersed in the divine love. Cf. *Azhi*, the deep sea; *Azhal*, being deep or being immersed.

[2] An educated Vaishṇava told me at Śrîrangam that devas and saints receive the same homage.

[3] It is possible that the poems attributed to Namm'âr̤vâr and other saints are really later compositions. See *Epig. Ind.* vol. VIII. p. 294.

[4] XI. 5. 38–40.

[5] Bhandarkar (*Vaishṇ. and Śaivism*, p. 50) thinks it probable that Kulaśekhara, one of the middle Âr̤vârs, lived about 1130. But the argument is not conclusive and it seems to me improbable that he lived after Nâthamuni.

[6] The first called Mudal-Âyiram consists of nine hymns ascribed to various saints such as Periyâr̤var and Andal. The second and third each consist of a single work the Periya-tiru-mor̤i and the Tiru-vay-mor̤i ascribed to Tiru-mangai and

extract consisting of 602 verses selected for use in daily worship is in part accessible[1]. This poetry shows the same ecstatic devotion and love of nature as the Tiruvaçagam. It contemplates the worship of images and a temple ritual consisting in awakening the god at morning and attending on him during the day. It quotes the Upanishads and Bhagavad-gîtâ, assumes as a metaphysical basis a vedantized form of the Sâṅkhya philosophy, and also accepts the legends of the pastoral Kṛishṇa but without giving much detail. Jains, Buddhists and Śaivas are blamed and the repetition of the name Govinda is enjoined. Though the hymns are not anti-Brahmanic they decidedly do not contemplate a life spent in orthodox observances and their reputed authors include several Śûdras, a king and a woman.

After the poet-saints came the doctors and theologians. Accounts of them, which seem historical in the main though full of miraculous details, are found in the Tamil biographies[2] illustrating the apostolic succession of teachers. It appears fairly certain that Râmânuja, the fourth in succession, was alive in 1118: the first, known as Nâthamuni, may therefore have lived 100–150 years earlier. None of his works are extant but he is said to have arranged the poems of the Âṛvârs for recitation in temple services. He went on a pilgrimage to northern India and according to tradition was an adept in Yoga, being one of the last to practise it in the south. Third in succession was his grandson Yamunârcârya (known as Âlavandâr or victor), who spent the first part of his life as a wealthy layman but was converted and resided at Śrîrangam. Here he composed several important works in Sanskrit including one written to establish the orthodoxy of the Pañcarâtra and its ritual[3].

Namm'âṛvâr respectively. The fourth part or Iyar-pa is like the first a miscellany containing further compositions by these two as well as by others.

[1] Nityânusandhânam series: edited with Telugu paraphrase and English translation by M. B. Srinivasa Aiyangar, Madras, 1898.

[2] The best known is the Guru-paramparâ-prabhâvam of Brahmatantra-svatantra-swâmi. For an English account of these doctors see T. Râjagopala Chariar, *The Vaishṇavite Reformers of India*, Madras, 1909.

[3] Âgamaprâmâṇya. He also wrote a well-known hymn called Âlavandâr-Stotram and a philosophical treatise called Siddhi-traya.

4

He was succeeded by Râmânuja, a great name in Indian theology both as the organizer of a most important sect and, if not the founder[1], at least the accepted exponent of the Viśishṭâdvaita philosophy. Râmânuja was born at Śrîperumbudur[2] near Madras, where he is still commemorated by a celebrated shrine. As a youth he studied Śivaite philosophy at Conjeevaram but abandoned it for Vishnuism. He appears to have been a good administrator. He made the definitive collection of the hymns of the Âṟvârs and is said to have founded 700 maṭhs and 89 hereditary abbotships, for he allowed the members of his order to marry. He visited northern India, including Kashmir if tradition may be believed, but his chief residence was Śrîrangam. Towards the end of the eleventh century however, the hostility of the Chola King Kulottunga, who was an intolerant Śivaite, forced him to retire to Mysore. Here he was protected by King Viṭṭala Deva whom he converted from Jainism and on the death of Kulottunga in 1118 he returned to Śrîrangam where he ended his days. In the temple there his tomb and a shrine where his image receives divine honours may still be seen. His best known work[3] is the Śrî Bhâshya or commentary on the Vedânta sûtras.

The sect which he founded is known as the Śrî Sampradâya and its members as the Śrî Vaishṇavas. As among the Śivaites revelation is often supposed to be made by Śiva through Śakti, so here the Lord is said to have revealed the truth to his consort Śrî or Lakshmî, she to a demigod called Visvaksena, and he to Namm'âṟvâr, from whom Râmânuja was eighth in spiritual descent. Though the members of the sect are sometimes called Ramaites the personality of Râma plays a small part in their faith, especially as expounded by Râmânuja. As names for the deity he uses Nârâyaṇa and Vâsudeva and he quotes freely from

[1] He states himself that he followed Boddhâyana, a commentator on the Sûtras of unknown date but anterior to Śaṅkara. He quotes several other commentators particularly Dramiḍa, so that his school must have had a long line of teachers.

[2] See *Gazetteer of India*, vol. XXIII. s.v. There is a Kanarese account of his life called Dibya-caritra. For his life and teaching see also Bhandarkar in *Berichte VIIth Int. Orient. Congress*, 1886, pp. 101 ff. Lives in English have been published at Madras by Alkondaville Govindâcârya (1906) and Kṛishṇaswami Aiyengar (? 1909).

[3] He also wrote the Vedârtha Saṅgraha, Vedârtha Pradîpa, Vedânta Sâra and a commentary on the Bhagavad-gîtâ.

the Bhagavad-gîtâ and the Vishṇu Purâṇa. Compared with the emotional deism of Caitanya this faith seems somewhat philosophic and reticent.

Râmânuja clearly indicates its principal points in the first words of his Śrî Bhâshya. "May my mind be filled with devotion towards the highest Brahman, the abode of Lakshmî; who is luminously revealed in the Upanishads: who in sport produces, sustains and reabsorbs the entire universe: whose only aim is to foster the manifold classes of beings that humbly worship him[1]." He goes on to say that his teaching is that of the Upanishads, "which was obscured by the mutual conflict of manifold opinions," and that he follows the commentary of Bodhâyana and other teachers who have abridged it.

That is to say, the form of Vishnuism which Râmânuja made one of the principal religions of India claims to be the teaching of the Upanishads, although he also affiliates himself to the Bhâgavatas. He interprets the part of the Vedânta Sûtras which treats of this sect[2] as meaning that the author states and ultimately disallows the objections raised to their teaching and he definitely approves it. "As it is thus settled that the highest Brahman or Nârâyaṇa himself is the promulgator of the entire Pancarâtra and that this system teaches the nature of Nârâyaṇa and the proper way of worshipping him, none can disestablish the view that in the Pancarâtra all the other doctrines are comprised[3]."

The true tradition of the Upanishads he contends has been distorted by "manifold opinions," among which the doctrine of Śaṅkara was no doubt the chief. That doctrine was naturally distasteful to devotional poets, and from the time of Nâthamuni onwards a philosophic reaction against it grew up in Śrîrangam. Râmânuja preaches the worship of a loving God, though when we read that God produces and reabsorbs the universe in sport, we find that we are farther from Christianity than we at first supposed. There is a touch of mythology in the mention of Lakshmî[4] but it is clear that Râmânuja himself had little liking for mythology. He barely mentions Râma and Kṛishṇa in the Śrî Bhâshya nor does he pay much attention to the consort of

[1] *S.B.E.* XLVIII. p. 3. [2] II. 2. 36–39. [3] II. 2. 43 *ad fin.*

[4] Râmânuja's introduction to the Bhagavad-gîtâ is more ornate but does not go much further in doctrine than the passage here quoted.

the deity. On the other hand he shows no sign of rejecting the ritual and regulations of the Brahmans. He apparently wished to prove that the doctrine of salvation by devotion to a personal god is compatible with a system as strictly orthodox as Śaṅkara's own.

I shall treat elsewhere of his philosophy, known as the Viśishṭâdvaita or non-duality, which yet recognizes a distinction between God and individual souls. The line of thought is old and at all periods is clearly a compromise, unwilling to deny that God is everything and yet dissatisfied with the idea that a personal deity and our individual transmigrating souls are all merely illusion. Devotional theism was growing in Râmânuja's time. He could not break with the Upanishads and Vedantic tradition but he adapted them to the needs of his day. He taught firstly that the material world and human souls are not illusion but so to speak the body of God who comprises and pervades them: secondly this God is omniscient, omnipresent, almighty and all-merciful, and salvation (that is mukti or deliverance from transmigration) is obtained by those souls who, assisted by his grace, meditate on him and know him; thirdly this salvation consists not in absorption into God but in blissful existence near him and in participation of his glorious qualities. He further held[1] that God exists in five modes, namely: (*a*) Para, the entire supreme spirit, (*b*) the fourfold manifestation as Vâsudeva, Saṅkarshaṇa, Pradyumna and Aniruddha, (*c*) incarnations such as Râma and Kṛishṇa, (*d*) the internal controller or Antaryâmin according to the text[2] "who abiding in the soul rules the soul within," (*e*) duly consecrated images.

The followers of Râmânuja are at present divided into two schools known as Tengalais and Vadagalais, or southern and northern[3]. The double residence of the founder is one reason for the division, since both Mysore and Trichinopoly could claim to have personal knowledge of his teaching. The really important difference seems to be that the Tengalai or southern school is inclined to break away from Sanskrit tradition, to ignore the Vedas in practice and to regard the Tamil Nâlâyiram as an

[1] This fivefold manifestation of the deity is a characteristic Pâncarâtra doctrine. See Schrader, *Int.* pp. 25, 51 and *Śrî Bhâshya*, II. 242.

[2] See Br. Ar. Up. III. 7. The Śrî Vaishṇavas attach great importance to this chapter.

[3] Only relatively northern and southern. Neither flourish in what we call northern India.

all-sufficient scripture, whereas the Vadagalais, though not rejecting the Nâlâyiram, insist on the authority of the Vedas. But both divisions are scrupulous about caste observances and the ceremonial purity of their food. They are separated by nice questions of doctrine, especially as to the nature of prapatti, resignation or self-surrender to the deity, a sentiment slightly different from bhakti which is active faith or devotion. The northerners hold that the soul lays hold of the Lord, as the young monkey hangs on to its mother, whereas the southerners say that the Lord picks up the helpless and passive soul as a cat picks up a kitten[1]. According to the northerners, the consort of Vishṇu is, like him, uncreated and equally to be worshipped as a bestower of grace: according to the southerners she is created and, though divine, merely a mediator or channel of the Lord's grace. Even more important in popular esteem is the fact that the Vadagalai sectarian mark ends between the eyebrows whereas the Tengalais prolong it to the tip of the nose. *Odium theologicum* is often bitterest between the sects which are most nearly related and accordingly we find that the Tengalais and Vadagalais frequently quarrel. They use the same temples but in many places both claim the exclusive right to recite the hymns of the Âṟvârs. The chief difference in their recitation lies in the opening verse in which each party celebrates the names of its special teachers, and disputes as to the legality of a particular verse in a particular shrine sometimes give rise to free fights and subsequent lawsuits.

The two schools reckon the apostolic succession differently and appear to have separated in the thirteenth century, in which they were represented by Piḷḷai Lokâcârya and Vedânta Desika[2] respectively. The Tengalai, of which the first-named teacher

[1] Hence the two doctrines are called markaṭa-nyâya and marjâra-nyâya, monkey theory and cat theory. The latter gave rise to the dangerous doctrine of Doshabhogya, that God enjoys sin, since it gives a larger scope for the display of His grace. Cf. Oscar Wilde in *De Profundis*, "Christ, through some divine instinct in him, seems "to have always loved the sinner as being the nearest possible approach to per-"fection in man....In a manner not yet understood of the world, he regarded sin "and suffering as being in themselves beautiful holy things and modes of per-"fection....Christ, had he been asked, would have said—I feel quite certain about "it—that the moment the prodigal son fell on his knees and wept, he made his "having wasted his substance with harlots, his swine herding and hungering for "the husks they ate beautiful and holy moments in his life."

[2] Also called Veṅkatanâtha. For some rather elaborate studies in the history of the Śrî-Vaishṇavas see V. Rangacharis' articles in *J. Bombay R.A.S.* 1915 and 1916 and *J. Mythic Society*, 1917, Nos. 2 ff.

was the practical founder, must be regarded as innovators, for in their use of Tamil as the language of religion they do not follow the example of Râmânuja. Lokâcârya teaches that the grace of God is irresistible and should be met not merely by active faith, but by self-surrender[1], and entire submission to the guidance of the spiritual teacher. He was the author of eighteen works called Rahasyas or secrets[2] but though he appears to have been the first to formulate the Tengalai doctrines, Manavala Mahâmuni (1370–1443 A.D.) is regarded by the sect as its chief saint. His images and pictures are frequent in south India and he wrote numerous commentaries and poems. Vedânta Desika, the founder of the Vadagalai, was a native of Conjeevaram but spent much of his life at Śrîrangam. He was a voluminous author and composed *inter alia* an allegorical play in ten acts, portraying the liberation of the soul under the auspices of King Viveka (discrimination) and Queen Sumati (Wisdom).

At the present day the two sects recognize as their respective heads two Âcâryas who are married, whereas all Smârta Âcâryas are celibates[3]. The Tengalai Âcârya resides near Tinnevelly, the Vadagalai in the district of Kurnool. They both make periodical visitations in their districts and have considerable ecclesiastical power. In the south Śrîrangam near Trichinopoly is their principal shrine: in the north Melucote in the Seringapatam district is esteemed very sacred.

5

It was only natural that Râmânuja's advocacy of qualified non-duality should lead some more uncompromising spirit to affirm the doctrine of Dvaita or duality. This step was taken by Madhva Âcârya, a Kanarese Brahman who was probably born in 1199 A.D.[4] In the previous year the great temple of

[1] Prapatti and âcâryâbhimâna.—The word *prapatti* seems not to occur in the Śrî Bhâshya and it is clear that Râmânuja's temperament was inclined to active and intelligent devotion. But *prapatti* is said to have been taught by Nathamuni and Sathagopa (Râjagopala Chariar, *Vaishṇavite Reformers*, p. 6). The word means literally *approaching*.

[2] The Artha-pañcaka and Tattva-traya are the best known. See text and translation of the first in *J.R.A.S.* 1910, pp. 565–607.

[3] Râmânuja set less store than Śankara on asceticism and renunciation of the world. He held the doctrine called *samucchaya* (or combination) namely that good works as well as knowledge are efficacious for salvation.

[4] Also called Ânandatîrtha and Pûrṅaprajña. According to others he was born in 1238 A.D. See for his doctrines Grierson's article Madhvas in *E.R.E.* and his own

Jagannatha at Puri had been completed and the Vishnuite movement was at its height. Madhva though educated as a Śaiva became a Vaishṇava. He denied absolutely the identity of the Supreme Being with the individual soul and held that the world is not a modification of the Lord but that he is like a father who begets a son. Yet in practice, rigid monotheism is not more prevalent among Madhva's followers than in other sects. They are said to tolerate the worship of Śivaite deities and of the lingam in their temples[1] and their ascetics dress like Śaivas.

Madhva travelled in both northern and southern India and had a somewhat troubled life, for his doctrine, being the flat contradiction of the Advaita, involved him in continual conflicts with the followers of Śaṅkara who are said to have even stolen his library. At any rate they anathematized his teaching with a violence unusual in Indian theology[2]. In spite of such lively controversy he found time to write thirty-seven works, including commentaries on the Upanishads, Bhagavad-gîtâ and Vedânta Sûtras. The obvious meaning of these texts is not that required by his system, but they are recognized by all Vaishṇavas as the three Prasthânas or starting-points of philosophy and he had to show that they supported his views. Hence his interpretation often seems forced and perverse. The most extraordinary instance of this is his explanation of the celebrated phrase in

commentaries on the Chândogya and Bṛihad Ar. Upanishads published in *Sacred Books of the Hindus*, vols. III. and XIV. For his date Bhandarkar, *Vaishṇ. and Śaivism*, pp. 58–59 and *I.A.* 1914, pp. 233 ff. and 262 ff. Accounts of his life and teaching have been written by Padmanabha Char. and Kṛishṇa Svami Aiyer (Madras, 1909). His followers maintain that he is not dead but still alive at Badarî in the Himalayas.

[1] See Padmanabha Char. *l.c.* page 12. Madhva condemned the worship of inanimate objects (*e.g.* com. Chând. Up. VII. 14. 2) but not the worship of Brahman *in* inanimate objects.

[2] In a work called the *Pâshanda capetikâ* or *A Slap for Heretics*, all the adherents of Madhva are consigned to hell and the Saurapurâṇa, chaps. XXXVIII.–XL. contains a violent polemic against them. See Jahn's *Analysis*, pp. 90–106 and Barth in *Mélanges Harlez*, pp. 12–25. It is curious that the Madhvas should have been selected for attack, for in many ways they are less opposed to Śivaites than are other Vishnuite sects but the author was clearly badly informed about the doctrines which he attacks and he was probably an old-fashioned Śivaite of the north who regarded Madhvism as a new-fangled version of objectionable doctrines.

The Madhvas are equally violent in denouncing Śankara and his followers. They miswrite the name Saṃkara, giving it the sense of mongrel or dirt and hold that he was an incarnation of a demon called Maṇimat sent by evil spirits to corrupt the world.

the Chândogya Upanishad Sa âtmâ tat tvam asi. He reads Sa âtmâ atat tvam asi and considers that it means "You are not that God. Why be so conceited as to suppose that you are[1]?" Monotheistic texts have often received a mystical and pantheistic interpretation. The Old Testament and the Koran have been so treated by Kabbalists and Sufis. But in Madhva's commentaries we see the opposite and probably rarer method. Pantheistic texts are twisted until they are made to express uncompromising monotheism.

The sect is often called Brahma-sampradâya, because it claims that its doctrine was revealed by Brahmâ from whom Madhva was the sixth teacher in spiritual descent. Its members are known as Mâdhvas but prefer to call themselves Sad-Vaishṇavas. Its teaching seems more rigid and less emotional than that of other Vishnuites and is based on the Pancabheda or five eternal distinctions between (*a*) God and the soul, (*b*) God and matter, (*c*) the soul and matter, (*d*) individual souls, (*e*) individual atoms of matter. God is generally called Vishṇu or Nârâyaṇa rather than Vâsudeva. Kṛishṇa is adored but not in his pastoral aspect. Vishṇu and his spouse Lakshmî are real though superhuman personalities and their sons are Brahmâ the creator and Vâyu[2]. Peculiar to this sect is the doctrine that except through Vâyu, the son of Vishṇu, salvation is impossible. Vâyu has been three times incarnate as Hanumat, the helper of Râma, as Bhîma and as Madhva himself[3]. Souls are separate, innumerable and related to God as subjects to a king. They are of three classes: those who are destined to eternal bliss in the presence of God: those who revolve eternally in the maze of transmigration: and those who tending ever downwards are doomed to eternal suffering.

[1] See his comment on Chând. Up. VI. 8. 7. Compare Bhag.-g. XV. 7. The text appears to say that the soul (Jîva) is a part (amsa) of the Lord. Madhva says it is so-called because it bears some reduced similitude to the Lord, though quite distinct from him. Madhva's exegesis is supported by a system of tantric or cabalistic interpretation in which every letter has a special meaning. Thus in the passage of the Chând. Up. mentioned above the simple words *sa ya eshah* are explained as equivalent to Sâra essence, yama the controller, and ishta the desired one. The reading atat tvam asi is said not to have originated with Madhva but to be found in a Bhâgavata work called the Sâmasamhitâ.

[2] In his commentary on the opening of the Chând. Up. Madhva seems to imply a Trinity consisting of Vishṇu, Ramâ (=Lakshmî) and Vâyu.

[3] This is expressly stated at the end of the commentary on the Brih. Ar. Upan.

This last doctrine, as well as the doctrine of salvation through Vâyu, the wind or spirit, has led many to suspect that Madhva was influenced by Christian ideas, but it is more probable that he owed something to Islam. Such influence would no doubt be distant and indirect, for a Brahman would not come into contact with Moslim doctors, though it is said that Madhva could speak Persian[1]. But some Moslim ideas such as the absolute separation of God from the world and the predestination of souls to eternal happiness and misery may have entered Brahman minds. Still, nearly all Madhva's views (with the possible exception of eternal punishment) have Indian analogies. The Yoga teaches that there are innumerable souls distinct from one another and from God and though salvation through the spirit sounds Christian, yet the Upanishads constantly celebrate Vâyu (wind) and Prâṇa (breath) as the pervading principle of the world and the home of the self. "By the wind (Vâyu) as thread, O Gautama, this world and the other world and all creatures are bound together[2]." Thus the idea that the wind is the universal mediator is old and it does not seem that Madhva regarded Vâyu as a redeemer or expiation for sin like Christ.

The Mâdhvas are still an energetic and important sect. Their headquarters are at Udipi in South Kanara and they also hold an annual conference at Tirupati at which examinations in theology are held and prizes given. At Udipi are eight maṭhs and a very sacred temple, dedicated by Madhva himself to Kṛishṇa. The head of each maṭh is charged in turn with the supervision of this temple during two years and the change of office is celebrated by a great biennial festival in January. The worship is more puritanical than in the temples of other sects, dancing girls for instance not being allowed, but great importance is attached to the practice of branding the body with the emblems of Vishṇu. The sect, like the Śrî Vaishṇavas, is divided

[1] *Life and teachings of Śrî-Madhvacharyar* by Padmanabha Char. 1909, p. 159. Some have suspected a connection between Madhva's teaching and Manicheism, because he attached much importance to an obscure demon called Manimat (see Mahâbh. III. 11,661) whom he considered incarnate in Śankara. It is conceivable that in his Persian studies he may have heard of Mani as an arch-heretic and have identified him with this demon but this does not imply any connection between his own system (or Śankara's either) and Manicheism.

[2] Brih. Ar. Upan. III. 7. 2.

into two parties, the Vyasakutas who are conservative and use Sanskrit scriptures[1], and the Dasakutas who have more popular tendencies and use sacred books written in Kanarese. Neither the Śrî Vaishṇavas nor the Mâdhvas are numerous in northern India.

[1] Among them are the Maṇimanjarî, the Madhvavijaya and the Vâyustuti, all attributed to a disciple of Madhva and his son.

CHAPTER XXX

LATER VISHNUISM IN NORTH INDIA

1

WITH the fifteenth century Hinduism enters on a new phase. Sects arise which show the influence of Mohammedanism, sometimes to such an extent that it is hard to say whether they should be classed as Hindu or Moslim, and many teachers repudiate caste. Also, whereas in the previous centuries the centre of religious feeling lay in the south, it now shifts to the north. Hinduism had been buffeted but not seriously menaced there: the teachers of the south had not failed to recognize by their pilgrimages the sanctity and authority of the northern seats of learning: such works as the Gîtâ-govinda testify to the existence there of fervent Vishnuism. But the country had been harassed by Moslim invasions and unsettled by the vicissitudes of transitory dynasties. The Jains were powerful in Gujarat and Rajputâna. In Bengal Śâktism and moribund Buddhism were not likely to engender new enthusiasms. But in a few centuries the movements inaugurated in the south increased in extension and strength. Hindus and Mohammedans began to know more of each other, and in the sixteenth century under the tolerant rule of Akbar and his successors the new sects which had been growing were able to consolidate themselves.

After Râmânuja and Madhva, the next great name in the history of Vishnuism, and indeed of Hinduism, is Râmânand. His date is uncertain[1]. He was posterior to Râmânuja, from whose sect he detached himself, and Kabir was his disciple,

[1] See Bhandarkar, *Vaishṇ. and Śaivism*, pp. 66 ff., Grierson in *Ind. Ant.* 1893, p. 226, and also in article Ramanandi in *E.R.E.*; Farquhar, *J.R.A.S.* 1920, pp. 185 ff. Though Indian tradition seems to be unanimous in giving 1299 A.D. (4400 Kali) as the date of Râmânand's birth, all that we know about himself and his disciples makes it more probable that he was born nearly a century later. The history of ideas, too, becomes clear and intelligible if we suppose that Râmânand, Kabir and Nanak flourished about 1400, 1450 and 1500 respectively. One should be cautious in allowing such arguments to outweigh unanimous tradition, but tradition also assigns to Râmânand an improbably long life, thus indicating a feeling that he influenced the fifteenth century. Also the traditions as to the number of teachers between Râmânuja and Râmânand differ greatly.

apparently his immediate disciple. Some traditions give Prayaga as his birthplace, others Melucote, but the north was the scene of his activity. He went on a lengthy pilgrimage, and on his return was accused of having infringed the rules of his sect as to eating, etc., and was excommunicated, but received permission from his Guru to found a new sect. He then settled in Benares and taught there. He wrote no treatise but various hymns ascribed to him are still popular[1]. Though he is not associated with any special dogma, yet his teaching is of great importance as marking the origin of a popular religious movement characterized by the use of the vernacular languages instead of Sanskrit, and by a laxity in caste rules culminating in a readiness to admit as equals all worshippers of the true God[2]. This God is Râma rather than Kṛishṇa. I have already pointed out that the worship of Râma as the Supreme Being (to be distinguished from respect for him as a hero) is not early: in fact it appears to begin in the period which we are considering. Of the human forms of the deity Kṛishṇa was clearly the most popular but the school of Râmânuja, while admitting both Râma and Kṛishṇa as incarnations, preferred to adore God under less mythological and more philosophic names such as Nârâyaṇa. Râmânand, who addressed himself to all classes and not merely to the Brahman aristocracy, selected as the divine name Râma. It was more human than Nârâyaṇa, less sensuous than Kṛishṇa. Every Hindu was familiar with the poetry which sings of Râma as a chivalrous and godlike hero. But he was not, like Kṛishṇa, the lover of the soul, and when Râmaism was divested of mythology by successive reformers it became a monotheism in which Hindu and Moslim elements could blend. Râmânand had twelve disciples, among whom were Kabir, a Raja called Pîpâ, Rai Das, a leather-seller (and therefore an outcast according to Hindu ideas) as well as Brahmans. The Râmats, as his followers were called, are a numerous and respectable body in north India, using the same sectarian mark as the Vadagalais from whom they do not differ materially, although a Hindu might consider that their small regard for caste is a vital distinction. They often call themselves Avadhûtas, that is, those who have shaken off orldly restrictions, and the more devout among them belong

[1] One of them is found in the Granth of the Sikhs.

[2] Râmânand's maxim was "Jâti pâti puchai nahikoi: Hari-ku bhajai so Hari-kau hoî." Let no one ask a man's caste or sect. Whoever adores God, he is God's own.

to an order divided into four classes of which only the highest is reserved to Brahmans and the others are open to all castes. They own numerous and wealthy maṭhs, but it is said that in some of these celibacy is not required and that monks and nuns live openly as man and wife[1].

An important aspect of the Râmat movement is its effect on the popular literature of Hindustan which in the fifteenth and even more in the sixteenth century blossoms into flowers of religious poetry. Many of these writings possess real merit and are still a moral and spiritual force. European scholars are only beginning to pay sufficient attention to this mighty flood of hymns which gushed forth in nearly all the vernaculars of India[2] and appealed directly to the people. The phenomenon was not really new. The psalms of the Buddhists and even the hymns of the Ṛig Veda were vernacular literature in their day, and in the south the songs of the Devaram and Nâlâyiram are of some antiquity. But in the north, though some Prâkrit literature has been preserved, Sanskrit was long considered the only proper language for religion. We can hardly doubt that vernacular hymns existed, but they did not receive the imprimatur of any teacher, and have not survived. But about 1400 all this changes. Though Râmânand was not much of a writer he gave his authority to the use of the vernacular: he did not, like Râmânuja, either employ or enjoin Sanskrit and the meagre details which we have of his circle lead us to imagine him surrounded by men of homely speech.

One current in this sea of poetry was Krishnaite and as such not directly connected with Râmânand. Vidyâpati[3] sang of the loves of Kṛishṇa and Râdhâ in the Maithili dialect and also in a form of Bengali. In the early fifteenth century (*c.* 1420) we have the poetess Mirâ Bai, wife of the Raja of Chitore who gained celebrity and domestic unhappiness by her passionate

[1] Bhattacharya, *Hindu Castes and Sects*, p. 445.

[2] Thus we have the poems of Kabir, Nânak and others contained in the Granth of the Sikhs and tending to Mohammedanism: the hymns wherein Mirâ Bai, Vallabha and his disciples praised Kṛishṇa in Râjputâna and Braj: the poets inspired by Caitanya in Bengal: Śaṅkar Deb and Madhab Deb in Assam: Namdev and Tukârâm in the Maratha country.

[3] See Beames, *J.A.* 1873, pp. 37 ff., and Grierson, *Maithili Christomathy*, pp. 34 ff., in extra No. to *Journ. As. Soc. Bengal*, Part I. for 1882 and Coomaraswamy's illustrated translation of Vidyâpati, 1915. It is said that a land grant proves he was a celebrated Pandit in 1400. The Bengali Vaishṇava poet Chaṇḍî Dâs was his contemporary.

devotion to the form of Kṛishṇa known as Ranchor. According to one legend the image came to life in answer to her fervent prayers, and throwing his arms round her allowed her to meet a rapturous death in his embrace. This is precisely the sentiment which we find later in the teaching of Vallabhâcârya and Caitanya. The hymns of the Bengali poets have been collected in the *Padakalpataru*, one of the chief sacred books of the Bengali Vaishṇavas. From Vallabhâcârya spring the group of poets who adorned Braj or the Muttra district. Pre-eminent among them is the blind Sur Das who flourished about 1550 and wrote such sweet lyrics that Kṛishṇa himself came down and acted as his amanuensis. A somewhat later member of the same group is Nâbhâ Das, the author of the Bhakta Mâlâ or Legends of the Saints, which is still one of the most popular religious works of northern India[1]. Almost contemporary with Sur Das was the great Tulsi Das and Grierson[2] enumerates thirteen subsequent writers who composed Râmâyaṇas in some dialect of Hindi. A little later came the Mahratta poet Tukarâm (born about 1600) who gave utterance to Krishnaism in another language.

Tulsi Das is too important to be merely mentioned as one in a list of poets. He is a great figure in Indian religion, and the saying that his Râmâyaṇa is more popular and more honoured in the North-western Provinces than the Bible in England is no exaggeration[3]. He came into the world in 1532 but was exposed by his parents as born under an unlucky star and was adopted by a wandering Sâdhu. He married but his son died and after this loss he himself became a Sâdhu. He began to write his Râmâyaṇa in Oudh at the age of forty-three, but moved to Benares where he completed it and died in 1623. On the Tulsi Ghat, near the river Asi, may still be seen the rooms which he occupied. They are at the top of a lofty building and command a beautiful view over the river[4].

[1] See Grierson, Gleanings from the Bhaktamâlâ, *J.R.A.S.* 1909 and 1910.

[2] *Modern Vernacular Literature of Hindustan*, 1889, p. 57.

[3] Similarly Dinesh Chandra Sen (*Lang. and Lit. of Bengal*, p. 170) says that Krittivâsa's translation of the Râmâyaṇa "is the Bible of the people of the Gangetic Valley and it is for the most part the peasants who read it." Krittivâsa was born in 1346 and roughly contemporary with Râmânand. Thus the popular interest in Râma was roused in different provinces at the same time.

[4] He also wrote several other poems, among which may be mentioned the Gîtâvalî and Kavittâvalî, dedicated respectively to the infancy and the heroic deeds of Râma, and the Vinaya Pattrikâ or petition, a volume of hymns and prayers.

His Râmâyaṇa which is an original composition and not a translation of Vâlmîki's work is one of the great religious poems of the world and not unworthy to be set beside *Paradise Lost.* The sustained majesty of diction and exuberance of ornament are accompanied by a spontaneity and vigour rare in any literature, especially in Asia. The poet is not embellishing a laboured theme: he goes on and on because his emotion bursts forth again and again, diversifying the same topic with an inexhaustible variety of style and metaphor. As in some forest a stream flows among flowers and trees, but pours forth a flood of pure water uncoloured by the plants on its bank, so in the heart of Tulsi Das the love of God welled up in a mighty fountain ornamented by the mythology and legends with which he bedecked it, yet unaffected by them. He founded no sect, which is one reason of his popularity, for nearly all sects can read him with edification, and he is primarily a poet not a theologian. But though he allows himself a poet's licence to state great truths in various ways, he still enunciates a definite belief. This is theism, connected with the name Râma. Since in the north he is the author most esteemed by the Vishnuites, it would be a paradox to refuse him that designation, but his teaching is not so much that Vishṇu is the Supreme Being who becomes incarnate in Râma, as that Râma, and more rarely Hari and Vâsudeva, are names of the All-God who manifests himself in human form. Vishṇu is mentioned as a celestial being in the company of Brahmâ[1], and so far as any god other than Râma receives attention it is Śiva, not indeed as Râma's equal, but as a being at once very powerful and very devout, who acts as a mediator or guide. "Without prayer to Śiva no one can attain to the faith which I require[2]." "Râma is God, the totality of good, imperishable, invisible, uncreated, incomparable, void of all change, indivisible, whom the Veda declares that it cannot define[3]." And yet, "He whom scripture and philosophy have sung and whom the saints love to contemplate, even the Lord God, he is the son of Dasarath, King of Kosala[4]." By the power of Râma exist Brahmâ, Vishṇu and Śiva, as also Mâyâ, the illusion which brings about the world. His "delusive power is

[1] See Growse's *Translation*, vol. I. pp. 60, 62.
[2] *Ib.* vol. III. p. 190, cf. vol. I. p. 88 and vol. III. pp. 66–67.
[3] *Ib.* vol. II. p. 54.
[4] *Ib.* vol. I. p. 77.

a vast fig-tree, its clustering fruit the countless multitude of worlds, while all things animate and inanimate are like the insects that dwell inside and think their own particular fig the only one in existence[1]." God has made all things: pain and pleasure, sin and merit, saints and sinners, Brahmans and butchers, passion and asceticism. It is the Veda that distinguishes good and evil among them[2]. The love of God and faith are the only road to happiness. "The worship of Hari is real and all the world is a dream[3]." Tulsi Das often uses the language of the Advaita philosophy and even calls God the annihilator of duality, but though he admits the possibility of absorption and identification with the deity, he holds that the double relation of a loving God and a loving soul constitutes greater bliss. "The saint was not absorbed into the divinity for this reason that he had already received the gift of faith[4]." And in a similar spirit he says, "Let those preach in their wisdom who contemplate Thee as the supreme spirit, the uncreate, inseparable from the universe, recognizable only by inference and beyond the understanding; but we, O Lord, will ever hymn the glories of thy incarnation." Like most Hindus he is little disposed to enquire what is the purpose of creation, but he comes very near to saying that God has evolved the world by the power of Mâyâ because the bliss which God and his beloved feel is greater than the bliss of impersonal undifferentiated divinity. It will be seen that Tulsi Das is thoroughly Hindu: neither his fundamental ideas nor his mythological embellishments owe anything to Islam or Christianity. He accepts unreservedly such principles as Mâyâ, transmigration, Karma and release. But his sentiments, more than those of any other Indian writer, bear a striking resemblance to the New Testament. Though he holds that the whole world is of God, he none the less bids men shun evil and choose the good, and the singular purity of his thoughts and style contrasts strongly with other Vishnuite works. He does not conceive of the love which may exist between the soul and God as a form of sexual passion.

[1] Growse, *l.c.* vol. II. p. 200, cf. p. 204. Mâyâ who sets the whole world dancing and whose actions no one can understand is herself set dancing with all her troupe, like an actress on the stage, by the play of the Lord's eyebrows. Cf. too, for the infinity of worlds, pp. 210, 211.

[2] Growse aptly compares St Paul, "I had not known evil but by the law."

[3] *Ib.* vol. II. p. 223.

[4] *Ib.* vol. II. p. 196.

2

The beginning of the sixteenth century was a time of religious upheaval in India for it witnessed the careers not only of Vallabhâcârya and Caitanya, but also of Nânak, the founder of the Sikhs. In the west it was the epoch of Luther and as in Europe so in India no great religious movement has taken place since that time. The sects then founded have swollen into extravagance and been reformed: other sects have arisen from a mixture of Hinduism with Moslem and Christian elements, but no new and original current of thought or devotion has been started.

Though the two great sects associated with the names of Caitanya and Vallabhâcârya have different geographical spheres and also present some differences in doctrinal details, both are emotional and even erotic and both adore Kṛishṇa as a child or young man. Their almost simultaneous appearance in eastern and western India and their rapid growth show that they represent an unusually potent current of ideas and sentiments. But the worship of Kṛishṇa was, as we have seen, nothing new in northern India. Even that relatively late phase in which the sports of the divine herdsman are made to typify the love of God for human souls is at least as early as the Gîtâ-govinda written about 1170. In the thirteenth and fourteenth centuries, the history of Kṛishṇa worship is not clear[1], but it persisted and about 1400 found speech in Bengal and in Rajputâna.

According to Vaishṇava theologians the followers of Vallabhâcârya[2] are a section of the Rudra-sampradâya founded in the early part of the fifteenth century by Vishṇusvâmi, an emigrant from southern India, who preached chiefly in Gujarat. The doctrines of the sect are supposed to have been delivered by the Almighty to Śiva from whom Vishṇusvâmi was fifteenth in spiritual descent, and are known by the name of *Śuddhâdvaita* or pure non-duality. They teach that God has three attributes—*sac-cid-ânanda*—existence, consciousness and bliss. In the human

[1] The Vishnuite sect called Nimâvat is said to have been exterminated by Jains (Grierson in *E.R.E.* sub. v. Bhakti-mârga, p. 545). This may point to persecution during this period.

[2] For Vallabhâcârya and his sect, see especially Growse, *Mathurâ, a district memoir*, 1874; *History of the sect of the Mahârâjas in western India* (anonymous), 1865. Also Bhandarkar, *Vaishṇ. and Saivism*, pp. 76–82 and Farquhar, *Outlines of Relig. Lit. of India*, pp. 312–317.

or animal soul bliss is suppressed and in matter consciousness is suppressed too. But when the soul attains release it recovers bliss and becomes identical in nature with God. For practical purposes the Vallabhâcâris may be regarded as a sect founded by Vallabha, said to have been born in 1470. He was the son of a Telinga Brahman, who had migrated with Vishṇusvâmi to the north.

Such was the pious precocity of Vallabha that at the age of twelve he had already discovered a new religion and started on a pilgrimage to preach it. He was well received at the Court of Vijayanagar, and was so successful in disputation that he was recognized as chief doctor of the Vaishṇava school. He subsequently spent nine years in travelling twice round India and at Brindaban received a visit from Kṛishṇa in person, who bade him promulgate his worship in the form of the divine child known as Bâla Gopâla. Vallabha settled in Benares and is said to have composed a number of works which are still extant[1]. He gained further victories as a successful disputant and also married and became the father of two sons. At the age of fifty-two he took to the life of a Sannyâsi, but died forty-two days afterwards.

Though Vallabha died as an ascetic, his doctrines are currently known as the Pushṭi Mârga, the road of well-being or comfort. His philosophy was more decidedly monistic than is usual among Vishnuites, and Indian monism has generally taught that, as the soul and God are one in essence, the soul should realize this identity and renounce the pleasures of the senses. But with Vallabhâcârya it may be said that the vision which is generally directed godwards and forgets the flesh, turned earthwards and forgot God, for his teaching is that since the individual and the deity are one, the body should be reverenced and indulged. Pushṭi[2] or well-being is the special grace of God and the elect are called Pushṭi-jîva. They depend entirely on God's grace and are contrasted with Maryâdâ-jîvas, or those who submit to moral discipline. The highest felicity is

[1] The principal of them are the Siddhânta-Rahasya and the Bhâgavata-Tîka-Subodhini, a commentary on the Bhâgavata Purâṇa. This is a short poem of only seventeen lines printed in Growse's *Mathurâ*, p. 156. It professes to be a revelation from the deity to the effect that sin can be done away with by union with Brahma (Brahma-sambandha-karaṇât). Other authoritative works of the sect are the Śuddhâdvaita mârtaṇḍa, Sakalâcâryamatasangraha and Prameyaratnârṇava, all edited in theChowkhamba Sanskrit series.

[2] Cf. the use of the word poshaṇam in the Bhâgavata Purâṇa, II. x.

not *mukti* or liberation but the eternal service of Kṛishṇa and eternal participation in his sports.

These doctrines have led to deplorable results, but so strong is the Indian instinct towards self-denial and asceticism that it is the priests rather than the worshippers who profit by this permission to indulge the body, and the chief feature of the sect is the extravagant respect paid to the descendants of Vallabhâcârya. They are known as Maharajas or Great Kings and their followers, especially women, dedicate to them *tan*, *dhan*, *man*: body, purse and spirit, for it is a condition of the road of well-being that before the devotee enjoys anything himself he must dedicate it to the deity and the Maharaj represents the deity. The daily prayer of the sect is "Om. Kṛishṇa is my refuge. I who suffer the infinite pain and torment of enduring for a thousand years separation from Kṛishṇa, consecrate to Kṛishṇa my body, senses, life, heart and faculties, my wife, house, family, property and my own self. I am thy slave, O Kṛishṇa[1]." This formula is recited to the Maharaj with peculiar solemnity by each male as he comes of age and is admitted as a full member of the sect. The words in which this dedication of self and family is made are not in themselves open to criticism and a parallel may be found in Christian hymns. But the literature of the Vallabhis unequivocally states that the Guru is the same as the deity[2] and there can be little doubt that even now the Maharajas are adored by their followers, especially by the women, as representatives of Kṛishṇa in his character of the lover of the Gopis and that the worship is often licentious[3]. Many Hindus denounce the sect and in 1862 one of the Maharajas brought an action for libel in the supreme court of Bombay on

[1] Growse, *Mathurâ*, p. 157, says this formula is based on the Nâradapancarâtra. It is called Samarpana, dedication, or Brahma-sambandha, connecting oneself with the Supreme Being.

[2] For instance "Whoever holds his Guru and Kṛishṇa to be distinct and different shall be born again as a bird." Harirayaji 32. Quoted in *History of the Sect of the Mahârâjas*, p. 82.

[3] In the ordinary ceremonial the Maharaj stands beside the image of Kṛishṇa and acknowledges the worship offered. Sometimes he is swung in a swing with or without the image. The hymns sung on these occasions are frequently immoral. Even more licentious are the meetings or dances known as Ras Mandali and Ras Lîlâ. A meal of hot food seasoned with aphrodisiacs is also said to be provided in the temples. The water in which the Maharaj's linen or feet have been washed is sold for a high price and actually drunk by devotees.

account of the serious charges of immorality brought against him in the native press. The trial became a *cause célèbre.* Judgment was delivered against the Maharaj, the Judge declaring the charges to be fully substantiated. Yet in spite of these proceedings the sect still flourishes, apparently unchanged in doctrine and practice, and has a large following among the mercantile castes of western India. The Râdhâ-Vallabhis, an analogous sect founded by Harivaṃsa in the sixteenth century, give the pre-eminence to Râdhâ, the wife of Kṛishṇa, and in their secret ceremonies are said to dress as women. The worship of Râdhâ is a late phase of Vishnuism and is not known even to the Bhâgavata Purâṇa[1].

Vallabhism owes much of its success to the family of the founder. They had evidently a strong dynastic sentiment as well as a love of missionary conquest—a powerful combination. Vallabhâcârya left behind him eighty-four principal disciples whose lives are recorded in the work called the *Stories of the Eighty-four Vaishṇavas,* and his authority descended to his son Vithalnath. Like his father, Vithalnath was active as a proselytizer and pilgrim and propagated his doctrines extensively in many parts of western India such as Cutch, Malwa, and Bijapur. His converts came chiefly from the mercantile classes but also included some Brahmans and Mussulmans. He is said to have abolished caste distinctions but the sect has not preserved this feature. In his later years he resided at Muttra or the neighbouring town of Gokul, whence he is known as Gokul Gosainji. This title of Gosain, which is still borne by his male descendants, is derived from Kṛishṇa's name Gosvâmin, the lord of cattle[2]. He had seven sons, in each of whom Kṛishṇa is said to have been incarnate for five years. They exercised spiritual authority in separate districts—as we might say in different dioceses—but the fourth son, Gokulnathji and his descendants claimed and still claim a special pre-eminence. The family is at present represented by about a hundred males who are accepted as

[1] Strictly speaking the Râdhâ-Vallabhis are not an offshoot of Vallabha's school, but of the Nimâvats or of the Mâdhva-sampradâya. The theory underlying their strange practices seems to be that Kṛishṇa is the only male and that all mankind should cultivate sentiments of female love for him. See Macnicol, *Indian Theism,* p. 134.

[2] But other explanations are current such as Lord of the senses or Lord of the Vedas.

incarnations and receive the title of Maharaja. About twenty reside at Gokul[1] or near Muttra: there are a few in Bombay and in all the great cities of western India, but the Maharaj of Nath Dwara in Rajputâna is esteemed the chief. This place is not an ancient seat of Kṛishṇa worship, but during the persecution of Aurungzeb a peculiarly holy image was brought thither from Muttra and placed in the shrine where it still remains.

A protest against the immorality of the Vallabhi sect was made by Swâminârâyaṇa, a Brahman who was born in the district of Lucknow about 1780[2]. He settled in Ahmedabad and gained so large a following that the authorities became alarmed and imprisoned him. But his popularity only increased: he became the centre of a great religious movement: hymns descriptive of his virtues and sufferings were sung by his followers and when he was released he found himself at the head of a band which was almost an army. He erected a temple in the village of Wartal in Baroda, which he made the centre of his sect, and recruited followers by means of periodical tours throughout Gujarat. His doctrines are embodied in an anthology called the Śikshâpatrî consisting of 212 precepts, some borrowed from accepted Hindu scriptures and some original and in a catechism called Vacanâmritam. His teaching was summed up in the phrase "Devotion to Kṛishṇa with observance of duty and purity of life" and in practice took the form of a laudable polemic against the licentiousness of the Vallabhis. As in most of the purer sects of Vishnuism, Kṛishṇa is regarded merely as a name of the Supreme Deity. Thus the Śikshâpatrî says "Nârâyaṇa and Śiva should be equally recognized as parts of one and the same supreme spirit, since both have been declared in the Vedas to be forms of Brahma. On no account let it be thought that difference in form or name makes any difference in the identity of the deity." The followers of Swâminârâyaṇa still number about 200,000 in western India and are divided into the laity and a body of celibate clergy. I have visited their religious establishments in Ahmedabad. It consists of a temple with a large and well-kept monastery in which are housed about 300 monks who wear costumes of reddish grey. Except in Assam I have not seen in India any parallel to this monastery

[1] See Growse, *Mathurâ*, p. 153. I can entirely confirm what he says. This mean, inartistic, dirty place certainly suggests moral depravity.

[2] His real name was Sahajânanda.

either in size or discipline. It is provided with a library and hospital. In the temple are images of Nara and Nârâyaṇa (explained as Kṛishṇa and Arjuna), Kṛishṇa and Râdhâ, Gaṇeśa and Hanuman[1].

3

The sect founded by Caitanya is connected with eastern India as the Vallabhis are with the west. Bengal is perhaps the native land of the worship of Kṛishṇa as the god of love. It was there that Jayadeva flourished in the last days of the Sena dynasty and the lyrical poet Chandîdâs at the end of the fourteenth century. About the same time the still greater poet Vidyâpati was singing in Durbhanga. For these writers, as for Caitanya, religion is the bond of love which unites the soul and God, as typified by the passion[2] that drew together Râdhâ and Kṛishṇa. The idea that God loves and seeks out human souls is familiar to Christianity and receives very emotional expression in well-known hymns, but the bold humanity of these Indian lyrics seems to Europeans unsuitable. I will let a distinguished Indian apologize for it in his own words:

"The paradox that has to be understood is that Kṛishṇa means God. Yet he is represented as a youth, standing at a gate, trying to waylay the beloved maiden, attempting to entrap the soul, as it were, into a clandestine meeting. This, which is so inconceivable to a purely modern mind, presents no difficulty at all to the Vaishṇava devotee. To him God is the lover himself: the sweet flowers, the fresh grass, the gay sound heard in the woods are direct messages and tokens of love to his soul, bringing to his mind at every instant that loving God whom he pictures as ever anxious to win the human heart[3]."

Caitanya[4] was born at Nadia in 1485 and came under the influence of the Mâdhva sect. In youth he was a prodigy of

[1] Caran Das (1703–1782) founded a somewhat similar sect which professed to abolish idolatry and laid great stress on ethics. See Grierson's article Caran Das in *E.R.E.*

[2] But Vishnuite writers distinguish *kâma* desire and *prema* love, just as ἔρως and ἀγάπη are distinguished in Greek. See Dinesh Chandra Sen, *l.c.* p. 485.

[3] Dinesh Chandra Sen, *History of Bengali Language and Literature*, pp. 134–5.

[4] For Caitanya see Dinesh Chandra Sen, *History of Bengali Language and Lit.* chap. v. and Jadunath Sarkar, *Chaitanya's Pilgrimages and teachings from the Caitanya-Caritâmrita* of Kṛishṇa Das (1590) founded on the earlier Caitanya-Caritra of Brindavan. Several of Caitanya's followers were also voluminous writers.

learning[1], but at the age of about seventeen while on a pilgrimage to Gaya began to display that emotional and even hysterical religious feeling which marked all his teaching. He swooned at the mention of Kṛishṇa's name and passed his time in dancing and singing hymns. At twenty-five he became a Sannyâsî, and at the request of his mother, who did not wish him to wander too far, settled in Puri near the temple of Jagannath. Here he spent the rest of his life in preaching, worship and ecstatic meditation, but found time to make a tour in southern India and another to Brindaban and Benares. He appears to have left the management of his sect largely to his disciples, Advaita, Nityânanda and Haridas, and to have written nothing himself. But he evidently possessed a gift of religious magnetism and exercised an extraordinary influence on those who heard him preach or sing. He died or disappeared before the age of fifty but apparently none of the stories about his end merit credence.

Although the teaching of Caitanya is not so objectionable morally as the doctrines of the Vallabhis, it follows the same line of making religion easy and emotional and it is not difficult to understand how his preaching, set forth with the eloquence which he possessed, won converts from the lower classes by thousands. He laid no stress on asceticism, approved of marriage and rejected all difficult rites and ceremonies. The form of worship which he specially enjoined was the singing of Kîrtans or hymns consisting chiefly in a repetition of the divine names accompanied by music and dancing. Swaying the body and repetition of the same formula or hymn are features of emotional religion found in the most diverse regions, for instance among the Rufais or Howling Dervishes, at Welsh revival meetings and in negro churches in the Southern States. It is therefore unnecessary to seek any special explanation in India but perhaps there is some connection between the religious ecstasies of Vaishṇavas and Dervishes. Within Caitanya's sect, caste was not observed. He is said to have admitted many Moslims to membership and to have regarded all worshippers of Kṛishṇa as equal. Though caste has grown up again, yet the old regulation is still in force inside the temple of Jagannath at Puri. Within the sacred enclosure all are treated as of one caste and eat the

[1] He married the daughter of a certain Vallabha who apparently was not the founder of the Sect, as is often stated.

same sacred food. In Caitanya's words "the mercy of God regards neither tribe nor family."

His theology[1] shows little originality. The deity is called Bhagavân or more frequently Hari. His majesty and omnipotence are personified as Nârâyaṇa, his beauty and ecstasy as Kṛishṇa. The material world is defined as *bhedâbhedaprakâśa*, a manifestation of the deity as separate and yet not separate from him, and the soul is *vibhinnâṁśa* or a detached portion of him. Some souls are in bondage to Prakṛiti or Mâyâ, others through faith and love attain deliverance. Reason is useless in religious matters, but *ruci* or spiritual feeling has a quick intuition of the divine.

Salvation is obtained by Bhakti, faith or devotion, which embraces and supersedes all other duties. This devotion means absolute self-surrender to the deity and love for him which asks for no return but is its own reward. "He who expects remuneration for his love acts as a trader." In this devotion there are five degrees: (*a*) sânti, calm meditation, (*b*) dâsya, servitude, (*c*) sâkhya, friendship, (*d*) vâtsalya, love like that of a child for its parent, (*e*) mâdhurya, love like that of a woman for a lover. All these sentiments are found in God and this combined ecstasy is an eternal principle identified with Hari himself, just as in the language of the Gospels, God is love. Though Caitanya makes love the crown and culmination of religion, the worship of his followers is not licentious, and it is held that the right frame of mind is best attained by the recitation of Kṛishṇa's names especially Hari.

The earlier centre of Caitanya's sect was his birthplace, Nadia, but both during his life and afterwards his disciples frequented Brindaban and sought out the old sacred sites which were at that time neglected. At the beginning of the nineteenth century Lala Baba, a wealthy Bengali merchant, became a mendicant and visited Muttra. Though he had renounced the world, he still retained his business instincts and bought up the villages which contained the most celebrated shrines and were most frequented by pilgrims. The result was a most profitable

[1] The theology of the sect may be studied in Baladeva's commentary on the Vedânta sûtras and his Prameya Ratnâvalî, both contained in vol. v. of the *Sacred Books of the Hindus*. It would appear that the sect regards itself as a continuation of the Brahma-sampradâya but its tenets have more resemblance to those of Vallabha.

speculation and the establishment of Caitanya's Church in the district of Braj, which thus became the holy land of both the great Krishnaite sects. The followers of Caitanya at the present day are said to be divided into Gosains, or ecclesiastics, who are the descendants of the founder's original disciples, the Vrikats or celibates, and the laity. Besides the celibates there are several semi-monastic orders who adopt the dress of monks but marry. They have numerous maṭhs at Nadia and elsewhere. Like the Vallabhis, this sect deifies its leaders. Caitanya, Nityânanda and Advaita are called the three masters (Prabhû) and believed to be a joint incarnation of Kṛishṇa, though according to some only the first two shared the divine essence. Six of Caitanya's disciples known as the six Gosains are also greatly venerated and even ordinary religious teachers still receive an almost idolatrous respect.

Though Caitanya was not a writer himself he exercised a great influence on the literature of Bengal. In the opinion of so competent a judge as Dinesh Chandra Sen, Bengali was raised to the status of a literary language by the Vishnuite hymn-writers just as Pali was by the Buddhists. Such hymns were written before the time of Caitanya but after him they became extremely numerous[1] and their tone and style are said to change. The ecstasies and visions of which they tell are those described in his biographies and this emotional poetry has profoundly influenced all classes in Bengal. But there was and still is a considerable hostility between the Śâktas and Vishnuites.

4

A form of Vishnuism, possessing a special local flavour, is connected with the Maratha country and with the names of Nâmdev, Tukârâm[2] and Râmdâs, the spiritual preceptor of Śivaji. The centre of this worship is the town of Pandharpur and I have not found it described as a branch of any of the four Vishnuite Churches: but the facts that Nâmdev wrote in Hindi as well as in Marathi, that many of his hymns are included in the Granth, and that his sentiments show affinities to the

[1] No less than 159 padakartâs or religious poets are enumerated by Dinesh Chandra Sen. Several collections of these poems have been published of which the principal is called Padakalpataru.

[2] See Bhandarkar, *Vaishṇ. and Śaivism*, pp. 87–99, and Nicol, *Psalms of Maratha Saints* which gives a bibliography. For Nâmdev see also Macauliffe, *The Sikh Religion*, vol. VI. pp. 17–76. For Ramdas see Rawlinson, *Sivaji the Maratha*, pp. 116 ff.

teaching of Nânak, suggest that he belonged to the school of Râmânand. There is however a difficulty about his date. Native tradition gives 1270 as the year of his birth but the language of his poems both in Marathi and Hindi is said to be too modern for this period and to indicate that he lived about 1400[1], when he might easily have felt the influence of Râmânand, for he travelled in the north.

Most of his poetry however has for its centre the temple of Pandharpur where was worshipped a deity called Viṭṭhala, Viṭṭoba or Pâṇḍurang. It is said that the first two names are dialectic variations of Vishṇu, but that Pâṇḍurang is an epithet of Śiva[2]. There is no doubt that the deity of Pandharpur has for many centuries been identified with Kṛishṇa, who, as in Bengal, is god the lover of the soul. But the hymns of the Marathas are less sensuous and Kṛishṇa is coupled not with his mistress Râdhâ, but with his wife Rukmiṇî. In fact Rukmiṇî-pati or husband of Rukmiṇî is one of his commonest titles. Nâmdev's opinions varied at different times and perhaps in different moods: like most religious poets he cannot be judged by logic or theology. Sometimes he inveigh's against idolatry—understood as an attempt to limit God to an image—but in other verses he sings the praises of Pâṇḍurang, the local deity, as the lord and creator of all. His great message is that God—by whatever name he is called—is everywhere and accessible to all, accessible without ceremonial or philosophy. "Vows, fasts and austerities are not needful, nor need you go on pilgrimage. Be watchful in your heart and always sing the name of Hari. Yoga, sacrifices and renunciation are not needful. Love the feet of Hari. Neither need you contemplate the absolute. Hold fast to the love of Hari's name. Says Nâmâ, be steadfast in singing the name and then Hari will appear to you[3]."

[1] Bhandarkar, *l.c.* p. 92. An earlier poet of this country was Jñâneśvara who wrote a paraphrase of the Bhagavad-gîtâ in 1290. His writings are said to be the first great landmark in Marathi literature.

[2] There is no necessary hostility between the worship of Śiva and of Vishṇu. At Pandharpur pilgrims visit first a temple of Śiva and then the principal shrine. This latter, like the temple of Jagannath at Puri, is suspected of having been a Buddhist shrine. It is called Vihâra, the principal festival is in the Buddhist Lent and caste is not observed within its precincts.

[3] Quoted by Bhandarkar, p. 90. The subsequent quotations are from the same source but I have sometimes slightly modified them and compared them with the original, though I have no pretension to be a Marathi scholar.

Tukârâm is better known than Nâmdev and his poetry which was part of the intellectual awakening that accompanied the rise of the Maratha power is still a living force wherever Marathi is spoken. He lived from 1607 to 1649 and was born in a family of merchants near Poona. But he was too generous to succeed in trade and a famine, in which one of his two wives died, brought him to poverty. Thenceforth he devoted himself to praying and preaching. He developed a great aptitude for composing rhyming songs in irregular metre[1], and like Caitanya he held services consisting of discourses interspersed with such songs, prepared or extempore. In spite of persecution by the Brahmans, these meetings became very popular and were even attended by the great Śivaji.

His creed is the same as that of Nâmdev and finds expression in verses such as these. "This thy nature is beyond the grasp of mind or words, and therefore I have made love a measure. I measure the Endless by the measure of love: he is not to be truly measured otherwise. Thou art not to be found by Yoga, sacrifice, fasting, bodily exertions or knowledge. O Keśava, accept the service which we render."

But if he had no use for asceticism he also feared the passions. "The Endless is beyond; between him and me are the lofty mountains of desire and anger. I cannot ascend them and find no pass." In poems which are apparently later, his tone is more peaceful. He speaks much of the death of self, of purity of heart, and of self-dedication to God. "Dedicate all you do to God and have done with it: Tukâ says, do not ask me again and again: nothing else is to be taught but this."

Maratha critics have discussed whether Tukârâm followed the monistic philosophy of Śaṅkara or not and it must be confessed that his utterances are contradictory. But the gist of the matter is that he disliked not so much monism as philosophy. Hence he says "For me there is no use in the Advaita. Sweet to me is the service of thy feet. The relation between God and his devotee is a source of high joy. Make me feel this, keeping me distinct from thee." But he can also say almost in the language of the Upanishads. "When salt is dissolved in water, what remains distinct? I have thus become one in joy with thee and have lost myself in thee. When fire and camphor are

[1] Called Abhangs.

brought together, is there any black remnant? Tukâ says, thou and I were one light."

5

There are interesting Vishnuite sects in Assam[1]. Until the sixteenth century Hinduism was represented in those regions by Śâktism, which was strong among the upper classes, though the mass of the people still adhered to their old tribal worships. The first apostle of Vishnuism was Śaṅkar Deb in the sixteenth century. He preached first in the Ahom kingdom but was driven out by the opposition of Śâktist Brahmans, and found a refuge at Barpeta. He appears to have inculcated the worship of Kṛishṇa as the sole divine being and to have denounced idolatry, sacrifices and caste. These views were held even more strictly by his successor, Madhab Deb, a writer of repute whose works, such as the Nâmghosha and Ratnâvalî, are regarded as scripture by his followers. Though the Brahmans of Assam were opposed to the introduction of Vishnuism and a section of them continued to instigate persecutions for two centuries or more, yet when it became clear that the new teaching had a great popular following another section were anxious that it should not pass out of sacerdotal control and organized it as a legitimate branch of Hinduism. While fully recognizing the doctrine of justification by faith, they also made provision for due respect to caste and Brahmanic authority.

According to the last census of India[2] the common view that Śaṅkar Deb drew his inspiration from Caitanya meets with criticism in Assam. His biographies say that he lived 120 years and died in 1569. It has been generally assumed that his age has been exaggerated but that the date of his death is correct. If it can be proved, as contended, that he was preaching in 1505, there would be no difficulty in admitting that he was independent of Caitanya and belonged to an earlier phase of the Vishnuite movement which produced the activity of Vallabha and the poetry of Vidyâpati. It is a further argument for this independence that he taught the worship of Vishṇu only and not of Râdhâ and discountenanced the use of images. On the other hand it is stated that he sojourned in Bengal and it

[1] See Eliot, Hinduism in Assam, *J.R.A.S.* 1910, pp. 1168–1186.
[2] *Census of India*, 1911, Assam, p. 41.

appears that soon after his death his connection with the teaching of Caitanya was recognized in Assam.

At present there are three sects in Assam. Firstly, the Mahâpurushias, who follow more or less faithfully the doctrines of Śaṅkar and Madhab. They admit Śûdras as religious teachers and abbots, and lay little stress on caste while not entirely rejecting it. They abstain almost entirely from the use of images in worship, the only exception being that a small figure of Kṛishṇa in the form of Vaikuṇṭha Nâtha is found in their temples. It is not the principal object of veneration but stands to the left of a throne on which lies a copy of the Nâmghosha[1]. This, together with the foot-prints of Śaṅkar and Madhab, receives the homage of the faithful. The chief centre of the Mahâpurushias is Barpeta, but they have also monasteries on the Majuli Island and elsewhere. Secondly, the Bamunia monasteries, with a large lay following, represent a brahmanized form of the Mahâpurushia faith. This movement began in the life-time of Madhab. Many of his Brahman disciples seceded from him and founded separate communities which insisted on the observance of caste (especially on the necessity of religious teachers being Brahmans) but tolerated image-worship and the use of some kinds of flesh as food. Though this sect was persecuted by the Ahom kings[2], they were strong enough to maintain themselves. A compromise was effected in the reign of Rudra Singh (1696–1714), by which their abbots were shown all honour but were assigned the Majuli Island in the upper Brahmaputra as their chief, if not only, residence. This island is still studded with numerous *Sattras* or monasteries, the largest of which contain three or four hundred monks, known as Bhakats (Bhaktas). They take no vows and wear no special costume but are obliged to be celibate while they remain in the sattra. The Mahâpurushia and Bamunia monasteries are of similar appearance, and in externals (though not in doctrine) seem to have been influenced by the Lamaism of the neighbouring regions of Sikhim and Tibet. The temples are long, low, wooden buildings, covered by roofs of corrugated iron or thatched, and

[1] Some authorities state that the sacred book thus venerated is the Bhagavad-gîtâ, but at Kamalabari I made careful enquiries and was assured it was the Nâmghosha.

[2] Especially Gadadhar Singh, 1681–96.

containing inside a nave with two rows of wooden pillars which leads to a sanctuary divided from it by a screen. The third sect are the Moamarias, of political rather than religious importance. They represent a democratic element, recruited from non-Hindu tribes, which seceded even in the life-time of Śaṅkar Deb. They appear to reject nearly all Hindu observances and to worship aboriginal deities as well as Kṛishṇa. Little is known of their religious teaching, if indeed they have anything worthy of the name, but in the latter half of the eighteenth century they distracted the kingdom of Assam with a series of rebellions which were suppressed with atrocious cruelty.

Caitanya is said to have admitted some Mohammedans as members of his sect. The precedent has not been followed among most branches of his later adherents but a curious half-secret sect, found throughout Bengal in considerable numbers and called Kartâbhajas[1], appears to represent an eccentric development of his teaching in combination with Mohammedan elements. Both Moslims and Hindus belong to this sect. They observe the ordinary social customs of the class to which they belong, but it is said that those who are nominal Moslims neither circumcize themselves nor frequent mosques. The founder, called Ram Smaran Pal, was born in the Nadia district about 1700, and his chief doctrine is said to have been that there is only one God who is incarnate in the Head of the sect or Kartâ[2]. For the first few generations the headship was invested in the founder and his descendants but dissensions occurred and there is now no one head: the faithful can select any male member of the founder's family as the object of their devotion. The Kartâ claims to be the owner of every human body and is said to exact rent for the soul's tenancy thereof. No distinction of caste or creed is recognized and hardly any ceremonies are prescribed but meat and wine are forbidden, the mantra of the sect is to be repeated five times a day and Friday is held sacred. These observances seem an imitation of Mohammedanism[3].

[1] See *Census of India,* 1901, Bengal, pp. 183–4 and Bhattacharya, *Hindu Castes and Sects*, pp. 485–488.

[2] Karta, literally doer, is the name given to the executive head of a joint family in Bengal. The sect prefer to call themselves Bhabajanas or Bhagawanis.

[3] Another mixed sect is that of the Dhâmis in the Panna state of Bundelkhand, founded by one Prannâth in the reign of Aurungzeb. Their doctrine is a combination of Hinduism and Islam, tending towards Krishnaism. See Russell, *Tribes and Castes of Central Provinces*, p. 217.

CHAPTER XXXI

AMALGAMATION OF HINDUISM AND ISLAM. KABIR AND THE SIKHS

1

THE Kartâbhajas mentioned at the end of the last chapter show a mixture of Hinduism and Mohammedanism, and the mixture[1] is found in other sects some of which are of considerable importance. A group of these sects, including the Sikhs and followers of Kabir, arose in the fifteenth and sixteenth centuries. Their origin can be traced to Râmânand but they cannot be called Vaishṇavas and they are clearly distinguished from all the religious bodies that we have hitherto passed in review. The tone of their writings is more restrained and severe: the worshipper approaches the deity as a servant rather than a lover: caste is rejected as useless: Hindu mythology is eschewed or used sparingly. Yet in spite of these differences the essential doctrines of Tulsi Das, Kabir and Nânak show a great resemblance. They all believe in one deity whom they call by various names, but this deity, though personal, remains of the Indian not of the Semitic type. He somehow brings the world of transmigration into being by his power of illusion, and the business of the soul is to free itself from the illusion and return to him. Almost all these teachers, whether orthodox or heterodox, had a singular facility for composing hymns, often of high literary merit, and it is in these emotional utterances, rather than in dogmatic treatises, that they addressed themselves to the peoples of northern India.

The earliest of these mixed sects is that founded by Kabir[2]. He appears to have been a Mohammedan weaver by birth,

[1] It is exemplified by the curious word an-had *limitless*, being the Indian negative prefix added to the arabic word *had* used in the Sikh Granth and by Caran Das as a name of God.

[2] See especially G. H. Westcott, *Kabir and the Kabir Panth*, and Macauliffe, *Sikh Religion*, vol. VI. pp. 122–316. Also Wilson, *Essays on the religion of the Hindus*, vol. I. pp. 68–98. Garcin de Tassy, *Histoire de la Littérature Hindoue*, II. pp. 120–134. Bhandarkar, *Vaishṇ. and Śaivism*, pp. 67–73.

though tradition is not unanimous on this point[1]. It is admitted, however, that he was brought up among Moslims at Benares but became a disciple of Râmânand. This suggests that he lived early in the fifteenth century[2]. Another tradition says that he was summoned before Sikander Lodi (1489–1517), but the details of his life are evidently legendary. We only know that he was married and had a son, that he taught in northern and perhaps central India and died at Maghar in the district of Gorakhpur. There is significance, however, in the legend which relates that after his decease Hindus and Mohammedans disputed as to whether his body should be burned or buried. But when they raised the cloth which covered the corpse, they found underneath it only a heap of flowers. So the Hindus took part and burnt them at Benares and the Moslims buried the rest at Maghar. His grave there is still in Moslim keeping.

In teaching Kabir stands midway between the two religions, but leaning to the side of Hinduism. It is clear that this Hindu bias became stronger in his followers, but it is not easy to separate his own teaching from subsequent embellishments, for the numerous hymns and sayings attributed to him are collected in compilations made after his death, such as the Bijak and the Âdigranth of the Sikhs. In hymns which sound authentic he puts Hindus and Moslims on the same footing.

"Kabir is a child of Ram and Allah," he says, "and accepteth all Gurus and Pirs." "O God, whether Allah or Ram, I live by thy name."

> "Make thy mind thy Kaaba, thy body its enclosing temple,
> Conscience its prime teacher.
> Then, O priest, call men to pray to that mosque
> Which hath five gates.
> The Hindus and Mussulmans have the same Lord."

But the formalities of both creeds are impartially condemned. "They are good riders who keep aloof from the Veda and Koran[3]." Caste, circumcision and idolatry are reprobated. The Hindu deities and their incarnations are all dead: God was not

[1] The name Kabir seems to me decisive.

[2] Dadu who died about 1603 is said to have been fifth in spiritual descent from Kabir.

[3] From a hymn in which the spiritual life is represented as a ride. Macauliffe, VI. p. 156.

in any of them[1]. Ram, it would seem, should be understood not as Râmacandra but as a name of God.

Yet the general outlook is Hindu rather than Mohammedan. God is the magician who brings about this illusory world in which the soul wanders[2]. "I was in immobile and mobile creatures, in worms and in moths; I passed through many various births. But when I assumed a human body, I was a Yogi, a Yati, a penitent, a Brahmacâri: sometimes an Emperor and sometimes a beggar." Unlike the Sikhs, Kabir teaches the sanctity of life, even of plants. "Thou cuttest leaves, O flower girl: in every leaf there is life." Release, as for all Hindus, consists in escaping from the round of births and deaths. Of this he speaks almost in the language of the Buddha[3].

> "Though I have assumed many shapes, this is my last.
> The strings and wires of the musical instrument are all worn out:
> I am now in the power of God's name.
> I shall not again have to dance to the tune of birth and death.
> Nor shall my heart accompany on the drum."

This deliverance is accomplished by the union or identification of the soul with God.

> "Remove the difference between thyself and God and thou shalt be united with him......
> Him whom I sought without me, now I find within me......
> Know God: by knowing him thou shalt become as he.
> When the soul and God are blended no one can distinguish them[4]."

But if he sometimes writes like Śaṅkara, he also has the note of the Psalms and Gospels. He has the sense of sin: he thinks of God in vivid personal metaphors, as a lord, a bridegroom, a parent, both father and mother.

> "Save me, O God, though I have offended thee......
> I forgot him who made me and did cleave unto strangers."

[1] But Hari is sometimes used by Kabir, especially in the hymns incorporated in the Granth, as a name of God.

[2] Though Kabir writes as a poet rather than as a philosopher he evidently leaned to the doctrine of illusion (*vivartavâda*) rather than to the doctrine of manifestation or development (*pariṇâmavâda*). He regards Mâyâ as something evil, a trick, a thief, a force which leads men captive, but which disappears with the knowledge of God. "The illusion vanished when I recognized him" (XXXIX.).

[3] He even uses the word nirvâṇa.

[4] From Kabir's acrostic. Macauliffe, VI. pp. 186 and 188. It is possible that this is a later composition.

"Sing, sing, the marriage song.
The sovereign God hath come to my house as my husband....
I obtained God as my bridegroom; so great has been my good fortune."

"A mother beareth not in mind
All the faults her son committeth.
O, God, I am thy child:
Why blottest thou not out my sins?"......

"My Father is the great Lord of the Earth;
To that Father how shall I go[1]?"

The writings of Kabir's disciples such as the Sukh Nidhan attributed to Srut Gopal (and written according to Westcott about 1729) and the still later Amar Mul, which is said to be representative of the modern Kabirpanth, show a greater inclination to Pantheism, though caste and idolatry are still condemned. In these works, which relate the conversion of Dharm Das afterwards one of Kabir's principal followers, Kabir is identified with the Creator and then made a pantheistic deity much as Kṛishṇa in the Bhagavad-gîtâ[2]. He is also the true Guru whose help is necessary for salvation. Stress is further laid on the doctrine of Śabda, or the divine word. Hindu theology was familiar with this expression as signifying the eternal self-existent revelation contained in the Vedas. Kabir appears to have held that articulate sound is an expression of the Deity and that every letter, as a constituent of such sound, has a meaning. But these letters are due to Mâyâ: in reality there is no plurality of sound. Ram seems to have been selected as the divine name, because its brevity is an approach to this unity, but true knowledge is to understand the Letterless One, that is the real name or essence of God from which all differentiation of letters has vanished. Apart from some special metaphors the whole doctrine set forth in the Sukh Nidhan

[1] Macauliffe, VI. pp. 230, 209, 202, 197.

[2] Westcott, *l.c.* p. 144, "I am the creator of this world......I am the seed and the tree......all are contained in me—I live within all and all live within me" and much to the same effect. Even in the hymns of the Âdi Granth we find such phrases as "Now thou and I have become one." (Macauliffe, VI. p. 180.)

This identification of Kabir with the deity is interesting as being a modern example of what probably happened in the case of Kṛishṇa. Similarly those who collected the hymns which form the sacred books of the Sikhs and Kabirpanthis repeated the process which in earlier ages produced the Ṛig Veda.

and Amar Mul is little more than a loose Vedantism, somewhat reminiscent of Sufiism[1].

The teaching of Kabir is known as the Kabirpanth. At present there are both Hindus and Mohammedans among his followers and both have monasteries at Maghar where he is buried. The sect numbers in all about a million[2]. It is said that the two divisions have little in common except veneration of Kabir and do not intermix, but they both observe the practice of partaking of sacred meals, holy water[3], and consecrated betel nut. The Hindu section is again divided into two branches known as Father (Bap) and Mother (Mai).

Though there is not much that is original in the doctrines of Kabir, he is a considerable figure in Hindi literature and may justly be called epoch-making as marking the first fusion of Hinduism and Islam which culminates and attains political importance in the Sikhs. Other offshoots of his teaching are the Satnâmîs, Râdhâ-swâmis and Dâdupanthis. The first were founded or reorganized in 1750 by a certain Jag-jivan-das. They do not observe caste and in theory adore only the True Name of God but in practice admit ordinary Hindu worship. The Râdhâ-swâmis, founded in 1861, profess a combination of the Kabirpanth with Christian ideas. The Dâdupanthis show the influence of the military spirit of Islam. They were founded by Dâdu, a cotton weaver of Ahmedabad who flourished in Akbar's reign and died about 1603. He insisted on the equality of mankind, vegetarianism, abstinence from alcohol and strict celibacy. Hence the sect is recruited by adopting boys, most of whom are trained as soldiers. In such conditions the Dâdupanthis cannot increase greatly but they number about nine thousand and are found chiefly in the state of Jaipur, especially in the town of Naraina[4].

[1] "The Âtmâ mingles with Paramâtmâ, as the rivers flow into the ocean. Only in this way can Paramâtmâ be found. The Âtmâ without Śabda is blind and cannot find the path. He who sees Âtmâ-Râm is present everywhere. All he sees is like himself. There is nought except Brahmâ. I am he, I am the true Kabir." Westcott, p. 168.

[2] The Census of 1901 gives 843,171 but there is reason to think the real numbers are larger.

[3] Consecrated by washing in it wooden sandals supposed to represent the feet of Kabir. It is stated that they believe they eat the body of Kabir at their sacred meal which perhaps points to Christian influence. See Russell, *l.c.* pp. 239–240.

[4] See Russell, *Tribes and Castes of Central Provinces*, p. 217, where it is said that some of them are householders.

2

The Sikh religion[1] is of special interest since it has created not only a political society but also customs so distinctive that those who profess it rank in common esteem as a separate race. The founder Nânak lived from 1469 to 1538 and was born near Lahore. He was a Hindu by birth but came under Mohammedan influence and conceived the idea of reconciling the two faiths. He was attracted by the doctrines of Kabir and did not at first claim to teach a new religion. He wished to unite Hindus and Moslims and described himself simply as Guru or teacher and his adherents as Sikhs or disciples.

He spent the greater part of his life wandering about India and is said to have reached Mecca. A beautiful story relates that he fell asleep with his feet turned towards the Kaaba. A mollah kicked him and asked how he dared to turn his feet and not his head towards God. But he answered, "Turn my feet in a direction where God is not." He was attended on his wanderings by Mardâna, a lute-player, who accompanied the hymns which he never failed to compose when a thought or adventure occurred to him. These compositions are similar to those of Kabir, but seem to me of inferior merit. They are diffuse and inordinately long; the Japji for instance, which every Sikh ought to recite as his daily prayer, fills not less than twenty octavo pages. Yet beautiful and incisive passages are not wanting. When at the temple of Jagannath, he was asked to take part in the evening worship at which lights were waved before the god while flowers and incense were presented on golden salvers studded with pearls. But he burst out into song[2].

"The sun and moon, O Lord, are thy lamps, the firmament thy salver and the orbs of the stars the pearls set therein.

"The perfume of the sandal tree is thy incense; the wind is thy fan; all the forests are thy flowers, O Lord of light."

Though Nânak is full of Hindu allusions he is more Mohammedan in tone than Kabir, and the ritual of Sikh temples is

[1] See especially Macauliffe, *The Sikh Religion*, six volumes.
[2] Macauliffe, I. p. 82.

modelled on the Mohammedan rather than on the Hindu pattern. The opening words of the Japji are: "There is but one God, whose name is true, the Creator[1]" and he is regarded rather as the ruler of the world than as a spirit finding expression in it. "By his order" all things happen. "By obeying him" man obtains happiness and salvation. "There is no limit to his mercy and his praises." In the presence of God "man has no power and no strength." Such sentiments have a smack of Mohammed and Nânak sometimes uses the very words of the Koran as when he says that God has no companion. And though the penetrating spirit of the Vedânta infects this regal monotheism, yet the doctrine of Mâyâ is set forth in unusual phraseology: "God himself created the world and himself gave names to things. He made Mâyâ by his power: seated, he beheld his work with delight."

In other compositions attributed to Nânak greater prominence is given to Mâyâ and to the common Hindu idea that creation is a self-expansion of the deity. Metempsychosis is taught and the divine name is Hari. This is characteristic of the age, for Nânak was nearly a contemporary of Caitanya and Vallabhâcârya. For Kabir, the disciple of Râmânanda, the name was Ram.

Nânak was sufficiently conscious of his position as head of a sect to leave a successor as Guru[2], but there is no indication that at this time the Sikhs differed materially from many other religious bodies who reprobated caste and idolatry. Under the fourth Guru, Ram Das, the beginnings of a change appear. His strong personality collected many wealthy adherents and with their offerings he purchased the tank of Amritsar[3] and built in its midst the celebrated Golden Temple. He appointed his son Arjun as Guru in 1581, just before his death: the succession was made hereditary and henceforth the Gurus became chiefs rather than spiritual teachers. Arjun assumed some of the insignia of royalty: a town grew up round the sacred

[1] The original is Kartâ purukh (=purusha), the creative male. This phrase shows how Hindu habits of thought clung to Nânak.

[2] The Guru of the Sikhs are: (*a*) Nânak, 1469–1538, (*b*) Angada, 1538–1552, (*c*) Amardas, 1552–1575, (*d*) Ramdas, 1575–1581, (*e*) Arjun, 1581–1606, (*f*) Har-Govind, 1606–1639, (*g*) Har-Rai, 1639–1663, (*h*) Har-Kisan, 1663–1666, (*i*) Teg-Bahadur, 1666–1675, (*j*) Govind Singh, 1675–1708.

[3] Amritasaras the lake of nectar.

tank and became the centre of a community; a tax was collected from all Sikhs and they were subjected to special and often salutary legislation. Infanticide, for instance, was strictly forbidden. With a view of providing a code and standard Arjun compiled the Granth or Sikh scriptures, for though hymns and prayers composed by Nânak and others were in use there was as yet no authorized collection of them. The example of Mohammedanism no doubt stimulated the desire to possess a sacred book and the veneration of the scriptures increased with time. The Granth now receives the same kind of respect as the Koran and the first sight of a Sikh temple with a large open volume on a reading-desk cannot fail to recall a mosque.

Arjun's compilation is called the Âdi-granth, or original book, to distinguish it from the later additions made by Guru Govind. It comprises hymns and prayers by Nânak and the four Gurus who followed him (including Arjun himself), Râmânand, Kabir and others, amounting to thirty-five writers in all. The list is interesting as testifying to the existence of a great body of oral poetry by various authors ranging from Râmânand, who had not separated himself from orthodox Vishnuism, to Arjun, the chief of the Sikh national community. It was evidently felt that all these men had one inspiration coming from one truth and even now unwritten poems of Nânak are current in Bihar. The Granth is written in a special alphabet known as Gurmukhi[1] and contains both prose and poetical pieces in several languages: most are in old western Hindi[2] but some are in Panjabi and Marathi.

But though in compiling a sacred book and in uniting the temporal and spiritual power Arjun was influenced by the spirit of Mohammedanism, this is not the sort of imitation which makes for peace. The combination of Hinduism and Islam resulted in the production of a special type of Hindu peculiarly distasteful to Moslims and not much loved by other Hindus. Much of Arjun's activity took place in the later years of the Emperor Akbar. This most philosophic and tolerant of princes abandoned Mohammedanism after 1579, remitted the special

[1] It appears to be an arbitrary adaptation of the Deva-nâgari characters. The shape of the letters is mostly the same but new values are assigned to them.

[2] This is the description of the dialect given by Grierson, the highest authority in such matters.

taxes payable by non-Moslims and adopted many Hindu observances. Towards the end of his life he promulgated a new creed known as the Din-i-ilahi or divine faith. This eclectic and composite religion bears testimony to his vanity as well as to his large sympathies, for it recognized him as the viceregent or even an incarnation of God. It would appear that the singular little work called the Allopanishad or Allah Upanishad[1] was written in connection with this movement. It purports to be an Upanishad of the Atharva Veda and can hardly be described as other than a forgery. It declares that "the Allah of the prophet Muhammad Akbar[2] is the God of Gods" and identifies him with Mitra, Varuṇa, the sun, moon, water, Indra, etc. Akbar's religion did not long survive his death and never flourished far from the imperial court, but somewhat later (1656) Muhammad Dara Shukoh, the son of Shah Jehan, caused a Persian translation of about fifty Upanishads, known as the Oupnekhat[3], to be prepared. The general temper of the period was propitious to the growth and immunity of mixed forms of belief, but the warlike and semi-political character of the Sikh community brought trouble on it.

Arjun attracted the unfavourable attention of Akbar's successor, Jehangir[4], and was cast into prison where he died. The Sikhs took up arms and henceforth regarded themselves as the enemies of the government, but their strength was wasted by internal dissensions. The ninth Guru, Teg-Bahadur, was executed by Aurungzeb. Desire to avenge this martyrdom and the strenuous character of the tenth Guru, Govind Singh (1675–1708), completed the transformation of the Sikhs into a church militant devoted to a holy war.

Though the most aggressive and uncompromising features of Sikhism are due to the innovations of Govind, he was so far from being a theological bigot that he worshipped Durgâ and

[1] See Rajendrala Mitra's article in *J.A.S.B.* XL. 1871, pp. 170–176, which gives the Sanskrit text of the Upanishad. Also Schrader, *Catalogue of Adyar Library*, 1908, pp. 136–7. Schrader states that in the north of India the Allopanishad is recited by Brahmans at the Vasantotsava and on other occasions: also that in southern India it is generally believed that Moslims are skilled in the Atharva Veda.

[2] *I.e.*, not the Allah of the Koran.

[3] This Persian translation was rendered word for word into very strange Latin by Anquetil Duperron (1801–2) and this Latin version was used by Schopenhauer.

[4] He is said to have prayed for the success of the Emperor's rebellious son.

was even said to have offered human sacrifices. But the aim of all his ordinances was to make his followers an independent body of fighting men. They were to return the salutation of no Hindu and to put to death every Mohammedan. The community was called Khalsa[1]: within it there was perfect equality: every man was to carry a sword and wear long hair but short trousers. Converts, or recruits, came chiefly from the fighting tribes of the Jats, but in theory admission was free. The initiatory ceremony, which resembled baptism, was performed with sugar and water stirred with a sword, and the neophyte vowed not to worship idols, to bow to none except a Sikh Guru, and never to turn his back on the enemy. To give these institutions better religious sanction, Govind composed a supplement to the Granth, called Daśama Pâdshâh ka Granth or book of the tenth prince. It consists of four parts, all in verse, and is said to inculcate war as persistently as Nânak had inculcated meekness and peace. To give his institutions greater permanence and prevent future alterations Govind refused to appoint any human successor and bade the Sikhs consider the Granth as their Guru. "Whatsoever ye shall ask of it, it will show you" he said, and in obedience to his command the book is still invested with a kind of personality and known as Granth Sahib.

Govind spent most of his time in wars with Aurungzeb marked by indomitable perseverance rather than success. Towards the end of his life he retired into Malwa and resided at a place called Damdama. The accounts of his latter days are somewhat divergent. According to one story he made his peace with the Mughals and accepted a military command under the successor of Aurungzeb but it is more commonly asserted that he was assassinated by a private enemy. Even more troublous were the days of his successor Banda. Since Govind had abolished the Guruship, he could not claim to be more than a temporal chief, but what he lacked in spiritual authority he made amends for in fanaticism. The eight years of his leadership were spent in a war of mutual extermination waged with the Moslims of the Panjab and diversified only by internal dissensions. At last he was captured and the sect was nearly annihilated by the Emperor Farukhsîyar. According to the

[1] This Arabic word is interpreted in this context as meaning the special portion (of God).

ordinary account this victory was followed by an orgy of torture and Banda was barbarously executed after witnessing during seven days the torments of his followers and kinsmen. We read with pleasure but incredulity that one division of the Sikhs believe that he escaped and promulgated his peculiar doctrines in Sind. Asiatics do not relish the idea that the chosen of God can suffer violent death.

The further history of the Sikhs is political rather than religious, and need not detain us here. Despite the efforts of the Mughals to exterminate them, they were favoured by the disturbed state of the country in the early decades of the eighteenth century, for the raids of Afghans and Persians convulsed and paralyzed the empire of Delhi. The government of the Khalsa passed into the hands of a body of fanatics, called Akâlis, but the decision of grave matters rested with a council of the whole community which occasionally met at Amritsar. Every Sikh claimed to have joined the confederacy as an independent soldier, bound to fight under his military leaders but otherwise exempt from control, and entitled to a share of land. This absolute independence, being unworkable in practice, was modified by the formation of Misals or voluntary associations, of which there were at one time twelve. From the middle of the eighteenth century onwards the Sikhs were masters of the Panjab and their great chief Ranjit Singh (1797–1839) succeeded in converting the confederacy into a despotic monarchy. Their power did not last long after his death and the Panjab was conquered by the British in the two wars of 1846 and 1849.

With the loss of political independence, the differences between the Sikhs and other Hindus tended to decrease. This was natural, for nearly all their strictly religious tenets can be paralleled in Hinduism. Guru Govind waged no war against polytheism but wished to found a religious commonwealth equally independent of Hindu castes and Mohammedan sultans. For some time his ordinances were successful in creating a tribe, almost a nation. With the collapse of the Sikh state, the old hatred of Mohammedanism remained, but the Sikhs differed from normal Hindus hardly more than such sects as the Lingâyats, and, as happened with decadent Buddhism, the unobtrusive pressure of Hindu beliefs and observances tended to obliterate those differences. The Census of India[1], 1901, enumerated three degrees of Sikhism. The first comprises a few zealots called Akâlis who observe all the precepts of Govind. The second class are the Guru Govind Sikhs, who observe the Guru's main commands, especially the prohibition to smoke and cut the hair. Lastly, there are a considerable number who profess a respect for the Guru but follow Hindu beliefs and usages wholly or in part. Sikhism indeed reproduces on a small scale the changeableness and complexity of Hinduism, and includes associations called Sabhâ, whose members aim at restoring or maintaining what they consider to be the true faith. In 1901 there was a tendency for Sikhs to give up their peculiarities and describe themselves as ordinary Hindus, but in the next decade a change of sentiment among these waverers caused the Sikh community as registered to increase by thirty-seven per cent. and a period of religious zeal is reported[2].

[1] *Census of India*, 1901, Panjab report, p. 122.
[2] *Provincial Geographies of India*, Panjab, Douie, 1916, p. 117.

CHAPTER XXXII

ŚÂKTISM[1]

AMONG the principal sub-divisions of Hinduism must be reckoned the remarkable religion known as Śâktism, that is the worship of Śakti or Śiva's spouse under various names, of which Devî, Durgâ and Kâlî are the best known. It differs from most sects in not being due to the creative or reforming energy of any one human founder. It claims to be a revelation from Śiva himself, but considered historically it appears to be a compound of Hinduism with un-Aryan beliefs. It acquired great influence both in the courts and among the people of north-eastern India but without producing personalities of much eminence as teachers or writers.

It would be convenient to distinguish Śâktism and Tantrism, as I have already suggested. The former means the worship of a goddess or goddesses, especially those who are regarded as forms of Śiva's consort. Vishnuites sometimes worship female deities, but though the worship of Lakshmî, Râdhâ and others may be coloured by imitation of Śâktist practices, it is less conspicuous and seems to have a different origin. Tantrism is a system of magical or sacramental ritual, which professes to attain the highest aims of religion by such methods as spells, diagrams, gestures and other physical exercises. One of its bases is the assumption that man and the universe correspond as microcosm and macrocosm and that both are subject to the mysterious power of words and letters.

These ideas are not modern nor peculiar to any Indian sect. They are present in the Vedic ceremonial, in the practices of the Yoga and even in the teaching of the quasi-mussulman sect of Kabir, which attaches great importance to the letters of the divine name. They harmonize with the common Indian view that some form of discipline or physical training is essential to

[1] See also chap. XXIV. as to Śâktism and Tantrism in Buddhism. Copious materials for the study of Śâktism and Tantrism are being made available in the series of tantric texts edited in Sanskrit and Tibetan, and in some cases translated by the author who uses the pseudonym A. Avalon.

the religious life. They are found in a highly developed form among the Nambutiris and other Brahmans of southern India who try to observe the Vedic rules and in the Far East among Buddhists of the Shingon or Chên-yen sect[1]. As a rule they receive the name of Tantrism only when they are elaborated into a system which claims to be a special dispensation for this age and to supersede more arduous methods which are politely set aside as practicable only for the hero-saints of happier times. Tantrism, like salvation by faith, is a simplification of religion but on mechanical rather than emotional lines, though its deficiency in emotion often finds strange compensations.

But Tantrism is analogous not so much to justification by faith as to sacramental ritual. The parallel may seem shocking, but most tantric ceremonies are similar in idea to Christian sacraments and may be called sacramental as correctly as magical. Even in the Anglican Church baptism includes sprinkling with water (abhisheka), the sign of the cross (nyâsa) and a formula (mantra), and if any one supposes that a child so treated is sure of heaven whereas the future of the unbaptized is dubious, he holds like the Tantrists that spiritual ends can be attained by physical means. And in the Roman Church where the rite includes exorcism and the use of salt, oil and lights, the parallel is still closer. Christian mysticism has had much to do with symbolism and even with alchemy[2], and Zoroastrianism, which is generally regarded as a reasonable religion, attaches extraordinary importance to holy spells[3]. So Indian religions are not singular in this respect, though the uncompromising thoroughness with which they work out this like other ideas leads to startling results.

The worship of female deities becomes prominent somewhat late in Indian literature and it does not represent—not to the same extent as the Chinese cult of Kwan-yin for example—the better ideals of the period when it appears. The goddesses of the Ṛig Veda are insignificant: they are little more than names, and grammatically often the feminine forms of their consorts. But this Veda is evidently a special manual of prayer from which many departments of popular religion were excluded. In

[1] See *Annales du Musée Guimet*, Tome VIII. Si-Do-In-Dzon. Gestes de l'officiant dans les cérémonies mystiques des sectes Tendai et Singon, 1899.

[2] See Underhill, *Mysticism*, chaps. VI. and VII.

[3] See Dhalla, *Zoroastrian Theology*, p. 116.

the Atharva Veda many spirits with feminine names are invoked and there is an inclination to personify bad qualities and disasters as goddesses. But we do not find any goddess who has attained a position comparable with that held by Durgâ, Cybele or Astarte, though there are some remarkable hymns[1] addressed to the Earth. But there is no doubt that the worship of goddesses (especially goddesses of fertility) as great powers is both ancient and widespread. We find it among the Egyptians and Semites, in Asia Minor, in Greece, Italy, and among the Kelts. The goddess Anahit, who was worshipped with immoral rites in Bactria, is figured on the coins of the Kushans and must at one time have been known on the north-western borders of India. At the present day Śîtalâ and in south India Mariamman are goddesses of smallpox who require propitiation, and one of the earliest deities known to have been worshipped by the Tamils is the goddess Koṭṭavai[2]. Somewhat obscure but widely worshipped are the powers known as the Mothers, a title which also occurs in Keltic mythology. They are groups of goddesses varying in number and often malevolent. As many as a hundred and forty are said to be worshipped in Gujarat. The census of Bengal (1901) records the worship of the earth, sun and rivers as females, of the snake goddesses Manasâ and Jagat Gaurî and of numerous female demons who send disease, such as the seven sisters, Ola Bibi, Jogini and the Churels, or spirits of women who have died in childbirth.

The rites celebrated in honour of these deities are often of a questionable character and include dances by naked women and offerings of spirituous liquors and blood. Similar features are found in other countries. Prostitution formed part of the worship of Astarte and Anahit: the Tauric Artemis was adored with human sacrifices and Cybele with self-inflicted mutilations. Similarly offerings of blood drawn from the sacrificer's own body are enjoined in the Kâlikâ Purâṇa. Two stages can be distinguished in the relations between these cults and Hinduism. In the later stage which can be witnessed even at the present day an aboriginal goddess or demon is identified with one of the aspects (generally a "black" or fierce aspect) of Śiva's

[1] Specially Ath. Veda, XII. 1.

[2] Village deities in south India at the present day are usually female. See Whitehead, *Village Gods*, p. 21.

spouse[1]. But such identification is facilitated by the fact that goddesses like Kâlî, Bhairavî, Chinnamastakâ are not products of purely Hindu imagination but represent earlier stages of amalgamation in which Hindu and aboriginal ideas are already compounded. When the smallpox goddess is identified with Kâlî, the procedure is correct, for some popular forms of Kâlî are little more than an aboriginal deity of pestilence draped with Hindu imagery and philosophy.

Some Hindu scholars demur to this derivation of Śâktism from lower cults. They point to its refined and philosophic aspects; they see in it the worship of a goddess, who can be as merciful as the Madonna, but yet, since she is the goddess of nature, combines in one shape life and death. May not the grosser forms of Śâktism be perversions and corruptions of an ancient and higher faith? In support of this it may be urged that the Buddhist goddess Târâ is as a rule a beautiful and benevolent figure, though she can be terrible as the enemy of evil and has clear affinities to Durgâ. Yet the history of Indian thought does not support this view, but rather the view that Hinduism incorporated certain ancient ideas, true and striking as ancient ideas often are, but without purging them sufficiently to make them acceptable to the majority of educated Indians.

The Yajur Veda[2] associates Rudra with a female deity called Ambikâ or mother, who is however his sister, not his spouse. The earliest forms of the latter seem to connect her with mountains. She is Umâ Haimavatî, the daughter of the Himalayas, and Pârvatî, she of the mountains, and was perhaps originally a sacred peak. In an interesting but brief passage of the Kena Upanishad (III. 12 and IV. 1) Umâ Haimavatî explains to the gods that a being whom they do not know is Brahman. In later times we hear of a similar goddess in the Vindhyas, Mahârânî Vindhyeśvarî, who was connected with human sacrifices and Thugs[3]. Śiva's consort, like her Lord, has many forms classified as white or benignant and black or terrible. Umâ belongs to the former class but the latter (such as Kâlî,

[1] Thus Cândî is considered as identical with the wood goddess Bâsulî, worshipped in the jungles of Bengal and Orissa. See *J.A.* 1873, p. 187.

[2] Vaj. Sanh. 3. 57 and Taittir. Br. I. 6. 10. 4.

[3] Crooke, *Popular Religion of Northern India*, I. 63. Monier Williams, *Brahm. and Hinduism*, p. 57 gives an interesting account of the shrine of Kâlî at Vindhyâcal said to have been formerly frequented by Thugs.

Durgâ, Câmundâ, Candâ and Karalâ) are more important[1]. Female deities bearing names like these are worshipped in most parts of India, literally from the Himalaya to Cape Comorin, for the latter name is derived from Kumârî, the Virgin goddess[2]. But the names Śâkta and Śâktism are usually restricted to those sects in Bengal and Assam who worship the Consort of Śiva with the rites prescribed in the Tantras.

Śâktism regards the goddess as the active manifestation of the godhead. As such she is styled Śakti, or energy (whence the name Śâkta), and is also identified with Mâyâ, the power which is associated with Brahman and brings the phenomenal world into being. Similar ideas appear in a philosophic form in the Sâṅkhya teaching. Here the soul is masculine and passive: its task is to extricate and isolate itself. But Prakṛiti or Nature is feminine and active: to her is due the evolution of the universe: she involves the soul in actions which cause pain but she also helps the work of liberation[3]. In its fully developed form the doctrine of the Tantras teaches that Śakti is not an emanation or aspect of the deity. There is no distinction between Brahman and Śakti. She is Parabrahman and *parâtparâ*, Supreme of the Supreme.

The birthplace of Śâktism as a definite sect seems to have been north-eastern India[4] and though it is said to be extending in the United Provinces, its present sphere of influence is still

[1] This idea that deities have different aspects in which they practically become different persons is very prevalent in Tibetan mythology which is borrowed from medieval Bengal.

[2] Though there are great temples erected to goddesses in S. India, there are also some signs of hostility to Śâktism. See the curious legends about an attendant of Śiva called Bhriṅgi who would not worship Pârvatî. Hultzsch, *South Indian Inscriptions*, II. ii. p. 190.

[3] There is a curious tendency in India to regard the male principle as quiescent, the female as active and stimulating. The Chinese, who are equally fond of using these two principles in their cosmological speculations, adopt the opposite view. The *Yang* (male) is positive and active. The *Yin* (female) is negative and passive.

[4] The Mahânirvâṇa Tantra seems to have been composed in Bengal since it recommends for sacrificial purposes (VI. 7) three kinds of fish said to be characteristic of that region. On the other hand Buddhist works called Tantras are said to have been composed in north-western India. Udyâna had an old reputation for magic and even in modern times Śâktism exists in western Tibet and Leh. It is highly probable that in all these districts the practice of magic and the worship of mountain goddesses were prevalent, but I find little evidence that a definite Śâkta sect arose elsewhere than in Bengal and Assam or that the Śâktist corruption of Buddhism prevailed elsewhere than in Magadha and Bengal.

chiefly Bengal and Assam[1]. The population of these countries is not Aryan (though the Bengali language bears witness to the strong Aryan influence which has prevailed there) and is largely composed of immigrants from the north belonging to the Tibeto-Burman, Mon-Khmer and Shan families. These tribes remain distinct in Assam but the Bengali represents the fusion of such invaders with a Munda or Dravidian race, leavened by a little Aryan blood in the higher castes. In all this region we hear of no ancient Brahmanic settlements, no ancient centres of Vedic or even Puranic learning[2] and when Buddhism decayed no body of Brahmanic tradition such as existed in other parts of India imposed its authority on the writers of the Tantras. Even at the present day the worship of female spirits, only half acknowledged by the Brahmans, prevails among these people, and in the past the national deities of many tribes were goddesses who were propitiated with human sacrifices. Thus the Chutiyas of Sadiya used to adore a goddess, called Kesai Khati—the eater of raw flesh. The rites of these deities were originally performed by tribal priests, but as Hindu influence spread, the Brahmans gradually took charge of them without modifying their character in essentials. Popular Bengali poetry represents these goddesses as desiring worship and feeling that they are slighted: they persecute those who ignore them, but shower blessings on their worshippers, even on the obdurate who are at last compelled to do them homage. The language of mythology could not describe more clearly the endeavours of a plebeian cult to obtain recognition[3].

The Mahâbhârata contains hymns to Durgâ in which she is said to love offerings of flesh and wine[4], but it is not likely that Śâktism or Tantrism—that is a system with special scriptures

[1] But the Brahmans of isolated localities, like Satara in the Bombay Presidency, are said to be Śâktas and the Kâñculiyas of S. India are described as a Śâktist sect.

[2] The law-giver Baudhâyana seems to have regarded Aṅga and Vaṅga with suspicion, I. 1. 13, 14.

[3] See especially the story of Manasâ Devi in Dinesh Chandra Sen (*Beng. Lang. and Lit.* 257), who says the earliest literary version dates from the twelfth century. But doubtless the story is much older.

[4] Virâtap. chap. VI. (not in all MSS.). Bhishmap. chap. XXIII. Also in the Harivaṃsa, *vv.* 3236 ff. Pargiter considers that the Devî-Mâhâtmya was probably composed in the fifth or sixth century. Chap. XXI. of the Lotus Sûtra contains a spell invoking a goddess under many names. Though this chapter is an addition to the original work, it was translated into Chinese between 265 and 316.

and doctrines—was prevalent before the seventh century A.D. for the Tantras are not mentioned by the Chinese pilgrims and the lexicon *Amara Kosha* (perhaps *c.* 500 A.D.) does not recognize the word as a designation of religious books. Bâṇa (*c.* 630) gives more than once in his romances lists of sectaries but though he mentions Bhâgavatas and Pâśupatas, he does not speak of Śâktas[1]. On the other hand Tantrism infected Buddhism soon after this period. The earlier Tibetan translations of the Tantras are attributed to the ninth century. MSS. of the Kubjikâmata and other Tantras are said to date from the ninth and even from the seventh century and tradition represents Sankarâcârya as having contests with Śâktas[2]. But many Tantras were written in the fifteenth century and even later, for the Yogini Tantra alludes to the Koch king Bishwa Singh (1515–1540) and the Meru Tantra mentions London and the English.

From the twelfth to the sixteenth century, when Buddhism, itself deeply infected with Tantrism, was disappearing, Śâktism was probably the most powerful religion in Bengal, but Vishnuism was gaining strength and after the time of Caitanya proved a formidable rival to it. At the beginning of the fifteenth century we hear that the king of the Ahoms summoned Brahmans to his Court and adopted many Hindu rites and beliefs, and from this time onward Śâktism was patronized by most of the Assamese Rajas although after 1550 Vishnuism became the religion of the mass of the people. Śâktism never inspired any popular or missionary movement, but it was powerful among the aristocracy and instigated persecutions against the Vishnuites.

The more respectable Tantras[3] show considerable resemblance to the later Upanishads such as the Nṛisinhatâpanîya and Râmatâpanîya, which mention Śakti in the sense of creative energy[4]. Both classes of works treat of magical formulæ (mantras)

[1] But he does mention the worship of the Divine Mothers. Harshacar. VII. 250 and Kâdamb. 134.

[2] Hymns to the Devî are also attributed to him but I do not know what evidence there is for his authorship.

[3] As pointed out elsewhere, though this word is most commonly used of the Śâkta scriptures it is not restricted to them and we hear of both Buddhist and Vaishṇava Tantras.

[4] The Adhyâtma Râmâyaṇa is an instance of Śâktist ideas in another theological setting. It is a Vishnuite work but Sîtâ is made to say that she is *Prakṛiti* who does all the deeds related in the poem, whereas Râma is *Purusha*, inactive and a witness of her deeds.

and the construction of mystic diagrams or yantras. This resemblance does not give us much assistance in chronology, for the dates of the later Upanishads are very uncertain, but it shows how the Tantras are connected with other branches of Hindu thought.

The distinction between Tantras and Purâṇas is not always well-marked. The Bhâgavata Purâṇa countenances tantric rites[1] and the Agni Purâṇa (from chapter XXI onwards) bears a strong resemblance to a Tantra. As a rule the Tantras contain less historical and legendary matter than the Purâṇas and more directions as to ritual. But whereas the Purâṇas approve of both Vedic rites and others, the Tantras insist that ceremonies other than those which they prescribe are now useless. They maintain that each age of the world has its own special revelation and that in this age the Tantra-śâstra is the only scripture. Thus in the Mahânirvâṇa Tantra Śiva says[2]: "The fool who would follow other doctrines heedless of mine is as great a sinner as a parricide or the murderer of a Brahman or of a woman....The Vedic rites and mantras which were efficacious in the first age have ceased to have power in this. They are now as powerless as snakes whose fangs have been drawn and are like dead things." The Kulârṇava Tantra (I. 79 ff.) inveighs against those who think they will obtain salvation by Vedic sacrifices or asceticism or reading sacred books, whereas it can be won only by tantric rites.

Various lists of Tantras are given and it is generally admitted that many have been lost. The most complete, but somewhat theoretical enumeration[3] divides India and the adjoining lands into three regions to each of which sixty-four Tantras are assigned. The best known names are perhaps Mahânirvâṇa[4], Sâradâtilaka[5], Yoginî, Kulârṇava[6] and Rudra-Yâmala. A Tantra

[1] XI. iii. 47–8; XI. v. 28 and 31. Probably Vishnuite not Śâktist Tantras are meant but the Purana distinguishes between Vedic revelation meant for previous sages and tantric revelation meant for the present day. So too Kullûka Bhaṭṭa the commentator on Manu who was a Bengali and probably lived in the fifteenth century says (on Manu II. i.) that Śruti is twofold, Vedic and tantric. *Śrutisca dvividhâ vaidikî tântrikîca.*

[2] II. 15.

[3] See for full list Avalon, *Principles of Tantra*, pp. lxv–lxvii. A collection of thirty-seven Tantras has been published at Calcutta by Babu Rasik Mohun Chatterjee and a few have been published separately.

[4] Translated by Avalon, 1913, also by Manmatha Nath Dutt, 1900.

[5] Analysed in *J.A.O.S.* XXIII. i. 1902.

[6] Edited by Târanâtha Vidyâratna, with introduction by A. Avalon, 1917.

is generally cast in the form of a dialogue in which Śiva instructs his consort but sometimes *vice versâ*. It is said that the former class are correctly described as Âgamas and the works where the Śakti addresses Śiva as Nigamas[1]. Some are also called Yâmalas and Dâmaras but I have found no definition of the meaning of these words. The Prapañcasâra Tantra[2] professes to be a revelation from Nârâyaṇa.

Śâktism and the Tantras which teach it are generally condemned by Hindus of other sects[3]. It is arguable that this condemnation is unjust, for like other forms of Hinduism the Tantras make the liberation of the soul their object and prescribe a life of religious observances including asceticism and meditation, after which the adept becomes released even in this life. But however much new tantric literature may be made accessible in future, I doubt if impartial criticism will come to any opinion except that Śâktism and Tantrism collect and emphasize what is superficial, trivial and even bad in Indian religion, omitting or neglecting its higher sides. If for instance the Mahânirvâṇa Tantra which is a good specimen of these works be compared with Śaṅkara's commentary on the Vedânta Sûtras, or the poems of Tulsi Das, it will be seen that it is woefully deficient in the excellences of either. But many tantric treatises are chiefly concerned with charms, spells, amulets and other magical methods of obtaining wealth, causing or averting disease and destroying enemies, processes which even if efficacious have nothing to do with the better side of religion[4].

The religious life prescribed in the Tantras[5] commences with initiation and requires the supervision of the Guru. The object of it is *Siddhi* or success, the highest form of which is spiritual perfection. *Siddhi* is produced by *Sâdhana*, or that method of

[1] See Avalon, *Principles of Tantra*, p. lxi. But these are probably special meanings attached to the words by tantric schools. *Nigama* is found pretty frequently, *e.g.* Manu, IV. 19 and Lalita-vistara, XII. But it is not likely that it is used there in this special sense.

[2] Edited by Avalon, 1914.

[3] Satirical descriptions of Śâktism are fairly ancient, *e.g.* Karpura Mañjarî, Harvard edition, pp. 25 and 233.

[4] Tantrism has some analogy to the Fêng-shui or geomancy of the Chinese. Both take ancient superstitions which seem incompatible with science and systematize them into pseudo-sciences, remaining blind to the fact that the subject-matter is wholly imaginary.

[5] For what follows as for much else in this chapter, I am indebted to Avalon's translation of the Mahânirvâṇa Tantra and introduction.

training the physical and psychic faculties which realizes their potentialities. Tantric training assumes a certain constitution of the universe and the repetition in miniature of this constitution in the human body which contains various nervous centres and subtle channels for the passage of energy unknown to vulgar anatomy. Thus the Śakti who pervades the universe is also present in the body as Kuṇḍalinî, a serpentine coil of energy, and it is part of Sâdhana to arouse this energy and make it mount from the lower to the higher centres. Kuṇḍalinî is also present in sounds and in letters. Hence if different parts of the body are touched to the accompaniment of appropriate mantras (which rite is called nyâsa) the various Śaktis are made to dwell in the human frame in suitable positions.

The Tantras recognize that human beings are not equal and that codes and rituals must vary according to temperament and capacity. Three conditions of men, called the animal, heroic and divine[1], are often mentioned and are said to characterize three periods of life—youth, manhood and age, or three classes of mankind, non-tantrists, ordinary tantrists, and adepts. These three conditions clearly correspond to the three Guṇas. Also men, or rather Hindus, belong to one of seven groups, or stages, according to the religious practices which it is best for them to follow. Śâktists apparently demur[2] to the statement commonly made by Indians as well as by Europeans that they are divided into two sects the Dakshiṇâcârins, or right-hand worshippers, whose ritual is public and decent, and the Vâmâcârins who meet to engage in secret but admittedly immoral orgies. But for practical purposes the division is just, although it must not be supposed that Dakshiṇâcârins necessarily condemn the secret worship. They may consider it as good for others but not for themselves. Śâktists apparently would prefer to state the matter thus. There are seven stages of religion. First come Vedic, Vishnuite and Śivaite worship, all three inferior, and then Dakshiṇâcâra, interpreted as meaning favourable worship, that is favourable to the accomplishment of higher purposes, because the worshipper now begins to understand the nature of Devî, the great goddess. These four kinds of worship are all said to belong to *pravritti* or active life. The other three, considered to be higher, require a special initiation and belong to *nivritti*, the

[1] Paśu-, vîra-, divya-bhâva.

[2] Avalon, Mahân. Tan. pp. lxxix, lxxx.

path of return in which passion and activity are suppressed[1]. And here is propounded the doctrine that passion can be destroyed and exhausted by passion[2], that is to say that the impulses of eating, drinking and sexual intercourse are best subjugated by indulging them. The fifth stage, in which this method is first adopted, is called Vâmâcâra[3]. In the sixth, or Siddhântâcâra[4], the adept becomes more and more free from passion and prejudice and is finally able to enter Kaulâcâra, the highest stage of all. A Kaula is one who has passed beyond all sects and belongs to none, since he has the knowledge of Brahman. "Possessing merely the form of man, he moves about this earth for the salvation of the world and the instruction of men[5]."

These are aspirations common to all Indian religion. The peculiarity of the Tantras is to suppose that a ritual which is shocking to most Hindus is an indispensable preliminary to their attainment[6]. Its essential feature is known as *pancatattva*, the five elements, or *pancamakâra* the five m's, because they all begin with that letter, namely, *madya*, *mâṃsa*, *matsya*, *mudrâ*, and *maithuna*, wine, meat, fish, parched grain and copulation. The celebration of this ritual takes place at midnight, and is called *cakra* or circle. The proceedings begin by the devotees seating themselves in a circle and are said to terminate in an indiscriminate orgy. It is only fair to say that some Tantras inveigh against drunkenness and authorize only moderate drinking[7]. In all cases it is essential that the wine, flesh, etc.,

[1] "The eternal rhythm of Divine Breath is outwards from spirit to matter and inwards from matter to spirit. Devî as Mâyâ evolves the world. As Mahâmâyâ she recalls it to herself.......Each of these movements is divine. Enjoyment and liberation are each her gifts." Avalon, Mahân. Tan. p. cxl.

[2] Yair eva patanam dravyaih siddhis tair eva coditâ—Kulârṇava Tantra, v. 48. There is probably something similar in Taoism. See Wieger, *Histoire des Croyances religieuses en Chine*, p. 409. The Indian Tantrists were aware of the dangers of their system and said it was as difficult as walking on the edge of a sword or holding a tiger.

[3] Vâmâcâra is said not to mean left-hand worship but woman (vâmâ) worship. This interpretation of Dakshiṇa and Vâmâcâra is probably fanciful.

[4] Sometimes two extra stages Aghora and Yogâcâra are inserted here.

[5] Mahân. Tan. x. 108. A Kaula may pretend to be a Vaishṇava or a Śaiva.

[6] Although the Tantras occasionally say that mere ritual is not sufficient for the highest religions, yet *indispensable preliminary* is often understood as meaning *sure means*. Thus the Mahânirvâṇa Tantra (x. 202, Avalon's transl.) says "Those who worship the Kaulas with *panca tattva* and with heart uplifted, cause the salvation of their ancestors and themselves attain the highest end."

[7] But on the other hand some Tantras or tantric treatises recommend crazy abominations.

should be formally dedicated to the goddess: without this preliminary indulgence in these pleasures is sinful. Indeed it may be said that apart from the ceremonial which they inculcate, the general principles of the Tantras breathe a liberal and intelligent spirit. Caste restrictions are minimized: travelling is permitted. Women are honoured: they can act as teachers: the burning of widows is forbidden[1]: girl widows may remarry[2] and the murder of a woman is peculiarly heinous. Prostitution is denounced. Whereas Christianity is sometimes accused of restricting its higher code to Church and Sundays, the opposite may be said of Tantrism. Outside the temple its morality is excellent.

A work like the Mahânirvâṇa Tantra presents a refined form of Śâktism modified, so far as may be, in conformity with ordinary Hindu usage[3]. But other features indubitably connect it with aboriginal cults. For instance there is a legend which relates how the body of the Śakti was cut into pieces and scattered over Assam and Bengal. This story has an uncouth and barbarous air and seems out of place even in Puranic mythology. It recalls the tales told of Osiris, Orpheus and Halfdan the Black[4] and may be ultimately traceable to the idea that the dismemberment of a deity or a human representative ensures fertility. Until recently the Khonds of Bengal used to hack human victims in pieces as a sacrifice to the Earth Goddess and throw the shreds of flesh on the fields to secure a good harvest[5]. In Sanskrit literature I have not found any authority for the dismemberment of Satî earlier than the Tantras or Upapurâṇas (*e.g.* Kâlikâ), but this late appearance does not mean that the legend is late in itself but merely that it was not countenanced by Sanskrit writers until medieval times. Various reasons for the dismemberment are given and the incident is rather awkwardly tacked on to other stories. One common version relates that when Satî (one of the many forms of Śakti) died of vexation because her husband Śiva was insulted by her

[1] Mahânir. Tant. x. 79. Bhartrâ saha kuleśâni na dahet kulakâminim.

[2] *Ib.* xi. 67.

[3] *E.g.* It does not prescribe human sacrifices and counsels moderation in the use of wine and *maithuna*.

[4] See Frazer's *Adonis, Attis and Osiris*, pp. 269–273 for these and other stories of dismemberment.

[5] See Frazer, *Golden Bough: Spirits of the Corn*, vol. i. 245 and authorities quoted.

father Daksha, Śiva took up her corpse and wandered distractedly carrying it on his shoulder[1]. In order to stop this penance Vishṇu followed him and cut off pieces from the corpse with his quoit until the whole had fallen to earth in fifty-one pieces. The spots where these pieces touched the ground are held sacred and called pîṭhs. At most of them are shown a rock supposed to represent some portion of the goddess's body and some object called a bhairabi, left by Śiva as a guardian to protect her and often taking the form of a lingam. The most important of these pîṭhs are Kâmâkhyâ near Gauhati, Faljur in the Jaintia Parganas, and Kalighat in Calcutta[2].

Though the Śakti of Śiva is theoretically one, yet since she assumes many forms she becomes in practice many deities or rather she is many deities combined in one or sometimes a sovereign attended by a retinue of similar female spirits. Among such forms we find the ten Mahâvidyâs, or personifications of her supernatural knowledge; the Mahâmâtris, Mâtrikâs or the Great Mothers, allied to the aboriginal goddesses already mentioned; the Nâyakas or mistresses; the Yoginîs or sorceresses, and fiends called Ḍâkinîs. But the most popular of her manifestations are Durgâ and Kâlî. The sects which revere these goddesses are the most important religious bodies in Bengal, where they number thirty-five million adherents. The Durgâpûja is the greatest festival of the year in north-eastern India[3] and in the temple of Kalighat at Calcutta may be seen the singular spectacle of educated Hindus decapitating goats before the image of Kâlî. It is a black female figure with gaping mouth and protruded tongue dancing on a prostrate body[4], and

[1] Images representing this are common in Assam.

[2] Hsüan Chuang (Watters, vol. I. chap. VII) mentions several sacred places in N.W. India where the Buddha in a previous birth was dismembered or gave his flesh to feed mankind. Can these places have been similar to the pîṭhs of Assam and were the original heroes of the legend deities who were dismembered like Satî and subsequently accommodated to Buddhist theology as Bodhisattvas?

[3] It is an autumnal festival. A special image of the goddess is made which is worshipped for nine days and then thrown into the river. For an account of the festival which makes its tantric character very clear see Durga Puja by Pratapachandra Ghosha, Calcutta, 1871.

[4] One explanation given is that she was so elated with her victories over giants that she began to dance which shook the Universe. Śiva in order to save the world placed himself beneath her feet and when she saw she was trampling on her husband, she stopped. But there are other explanations.

Another of the strangely barbaric legends which cluster round the Śakti is

adorned with skulls and horrid emblems of destruction. Of her four hands two carry a sword and a severed head but the other two are extended to give blessing and protection to her worshippers. So great is the crowd of enthusiastic suppliants that it is often hard to approach the shrine and the nationalist party in Bengal who clamour for parliamentary institutions are among the goddess's devotees.

It is easy to criticize and condemn this worship. Its outward signs are repulsive to Europeans and its inner meaning strange, for even those who pray to the Madonna are startled by the idea that the divine nature is essentially feminine[1]. Yet this idea has deep roots in the heart of Bengal and with it another idea: the terrors of death, plague and storm are half but only half revelations of the goddess-mother who can be smiling and tender as well. Whatever may be the origin of Kâlî and of the strange images which represent her, she is now no she-devil who needs to be propitiated, but a reminder that birth and death are twins, that the horrors of the world come from the same source as its grace and beauty and that cheerful acceptance of the deity's terrible manifestations is an essential part of the higher spiritual life[2]. These ideas are best expressed in the songs of Râma Prasâda Sen (1718–1775) which "still reign supreme in the villages" of Bengal and show that this strange worship has really a hold on millions of Indian rustics[3]. The directness and childlike simplicity of his poems have caused an Indian critic to compare him to Blake. "Though the mother beat the child," he sings, "the child cries mother, mother, and clings still

illustrated by the figure called Chinnamastakâ. It represents the goddess as carrying her own head which she has just cut off, while from the neck spout fountains of blood which are drunk by her attendants and by the severed head itself.

[1] Yet the English mystic Julian, the anchoress of Norwich (*c.* 1400), insists on the motherhood as well as the fatherhood of God. "God is our mother, brother and Saviour." "As verily God is our father, so verily God is our mother."

So too in an inscription found at Capua (C.I.N. 3580) Isis is addressed as *una quae es omnia*.

The Power addressed in Swinburne's poems *Mater Triumphalis, Hertha, The Pilgrims* and *Dolores* is really a conception very similar to Śakti.

[2] These ideas find frequent expression in the works of Bunkim Chandra Chatterjee, Dinesh Chandra Sen and Sister Nivedita.

[3] See Dinesh Chandra Sen, *Hist. Beng. Lang. and Lit.* pp. 712–721. Even the iconoclast Devendranath Tagore speaks of the Universal Mother. See *Autobiog.* p. 240.

tighter to her garment. True, I cannot see thee, yet I am not a lost child. I still cry mother, mother."

"All the miseries that I have suffered and am suffering, I know, O mother, to be your mercy alone."

I must confess that I cannot fully sympathize with this worship, even when it is sung in the hymns of Râma Prasâda, but it is clear that he makes it tolerable just because he throws aside all the magic and ritual of the Tantras and deals straight with what are for him elemental and emotional facts. He makes even sceptics feel that he has really seen God in this strange guise.

The chief sanctuary of Śâktism is at Kâmâkhyâ (or Kâmâkshâ) on a hill which stands on the banks of the Brahmaputra, about two miles below Gauhati. It is mentioned in the Padma Purâṇa. The temples have been rebuilt several times, and in the eighteenth century were munificently endowed by an Ahom king, and placed under the management of a Brahman from Nadia in Bengal, with reversion to his descendants who bear the title of Parbatiya Gosains. Considerable estates are still assigned to their upkeep. There are ten[1] shrines on the hill dedicated to various forms of the Śakti. The situation is magnificent, commanding an extensive prospect over the Brahmaputra and the plains on either bank, but none of the buildings are of much architectural merit. The largest and best is the temple dedicated to Kâmâkhyâ herself, the goddess of sexual desire. It is of the style usual in northern India, an unlighted shrine surmounted by a dome, and approached by a rather ample vestibule, which is also imperfectly lighted. An inscription has been preserved recording the restoration of the temple about 1550 but only the present basement dates from that time, most of the superstructure being recent. Europeans may not enter but an image of the goddess can be seen from a side door. In the depths of the shrine is said to be a cleft in the rock, adored as the Yoni of Śakti. In front of the temple are two posts to which a goat is tied, and decapitated daily at noon. Below the principal shrine is the temple of Bhairavî. Human sacrifices were offered here in comparatively recent times, and it is not denied that they would be offered now if the law allowed. Also it is not denied

[1] So I was told, but I saw only six, when I visited the place in 1910.

that the rites of the "five m's" already mentioned are frequently performed in these temples, and that Aghoris may be found in them. The spot attracts a considerable number of pilgrims from Bengal, and a wealthy devotee has built a villa on the hill and pays visits to it for the purpose of taking part in the rites. I was informed that the most esteemed scriptures of the sect are the Yoginî Tantra, the Mahânirvâṇa Tantra, and the Kâlikâ Purâṇa. This last work contains a section or chapter on blood[1], which gives rules for the performance of human sacrifices. It states however that they should not be performed by the first three castes, which is perhaps a way of saying that though they may be performed by non-Aryans under Brahmanic auspices they form no part of the Aryan religion. But they are recommended to princes and ministers and should not be performed without the consent of princes. The ritual bears little resemblance to the Vedic sacrifices and the essence of the ceremony is the presentation to the goddess of the victim's severed head in a vessel of gold, silver, copper, brass or wood but not of iron. The axe with which the decapitation is to be performed is solemnly consecrated to Kâlî and the victim is worshipped before immolation. The sacrificer first thinks of Brahmâ and the other gods as being present in the victim's body, and then prays to him directly as being all the gods in one. "When this has been done" says Śiva, who is represented as himself revealing these rules, "the victim is even as myself." This identification of the human victim with the god has many analogies elsewhere, particularly among the Khonds[2].

It is remarkable that this barbarous and immoral worship, though looked at askance except in its own holy places, is by no means confined to the lower castes. A series of apologies composed in excellent English (but sometimes anonymous) attest the sympathy of the educated. So far as theology and metaphysics are concerned, these defences are plausible. The Śakti is identified with Prakṛiti or with the Mâyâ of the Advaita philosophy and defined as the energy, coexistent with Brahman, which creates the world. But attempts to palliate the ceremonial, such as the argument that it is a consecration and limitation of the appetites because they may be gratified only in the service

[1] Rudhirâdhyâya. Translated in *As. Researches*, v. 1798, pp. 371–391.

[2] See Frazer, *op. cit.* p. 246.

of the goddess, are not convincing. Nor do the Śâktas, when able to profess their faith openly, deny the nature of their rites or the importance attached to them. An oft-quoted tantric verse represents Śiva as saying *Maithunena mahâyogî mama tulyo na saṁśayaḥ*. And for practical purposes that is the gist of Śâktist teaching.

The temples of Kâmâkhyâ leave a disagreeable impression—an impression of dark evil haunts of lust and bloodshed, akin to madness and unrelieved by any grace or vigour of art. For there is no attempt in them to represent the terrible or voluptuous aspects of Hinduism, such as find expression in sculpture elsewhere. All the buildings, and especially the modern temple of Kâlî, which was in process of construction when I saw the place, testify to the atrophy and paralysis produced by erotic forms of religion in the artistic and intellectual spheres, a phenomenon which finds another sad illustration in quite different theological surroundings among the Vallabhâcârya sect at Gokul near Muttra.

It would be a poor service to India to palliate the evils and extravagances of Śâktism, but still it must be made clear that it is not a mere survival of barbaric practices. The writers of the Tantras are good Hindus and declare that their object is to teach liberation and union with the Supreme Spirit. The ecstasies induced by tantric rites produce this here in a preliminary form to be made perfect in the liberated soul. This is not the craze of a few hysterical devotees, but the faith of millions among whom many are well educated. In some aspects Śâktism is similar to the erotic Vishnuite sects, but there is little real analogy in their ways of thinking. For the essence of Vishnuism is passionate devotion and self-surrender to a deity and this idea is not prominent in the Tantras. The strange inconsistencies of Śâktism are of the kind which are characteristic of Hinduism as a whole, but the contrasts are more violent and the monstrosities more conspicuous than elsewhere; wild legends and metaphysics are mixed together, and the peace that passes all understanding is to be obtained by orgies and offerings of blood.

CHAPTER XXXIII

HINDU PHILOSOPHY

1

PHILOSOPHY is more closely connected with religion in India than in Europe. It is not a dispassionate scientific investigation but a practical religious quest. Even the Nyâya school, which is concerned chiefly with formal logic, promises that by the removal of false knowledge it can emancipate the soul and give the bliss of salvation. Nor are the expressions system or school of philosophy, commonly used to render *darśana*, altogether happy. The word is derived from the root *dṛiś*, to see, and means a way of looking at things. As such a way of looking is supposed to be both comprehensive and orderly, it is more or less what we call philosophical, but the points of view are so special and so various that the result is not always what we call a philosophical system. Mâdhava's[1] list of Darśanas includes Buddhism and Jainism, which are commonly regarded as separate religions, as well as the Pâśupata and Śaiva, which are sects of Hinduism. The Darśana of Jaimini is merely a discussion of general questions relating to sacrifices: the Nyâya Darśana examines logic and rhetoric: the Pâṇiniya Darśana treats of grammar and the nature of language, but claims that it ought to be studied "as the means for attaining the chief end of man[2]."

Six of the Darśanas have received special prominence and are often called the six Orthodox Schools. They are the Nyâya and Vaiśeshika, Sâṅkhya and Yoga, Pûrva and Uttara Mîmâṃsâ,

[1] In the Sarva-darśana-saṅgraha, the best known compendium of Indian philosophy.

[2] J. C. Chatterji's definition of Indian philosophy (in his *Indian Realism*, p. 1) is interesting. "By Hindu philosophy I mean that branch of the ancient learning "of the Hindus which demonstrates by reasoning propositions with regard to "(*a*) what a man ought to do in order to gain true happiness... or (*b*) what he "ought to realize by direct experience in order to be radically and absolutely freed "from suffering and to be absolutely independent, such propositions being already "given and lines of reasoning in their support being established by duly qualified "authorities."

or Vedânta. The rest are either comparatively unimportant or are more conveniently treated of as religious sects. The six placed on the select list are sufficiently miscellaneous and one wonders what principle of classification can have brought them together. The first two have little connection with religion, though they put forward the emancipation of the soul as their object, and I have no space to discuss them. They are however important as showing that realism has a place in Indian thought in spite of its marked tendency to idealism[1]. They are concerned chiefly with an examination of human faculties and the objects of knowledge, and are related to one another. The special doctrine of the Vaiśeshika is the theory of atoms ascribed to Kaṇâda. It teaches that matter consists of atoms (aṇu) which are eternal in themselves though all combinations of them are liable to decompose. The Sâṅkhya and Yoga are also related and represent two aspects of the same system which is of great antiquity and allied to Buddhism and Jainism. The two Mîmâṃsâs are consecutive expositions of the teaching scattered throughout the Vedic texts respecting ceremonial and the knowledge of God respectively. The second Mîmâṃsâ, commonly called the Vedânta, is by far the more interesting and important.

The common feature in these six systems which constitutes their orthodoxy is that they all admit the authority of the Veda. This implies more than our phrases revelation or inspiration of the Bible. Most of the Darśanas attach importance to the *pramâṇas*, sources or standards of knowledge. They are variously enumerated, but one of the oldest definitions makes them three: perception (pratyaksha), inference (anumâna) and scripture (śabda). The Veda is thus formally acknowledged to have the same authority as the evidence of the senses. With this is generally coupled the doctrine that it is eternal. It was not composed by human authors, but is a body of sound existing from eternity as part of Brahman and breathed out by him when he causes the whole creation to evolve at the beginning of a world period. The reputed authors are simply those who have, in Indian language, seen portions of this self-existent teaching. This doctrine sounds more reasonable if restated in the form that words are the expression of thought, and that if thought is the eternal essence of both Brahman and the soul,

[1] See Chatterji's work above cited.

a similar eternity may attach to words. Some such idea is the origin of the Christian doctrine of the Logos, and in many religions we find such notions as that words have a creative efficacy[1], or that he who knows the name of a thing has power over it. Among Mohammedans the Koran is supposed to be not merely an inspired composition but a pre-existing book, revealed to Mohammed piecemeal.

It is curious that both the sacred texts—the Veda and the Koran—to which this supernatural position is ascribed should be collections of obviously human, incongruous, and often insignificant documents connected with particular occasions, and in no way suggesting or claiming that they are anterior to the ordinary life of man on earth. It is still more extraordinary that systems of philosophy should profess to base themselves on such works. But in reality Hindu metaphysicians are not more bound by the past than their colleagues in other lands. They do not take scripture and ask what it means, but evolve their own systems and state that they are in accordance with it. Sometimes scripture is ignored in the details of argument. More often the metaphysician writes a commentary on it and boldly proves that it supports his views, though its apparent meaning may be hostile. It is clear that many philosophic commentaries have been written not because the authors really drew their inspiration from the Upanishads or Bhagavad-gîtâ but because they dared not neglect such important texts. All the Vedântist schools labour to prove that they are in harmony not only with the Upanishads but with the Brahma-sûtras. The philosophers of the Sâṅkhya are more detached from literature but though they ignore the existence of the deity, they acknowledge the Veda as a source of knowledge. Their recognition, however, has the air of a concession to Brahmanic sentiment. Isolated theories of the Sâṅkhya can be supported by isolated passages of the Upanishads, but no impartial critic can maintain that the general doctrines of the two are compatible. That the Brahmans should have been willing to admit the Sâṅkhya as a possible form of orthodoxy is a testimony both to its importance and to their liberality.

[1] It is this idea which disposes educated Hindus to believe in the magical or sacramental power of mystic syllables and letters, though the use of such spells seems to Europeans incredible folly.

It is remarkable that the test of orthodoxy should have been the acceptance of the authority of the Veda and not a confession of some sort of theism. But on this the Brahmans did not insist. The Vedânta is truly and intensely pantheistic or theistic, but in the other philosophies the Supreme Being is either eliminated or plays a small part. Thus while works which seem to be merely scientific treatises (like the Nyâya) set before themselves a religious object, other treatises, seemingly religious in scope, ignore the deity. There is a strong and ancient line of thought in India which, basing itself on the doctrine of Karma, or the inevitable consequences of the deed once done, lays stress on the efficacy of ceremonies or of asceticism or of knowledge without reference to a Supreme Being because, if he exists, he does not interfere with the workings of Karma, or with the power of knowledge to release from them.

Even the Vedânta, although in a way the quintessence of Indian orthodoxy, is not a scholastic philosophy designed to support recognized dogma and ritual. It is rather the orthodox method of soaring above these things. It contemplates from a higher level the life of religious observances (which is the subject of the Pûrva Mîmâṃsâ) and recognizes its value as a preliminary, but yet rejects it as inadequate. The Sannyâsi or adept follows no caste observances, performs no sacrifices, reads no scriptures. His religion is to realize in meditation the true nature, and it may be the identity, of the soul and God. Good works are of no more importance for him than rites, though he does well to employ his time in teaching. But Karma has ceased to exist for him: "the acts of a Yogi are neither black nor white," they have no moral quality nor consequences. This is dangerous language and the doctrine has sometimes been abused. But the point of the teaching is not that a Sannyâsi may do what he likes but that he is perfectly emancipated from material bondage. Most men are bound by their deeds; every new act brings consequences which attach the doer to the world of transmigration and create for him new existences. But the deeds of the man who is really free have no such trammelling effects, for they are not prompted by desire nor directed to an object. But since to become free he must have suppressed all desire, it is hardly conceivable that he should do anything which could be called a sin. But this conviction that the task of the sage is not to perfect any form of good conduct but to rise above both good and evil, imparts to the Darśanas and even to the Upanishads a singularly non-ethical and detached tone. The Yogi does no harm but he has less benevolence and active sympathy than the Buddhist monk. It was a feeling that such an attitude has its dangers and is only for the few who have fought their way to the heights where it can safely be adopted, that led the Brahmans in all ages to lay stress on the householder's life as the proper preparation for a philosophic old age. Despite utterances to the contrary, they never as a body approved the ideal of a life entirely devoted to asceticism and not occupied with social duties during one period. The extraordinary ease with which the higher phases of Indian thought shake off all formalities, social, religious and ethical, was counterbalanced by the multitudinous regulations devised to keep the majority in a law-abiding life.

None of the six Darśanas concern themselves with ethics. The more important deal with the transcendental progress of sages who have avowedly abandoned the life of works, and even those which treat of that lower life are occupied with ritual and logic rather than with anything which can be termed moral science. We must not infer that Indian literature is altogether unmoral. The doctrine of Karma is intensely ethical and ethical discussions are more prominent in the Epics than in Homer, besides being the subject of much gnomic and didactic poetry. But there is no mistaking the fact that the Hindu seeks for salvation by knowledge. He feels the power of deeds, but it is only the lower happiness which lies in doing good works and enjoying their fruits. The higher bliss consists in being entirely free from the bondage of deeds and Karma.

All the Darśanas have as a common principle this idea of Karma with the attendant doctrines that rebirth is a consequence of action and that salvation is an escape from rebirth. They all treat more or less of the sources and standards of knowledge, and all recognize the Veda as one of them. There is not much more that can be said of them all in common, for the Vedânta ignores matter and the Sâṅkhya ignores God, but they all share a conviction which presents difficulties to Europeans. It is that the state in which the mind ceases to think discursively and is concentrated on itself is not only desirable but the *summum bonum*. The European is inclined to say that such a state is distinguished from non-existence only by not being permanent. But the Hindu will have none of this. He holds that mind and thought are material though composed of the subtlest matter, and that when thought ceases, the immaterial soul (purusha or âtman) far from being practically non-existent is more truly existent than before and enjoys untroubled its own existence and its own nature.

Of the three most important systems, the Sâṅkhya, Yoga and Vedânta, the first and last are on most points opposed: both are ancient, but perhaps the products of different intellectual centres. In one sense the Yoga may be described as a theistic modification of the Sâṅkhya: from another and perhaps juster point of view it appears rather as a very ancient science of asceticism and contemplation, susceptible of combination with various metaphysical theories.

2

We may consider first of all the Sâṅkhya[1]. Tradition ascribes its invention to Kapila, but he is a mere name unconnected with any date or other circumstance. It is probable that the principal ideas of the Sâṅkhya germinated several centuries before our era but we have no evidence whatever as to when they were first formulated in Sûtras. The name was current as the designation of a philosophical system fairly early[2] but the accepted text-books are all late. The most respected is the Sâṅkhya-pravacana[3], attributed to Kapila but generally assigned by European critics to the fourteenth century A.D. Considerably more ancient, but still clearly a metrical epitome of a system already existing, is the Sâṅkhya-Kârikâ, a poem of seventy verses which was translated into Chinese about 560 A.D. and may be a few centuries older. Max Müller regarded the Tattva-samâsa, a short tract consisting chiefly of an enumeration of

[1] See especially Garbe, *Die Sâṅkhya Philosophie*, 1894; and Keith, *The Sâṁkhya System*, 1919, which however reached me too late for me to make any use of it.

[2] *E.g.* in the Bhagavad-gîtâ and Śvetâśvatara Upanishads. According to tradition Kapila taught Asuri and he, Pañcaśikha, who made the system celebrated. Garbe thinks Pañcaśikha may be assigned to the first century A.D.

[3] This appears to be the real title of the Sûtras edited and translated by Ballantyne as "The Sâṅkhya Aphorisms of Kapila."

topics, as the most ancient Sâṅkhya formulary, but the opinion of scholars as to its age is not unanimous. The name Sâṅkhya is best interpreted as signifying enumeration in allusion to the predilection of the school for numbered lists, a predilection equally noticeable in early Buddhism.

The object of the system set forth in these works is strictly practical. In the first words of the Sâṅkhya-pravacana, the complete cessation of suffering is the end of man, and the Sâṅkhya is devised to enable him to attain it. Another formula divides the contents of the Sâṅkhya into four topics—(*a*) that from which man must liberate himself, or suffering, (*b*) liberation, or the cessation of suffering, (*c*) the cause of suffering, or the failure to discriminate between the soul and matter, (*d*) the means of liberation, or discriminating knowledge. This division obviously resembles the four Truths of Buddhism. The object proposed is the same and the method analogous, though not identical, for Buddhism speaks as a religion and lays greater stress on conduct.

The theory of the Sâṅkhya, briefly stated, is this. There exist, uncreated and from all eternity, on the one side matter and on the other individual souls. The world, as we know it, is due entirely to the evolution of matter. Suffering is the result of souls being in bondage to matter, but this bondage does not affect the nature of the soul and in one sense is not real, for when souls acquire discriminating knowledge and see that they are not matter, then the bondage ceases and they attain to eternal peace.

The system is thus founded on dualism, the eternal antithesis between matter and soul. Many of its details are comprised in the simple enumeration of the twenty-five Tattvas or principles[1] as given in the Tattva-samâsa and other works. Of these, one is Purusha, the soul or self, which is neither produced nor productive, and the other twenty-four are all modifications of Prakṛiti or matter, which is unproduced but productive. Prakṛiti means the original ground form of external existence (as distinguished from Vikṛiti, modified form). It is uncreated and indestructible, but it has a tendency to variation or evolu-

[1] Or topics. It is difficult to find any one English word which covers the twenty-five tattvas, for they include both general and special ideas, mind and matter on the one hand; special organs on the other.

tion. The Sâṅkhya holds in the strictest sense that *ex nihilo nihil fit*. Substance can only be produced from substance and properly speaking there is no such thing as origination but only manifestation. Causality is regarded solely from the point of view of material causes, that is to say the cause of a pot is clay and not the action of the potter. Thus the effect or product is nothing else than the cause in another shape: production is only manifestation and destruction is the resolution of a product into its cause. Instead of holding like the Buddhists that there is no such thing as existence but only becoming, the Sâṅkhya rather affirms that there is nothing but successive manifestations of real existence. If clay is made into a pot and the pot is then broken and ground into clay again, the essential fact is not that a pot has come into existence and disappeared but that the clay continuously existing has undergone certain changes.

The tendency to evolution inherent in matter is due to the three *guṇas*. They are *sattva*, explained as goodness and happiness; *rajas*, as passion and movement; and *tamas*, as darkness, heaviness and ignorance. The word Guṇa is not easy to translate, for it seems to mean more than quality or mode and to signify the constituents of matter. Hence one cannot help feeling that the whole theory is an attempt to explain the unity and diversity of matter by a phrase, but all Hinduism is permeated by this phrase and theory. When the three guṇas are in equilibrium then matter—Prakṛiti—is quiescent, undifferentiated and unmanifested. But as soon as the equilibrium is disturbed and one of the guṇas becomes preponderant, then the process of differentiation and manifestation begins. The disturbance of equilibrium is due to the action of the individual Purushas or souls on Prakṛiti, but this action is mechanical and due to proximity not to the volition of the souls and may be compared to the attraction of a magnet for iron[1]. Thus at the beginning of the evolutionary process we have quiescent matter in equilibrium: over against this are souls innumerable, equally quiescent but exerting on matter a mechanical force. This upsets the equilibrium and creates a movement which takes at first the form of development and later of decay and collapse. Then matter returns to its quiescent state to be again excited by the Purushas and commence its world-making evolution anew. The

[1] Sâṅkh. Pravac. I. 96.

doctrine that evolution, dissolution and quiescence succeed one another periodically is an integral part of the Sâṅkhya[1].

The unmodified Prakṛiti stands first on the list of twenty-five principles. When evolution begins it produces first Buddhi or intellect, secondly Ahaṃkâra, which is perhaps best rendered by individuality, and next the five Tanmâtras or subtle elements. Buddhi, though meaning intellect, is used rather in the sense of ascertaining or perception. It is the faculty by which we distinguish objects and perceive what they are. It differs also from our conception of intellect in being, like Ahaṃkâra and all the subsequent developments of Prakṛiti, material, and must not be confused with the immaterial Purusha or soul. It is in fact the organ of thought, not in the sense of the brain or anything tangible, but a subtle substratum of all mental processes. But in what sense is it possible to say that this Buddhi exists apart from individuals, who have not come into being at this stage of cosmic evolution? This difficulty is not met by talking, as some commentators do, of cosmic as well as individual Buddhi, for even if all Prakṛiti is illuminated by Buddhi at this stage it is difficult to see what result can occur. To make the process of development coherent we must think of it not as a series of chronologically successive stages but rather as a logically connected series and an analysis of completely evolved beings, just as we might say that bones are covered with flesh and flesh with skin, without affirming that the bones have a separate and prior existence. Ahaṃkâra, which is, like Buddhi, strictly speaking a physical organ, means Ego-maker and denotes the sense of personality and individuality, almost the will. In the language of Indian philosophy it is the delusion or misconception which makes the soul imagine itself a personal agent and think, *I* see, *I* hear, *I* slay, *I* am slain, whereas the soul is really incapable of action and the acts are those of Prakṛiti.

The five subtle elements are the essences of sound, touch, colour, savour and odour conceived as physical principles, imperceptible to ordinary beings, though gods and Yogis can perceive them. The name Tanmâtra which signifies *that only* indicates that they are concerned exclusively with one sense.

[1] Garbe, *Die Sâṅkhya Philosophie*, p. 222. He considers that it spread thence to other schools. This involves the assumption that the Sâṅkhya is prior to Buddhism and Jainism.

Thus whereas the gross elements, such as earth, appeal to more than one sense and can be seen, felt and smelt, the subtle element of sound is restricted to the sense of hearing. It exists in all things audible but has nothing to do with their tangibility or visibility. There remain sixteen further modifications to make up the full list of twenty-four. They are the five organs of sense[1], the five organs of action[2], Manas or mind, regarded as a sixth and central sense, and also as the seat of will, and the five gross elements—earth, water, light, air and ether. The Sâṅkhya distinguishes between the gross and the subtle body. The latter, called lingaśarîra, is defined in more than one way, but it is expressly stated in the Kârikâs[3] that it is composed of "Buddhi and the rest, down to the subtle elements." It practically corresponds to what we call the soul, though totally distinct from Purusha or soul in the Sâṅkhya sense. It constitutes the character and essential being of a person. It is the part which transmigrates from one gross body to another, and is responsible for the acts committed in each existence. Its union with a gross body constitutes birth, its departure death. Except in the case of those who attain emancipation, its existence and transmigration last for a whole world-period at the end of which come quiescence and equilibrium. In it are imprinted the Saṃskâraś[4], the predispositions which pass on from one existence to another and are latent in the new-born mind like seeds in a field.

By following the evolution of matter we have now accounted for intellect, individuality, the senses, the moral character, will, and a principle which survives death and transmigrates. It might therefore be supposed that we have exhaustively analysed the constitution of a human being. But that is not the view of the Sâṅkhya. The evolution of Buddhi, Ahaṃkâra, the subtle body and the gross body is a physical process and the result is also physical, though parts of it are of so fine a substance that ordinary senses cannot perceive them. This physical organism becomes a living being (which term includes gods and animals) when it is connected with a soul (purusha) and consciousness depends on this connection, for neither is matter when isolated conscious, nor is the soul, at least not in our sense of the word.

[1] Ears, skin, eyes, tongue and nose.

[2] Voice, hands, feet, organs of excretion and generation.

[3] Verse 40. [4] Cf. the Buddhist Sankhâras.

Though the soul is neither the life which ends at death (for that is the gross body) nor yet the life which passes from existence to existence (for that is the subtle body) yet it is the vitalizing element which renders life possible.

The Sâṅkhya like Jainism regards souls as innumerable and distinct from one another. The word Purusha must have originally referred to the manikin supposed to inhabit the body, and there is some reason to think that the earliest teachers of the Sâṅkhya held that it was infinitely small. But in the existing text-books it is described as infinitely large. It is immaterial and without beginning, end, parts, dimensions, or qualities, incapable of change, motion, or action. These definitions may be partly due to the influence of the Vedânta and, though we know little about the historical development of the Sâṅkhya, there are traces of a compromise between the old teaching of a soul held in bondage and struggling for release and later conceptions of a soul which, being infinite and passionless, hardly seems capable of submitting to bondage. Though the soul cannot be said to transmigrate, to act, or to suffer, still through consciousness it makes the suffering of the world felt and though in its essence it remains eternally unchanged and unaffected, yet it experiences the reflection of the suffering which goes on. Just as a crystal (to use the Indian simile) allows a red flower to be seen through it and remains unchanged, although it seems to become red, so does the soul remain unchanged by sorrow or joy, although the illusion that it suffers or rejoices may be present in the consciousness.

The task of the soul is to free itself from illusion, and thus from bondage. For strictly speaking the bondage does not exist: it is caused by want of discrimination. Like the Vedânta, the Sâṅkhya regards all this troubled life as being, so far as the soul is concerned, mere illusion. But while the Vedânta bids the soul know its identity with Brahman, the Sâṅkhya bids it isolate itself and know that the acts and feelings which seem to be its own have really nothing to do with it. They are for the soul nothing but a spectacle or play originating in its connection with Prakṛiti, and it is actually said[1], "Wherefore no soul is bound, or is liberated or transmigrates. It is Prakṛiti, which has many bodily forms, which is bound, liberated and trans-

[1] Sâṅkh. Kâr. 62.

migrates." It is in Buddhi or intellect, which is a manifestation of Prakṛiti, that the knowledge of the difference between the soul and Prakṛiti must arise. Thus though the Sâṅkhya reposes on a fundamental dualism, it is not the dualism of good and evil. Soul and matter differ not because the first is good and the second bad, but because the first is unchangeable and the second constantly changing. Matter is often personified as a woman. Her motives are unselfish and she works for the liberation of the soul. "As a dancer after showing herself on the stage ceases to dance, so does Prakṛiti cease when she has made herself manifest to the soul." That is to say, when a soul once understands that it is distinct from the material world, that world ceases to exist for that particular soul, though of course the play continues for others. "Generous Prakṛiti, endowed with Guṇas, causes by manifold means without benefit to herself, the benefit of the soul, which is devoid of Guṇas and makes no return[1]." The condition of the liberated soul, corresponding to the *moksha* and *nirvâṇa* of other systems, is described as Kaivalya, that is, complete separation from the material world, but, as among Buddhists and Vedântists, he who has learnt the truth is liberated even before death, and can teach others. He goes on living, just as the wheel continues to revolve for some time after the potter has ceased to turn it. After death, complete liberation without the possibility of re-birth is attained. The Sâṅkhya manuals do not dwell further on the character of this liberation: we only know that the eternal soul is then completely isolated and aloof from all suffering and material things. Liberation is compared to profound sleep, the difference being that in dreamless sleep there is a seed, that is, the possibility of return to ordinary life, whereas when liberation is once attained there is no such return.

Both in its account of the world process and in its scheme of salvation the Sâṅkhya ignores theism in the same way as did the Buddha. Indeed the text-books go beyond this and practically deny the existence of a personal supreme deity. We are told[2] that the existence of God cannot be proved, for whatever exists must be either bound or free and God can be neither. We cannot think of him as bound and yet he cannot be free like an emancipated soul, for freedom implies the absence of desire and hence

[1] Sâṅkh. Kâr. 59–61. [2] Sâṅkh. Pravac. I. 92–95.

of the impulse to create. Similarly[1] the consequences of good and evil deeds are due to Karma and not to the government of God. Such a ruler is inconceivable, for if he governs the world according to the action of Karma his existence is superfluous, and if he is affected by selfish motives or desire, then he cannot be free. It is true that these passages speak of there being no proof of God's existence and hence commentators both Indian and European who skrink from atheism represent the Sâṅkhya as suspending judgment. But if a republican constitution duly describes the President and other authorities in whom the powers of government are vested, can we argue that it is not unmonarchical because it does not expressly say there is no king? In the Sâṅkhya there is no more place for a deity than for a king in a republican constitution. Moreover, the Sûtras endeavour to prove that the idea of God is inconceivable and self-contradictory and some commentaries speak plainly on this subject[2]. Thus the Sâṅkhya-tattva-kaumudi commenting on Kârikâ 57 argues that the world cannot have been created by God, whether we suppose him to have been impelled by selfishness or kindness. For if God is perfect he can have no need to create a world. And if his motive is kindness, is it reasonable to call into existence beings who while non-existent had no suffering, simply in order to show kindness in relieving them from suffering? A benevolent deity ought to create only happy creatures, not a mixed world like the one we see[3].

Arguments like this were not condemned by the Brahmans so strongly as we should expect, but they did not like them and though they did not excommunicate the Sâṅkhya in the same way as Buddhism, they greatly preferred a theistic variety of it called Yoga.

The Yoga and Sâṅkhya are mentioned together in the Śvetâśvatara Upanishad[4], and the Bhagavad-gîtâ[5] says that he sees truly who sees them as one. The difference lies in treatment

[1] Sâṅkh. Pravac. v. 2–12.

[2] Thus Sâṅkh. Pravac. v. 46, says Tatkartuḥ purushasyâbhâvât and the commentary explains Îśvara-pratishedhâd iti śeshah "supply the words, because we deny that there is a supreme God."

[3] Nevertheless the commentator Vijñâna-Bhikshu (*c.* 1500) tries to explain away this atheism and to reconcile the Sâṅkhya with the Vedânta. See Garbe's preface to his edition of the Sâṅkhya-pravacana-bhâshya.

[4] VI. 13.

[5] V. 5.

rather than in substance. Whereas the Sâṅkhya is mainly theoretical, the principal topic of the Yoga is the cultivation of that frame of mind which leads to emancipation and the methods and exercises proper to this end. Further, the Yoga recognizes a deity. This distinction may seem of capital importance but the god of the Yoga (called Îśvara or the Lord) is not its foundation and essence as Brahman is of the Vedânta[1]. Devotion to God is recognized as one among other methods for attaining emancipation and if this particular procedure, which is mentioned in relatively few passages, were omitted, the rest of the system would be unaffected. It is therefore probable that the theistic portions of the Yoga are an addition made under Brahmanic influence. But taking the existing Sûtras of the two philosophies, together with their commentaries, it may be said that the Yoga implies most of the Sâṅkhya theory and the Sâṅkhya most of the Yoga practice, for though it does not go into details it prescribes meditation which is to be perfected by regulating the breathing and by adopting certain postures. I have already spoken of the methods and discipline prescribed by the Yoga and need not dwell further on the topic now.

That Buddhism has some connection with the Sâṅkhya and Yoga has often been noticed[2]. Some of the ideas found in the Sâṅkhya and some of the practices prescribed by the Yoga are clearly anterior to Gotama and may have contributed to his mental development, but circumspection is necessary in the use of words like Yoga, Sâṅkhya and Vedânta. If we take them to mean the doctrinal systems contained in certain sûtras, they are clearly all later than Buddhism. But if we assume, as we may safely do, that the doctrine is much older than the manuals in which we now study it, we must also remember that when we leave the texts we are not justified in thinking of a system but merely of a line of thought. In this sense it is clear that many ideas of the Sâṅkhya appear among the Jains, but the Jains know nothing of the evolution of matter described by the Sâṅkhya manuals and think of the relation of the soul to matter

[1] Îśvara is apparently a purusha like others but greater in glory and untouched by human infirmities. Yoga sûtras, I. 24–26.

[2] It is a singular fact that both the Sâṅkhya-kârikâ-bhâshya and a treatise on the Vaiśeshika philosophy are included in the Chinese Tripitaka (Nanjio, Cat. Nos. 1300 and 1295). A warning is however added that they are not "the law of the Buddha."

in a more materialistic way. The notion of the separate eternal soul was the object of the Buddha's persistent polemics and was apparently a popular doctrine when he began preaching. The ascetic and meditative exercises prescribed by the Yoga were also known before his time and the Piṭakas do not hide the fact that he received instruction from two Yogîs. But though he was acquainted with the theories and practices which grew into the Yoga and Sâṅkhya, he did not found his religion on them for he rejected the idea of a soul which has to be delivered and did not make salvation dependent on the attainment of trances. If there was in his time a systematic Sâṅkhya philosophy explaining the nature of suffering and the way of release, it is strange that the Piṭakas contain no criticism of it, for though to us who see these ancient sects in perspective the resemblance of Buddhism to the Sâṅkhya is clear, there can be little doubt that the Buddha would have regarded it as a most erroneous heresy, because it proposes to attain the same objects as his own teaching but by different methods.

Sâṅkhya ideas are not found in the oldest Upanishads, but they appear (though not in a connected form) in those of the second stratum, such as the Śvetâśvatara and Kaṭhâ. It therefore seems probable, though not proven, that the origin of these ideas is to be sought not in the early Brahmanic schools but in the intellectual atmosphere non-theistic, non-sacerdotal, but audaciously speculative which prevailed in the central and eastern part of northern India in the sixth century B.C. The Sâṅkhya recognizes no merit in sacrifices or indeed in good works of any kind, even as a preliminary discipline, and in many details is un-Brahmanic. Unlike the Vedânta Sûtras, it does not exclude Śûdras from higher studies, but states that there are eight classes of gods and five of animals but only one of men. A teacher must have himself attained emancipation, but there is no provision that he must be a Brahman. Perhaps the fables and parables which form the basis of the fourth book of the Sâṅkhya Sûtras point to some more popular form of instruction similar to the discourses of the Buddha. We may suppose that this ancient un-Brahmanic school took shape in several sects, especially Jainism and Buddhism, and used the Yoga discipline. But the value and efficacy of that discipline were admitted almost universally and several centuries later it was formulated in the Sûtras which bear the name of Patañjali in a shape acceptable to Brahmans, not to Buddhists. If, as some scholars think, the Yoga sûtras are not earlier than 450 A.D.[1] it seems probable that it was Buddhism which stimulated the Brahmans to codify the principles and practice of Yoga, for the Yogâcâra school of Buddhism arose before the fifth century. The Sâṅkhya is perhaps a somewhat similar brahmanization of the purely speculative ideas which may have prevailed in Magadha and Kosala[2]. Though these districts were not strongholds of Brahmanism, yet it is clear from the Piṭakas that they contained a considerable Brahman population who must have been influenced by the ideas current around them but also must have wished to keep in touch with other Brahmans. The Sâṅkhya of our manuals represents such an attempt at conciliation. It is an elaboration in a different shape of some of the ideas out of which Buddhism sprung but in its later history it is connected with Brahmanism rather than Buddhism. When it is set forth in Sûtras in a succinct and isolated form, its divergence from ordinary Brahmanic thought is striking and in this form it does not seem to have ever been influential and now is professed by only a few Pandits, but, when combined in a literary and eclectic spirit with other ideas which may be incompatible with it in strict logic, it has been a mighty influence in Indian religion, orthodox as well as unorthodox. Such conceptions as Prakṛiti and the Guṇas colour most of the post-Vedic religious literature. Their working may be plainly traced in the Mahâbhârata, Manu and the Purâṇas[3], and the Tantras identify with Prakṛiti the goddesses whose worship they teach. The unethical character of the Sâṅkhya enabled it to form the strangest alliances with aboriginal beliefs.

[1] See Jacobi, *J.A.O.S.* Dec. 1910, p. 24. But if Vasubandhu lived about 280–360, as is now generally believed, allusions to the Yogâcâra school in the Yoga sûtras do not oblige us to place the sûtras much later than 300 A.D. since the Yogâcâra was founded by Asanga, the brother of Vasubandhu.

[2] I find it hard to accept Deussen's view (*Philosophy of the Upanishads*, chap. x) that the Sâṅkhya has grown out of the Vedânta.

[3] See *e.g.* Vishṇu Purâṇa, I. chaps. 2, 4, 5. The Bhagavad-gîtâ, though almost the New Testament of Vedantists, uses the words Sâṅkhya and Yoga in several passages as meaning speculative truth and the religious life and is concerned to show that they are the same. See II. 39; III. 3; V. 4, 5.

3

Unlike the Sâṅkhya, the Vedânta is seen in its most influential and perhaps most advantageous aspect when stated in its most abstract form. We need not enquire into its place of origin for it is clearly the final intellectual product of the schools which produced the Upanishads and the literature which preceded them, and though it may be difficult to say at what point we are justified in applying the name Vedânta to growing Brahmanic thought, the growth is continuous. The name means simply End of the Veda. In its ideas the Vedânta shows great breadth and freedom, yet it respects the prejudices and proprieties of Brahmanism. It teaches that God is all things, but interdicts this knowledge to the lower castes: it treats rites as a merely preliminary discipline, but it does not deny their value for certain states of life.

The Vedânta is the boldest and the most characteristic form of Indian thought. For Asia, and perhaps for the world at large, Buddhism is more important but on Indian soil it has been vanquished by the Vedânta, especially that form of it known as the Advaita. In all ages the main idea of this philosophy has been the same and may be summed up in the formula that the soul is God and that God is everything. If this formula is not completely accurate[1]—and a sentence which both translates and epitomizes alien metaphysics can hardly aspire to complete accuracy—the error lies in the fact to which I have called attention elsewhere that our words, God and soul, do not cover quite the same ground as the Indian words which they are used to translate.

Many scholars, both Indian and European, will demur to the high place here assigned to the Advaita philosophy. I am far from claiming that the doctrine of Śaṅkara is either primitive or unchallenged. Other forms of the Vedânta existed before him and became very strong after him. But so far as a synthesis of opinions which are divergent in details can be just, he gives a just synthesis and elaboration of the Upanishads. It is true that his teaching as to the higher and lower Brahman and as to Mâyâ has affinities to Mahayanist Buddhism, and that later sects were

[1] It is perhaps hardly necessary to add that there has been endless discussion as to the sense and manner in which the soul is God.

repelled by the severe and impersonal character of his philosophy, but the doctrine of which he is the most thorough and eminent exponent, namely that God or spirit is the only reality and one with the human soul, asserts itself in almost all Hindu sects, even though their other doctrines may seem to contradict it.

This line of thought is so persistent and has so many ramifications, that it is hard to say what is and what is not Vedânta. If we take literature as our best guide we may distinguish four points of importance marked by the Upanishads, the Brahma-Sûtras, Śaṅkara and Râmânuja.

I have said something elsewhere of the Upanishads. These works do not profess to form a systematic whole (though later Hinduism regards them as such) and when European scholars speak of them collectively, they generally mean the older members of the collection. These may justly be regarded as the ancestors of the Vedânta, inasmuch as the tone of thought prevalent in them is incipient Vedântism. It rejects dualism and regards the universe as a unity not as plurality, as something which has issued from Brahman or is pervaded by Brahman and in any case depends on Brahman for its significance and existence. Brahman is God in the pantheistic sense, totally disconnected with mythology and in most passages impersonal. The knowledge of Brahman is salvation: he who has it, goes to Brahman or becomes Brahman. More rarely we find statements of absolute identity such as "Being Brahman, he goes to Brahman[1]." But though the Upanishads say that the soul goes to or is Brahman, that the world comes from or is Brahman, that the soul is the whole universe and that a knowledge of these truths is the one thing of importance, these ideas are not combined into a system. They are simply the thoughts of the wise, not always agreeing in detail, and presented as independent utterances, each with its own value.

One of the most important of these wise men is Yâjñavalkya[2], the hero of the Bṛihad Âranyaka Upanishad and a great name, to whom are ascribed doctrines of which he probably never heard. The Upanishad represents him as developing and completing the views of Śâṇḍilya and Uddâlaka Âruṇi. The former taught[3] that the Âtman or Self within the heart, smaller than

[1] Bṛihad Âran. IV. 4. 6; *ib.* I. iv. 10. "I am Brahman."

[2] See above Book II. chaps. V and VI.

[3] Chând. Up. III. 14.

a grain of mustard seed, is also greater than all worlds. The brief exposition of his doctrine which we possess starts from and emphasizes the human self. This self is Brahman. The doctrine of Uddâlaka[1] takes the other side of the equation: he starts with Brahman and then asserts that Brahman is the soul. But though he teaches that in the beginning there was one only without a second, yet he seems to regard the subsequent products of this Being as external to it and permeated by it. But to Yâjñavalkya is ascribed an important modification of these doctrines, namely, that the Âtman is unknowable and transcendental[2]. It is unknowable because since it is essentially the knowing subject it can be known only by itself: it can never become the object of knowledge and language is inadequate to describe it. All that can be said of it is *neti*, *neti*, that is no, no: it is not anything which we try to predicate of it. But he who knows that the individual soul is the Âtman, becomes Âtman; being it, he knows it and knows all the world: he perceives that in all the world there is no plurality. Here the later doctrine of Mâyâ is adumbrated, though not formulated. Any system which holds that in reality there is no plurality or, like some forms of Mahayanist Buddhism, that nothing really exists implies the operation of this Mâyâ or illusion which makes us see the world as it appears to us. It may be thought of as mere ignorance, as a failure to see the universe as it really is: but no doubt the later view of Mâyâ as a creative energy which fashions the world of phenomena is closely connected with the half-mythological conceptions found in the Pâncarâtra and Śaiva philosophy which regard this creative illusion as a female force—a goddess in fact—inseparably associated with the deity.

The philosophy of the Upanishads, like all religious thought in India, is avowedly a quest of happiness and this happiness is found in some form of union with Brahman. He is perfect bliss, and whatever is distinct from him is full of suffering[3]. But this sense of the suffering inherent in existence is less marked in the older Upanishads and in the Vedânta than in Buddhism and the Sâṅkhya. Those systems make it their basis and first principle: in the Vedânta the temperament is the same

[1] Chând. Up. VI.

[2] See Deussen, *Philosophy of the Upanishads.*

[3] Ato'nyad ârtam. Bṛihad Âr. III. several times.

but the emphasis and direction of the thought are different. The Sâṅkhya looks at the world and says that salvation lies in escape into something which has nothing in common with it. But the Vedântist looks towards Brahman, and his pessimism is merely the feeling that everything which is not wholly and really Brahman is unsatisfactory. In the later developments of the system, pessimism almost disappears, for the existence of suffering is not the first Truth but an illusion: the soul, did it but know it, is Brahman and Brahman is bliss. So far as the Vedânta has any definite practical teaching, it does not wholly despise action. Action is indeed inferior to knowledge and when knowledge is once obtained works are useless accessories, but the four stages of a Brahman's career, including household life, are approved in the Vedânta Sûtras, though there is a disposition to say that he who has the necessary religious aptitudes can adopt the ascetic life at any time. The occupations of this ascetic life are meditation and absorption or samâdhi, the state in which the meditating soul becomes so completely blended with God on whom it meditates, that it has no consciousness of its separate existence[1].

As indicated above the so-called books of Śruti or Vedic literature are not consecutive treatises, but rather *responsa prudentium*, utterances respecting ritual and theology ascribed to poets, sacrificers and philosophers who were accepted as authorities. When these works came to be regarded as an orderly revelation, even orthodoxy could not shut its eyes to their divergences, and a comprehensive exegesis became necessary to give a conspectus of the whole body of truth. This investigation of the meaning of the Veda as a connected whole is called Mîmâṃsâ, and is divided into two branches, the earlier (pûrva) and the later (uttara). The first is represented by the Pûrva-mîmâṃsâ-sûtras of Jaimini[2] which are called earlier (pûrva) not in the chronological sense but because they deal with rites which come before knowledge, as a preparatory stage. It is interesting to find that Jaimini was accused of atheism and defended by Kumârila Bhaṭṭa. The defence is probably just, for Jaimini does

[1] Maitrâyaṇa. Brâh. Upanishad, VI. 20. "Having seen his own self as The Self he becomes selfless, and because he is selfless he is without limit, without cause, absorbed in thought."

[2] There is nothing to fix the date of this work except that Kumârila in commenting on it in the eighth century treats it as old and authoritative. It was perhaps composed in the early Gupta period.

not so much deny God as ignore him. But what is truly extraordinary, though characteristic of much Indian literature about ritual, is that a work dealing with the general theory of religious worship should treat the deity as an irrelevant topic. The Pûrva-mîmâṃsa discusses ceremonies prescribed by an eternal self-existing Veda. The reward of sacrifice is not given by God. When the result of an act does not appear at once, Jaimini teaches that there is all the same produced a supersensuous principle called *apûrva*, which bears fruit at a later time, and thus a sacrifice leads the offerer to heaven. This theory is really tantamount to placing magic on a philosophic basis.

Bâdarâyaṇa's sûtras, which represent the other branch of the Mîmâṃsâ, show a type of thought more advanced and profound than Jaimini's. They consist of 555 aphorisms—less than a fifth of Jaimini's voluminous work—and represent the outcome of considerable discussion posterior to the Upanishads, for they cite the opinions of seven other teachers and also refer to Bâdarâyaṇa himself by name. Hence they may be a compendium of his teaching made by his pupils. Their date is unknown but Śaṅkara evidently regards them as ancient and there were several commentators before him[1]. Like most sûtras these aphorisms are often obscure and are hardly intended to be more than a mnemotechnic summary of the doctrine, to be supplemented by oral instruction or a commentary. Hence it is difficult to define the teaching of Bâdarâyaṇa as distinguished from that of the Upanishads on the one hand, and that of his commentators on the other, or to say exactly what stage he marks in the development of thought, except that it is the stage of attempted synthesis[2]. He teaches that Brahman is the origin of the world and that with him should all knowledge, religion and effort be concerned. By meditation on him, the soul is released and somehow associated with him. But it is not clear that we have any warrant for finding in the sûtras (as does Śaṅkara) the distinction between the higher and lower Brahman, or the doctrine of the unreality of the world (Mâyâ) or the absolute identity of the individual soul with Brahman. We are

[1] Keith in *J.R.A.S.* 1907, p. 492 says it is becoming more and more probable that Bâdarâyaṇa cannot be dated after the Christian era. Jacobi in *J.A.O.S.* 1911, p. 29 concludes that the Brahma-sûtras were composed between 200 and 450 A.D.

[2] Such attempts must have begun early. The Maitrâyana Upanishad (II. 3) talks of Sarvopanishadvidyâ, the science of all the Upanishads.

told that the state of the released soul is non-separation (avibhâga) from Brahman, but this is variously explained by the commentators according to their views. Though the sûtras are the acknowledged text-book of Vedântism, their utterances are in practice less important than subsequent explanations of them. As often happens in India, the comment has overgrown and superseded the text.

The most important of these commentators is Śankarâcarya[1]. Had he been a European philosopher anxious that his ideas should bear his name, or a reformer like the Buddha with little respect for antiquity, he would doubtless have taken his place in history as one of the most original teachers of Asia. But since his whole object was to revive the traditions of the past and suppress his originality by attempting to prove that his ideas are those of Bâdarâyaṇa and the Upanishads, the magnitude of his contribution to Indian thought is often under-rated. We need not suppose that he was the inventor of all the ideas in his works of which we find no previous expression. He doubtless (like the Buddha) summarized and stereotyped an existing mode of thought but his summary bears the unmistakeable mark of his own personality.

Śaṅkara's teaching is known as Advaita or absolute monism. Nothing exists except the one existence called Brahman or Paramâtman, the Highest Self. Brahman is pure being and thought (the two being regarded as identical), without qualities. Brahman is not intelligent but is intelligence itself. The human soul (jîva) is identical with the Highest Self, not merely as a part of it, but as being itself the whole universal indivisible Brahman. This must not be misunderstood as a blasphemous assertion that man is equal to God. The soul is identical with Brahman only in so far as it forgets its separate human existence, and all that we call self and individuality. A man who has any pride in himself is *ipso facto* differentiated from Brahman as much as is possible. Yet in the world in which we move we see not only differentiation and multiplicity but also a plurality of individual souls apparently distinct from one another and from Brahman. This appearance is due to the principle of Mâyâ which is associated with Brahman and is the cause of the phenomenal world. If Mâyâ is translated by illusion it must

[1] See above, p. 207 ff.

be remembered that its meaning is not so much that the world and individual existences are illusory in the strict sense of the word, as phenomenal. The only true reality is self-conscious thought without an object. When the mind attains to that, it ceases to be human and individual: it *is* Brahman. But whenever it thinks of particular objects neither the thoughts nor the objects of the thoughts are real in the same sense. They are appearances, phenomena. This universe of phenomena includes not only all our emotions and all our perceptions of the external world, but also what might be supposed to be the deepest truths of religion, such as the personality of the Creator and the wanderings of the soul in the maze of transmigration. In the same sense that we suffer pain and pleasure, it is true that there is a personal God (Îśvara) who emits and reabsorbs the world at regular intervals, and that the soul is a limited existence passing from body to body. In this sense the soul, as in the Sâṅkhya philosophy, is surrounded by the *upâdhis,* certain limiting conditions or disguises, which form a permanent psychical equipment with which it remains invested in all its innumerable bodies. But though these doctrines may be true for those who are in the world, for those souls who are agents, enjoyers and sufferers, they cease to be true for the soul which takes the path of knowledge and sees its own identity with Brahman. It is by this means only that emancipation is attained, for good works bring a reward in kind, and hence inevitably lead to new embodiments, new creations of Mâyâ. And even in knowledge we must distinguish between the knowledge of the lower Brahman or personal Deity (Îśvara) and of the higher indescribable Brahman[1]. For the orthodox Hindu this distinc-

[1] The same distinction occurs in the works of Meister Eckhart († 1327 A.D.) who in many ways approximates to Indian thought, both Buddhist and Vedântist. He makes a distinction between the Godhead and God. The Godhead is the revealer but unrevealed: it is described as "wordless" (Yâjnavalkya's *neti, neti*), "the nameless nothing," "the immoveable rest." But God is the manifestation of the Godhead, the uttered word. "All that is in the Godhead is one. Therefore we can say nothing. "He is above all names, above all nature. God works, so doeth not the Godhead. "Therein are they distinguished, in working and in not working. The end of all "things is the hidden darkness of the eternal Godhead, unknown and never to be "known." (Quoted by Rufus Jones, *Studies in Mystical Religion*, p. 225.) It may be doubted if Śankara's distinction between the Higher and Lower Brahman is to be found in the Upanishads but it is probably the best means of harmonizing the discrepancies in those works which Indian theologians feel bound to explain away.

tion is of great importance, for it enables him to reconcile passages in the scriptures which otherwise are contradictory. Worship and meditation which make Îśvara their object do not lead directly to emancipation. They lead to the heavenly world of Îśvara, in which the soul, though glorified, is still a separate individual existence. But for him who meditates on the Highest Brahman and knows that his true self is that Brahman, Mâyâ and its works cease to exist. When he dies nothing differentiates him from that Brahman who alone is bliss and no new individual existence arises.

The crux of this doctrine is in the theory of Mâyâ. If Mâyâ appertains to Brahman, if it exists by his will, then why is it an evil, why is release to be desired? Ought not the individual souls to serve Brahman's purpose, and would not it be better served by living gladly in the phenomenal world than by passing beyond it? But such an idea has rarely satisfied Indian thinkers. If, on the other hand, Mâyâ is an evil or at least an imperfection, if it is like rust on a blade or dimness in a mirror, if, so to speak, the edges of Brahman are weak and break into fragments which are prevented by their own feebleness from realizing the unity of the whole, then the mind wonders uneasily if, in spite of all assurances to the contrary, this does not imply that Brahman is subject to some external law, to some even more mysterious Beyond. But Śaṅkara and the Brahma-sûtras will not tolerate such doubts. According to them, Brahman in making the world is not actuated by a motive in the ordinary sense, for that would imply human action and passion, but by a sportive impulse[1]: "We see in every-day life," says Śaṅkara, "that certain doings of princes, who have no desires left unfulfilled, have no reference to any extraneous purpose but proceed from mere sportfulness. We further see that the process of inhalation and exhalation is going on without reference to any extraneous purpose, merely following the law of its own nature. Analogously, the activity of the Lord also may be supposed to be mere sport, proceeding from his own nature without reference to any purpose[2]." This

[1] Vedânta sûtras, II. 1. 32–3, and Śaṅkaras's commentary, *S.B.E.* vol. XXXIV. pp. 356–7. Râmânuja holds a similar view and it is very common in India, *e.g.* Vishṇu Pur. I. chap. 2.

[2] See too a remarkable passage in his comment on Brahma-sûtras, II. 1. 23. "As soon as the consciousness of non-difference arises in us, the transmigratory "state of the individual soul and the creative quality of Brahman vanish at once,

is no worse than many other explanations of the scheme of things and the origin of evil but it is not really an explanation. It means that the Advaita is so engrossed in ecstatic contemplation of the omnipresent Brahman that it pays no attention to a mere by-product like the physical universe. How or why that universe with all its imperfections comes to exist, it does not explain.

Yet the boldness and ample sweep of Śaṅkara's thought have in them something greater than logic[1], something recalling the grandeur of plains and seas limited only by the horizon, nay rather those abysses of space wherein on clear nights worlds and suns innumerable are scattered like sparks by what he would call God's playfulness. European thought attains to these altitudes but cannot live in them for long: it demands and fancies for itself just what Śaṅkara will not grant, the motive of Brahman, the idea that he is working for some consummation, not that he was, is and will be eternally complete, unaffected by the drama of the universe and yet identical with souls that know him.

Even in India the austere and impersonal character of Śaṅkara's system provoked dissent: He was accused of being a Buddhist in disguise and the accusation raises an interesting question[2] in the history of Indian philosophy to which I have referred in a previous chapter. The affinity existing between the Mâdhyamika form of Buddhist metaphysics and the earlier Vedânta can hardly be disputed and the only question is which borrowed from the other. Such questions are exceedingly difficult to decide, for from time to time new ideas arose in India, permeated the common intellectual atmosphere, and were worked up by all sects into the forms that suited each best. In the present instance all that can be said is that certain ideas about the unreality of the world and about absolute and relative

"the whole phenomenon of plurality which springs from wrong knowledge being "sublated by perfect knowledge and what becomes then of the creation and the "faults of not doing what is beneficial and the like?"

[1] Although Śaṅkara's commentary is a piece of severe ratiocination, especially in its controversial parts, yet he holds that the knowledge of Brahman depends not on reasoning but on scripture and intuition. "The presentation before the mind of the Highest Self is effected by meditation and devotion." Brah. Sut. III. 2. 24. See too his comments on I. 1. 2 and II. 1. 11.

[2] See Sukhtankar, *Teachings of Vedânta according to Râmânuja*, pp. 17–19. Walleser, *Der aeltere Vedânta*, and De la Vallée Poussin in *J.R.A.S.* 1910, p. 129.

truth appear in several treatises both Brahmanic and Buddhist, such as the works of Śaṅkara and Nâgârjuna and the Gauḍapâdakârikâs, and of these the works attributed to Nâgârjuna seem to be the oldest. It must also be remembered that according to Chinese accounts Bodhidharma preached at Nanking in 520 a doctrine very similar to the *advaita* of Śaṅkara though expressed in Buddhist phraseology.

Of other forms of Vedântism, the best known is the system of Râmânuja generally called Viśishṭâdvaita[1]. It is an evidence of the position held by the Vedânta philosophy that religious leaders made a commentary on the Sûtras of Bâdarâyaṇa the vehicle of their most important views. Unlike Śaṅkara, Râmânuja is sectarian and identifies his supreme deity with Vishṇu or Nârâyaṇa, but this is little more than a matter of nomenclature. His interpretation is modern in the sense that it pursues the line of thought which leads up to the modern sects. But that line of thought has ancient roots. Râmânuja followed a commentator named Bodhâyana who was anterior to Śaṅkara, and in the opinion of so competent a judge as Thibaut he gives the meaning of Bâdarâyaṇa in many points more exactly than his great rival. On the other hand his interpretation often strains the most important utterances of the Upanishads.

Râmânuja admits no distinction between Brahman and Îśvara, but the distinction is abolished at the expense of abolishing the idea of the Higher Brahman, for his Brahman is practically the Îśvara of Śaṅkara. Brahman is not without attributes but possessed of all imaginable good attributes, and though nothing exists apart from him, like the antithesis of *purusha* and *prakṛiti* in the Sâṅkhya, yet the world is not as in Śaṅkara's system merely Mâyâ. Matter and souls (*cit* and *acit*) form the body of Brahman who both comprises and pervades

[1] This term is generally rendered by qualified, that is not absolute, Monism. But South Indian scholars give a slightly different explanation and maintain that it is equivalent to *Viśishṭayor advaitam* or the identity of the two qualified (*viśishṭa*) conditions of Brahman. Brahman is qualified by *cit* and *acit*, souls and matter, which stand to him in the relation of attributes. The two conditions are *Kâryâvasthâ* or period of cosmic manifestation in which *cit* and *acit* are manifest and *Karaṇâvasthâ* or period of cosmic dissolution, when they exist only in a subtle state within Brahman. These two conditions are not different (*advaitam*). See Śrinivas Iyengar, *J.R.A.S.* 1912, p. 1073 and also *Sri Râmânujâcârya: His Philosophy* by Rajagopalacharyar.

all things, which are merely modes of his existence[1]. He is the inner ruler (antaryâmin) who is in all elements and all human souls[2]. The texts which speak of Brahman as being one only without a second are explained as referring to the state of pralaya or absorption which occurs at the end of each Kalpa. At the conclusion of the period of pralaya he re-emits the world and individual souls by an act of volition and the souls begin the round of transmigration. Salvation or release from this round is obtained not by good works but by knowledge and meditation on the Lord assisted by his grace. The released soul is not identified with the Lord but enjoys near him a personal existence of eternal bliss and peace. This is more like European theism than the other doctrines which we have been considering. The difference is that God is not regarded as the creator of matter and souls. Matter and souls consist of his substance. But for all that he is a personal deity who can be loved and worshipped and whereas Śaṅkara was a religious philosopher, Râmânuja was rather a philosophic theologian and founder of a church. I have already spoken of his activity in this sphere.

4

The epics and Purâṇas contain philosophical discussions of considerable length which make little attempt at consistency. Yet the line of thought in them all is the same. The chief tenets of the theistic Sâṅkhya-Yoga are assumed: matter, soul and God are separate existences: the soul wishes to move towards God and away from matter. Yet when Indian writers glorify the deity they rarely abstain from identifying him with the universe. In the Bhagavad-gîtâ and other philosophical cantos of the Mahâbhârata the contradiction is usually left without an attempt at solution. Thus it is stated categorically[3] that the world consists of the perishable and imperishable, *i.e.*, matter and soul, but that the supreme spirit is distinct from both.

[1] Compare the phrase of Keats in a letter quoted by Bosanquet, *Gifford Lectures for* 1912, p. 66. "As various as the lives of men are, so various become their souls and thus does God make individual beings, souls, identical souls of the sparks of his own essence."

[2] This tenet is justified by Bṛihad Aran. Up. iii. 3 ff. which is a great text for Râmânuja's school. "He who dwells in the earth (water, etc.) and within the earth (or, is different from the earth) whom the earth knows not, whose body the earth is, who rules the earth within, he is thyself, the ruler within, the immortal."

[3] Bhag.-gîtâ, xv. 16, 17.

Yet in the same poem we pass from this antithesis to the monism which declares that the deity is all things and "the self seated in the heart of man." We have then attained the Vedantist point of view. Nearly all the modern sects, whether Śivaite or Vishnuite, admit the same contradiction into their teaching, for they reject both the atheism of the Sâṅkhya and the immaterialism of the Advaita (since it is impossible for a practical religion to deny the existence of either God or the world), while the irresistible tendency of Indian thought makes them describe their deity in pantheistic language. All strive to find some metaphysical or theological formula which will reconcile these discrepant ideas, and nearly all Vishnuites profess some special variety of the Vedânta called by such names as Viśishṭâdvaita, Dvaitâdvaita, Śuddhâdvaita and so on. They differ chiefly in their definition of the relation existing between the soul and God. Only the Mâdhvas entirely discard monism and profess duality (Dvaita) and even Madhva thought it necessary to write a commentary on the Brahma-sûtras to prove that they support his doctrine and the Śivaites too have a commentator, Nîlakaṇṭha, who interprets them in harmony with the Śaiva Siddhânta. There is also a modern commentary by Somanaradittyar which expounds this much twisted text agreeably to the doctrines of the Lingâyat sect.

In most fundamental principles the Śivaite and Śâktist schools agree with the Viśishṭâdvaita but their nomenclature is different and their scope is theological rather than philosophical. In all of them are felt the two tendencies, one wishing to distinguish God, soul and matter and to adjust their relations for the purposes of practical religion, the other holding more or less that God is all or at least that all things come from God and return to him. But there is one difference between the schools of sectarian philosophy and the Advaita of Śaṅkara which goes to the root of the matter. Śaṅkara holds that the world and individual existences are due to illusion, ignorance and misconception: they vanish in the light of true knowledge. Other schools, while agreeing that in some sense God is all, yet hold that the universe is not an illusion or false presentment of him but a process of manifestation or of evolution starting from him[1]. It is not precisely evolution in the European sense, but rather

[1] The two doctrines are called *Vivartavâda* and *Pariṇâmavâda*.

a rhythmic movement, of duration and extent inexpressible in figures, in which the Supreme Spirit alternately emits and re-absorbs the universe. As a rule the higher religious life aims at some form of union or close association with the deity, beyond the sphere of this process. In the evolutionary process the Vaishṇavas interpolate between the Supreme Spirit and the phenomenal world the phases of conditioned spirit known as Saṅkarshana, etc.; in the same way the Śivaite schools increase the twenty-four *tattvas* of the Sânkhya to thirty-six[1]. The first of these *tattvas* or principles is Śiva, corresponding to the highest Brahman. The next phase is Sadâśiva in which differentiation commences owing to the movement of Śakti, the active or female principle. Śiva in this phase is thought of as having a body composed of *mantras*. Śakti, also known as Bindu or Śuddhamâyâ, is sometimes regarded as a separate *tattva* but more generally as inseparably united with Śiva. The third *tattva* is Îśvara, or Śiva in the form of a lord or personal deity, and the fourth is Śuddhavidyâ or true knowledge, explained as the principle of correlation between the experiencer and that which is experienced. It is only after these that we come to Mâyâ, meaning not so much illusion as the substratum in which Karma inheres or the protoplasm from which all things grow. Between Mâyâ aṇd Purusha come five more *tattvas*, called envelopes. Their effect is to enclose and limit, thus turning the divine spirit into a human soul.

Śâktist accounts of the evolutionary process give greater prominence to the part played by Śakti and are usually meta-physiological, if the word may be pardoned, inasmuch as they regard the cosmic process as the growth of an embryo, an idea which is as old as the Vedas[2]. It is impossible to describe even in outline these manifold cosmologies but they generally speak of Śakti, who in one sense is identical with Śiva and merely his active form but in another sense is identified with Prakṛiti, coming into contact with the form of Śiva called Prakâśa or light and then solidifying into a drop (Bindu) or germ which divides. At some point in this process arise Nâda or sound, and

[1] These are only the more subtle *tattvas*. There are also 60 gross ones. See for the whole subject Schomerus Der Çaiva-Siddhânta, p. 129.

[2] It also finds expression in myths about the division of the deity into male and female halves, the cosmic egg, etc., which are found in all strata of Indian literature.

Śabda-brahman, the sound-Brahman, which manifests itself in various energies and assumes in the human body the form of the mysterious coiled force called Kuṇḍalinî[1]. Some of the older Vishnuite writings use similar language of Śakti, under the name of Lakshmî, but in the Viśishṭâdvaita of Râmânuja and subsequent teachers there is little disposition to dwell on any feminine energy in discussing the process of evolution.

Of all the Darśanas the most extraordinary is that called Raseśvara or the mercurial system[2]. According to it quicksilver, if eaten or otherwise applied, not only preserves the body from decay but delivers from transmigration the soul which inhabits this glorified body. Quicksilver is even asserted to be identical with the supreme self. This curious Darśana is represented as revealed by Śiva to Śakti and it is only an extreme example of the tantric doctrine that spiritual results can be obtained by physical means. The practice of taking mercury to secure health and long life must have been prevalent in medieval India for it is mentioned by both Marco Polo and Bernier[3].

5

A people among whom the Vedânta could obtain a large following must have been prone to think little of the things which we see compared with the unseen of which they are the manifestation. It is, therefore, not surprising if materialism met with small sympathy or success among them. In India the extravagances of asceticism and of mystic sensualism alike find devotees, but the simple philosophy of Let us eat and drink for to-morrow we die, does not commend itself. Nevertheless it is not wholly absent and was known as the doctrine of Brihaspati. Those who professed it were also called Cârvâkas and Lokâyatikas[4]. Brihaspati was the preceptor of the gods and his

[1] An account of tantric cosmology can be found in Avalon, *Mahân. Tantra*, pp xix–xxxi. See also Avalon, *Prapancasâra Tantra*, pp. 5 ff.; Śrinivâsa Iyengar, *Indian Philosophy*, pp. 143 and 295 ff.; Bhandarkar, *Vaishṇ. and Śaivism*, pp. 145 ff.

[2] Sarva-darśana-saṅgraha, chap. IX. For this doctrine in China see Wieger *Histoire des Croyances religieuses en Chine*, p. 411.

[3] See Yule's *Marco Polo*, II. pp. 365, 369.

[4] See Rhys Davids' note in his *Dialogues of the Buddha on Dîgha Nikâya*, Sutta V. pp. 166 ff. He seems to show that Lokâyata meant originally natural philosophy as a part of a Brahman's education and only gradually acquired a bad meaning. The Arthasâstra also recommends the Sânkhya, Yoga and Lokâyata systems.

connection with this sensualistic philosophy goes back to a legend found in the Upanishads[1] that he taught the demons false knowledge whose "reward lasts only as long as the pleasure lasts" in order to compass their destruction. This is similar to the legend found in the Purâṇas that Vishṇu became incarnate as Buddha in order to lead astray the Daityas. But though such words as Ćârvâka and Nâstika are used in later literature as terms of learned abuse, the former seems to denote a definite school, although we cannot connect its history with dates, places or personalities. The Cârvâkas are the first system examined in the Sarva-darśana-saṅgraha, which is written from the Vedântist standpoint, and beginning from the worst systems of philosophy ascends to those which are relatively correct. This account contains most of what we know about their doctrines[2], but is obviously biassed: it represents them as cynical voluptuaries holding that the only end of man is sensual enjoyment. We are told that they admitted only one source of knowledge, namely perception, and four elements, earth, water, fire and air, and that they held the soul to be identical with the body. Such a phrase as *my body* they considered to be metaphorical, as apart from the body there was no ego who owned it. The soul was supposed to be a physical product of the four elements, just as sugar combined with a ferment and other ingredients produces an intoxicating liquor. Among verses described as "said by Brihaspati" occur the following remarkable lines:

> "There is no heaven, no liberation, nor any soul in another world,
> Nor do the acts of the âśramas or castes produce any reward.
> If the animal slain in the Jyotishtoma sacrifice will go to heaven,
> Why does not the sacrificer immolate his own father?
> While life remains let a man live happily: let him feed on butter even if he runs into debt.
> When once the body becomes ashes, how can it ever return?"

The author of the Dabistân, who lived in the seventeenth century, also mentions the Cârvâkas in somewhat similar terms[3].

Brahmanical authors often couple the Cârvâkas and Buddhists. This lumping together of offensively heretical sects may

[1] Maitr. Up. VII. 8.

[2] See also Suali in *Muséon*, 1908, pp. 277 ff. and the article Materialism (Indian) in *E.R.E.* For another instance of ancient materialism see the views of Pâyâsi set forth in Dig. Nik. XXIII. The Bṛihad Ar. Up. III. 2. 13 implies that the idea of body and spirit being disintegrated at death was known though perhaps not relished.

[3] Translation by Shea and Troyer, vol. II. pp. 201–2.

be merely theological animus, but still it is possible that there may be a connection between the Cârvâkas and the extreme forms of Mahayanist nihilism. Schrader[1] in analysing a singular work, called the Svasaṃvedyopanishad, says it is "inspired by the Mahâyânist doctrine of vacuity (*śûnya-vâda*) and proclaims a most radical agnosticism by asserting in four chapters (*a*) that there is no reincarnation (existence being bubble-like), no God, no world: that all traditional literature (*Śruti* and *Smṛiti*) is the work of conceited fools; (*b*) that Time the destroyer and Nature the originator are the rulers of all existence and not good and bad deeds, and that there is neither hell nor heaven; (*c*) that people deluded by flowery speech cling to gods, sacred places, teachers, though there is in reality no difference at all between Vishṇu and a dog; (*d*) that though all words are untrue and all ideas mere illusions, yet liberation is possible by a thorough realization of *Bhâvâdvaita*." But for this rather sudden concession to Hindu sentiment, namely that deliverance is possible, this doctrine resembles the tenets attributed to the Cârvâkas.

[1] *Sanskrit Manuscripts in the Adyar Library*, 1908, pp. 300–1.